WILLY BRANDT

Willy Brandt
portrait of a statesman

Terence Prittie

SCHOCKEN BOOKS · NEW YORK

First SCHOCKEN edition 1974

Library of Congress Cataloging in Publication Data

Prittie, Hon. Terence Cornelius Farmer, 1913–
    Willie Brandt; portrait of a statesman.

    Bibliography: p.
    1. Brandt, Willy, 1913–
DD259.7.B7P74   1975   943.087′092′4   [B]   74–9229

Contents

Illustrations

Author's Note

In writing this book I have sought only to give an interim report on the career of Herr Willy Brandt, chancellor of the Federal Republic of Germany from 1969 to 1974. At the time of writing, 1973, Herr Brandt was only fifty-nine years old and should have had a good many years of active political life ahead of him. And still, the 'last line' of his biography is yet to be written. But his life story so far is worth recording at this moment in history for one principal reason: in November 1972 the people of the Federal Republic of Germany gave, for the first time, a clear-cut decision in favour of social democracy, in the shape of a party that demands social progress and a leader who actively opposed Nazi tyranny and left Germany in order to carry on the struggle against Hitler from foreign soil. This popular decision constituted a final break with a tragic and terrible past.

I should like to thank the members of the Federal Chancellery, in particular Herr Gerd Reuschenbach, for the very considerable help they gave me in collecting material for this book. My thanks are due, too, to the press and information officers of the Federal Government, the city of Berlin and the Social Democratic Party, and to the custodian of the Willy Brandt Archives in Bonn, Herr Gerd Boerner. I owe much to the help and encouragement of the Federal German Embassy in London, to the German Institute in London and to the Norwegian Embassy in London, who kindly translated letters written by Herr Brandt in Norwegian. I owe a very special debt of gratitude to Rolf Breitenstein, of the Federal German Embassy, for reading the manuscript and making some very valuable suggestions and corrections.

Others to whom my sincere thanks are due include: Frau Paula Bartels-Heine, Herr Fritz Benke, Herr Egon Bahr, Professor Arnulf Baring, Herr Heinrich Böll, Lord Brockway, Herr Erich Brost, Mr McGeorge Bundy, Mr Johan Cappelen, General

Lucius Clay, Mr Norman Crossland, General Sir Rohan Dela-comb, the late Dr G. F. Duckwitz, Mr Tage Erlander, Herr Jens Feddersen, Hans-Werner Graf Finck von Finckenstein, Frau Luise Flägel, Mr Herbert George, Lord George-Brown, General Barksdale Hamlett, Herr Hanns-Peter Herz, Dr Helmut Jaesrich, Dr Bruno Kreisky, Frau Gerda Landerer, Prinz Hubertus zu Löwenstein, Professor Rex Löwenthal, Dr Joseph Luns, Herr Erich Lüth, Mr John McCloy, Mr George McGhee, Dr Erich Mende, Mr James O'Donnell, Mr Walter Padley, Mr John Paice, General Sir David Peel-Yates, Frau Tilli Pensel, Mr Lance Pope, Herr Fritz Sänger, Mr Inge Scheflo, Herr Rolf Schwedler, Dr Karl Silex, Herr Theo Sommer, Herr Dietrich Spagenberg, Mr Michael Stewart, Mr Shepard Stone, Herr Günter Struwe, Mr Herbert Sulzbach, Herr Otto Theuner, Herr Joachim Unger, Herr Herbert Wehner and the Rt Hon. Harold Wilson.

I have drawn on my own reports for the *Manchester Guardian* (subsequently the *Guardian*) from October 1946 to June 1963, and the bibliography and quoted source references will show how much I owe to books, memoranda, letters and other writings made available to me with the kind permission of Herr Willy Brandt.

Finally, I should like to add my special thanks to Lady Elizabeth Sutherland and her husband, Mr Charles Janson, for their kindness and generosity in allowing me to finish this book in quiet and beautiful surroundings.

TERENCE C. F. PRITTIE

House of Tongue

Tongue

County Sutherland

November 1972

Foreword

It is an appropriate moment to tell the story of Willy Brandt's strange career and assess its importance. During his time as chancellor of the Federal German Republic, his government gave the great bulk of the German people a fresh start of the right kind. It was the first since the Second World War that was representative of the 'new' Germany, the first whose members were in no way burdened by German misdeeds of the past.

Brandt was born on 18 December 1913 as one of the most under-privileged citizens of the immensely powerful German Empire. He grew to manhood and maturity while two world wars destroyed his country's power and influence and left it apparently irrevocably divided between the western world and the Soviet bloc. The Germany of his youth bitterly resented a lost war and a Treaty of Versailles that it regarded as unjust. Brandt grew up in an atmosphere of deep frustration and sullen anger, in a country racked by internal divisions and the economic catastrophies of the 1922–3 inflation, and the chronic state of crisis that began in 1929. Still only a youth, he opposed the Nazis actively and had to go into exile when they seized power. He continued to oppose Nazism by every means within his power and returned after the Second World War to become a citizen again of a country that was destitute, despised and divided. He took an always prominent part in the German nation's slow and painful rebirth, in which a genuinely democratic form of government became firmly entrenched, a free press became a part of the German way of life and the individual German grew to appreciate his own rights and duties and his obligation to contribute to the aims and ideals of an emerging European community.

To his tasks as chancellor Brandt brought a wealth of human and political experience and a real understanding of the era of German history through which he has lived. He took charge of a Federal Republic that has taken fourth place among the industrial nations of the world, has proved itself a reliable partner in the Western Alliance and has made the real friends that Imperial Germany lacked and Nazi Germany never sought. The policies on which he embarked are described later in this book; they are complementary to and not in conflict with what has already been done. They give the writing of this book its special purpose.

WILLY BRANDT

I

Twenty Years A-Growing

Willy Brandt's life began in the working-class quarter of St Lorenz, in the old city of Lübeck. Its inhabitants were mostly employed in the docks, the railway yards, the city gasworks and the large breweries. Lübeck is about 15 miles from the Baltic Sea and the river Trave was navigable for sizeable vessels. What had been a primitive Wendish settlement grew quickly in an era of shipbuilding and trade into a large port, becoming a naval power in its own right and the most important member of the Hanseatic League of seaports and riverine cities. At the height of its power the League comprised eighty-one different places, spread along the shores of the Baltic and the North Sea, had factories in places as far apart as London and the Russian town of Novgorod, and in the fourteenth century conquered the whole habitable part of southern Sweden. Lübeck was hit heavily by the Thirty Years War and declined steadily from the mid-seventeenth century onwards. It continued, however, to maintain its status of a free city of the Holy Roman Empire, and its sense of independence went beyond that; it was the home of seafaring, outward-looking people and went through 'democratic' phases when government was shared by delegated representatives of the people. The people of northern Germany are traditionally reserved in manner, sparing with words, but adventurous and sturdily independent in character. If this sounds like a ready-made description of Willy Brandt in person one may adduce that environment played some part in the moulding of his character.

His mother was Martha Frahm, a salesgirl in a Lübeck co-operative store.[1] He was born illegitimate. According to one published account[2] he never knew who his father was, never asked his mother and never wanted to find out. Beyond one fleeting reference to having 'heard his father's name', he has said nothing on the subject.[3] He was christened Herbert Ernst Karl Frahm, which remained, at least officially, his name for over thirty years of his life. Martha Frahm died in 1969, having married and had one son by this marriage, Willy Brandt's half-brother. Brandt has never been close to him or, for that matter, to his mother. But he maintained friendly relations with her, in which a certain distance was indicated by the shyly businesslike tone of his letters.[4] Wilhelminian Germany was socially orthodox and strict in a Victorian way and while illegitimacy was not a crime, it was certainly frowned upon. Children can be very cruel, in a petty way, and illegitimacy was an obvious subject for gibes. Brandt has admitted: 'I missed having a father, in different ways, but . . . there were boys who were worse off than I was.'[5] Again: 'I had many friends, but not one who was really close to me. I felt it difficult to confide in other people. From my early years, I maintained this reserve. Accustomed to live within myself, I found it not easy to share my sentiments and inner thoughts with others.'[6]

His mother had to go on working and he was put in the charge of a woman from a street nearby during the week. Paula Bartels-Heine took him in on Sunday evening and kept him until the following Saturday afternoon, when his mother finished work.[7] During the week his mother washed and mended his clothes, knitted socks for him, but he must have missed her. Nor was there much of a family circle: his grandfather was away in the wars and his grandmother took no interest in him,[8] possibly because of his illegitimate birth. A child is instantly aware if anyone shuns him.

His mother's home was very humble, a flat with one room and a kitchen. Brandt's earliest memory of all is of coming into the kitchen, thinking of food.[9] In his mind's eye, years later, there was a pile of it on the kitchen table, but this memory must be from the war years, 1914–18, when food was very short and a single woman would have had no chance of scrounging anything extra. Still Brandt was a very normal child. Frau Bartels-Heine found him 'a proper youngster, ready to throw his weight about and with very much a mind of his own'.[10] Frau Flägel, a cousin of his mother, first saw him when he was just two hours old, and often thereafter.[11] What struck her most was that 'only for a very short time indeed did he have a baby-face; by the time he was eighteen months old he was already a serious, thoughtful youngster'. Later on, he was 'very quiet, very pensive and never

2

blurted out his thoughts'. He was certainly no trouble to bring up. He ate his food and grew quickly into a tough, upstanding boy. At three he was sturdy and tall for his age, with a big head, wide mouth and a habit of cocking his head quizzically to one side. A year or so later one photograph traps him in a happy moment, a gay little figure wearing a sailor suit and a beaming grin. Before he was ten he had developed remarkably mature features, with a broad forehead, strong chin and a mop of unruly hair.

In 1918 grandfather Frahm came back from the wars, remarried when his first wife died, found a job as a lorry-driver with the firm of Draeger and took his grandson to live with him. The boy was really fond of him, called him 'papa' and settled down happily in his new home. His mother looked in a couple of evenings a week. Grandfather Frahm was a man of character and ideas. He had been brought up in the Mecklenburg countryside, and worked as a farm labourer on a count's estate and moved to Lübeck to escape from its feudal atmosphere. His most bitter memory was of his own father being publicly whipped. He became a socialist, learnt something of Karl Marx, August Bebel and Ferdinand Lassalle, and distinguished himself in one Reichstag election by overturning the soup tureen into which his fellow farm labourers had dropped their voting slips, because the count's overseer was checking slips from the list of farm-hands on the estate. To vote socialist on a Mecklenburg nobleman's estate was a deadly sin.

Grandfather Frahm was a proud man and Brandt has recalled[12] one dramatic incident during a strike in 1921. Brandt was standing outside a baker's when a Draeger works director, passing by, recognized him, took him into the shop and bought him a couple of loaves. His grandfather told him sternly to take the bread back—he would not accept alms; the bread, he told the boy, was a bribe. So Brandt took the loaves back and proudly handed them over the counter. This was a stormy period in German history and even as an eight-year-old Brandt remembers the 'troubled political atmosphere, with a persistent undercurrent of unrest and internal conflict'.[13] He remembers, too, a workers' council taking over temporary control of municipal buildings, including the police station where his grandfather was in charge.

3

Brandt brought him his lunch that day, in an atmosphere that he described as a mixture of adventure and serious business.

Well before this date he was going to school; from the very beginning he was an excellent pupil, alert, intelligent and eager to learn. Generally at or near the top of his class, he put in extra work studying political ideas, particularly those of his chosen heroes, Lassalle and Bebel, the spokesmen of the underdog. At thirteen he won a place at a *Realschule,* or secondary modern school, with no fees charged since he came to it as top of his class. After one year he moved on to the Johanneum, Lübeck's only *Realgymnasium,* or secondary school with a scientific basis. He was to spend four years there, a citadel of privilege, as one of the very few pupils of working-class origin. He was well taught at the Johanneum, 'learnt naturally' and developed a remarkable memory, and an even more remarkable capacity for setting his thoughts down concisely and without adornment. But he was bound to feel isolated. His former foster mother felt that 'it must have been very hard on him. His schoolmates all came from a different background, had quite different political ideas; and he must have been very much alone, and had to solve his problems on his own. Still, he just went on following his own straight course!'[14] His mother's cousin, Frau Flägel, noted the development, round this time, of 'his colossal sense of justice'.[15]

He asserted his independence by joining the Sozialistische Arbeiter-Jugend (SAJ), the socialist youth movement, on one occasion coming to school dressed in its uniform of blue shirt and red tie. The other boys did not approve, while a teacher, Professor Kramer, was deeply perturbed when Brandt asked, 'Why shouldn't a poor man ask for sausage to put on his bread?' The professor told Brandt's mother that politics would be the ruin of him![16] The teaching staff were mainly hostile to the Weimar Republic and only the history and German professors were friendly and liberal-minded; history and German, along with, surprisingly, religious studies, became Brandt's best subjects. At his final examination he had a choice of three subjects for the all-important German essay – a historical essay, the poet Goethe, and the statement of a former pupil: 'When we look back on our years at school we must say that they gave us nothing for our future life.' Ready to be controversial, he chose the last. He was one of only two pupils who did so, but whereas the other praised school

4

in order to get good marks Brandt was highly critical. Even so he passed his exams. His own comment – it might have been a bad advertisement for the school had he, an outstanding student, been failed.[17]

What of his life out of school? His mother had married by now; her husband was a bricklayer from Mecklenburg called Kühlmann. His grandfather had been on the dole, then found *Notstandsarbeit* or temporary relief work. Real poverty had already been amply apparent during the inflation period, when from late in 1922 to the end of 1923 the Reichsmark currency lost all purchasing power. Brandt and other youngsters were able, when the new marks were introduced, to earn one lollipop for every 10,000 million of old, worthless Reichsmarks they collected. Inflation hit the working class as hard as anybody else.

He had begun to smoke at the age of seventeen and fairly soon took to a pipe. He drank a glass of beer when he felt like it and had an eye for the girls. He was a handsome young man by the time he left school and was earning some money on the side from writing. He had earlier become a voracious reader of books 'which had something to say',[18] Thomas Mann and Erich Maria Remarque being his favourites. Reading, and his interest in politics, encouraged him to write his first pieces for the press; short features and essays for the local Social Democratic (SPD) newspaper, the *Volksbote*. The first was published when he was under fifteen and he later won a prize, a copy of Fenimore Cooper's *Leather Stocking*. He was very proud of the small sums he earned from his journalism. He was encouraged to read and learn by his history teacher, Professor Eilhard Erich Pauls and as a result his reading was never an escape, but always a means to inform himself.

His interest in politics produced, in turn, an impatience with school, a desire to get out into the bigger world beyond. An impatience to get things done has stayed with him, for life. He has explained his early interest in politics in simple terms:

I suppose I inherited a desire for social justice and political progress. That brought me into the workers' movement. It duplicated every form of social activity, even down to collecting postage stamps. It was an alternative society of its own, in cultural affairs, in sport and in social activities of every kind. I

5

may have deviated from 'straight' politics for a time – I got interested in a *Verein für das Deutschtum in Ausland* [union of Germans abroad] – rather right wing from the SPD point of view. Then I had a fleeting interest in helping a German school in North Schleswig, which had been ceded to Denmark after the First World War.[19]

From an even earlier age he had taken part in socialist youth activities. He joined the Kinderfreunde (Children's Friends), then the Workers' Mandolin Club, for music and political discussion, then – still under fourteen – the SPD Falken, or 'falcons'. He enjoyed life in the open and in tents, hiking and climbing, songs at the campfire, sport, comradeship. He learnt to swim really well and as a runner won a 10,000-metre race as the only entrant![20] He believes that the Falken taught him the value of open discussion, voluntary discipline, self-reliance and co-operation with friends. These young German socialists were not welfare-minded: 'We had to rely on our own ability and means; we did not expect to be helped or supported by the state.'[21]

The city's Youth Affairs Office sent him, as a member of a group, for the first time to Scandinavia, which was to play so big a role in his later life. He went to Denmark in the summer of 1927 and it may be relevant that he recalls having, possibly, heard his father's name at about this time and that it 'sounded Scandinavian'.[22] More important, membership of the Falken brought him into close touch with the SPD and with its leader in Lübeck, Julius Leber. Leber was the third and by far the most formative influence so far in Brandt's life. His grandfather taught him about life, Professor Pauls about history* and now Leber gave him the substance of a political creed.

Leber was born in 1891 in Alsace, at that time in Germany. He volunteered for military service in 1914, was commissioned and decorated for bravery. A staunch and imaginative socialist, he came to Lübeck at the age of thirty to take a job on the *Volksbote*

---

* Brandt has never been a man to forget anybody who helped him in any way. In February 1972, the best part of half a century after Professor Pauls had taught him history, he spoke of his old teacher in glowing terms in a speech in Lübeck Town Hall, when receiving the freedom of the city. He laid a wreath on the professor's grave. The widow, Frau Adele Pauls, said in a letter of thanks that the professor had never been disappointed in the boy whom he had taught.

6

and became its editor. When Brandt first met him he was moving away from out-dated ideology and bureaucracy and concentrating on the defence of freedom, justice, authority and the rule of law. He believed, too, that the SPD had to attract the middle-class vote in order to halt the march of Nazism. Brandt owed much to Leber, who took him under his wing, encouraged his writing and launched him on an active political career. He saw in Leber a dynamic figure – a Latin in looks with sharply cut features, high forehead, burning eyes, a strong jaw and a soft, sensual mouth.[23] He was both realist and man of action. And a man of action was badly needed, for the Nazis were in full cry in their victorious drive to power. Brandt noticed them first in 1927 when the Hitler Youth were becoming active, and brawls were beginning to take place between them and the less closely organized SPD youth.

In 1928 Brandt became the leader of the Karl Marx Group of the SAJ. In the same year he had created a stir by being temporarily expelled from school for appearing on the anniversary of the foundation of the Reich to read a poem in public wearing his bright red SAJ tie. In 1929, when the economic crisis was at its height and there were thousands of unemployed in Lübeck alone, Leber gave him a semi-honorary post on the *Lübecker Volksbote* and in 1930 sponsored his recruitment as a fully-fledged member of the SPD. Brandt had developed into an excellent public speaker and a natural leader of his youthful contemporaries.

In 1930 the Nazis made their predictable breakthrough in the Reichstag elections, capturing 107 seats against the twelve they had held before. Brandt's view:

> The election results were a shock. The Nazis were talking of putting an end to the Republic, abolishing the free vote, using force. Their so-called 'socialism' meant nothing to us – it was an obvious fraud. I had one school-friend who was an ardent Nazi; he was honest and sincere. I talked to him in order to learn about the Nazis. I came to the conclusion that they represented an unbridled nationalism, devoid of spiritual content. Nazism was brutal and scorned humanity; it was steering in the direction of a new war.[24]

By 1931 Brandt was, as he put it, *stark engagiert* – deeply involved – in the struggle against Nazism. But a certain schizophrenia assailed the Social Democrats – 'Our Social Democratic

7

leader in the Reichstag, Otto Wels, coined the phrase, "rough fellows don't rule for long"; like others, I too hoped that the Nazis "might not last". It's easy to be wise after the event; but who guessed that the Nazis would be "in" for twelve long years or just what they would do in that time?'[25]

Leber recognized the deadly danger of Nazism. Brandt has paid tribute to his fiery courage – 'He was a wonderful man, a modern, very active man. He would belong to what one would call the right wing of his party, but he was an activist too. People liked him, even loved him, and I was very much impressed by his activism.'[26] Yet, tragically, Brandt broke with him – politically only, for they remained on reasonable personal terms. It was an act that required great courage; Leber was his mentor as well as his friend, and it caused consternation among the editorial staff of the *Lübecker Volksbote*. According to one member, Karl Albrecht, 'We were all amazed at the time. This young fellow dared to criticize even the great Julius Leber. But civic courage was always Willy Brandt's strong suit – and absolute honesty.'[27] Brandt left the newspaper and joined a shipbrokers' firm in Lübeck, F. H. Bertling, at a princely wage of 15 Marks a week, something under £1 or about $4. The work was mainly dull and the only consolation was plenty of foreign business – so that Brandt had the chance to brush up his English, and to learn a little Dutch, Swedish and Norwegian.

To understand why he felt obliged to break with Leber one must go back in history. The SPD was officially founded at the Gotha Conference of 1875. Its foundation brought instant repressive measures by the Iron Chancellor, Otto von Bismarck. Under the *Sozialisten-gesetze*, the anti-socialist laws of 1878 to 1890, 1,300 SPD publications were banned, 900 party members were deported and 1,500 people were sentenced to terms of imprisonment.[28] Bismarck's laws lapsed when he fell from power in 1890, and in the 1903 elections the party collected 3 million votes, 32 per cent of the poll, and 81 Reichstag seats. In 1912 the SPD vote was $4\frac{1}{2}$ million, with 110 out of 397 seats in the Reichstag. Party membership, illegal in Bismarck's day, rose to 1,085,000 in 1914. There were 91 SPD newspapers, with over $1\frac{1}{2}$ million subscribers. But there were fatal weaknesses behind this fine façade. One historian called the SPD 'a party of officials, who acquired their own sort of white-collar status', and 'an expanding bureaucracy, for whom the organization, rather than its aims, was becoming an end in itself'.[29] There was an inhibiting urge towards respectability, an inevitable trend towards middle-class materialism and a strong aversion to activist theory and practice.[30] And there were other flaws than a loss of contour and purpose in the domestic field. On 4 August 1914 the SPD parliamentary group voted 97 to 14 in favour of war credits. Over 50 per cent of male members of the SPD were to be mobilized for military service and an SPD deputy, Ludwig Frank, was the first member of the Reichstag to fall in action.[31] It was of no consequence to a party that preached and indeed believed in human rights that a small and neutral country, Belgium, was invaded simply because it 'got in the way' of the German advance into France. In December twenty members of the SPD boldly contested the grant of further war credits. This group subsequently formed the independent Socialist Party and opposed the shockingly harsh treaty of Brest-Litovsk, imposed on Russia in 1918.[32]

One may qualify criticism of the SPD. Tsarist Russia, the citadel of political reaction, was in 1914 the principal enemy. France was, indeed, hungering for *revanche,* and Frenchmen were thinking in terms of a *guerre à l'outrance,* involving a crushingly swift attack on Germany.[33] Should one blame simple socialists for being myopic when a man like Thomas Mann called the war 'a purification, a liberation, an enormous hope'?

The SPD, as the party of progress, reform and common sense, should have come into its own after the First World War. Never a party of action, they were called upon to play a major role at a time when action was imperative. The workers', sailors' and soldiers' councils hastily organized at the end of the war had no clear-cut plans and no possibility of survival. Localized 'revolutions' that took place all over Germany were unco-ordinated, unaimed. The failure of the attempted Spartacist coups at Christmas 1918 and in January 1919 had ensured that the SPD, now committed to crushing proletarian revolution, would carry on its pre-1914 tradition of graduated reform. In the January 1919 elections for a National Assembly they won 165 out of 423 seats, and the Independent Socialists 22. The left-liberal Democrats had 74; it seemed that the Weimar Republic had been launched with a strong majority supporting progressive government. But the left-liberal Democrats vanished into obscurity, while the Independent Socialists became the core of an anti-establishment, fundamentally anti-democratic Communist Party. In the June 1920 elections the parties that had played the main part in drafting the Weimar constitution (SPD, Democrats and Catholic Centre) lost their majority in the Reichstag. The subsequent story of the Weimar Republic was one of consistent failure to form a stable and reasonably progressive government.

By 1931 the SPD was still the strongest single party in the Reichstag, with 143 seats. But the extreme Right (Nazis and Nationalists) had 151, and the extreme Left, in the shape of the Soviet-steered Communist Party (KPD), 77. In theory government by the middle-of-the-road parties should still have been possible, but the SPD had already abdicated. From September 1930 the chancellor, Heinrich Brüning, governed by emergency decrees approved by the Reich president, Hindenburg. The SPD openly connived at and tolerated the development of authoritarian rule and so signed the death warrant of the Weimar Republic.

Young militants like Willy Brandt rejected this abject abdication of political responsibility. To them, the great party that had proclaimed a doctrine of peaceful class struggle was dead and buried. Instinct is more aware in young bones and in young minds. They wanted action and they had to look round for an alternative to the SPD. But first they had to take their leave of Leber, an unhappy, even heart-rending business. It is only very occasionally that a young man and a man much older experience an instinctive understanding and a reciprocal admiration. Leber was, like Brandt, all for action, but he was convinced that the SPD had to stand united. He was to show his own mettle in July 1932. In a stirring speech he called on thousands of Lübeck workers to oppose the Nazis by every means in their power. On 1 February 1933 he put up a gallant fight against Nazi thugs who attacked him and his friends in the street when they were on their way home from the Reichstag. In the mêlée one of the Nazis was killed. Leber's nose was broken, but in spite of the fact that he had been physically assaulted and possessed immunity from arrest as a member of the Reichstag, he was flung into gaol by the Nazis. Hitler had been proclaimed chancellor on 30 January; the Nazis were in virtually total control. Brandt organized demonstrations on Leber's behalf and appealed to the trade unions for a general strike. The trade unions, with a lack of civic courage, refused. But a few weeks later they were ready to participate in the biggest demonstration in the history of Lübeck, when fifteen thousand people assembled on the Burgfeld on 19 February. Leber was let out on bail in time for the meeting but was debarred from speaking in public. With his head still bandaged, he appeared on the platform, raising his arm and crying out the single word *Freiheit*, freedom. Not a speech, but a superb gesture of defiance.

Brandt never saw him again. Leber was to spend much of the early years of the Nazi era in prisons and concentration camps. When the resistance movement against Hitler formed during the Second World War he became one of its leading members. Brandt managed to restore contact with him, briefly, through Theodor Steltzer, a progressive conservative who in 1943 visited Stockholm, where Brandt was living. This was a matter only of messages exchanged. Leber was to be arrested on 5 July 1944, fifteen days before Count Stauffenberg's bomb so nearly put an end to Hitler's life. He was tried and hanged by the Nazis, after being tortured for weeks on end.

Years later Brandt was to say of Julius Leber: 'He came to the conclusion that if you fight for a thing that is right and honest, then you have eventually also to take the consequence, which means to give your life. Many of us felt that way during those years.'[34]

Brandt had to find a new political home when he left the SPD. He may have prepared himself, unconsciously, for his own choice when he visited Norway in the summer of 1931. He roamed everywhere and saw practical democracy in action. He revelled in the wild beauty and the sheer emptiness of Norway. He liked the simplicity and quiet dignity of the Norwegians, and most of all their natural toleration of one another.[35] The Norwegian Social Democratic Party were more radical and progressive than his own SPD. Their leaders were more imaginative, more adventurous. They had qualities that the uninspired, ageing SPD leadership sadly lacked. Although he left the SPD months later Brandt's mind was probably already made up when he returned to Lübeck from this holiday.

By the end of 1931 a dozen left-wing socialist groups had

broken away from the SPD. Brandt took his time looking round. There was plenty of political work to get on with. He was chairman of the local branch of the SAJ, and he organized major demonstrations in Lübeck-Blankensee and the neighbouring town of Neustadt. He was a born organizer, with patience and toleration,[36] and his powers of leadership enabled him to build an effective team. During 1931, too, he headed a vigorous campaign against rearmament and there were clashes between the Hitler Youth and the SAJ, with banners inscribed *'Gegen Panzerkreuzerbau! Für Völkerfrieden!'* ('Against the building of pocket battleships! For peace among nations!')[37]

At the end of 1931 SPD activists met in Berlin and formed the Sozialistische Arbeiter Partei (SAP) or Socialist Workers' Party. These young men had been contemplating leaving the SPD ever since Brüning began to govern by decree. They were disgusted by SPD leaders like Rudolf Breitscheid and his formula: 'We tolerate the damage done to democratic form, in order to safeguard the democratic content of the constitution.'[38] The SAP leaders wanted to create a Marxist revolutionary party, and the new party managed with difficulty to get off the ground. In October 1931 they claimed fifty thousand members – probably an exaggeration – and countless more supporters.[39] Their strong points were in Saxony, Berlin, Breslau and Frankfurt and they found immediate and enthusiastic support among socialist youth. Brandt joined the new party at the end of 1931 and his drive and influence were quickly felt in its youth activities and in the publication of a paper, the *Marxistische Tribüne*.

Both the Social Democrats and the Communists were infuriated by the foundation of the SAP. The Social Democrats accused the new party of preaching dissension and tried, too, to tar them with the communist brush. The SAP, indeed, laid themselves open to the charge of being a camouflaged communist body by such slogans as: 'A thousand times sooner with the Communists than with the capitalists'.[40] The Communists were angered by the SAP precisely because they refused to merge with the KPD and bring in thousands of young activists. To the KPD political philosophy was a matter of accepting Soviet orders. In addition the SAP acted as a focus for KPD dissidents and were joined in mid-1932 by some members of one group that entitled itself the 'KP Opposition'. The KPD wanted to unify the working class under their banner. Their leaders called the SPD such fanciful names as the 'battering-ram of fascism'[41] and 'social fascists'. The bickerings of the left-wing parties inevitably extended to the ideological field. A vast amount of fruitless talk went on about Marxist and Leninist principles, with the Nazi enemy at the gate and parliamentary democracy in a state of dissolution. There was, too, a strong Trotskyist contingent in the SAP, though not in the KPD, and there was much aimless discussion of a 'popular front' of working-class parties.

The SAP did, admittedly, put forward constructive ideas when one hundred delegates met at Easter 1932. They agreed to campaign for workers' rights and social justice, against Nazism, remilitarization and rule by emergency decree. But a crippling lack of finance was indicated by their appeal: 'Where is your dime?' They failed completely at the Prussian state elections in April 1932, polling only eighty thousand votes, or 0.4 per cent. They did even worse in the Reichstag elections in July, with seventy-two thousand, and their vote dropped to forty-five thousand in the Reichstag elections in November. They did better at local elections in Saxony a week later, but this was their last fling. Within a few months the Nazis succeeded in banning and dissolving all other political parties and all trade unions, passed an enabling act that gave Hitler the powers of a dictator and embarked on a campaign of wholesale intimidation and arrests of political opponents.

In March 1933 Brandt went to Berlin, to take part in an SAP congress held in secret. In fact the congress was shifted to Dresden at the last moment. The delegates who assembled under fear of arrest and imprisonment bitterly blamed the SPD and KPD for the Nazi seizure of power – the SPD for woolly-minded reformism, the KPD for slavish acceptance of Stalinism. The party officially dissolved itself but its 'activist' leaders decided to go underground inside Germany, establishing a main base in Berlin under Klaus Zweiling, Max Kohler and Walter Fabian. At the same time they proposed organizing three centres outside Germany – in Paris, Prague and Oslo.[42] Contact was to be maintained between Germany and the outside world by building up a courier service.

Brandt was bitterly disappointed by the failure of the democratic force in the Weimar Republic to resist. Even early in 1933 there was still talk about calling a general strike. Nothing was done; his subsequent comment was: 'To be defeated in battle is tragic; to surrender without a fight makes the tragedy a farce. It robs the victim of his last, most precious possession: his self-respect.'[43] The SPD failed; as one authority put it, 'The party, by 1933, was organized not to fight, but simply to exist.'[44]

The secret SAP congress had brought Brandt to Berlin for the first time in his life. What he saw depressed him. The tempo of life seemed erratic, even hectic, and he saw the broad esplanade of the Kurfürstendamm as the 'made-up mistress of a war-profiteer'.[45] A great many people, he noted, talked in whispers, looked furtively about them; the cafés habitually frequented by Berlin's intellectuals were empty. He went from the bright lights of the Kurfürstendamm to the workers' quarters in the 'red' borough of Wedding: 'What a contrast! Ugly and bare, those endless streets with the large tenement houses and the sunless backyards. But on that day they looked as if they were illuminated by an inner light. No flags, no banners relieved the general greyness – it was as if the houses wanted to show that they were not ashamed of their poverty.'[46] At a later date he was to speak of the 'hurt honour' and unhappiness of 'brave and honest' Berliners.[47]

With a heightened sense of doom and misery he went on to Dresden, to learn what had happened to his friends. The news was devastating: some were simply missing, others had been arrested by the Nazis; there were stories of people having been tortured and murdered in Nazi *Untersuchungshaft*, or 'investigatory arrest'. Jews were being persecuted, and – revealingly – this was a new problem to Brandt.[48] In his native liberal-minded Lübeck people had been genuinely unaware of a Jewish 'problem'. Yet Brandt was to see Dr Fritz Solmitz, former political editor of the *Lübecker Volksbote,* being driven through the streets with an obscenely anti-Semitic placard tied round his neck. Solmitz, as it happens, had expressed the view that the seventeen-year-old Brandt, when he began work on the *Lübecker Volksbote,* was *vielversprechend,* very promising.[49]

Both in Berlin and Dresden Brandt travelled, for the first time, under the name that he later took for life. He chose Willy Brandt as a *nom de guerre,* as he later called it,[50] a 'party name' – for the

SAP was banned and proscribed. That he kept it for life was natural, for it represented essentially his decision to oppose Nazism and, if necessary, leave Germany. Willy Brandt was the name under which he lived during the twelve years of Nazi rule in Germany. It came to mean all the more to him for that, and it stuck.

His decision to leave Germany has been criticized by political opponents. His duty, they have argued, was to stay in his own country and oppose the Nazis there. He has even been accused of running away. Yet he did not leave in a panic, but only after careful deliberation; he was to prove his high courage by returning three years later to take part in underground work against the Nazis. Had he remained in Germany in 1933 he would certainly have been arrested, whether or not his name was on the central Nazi black list, the *Fahndungsliste*. For he was well known to the Lübeck Nazis as a young man who was their declared enemy. He might have been released by the Nazis in the course of time, but his character was such that he would never have agreed to toe the Nazi line, or even to stay silent. His life would almost certainly have ended in a concentration camp.

The SAP tried to send Paul Fröhlich to Oslo, to organize a party bureau there; but he was caught on the Baltic island of Fehmarn. Escaping from Hitler's Germany was already hazardous. Brandt made his plans only after a warning from a lawyer, Emil Peters, that he was under official suspicion. Peters' view, in retrospect, was that 'had he stayed on, then he would certainly have been flung into a concentration camp, and would have never come out of it again'.[51] Brandt, years later, was inclined to agree.[52]

On 1 April 1933 one of his friends working for his grandfather's old firm of Draeger, Carl Giesenhagen, sent Brandt, who took Peters along with him, to a fisherman in Travemünde, Paul Stoosz. Stoosz decided to take his boat out that night and sail across the Baltic to the nearest Danish island, Laaland, twenty miles away across the Fehmarn Belt. It was a cutter, the property of Dr Draeger. Stoosz worked under a Herr Johannes Johannsen, his stepfather – and he proposed hiding Brandt behind cases of stores and fishing equipment and sailing after dark.[53] Boats putting out to sea from German ports were generally searched when they applied for clearance – sometimes at sea too. There was one ugly moment before they left. They had gone along to a bar, to drink a glass of beer. There Brandt was recognized by an acquaintance, a young man who had joined the Hitler Youth. Fortunately there was nothing particularly suspicious about Brandt's appearance. He was not dressed for a rough journey – there was a strong northerly wind blowing – and all that he in fact had with him was a briefcase with a few shirts in it and a copy of the first volume of Karl Marx's *Das Kapital*. The book, Brandt wryly wrote subsequently, 'never succeeded in turning me into an orthodox Marxist'.[54]

They sailed at dawn. The boat was perfunctorily inspected in the harbour by customs officials. Patrol boats were not out on this blustery morning but the journey was miserable. It took nearly five hours, twice as long as usual, and Brandt was horribly seasick. He landed at Rödbyhavn, on the island of Laaland, with his briefcase and a wallet with 100 marks in it (£5 or $25), green in the face with seasickness and walking tipsily in the gale. Such was the beginning of what was for him a new life.

He carried a couple of addresses in his head, one in Copenhagen and one in Oslo. He was still only nineteen years old, a tall, tough young man, handsome and carrying himself well. He had applied his mind from an early age to serious problems. Thought had led on to action; he had opposed Nazism wholeheartedly and for reasons that he thoroughly understood. He had not fled from Germany to save himself; he escaped with a real purpose.

2

A New Home, a New Life

The day before he left Germany Willy Brandt tried to talk a young friend of his in the SAP, Heinrich Bruhn, into coming to Norway with him. He told him: 'Heini, you don't realize how the Nazis will exploit their power. Better come with me; don't stick on here!'[1] Brandt was more successful with a girl-friend, Gertrud Meyer, a fellow member of the local SAJ youth group. She promised to follow him to Norway and did so a little later. At nineteen Brandt was very popular with the girls. Long, long after, this very simple fact was to be exploited by political opponents. Still, when he arrived in Denmark he was totally alone.

Of the two addresses he carried in his head the first brought him to Copenhagen, where he stayed with Oscar Hansen, a Danish poet. He spent only a few days there; his aim was to get to Oslo. No trouble about that – he travelled openly on his German passport, which he held for another year. His second address was that of Finn Moe, foreign editor of the *Arbeiderbladet,* the principal newspaper of the Norwegian Labour Party. Moe found him a place to live and gave him a job – at 30 krone a month (about £8 or $40) – which entailed helping to look after political refugees. This work was unexciting, but it gave him the chance to stand on his own feet and to learn Norwegian. He was a ready pupil, for three reasons. The first was the impression formed of Norway on his only previous visit: 'During the summer holidays of 1931 I had travelled across Scandinavia and seen with my own eyes the incomparable beauty of the Norwegian landscape. . . . I was attracted by the unforced friendliness, reserve and natural sense of justice of the fjord and mountain people.'[2] Secondly, he was a natural linguist. Within about three months he was writing articles for the *Arbeiderbladet.* A little later he made his first public speech in Norwegian. The third reason for his acclimatization was political. He found that

17

his own SAP had much in common with the Norwegian Labour Party (NAP): they both stood 'somewhere between the Social Democrats and the Communists'.[3] The NAP decided, after the First World War, to join the Comintern but broke away in 1923. By 1928 they were the most powerful party in Norway. What Brandt liked best was that they carried democracy down into small communities, into the life of the people. This doubtless contributed to the special solidarity in the Norwegian labour movement – industrial workers, farmers and fishermen had more in common than they did in bigger democracies.[4]

There was a less obvious reason why he was able to make his way so quickly in Norway. His new life there really was new. It gave him the 'chance to learn something, to collect experience'.[5] He was young, very young, and the kind of person who enjoyed adventure.

There was much to do, much to plan. Many exiles were wildly over-optimistic in assessing the length of the Nazi tenure of power. This was one reason why so many of them failed to learn to speak a foreign language. When Rudolf Breitscheid, of the SPD, heard that Hitler had been appointed chancellor he believed he would be overwhelmed by problems and 'would soon be finished'.[6] Others thought the Nazis would have to 'liberalize'. Others, again, had the improbable notion that the Nazis were being used by reactionary capitalism in its last fling.[7] Brandt was more down to earth, although sometimes subject to wishful thinking.* The fact was that he had a tremendously active mind. He intended to learn Norwegian, to interest himself in Norwegian social and political history, pick up his journalistic activities, find out more about Europe as a whole and, most important of all, help to rally world opinion against the Nazis.

He learnt to speak Norwegian perfectly. He became acquainted with a progressive intellectual group, Mot Dag (Towards the Day), whose members encouraged him to study at

* Brandt himself has since admitted: 'I never dimly dreamt that the Nazi era would last twelve years. I remember – it must have been some time fairly soon after I came to Norway – walking along a fjord, reciting the speech which I intended to make when I got back to Lübeck.' (Willy Brandt, in personal conversation with the author.) One friend said that Brandt 'was afraid' that the Nazi era was going to last as long as the First World War – in fact, four years – 'and he was considered to be very much a pessimist'.

Oslo University. He took his intermediate examination in 1934 and passed, but did not sit for his finals in history. Instead he returned to active journalism and politics. But he learnt much about Norway at Oslo University and he made useful friends. They included Einer Gerhardsen, prime minister after the war, Trygve Bratteli, later chairman of the Labour Party, Halvard Lange, a future Norwegian foreign minister, and the grand old man of Norwegian socialism, Martin Tranmäl. He moved, as he put it himself, in 'bourgeois' as well as socialist circles.[8] Quite simply he liked the Norwegians, and they liked him.*

Journalism and anti-Nazi activity were to be his two main interests during his twelve years in exile. They combined in the sense that journalism gave him the chance to express his anti-Nazi views and the means to earn a living. He was intensely busy. Already he had a habit of burying himself in his work, often to the total exclusion of all else. This habit was to lose him one faithful girl-friend who would dearly have loved to marry him and, later, his first wife. A single-minded determination to get the job done and an ability to work very nearly round the clock under pressure are tremendous assets; they may not contribute towards a cosy home life.

He quickly became a link-man between the German socialists in exile and the Norwegian Labour Party. One Norwegian friend, Johan Cappelen, later ambassador to Belgrade, remembers his contributions to discussion of foreign policy in the 'somewhat limited foreign affairs milieu of Oslo'.[9] Not yet a Norwegian citizen – the Nazis deprived him of German nationality by decree only in 1936 – Brandt could play no real part in the Norwegian labour movement. But his wide circle of Norwegian friends

---

* One thing that Brandt liked especially about the Norwegians was that they never wasted words. His favourite Norwegian story (as told to the author) concerns the farmer who was sitting in the wilds and was sitting at home one evening when there was a knock on the door. It was his nearest neighbour from three or four miles away up the fjord. The farmer opened the door and wordlessly motioned his friend inside, sitting him down at the kitchen table. As they sat in silence he noticed that his friend was staring fixedly up at a shelf. He looked up at it too, saw a bottle of aquavit on it, got the bottle down, poured out two glasses of it. Then they drank steadily and in silence until the bottle was nearly empty.

When the farmer poured out the last two glasses his friend at last spoke. '*Skol*!' was all that he said, but it was one word too many for the farmer. 'You wretched chatterbox!' he said. 'Did you come here for a decent drink, or to talk a load of rubbish?'

meant that he had influence. In the meantime he had to keep the SAP organization in Oslo going, and canalize their efforts to work against the Nazi regime in Germany. As a mere offshoot of the SPD, the SAP might have played only a minor role in the desperate efforts of the Germans in exile to warn the outside world against Nazism. This was not the case. They had a high percentage of young people in their ranks and many went into exile determined to do active work. The convinced SAP members who stayed in Germany felt the same way. The SAP, as a kind of activist élite, were able to fulful themselves far more successfully after Hitler had come into power than before.

From its centres in Paris, Prague and Oslo the party maintained crucially important links with Germany.[10] There was a busy correspondence, using code and invisible ink. Literature that the Nazis had banned was sent into Germany in suitcases with false bottoms, or through the post, with bogus bindings. Meetings were arranged, outside Germany's borders. For the SAP in Oslo, Copenhagen became the most obvious half-way meeting-place; it was so easily reached from Germany. In exile they collected money and sent it to Paris to use on behalf of the victims of Nazism in Germany. Those victims were usually in prison or concentration camps; generally the money went to wives and families. They secured Norwegian help when protesting against the trial in Berlin of Max Kohler and Stefan Szende for alleged subversion. The outcome was light sentences and both of them were later able to escape from Germany.

A much more striking action was undertaken on behalf of Carl von Ossietsky. A member of an aristocratic Prussian family, he became a pacifist after the First World War and his outspoken comments in the *Weltbühne*, a left-wing weekly that he edited, resulted in his arrest, trial and imprisonment with an eighteen-month sentence. This was in 1931 and he could have left Germany when he was released. He stayed and was rearrested on the night of the burning of the Reichstag in February 1933. In 1935, while in a concentration camp, he was awarded a Nobel Peace Prize. The Nazis took him from the gaol and offered him his freedom if he would recant his pacifist views.[11] He refused, and went back to gaol. Brandt collected signatures from Norwegian parliamentarians, and sixty-nine members of the Storting, the Norwegian parliament, as well as fifty-nine members of the Swedish parliament, the Riksdag, asked for his release. The Nazis gave way; Ossietsky came out of gaol, if only to die in May 1938 in hospital. Hitler ordained that no German citizen should in future be allowed to accept a Nobel Prize.

Brandt referred briefly to his own part in the affair in December 1971, when he himself received the Nobel Peace Prize in Oslo.[12] He recalled that he had secured the help of friends in bringing Ossietsky's case to the attention of the Nobel Prize Committee before Ossietsky received his prize, in fact in 1935. The prize was sent by the committee on 23 November 1936 and he would, had he not been in gaol, have received it in Oslo.

Much time was taken up in the spasmodic and hopeless efforts of the German left-wing groups in exile to secure unity of action. The reason why these failed was that the two major parties-in-exile, the SPD and the KPD, began the Nazi era as sworn enemies. SPD leaders preached working-class solidarity. But the KPD regarded the SPD as the natural ally of the bourgeoisie,[13] blocking working-class unity. In addition the SPD was politically inept – the communist leader, Wilhelm Pieck, coined the phrase: 'Every Communist should be the leader of five Social Democratic workers.'[14]

The two major parties-in-exile were also separated by geography. The SPD made their headquarters in Prague, the capital of a democratic country closest to Berlin; the KPD in exile were theoretically based in Paris, but gravitated towards Moscow. The Soviet government, for the time being, wanted a 'popular front' – of course under KPD leadership. This Moscow line persisted from 1934 to 1937. By that time the Soviet leaders decided a popular front was a pipe dream. On 12 November 1937 Georgi Dimitroff, a defendant in the 1933 Reichstag fire trial, wrote in *L'Humanité*, the organ of the French Communist Party, that Stalin was right in saying capitalism would be defeated only when the SPD was stamped out of the working-class movement.[15] Walter Ulbricht contributed to the Soviet campaign to secure KPD predominance in the *Kommunistische Internationale*[16] by attacking his 'Trotskyist' rivals. He declared: 'Counter-revolutionary Trotskyism, in alliance with German Fascism, is the chief warmonger in the world; also the mortal enemy of the Soviet Union and of the international proletariat.'

In Prague the SPD quickly became involved in their own

internal conflicts. At first this did not seem likely to happen. An executive of six members was formed in June 1933, comprising three 'moderates' and three 'progressives'. On 18 June they produced a manifesto with a revolutionary ring[17] and published the first issue of their newspaper, the *Neuer Vorwärts*. A miniature newspaper, *Sozialistische Aktion,* was smuggled across the frontier into Germany, printed on thin, almost tissue paper, with eight small pages and about twenty-five thousand words in all. Around two million copies were distributed in Germany during the first year of publication. Very soon the SPD opened a printing plant at Karlsbad (Karlovy Vary). Meanwhile the party had established close working relations with its Sudentenland socialist colleagues inside Czecho-Slovakia, and a courier service across the German frontier, supervised by *Grenzsekretäre* (literally 'frontier secretaries') posted at strategically favourable crossing-points. Later, crossing-points from Polish, French, Swiss, Belgian, Dutch and Danish territory were also used.

This was an impressive initial performance, but difficulties began to loom. There was a great deal of underlying anti-German feeling among the Czech population, which explains the growing sense of isolation of the SPD leadership in Prague. Bickerings broke out inside the party. They started with a struggle between the executive and the so-called Old Left. At the same time the leadership was being assailed by a New Left group, *Neu Beginnen,* which wanted to use the period of exile to plan a radical reform of society. Under pressure the SPD leaders published a manifesto in January 1934 that stressed Marxist ideology, the class struggle and the evolution of a powerful and united revolutionary socialist party. It radiated an optimism that the men who framed it can scarcely have felt, although they talked bravely of the impending fragmentation of the Nazi movement, of the insurmountable economic difficulties confronting the Nazis, of stiffening foreign resistance to the Nazi regime and of the possible defection of the German army. When the August 1934 Nazi plebiscite produced an overwhelming majority for Hitler taking over the post of chief of state in place of the dead Hindenburg, the *Neuer Vorwärts* claimed that 4,300,000 Germans opposed Hitler's nomination and a million more spoiled their ballot papers, showing that there were 'five million mortal opponents of Hitler'.

In Prague the SPD leaders returned to pleas for moderation, while instructions across the frontier to the underground were to concentrate on the collection and exchange of information, improvement of cell and cadre organization, helping comrades and their families in need, and conversation of forces in place of overt acts of opposition. These instructions were eminently sensible, but to some extent a tacit admission that the Nazi regime had come to stay.

Where did Brandt and the SAP fit into this picture of SPD-KPD rivalry and lack of working-class solidarity? What distinguished members of the SAP was their activism, their determination to get on with useful work. In 1934 they began publication of a paper, *Neue Front,* and a 'youth journal', *Jugend Korrespondenz,* later to become the *Sozialistische Jugend,* was founded in Oslo. Both of these Oslo publications owed much to Brandt's ideas and energy. They produced, too, a journal called *Kampfbereit* for key youth members and clandestine circulation in Germany, and in 1935 yet another newspaper, *Marxistische Tribüne,* was founded in Paris. Brandt became a major contributor to it.

The SAP were at first protagonists of working-class solidarity and the creation of a 'pure' Communist International based on the Marx-Engels *Communist Manifesto.* In this sense the party stood much closer to the Communists than to the Social Democrats. But they stood even closer to the Trotskyists, as an article written by Brandt for *Marxistische Tribüne* in 1936 indicates.[18] Brandt warned against Stalinism and Communist 'centrism' and cited the recent Moscow trials, which brought death sentences for so-called 'deviationists', as a depressing example of Stalinism in action. He wanted organizational independence from Moscow, but links with the best elements in the Communist International. The themes in this article might indicate immaturity of judgement. He maintained that the SAP were picking up support all the time from the SPD and KPD, whereas they were still a closely knit élite party. And he felt that where ideology was concerned Trotskyism assumed that it 'gave all the answers'. Trotskyism never did that. He certainly believed in international co-operation among the working class. In February 1934 the International Bureau of Revolutionary Youth Organizations was founded. He became an active participant in its discussions and plans. In the same month he attended a conference of left-wing socialist youth groups at Laaren, in Holland. It nearly ended in tragedy for him, and he was probably saved by the fact that he had come from Norway and was not at once recognizable as a German.[19] The pro-Nazi mayor of Laaren handed over four young Germans to the police, as 'undesirable aliens', and they were taken to the German frontier in handcuffs and surrendered to the Gestapo. Others, including Brandt himself, were taken to Amsterdam, interrogated there and expelled from Holland.

Brandt returned from Holland to the never-never land of socialist discussion of socialist strategy in the realization of socialist ideals. This barren exercise has been described, in a kind of instant bird's-eye view, by Günther Markscheffel, a close friend of Brandt. In his memorandum[20] Markscheffel gives a graphic picture of the endless, pointless talk that went on in émigré circles. He and his friends met once a week in the Rue Richer in Paris, close to the Folies-Bergères, paradoxically for serious discussion. They called the dark little hole of a room in which they met the Office of the Free German Youth (the title Free German Youth, FDJ, was annexed by the Communists and subsequently used in East Germany after the end of the Second World War). Their discussion led nowhere, but Markscheffel and his wife stayed sane for two reasons. They had to work for a living, he as a building worker, she as a cleaner. And Markscheffel travelled periodically to Germany in order to make contact with the underground there, crossing the frontier at Forbach, on the Saar. He vividly remembers Brandt's appearance one night at their discussions. He made an instant impression – 'after a few minutes he had the meeting in his pocket'. And his message was utterly to the point: young Germans in exile had to do something besides talking, best of all produce a journal that would develop their thinking about the future for Germany and Europe. The immediate result was *Freie Deutsche Jugend*, which ran for a time but folded up for lack of funds. Markscheffel lost touch with it all; he was arrested in Forbach by the French police for 'disturbing Franco-German relations', while acting as a *Grenzsekretär* supervising the courier service across the German frontier.

Brandt's life might have gone on being spent in this kind of unproductive, though well-meant, political activity up to the outbreak of the Second World War. But in the summer of 1936 he was sent to Berlin to re-establish contact with the socialist underground there, in charge temporarily of the SAP organization, the Metro. He had discarded his German passport in 1935, about a year before he was officially deprived of German citizenship. He carried, from then on, a 'strangers' passport' (*Fremdenpass*), made out in Norway for stateless persons. It happened to look very similar to a Norwegian passport.

His girl-friend, Gertrud Meyer, who in 1933 had followed him into exile from Lübeck, fortuitously came into his life again at this point. She had been in love with Brandt, wanted indeed to marry him. By 1936 she may have begun to realize that he was too much bound up in political work, perhaps also too independent in his way of life to marry her. She decided to marry an obliging Norwegian, Gunnar Gaasland, in order to get a work permit and the right to claim Norwegian citizenship. It was purely a marriage of convenience and in 1939 Gertrud emigrated to the United States. One friend of Brandt believed that she was still heartbroken over him.[21] Her husband Gunnar, at all events, agreed that Brandt should use his passport for his tour of duty in Berlin. Brandt, alias Gaasland, was ostensibly a Norwegian student, in Berlin to study German history at the Humboldt University.

He lodged with a Frau Hamel, 'a delightful lady',[22] at 20 Kurfürstendamm. He had to move with extreme circumspection, for the Gestapo had become expert since 1933 in tracking down opponents of Nazi tyranny. Nazi security operated at a score of different levels. There were Nazi agents in the factories; others infiltrated resistance groups, especially of the communist underground. The Nazis appointed their 'men of confidence' (*Vertrauensmänner*) even in blocks of flats, where they were designated as *Blockwart* (watchmen). The Gestapo kept, in addition, a careful watch on all meeting-places and drew up meticulous black lists of known and suspected opponents. In the course of three years security had become a fine art.

The Communists were hit hardest by Nazi round-ups. The SAP and its SJV (*Sozialistischer Jugendverein*) youth organization suffered heavily too. The Nazis struck whenever resistance was organized to the point of producing illegal literature. Whenever this happened the Gestapo sooner or later found a lead and followed it up. After an early SAP leaflet action they pounced in August 1933, arresting ninety-one leading members of the underground. The same thing happened in Breslau, where an illegal newspaper with a circulation of over four thousand was being produced. At the end of 1933 there was a wave of arrests in Berlin and ringleaders were brought to trial towards the end of 1934.[23] Details were smuggled out of Germany and there were protests in European countries. As a result foreign journalists were allowed to report the trials and the accused were given relatively mild sentences.

In 1935 Nazi 'justice' grew tougher. In Hamm eighteen SAP members, all between the ages of seventeen and twenty, were sentenced to a total of ninety years' imprisonment. SAP resisters became involved with communist and social democratic groups. Inter-party links made resistance groups easier for the Nazis to infiltrate. More than four hundred left-wing opponents of the regime were caught in Zeitz, and 140 in Magdeburg. Two years earlier, according to SAP leaders in exile,[24] about fourteen thousand SAP members had still been politically active; 1936 was a turning point for left-wingers in Germany. They were left with the alternatives of organizing on the most secret basis possible, or ceasing political activity and sitting out the Nazi era.

This was the situation that Brandt found when he arrived in Berlin. He crossed by boat, the regular train-ferry service, from the Danish island of Gedser to the port of Warnemünde. From Berlin he went, briefly, to Paris, then returned to the Reich capital. He has admitted feeling some fear;[25] indeed it could hardly have been otherwise. He was putting his head into the lion's mouth and the talks with friends in Paris had been thoroughly depressing. His name was by now on the central and key black list kept by the Nazis. He could be recognized by former associates who had gone over to the Nazi side. He carried a false passport, which might not stand inspection. To return to Germany, as a wanted man who could expect no mercy if he were caught, required great courage.

He has given his own account of his task.[26] The underground known as the Metro consisted of a number of cells kept very

26

small for security reasons – generally of four or five members only. Members used *Decknamen*, cover names, even when dealing with one another. Generally addresses were kept secret too; therefore a member of the underground who was caught and tortured by the Gestapo would be literally unable to say where his associates lived. Members of cells met at selected places, a café, a bookshop, a public building or railway station. Organization in small cells was the only possible answer to the untiring Nazi surveillance. Inevitably work carried out by the Metro and similar organizations was limited in scope. The first and most necessary task of all was to keep cells in existence and organize links between them. The development of cells in factories was of primary importance, although these – by virtue of everyone knowing everybody else personally – were more vulnerable than the groups that met clandestinely in the heart of big cities. Next, the cells accumulated information and passed it on, both within and outside Germany, using courier services across the frontier. This was part of the 'offensive of truth' waged against Nazism.[27] Ideally the dissemination of facts was best carried out by leaflets and illegal newspapers. But their production became steadily more risky, even suicidally so, and messages were increasingly transmitted by word of mouth or in invisible ink.

One of Brandt's associates in Berlin was Joachim Unger, a Trotskyist who became a member of the SAP in 1935. Unger's story shows how Hitler's left-wing opponents operated:

> I was an opponent of the Nazis in my teens, even before they came into power. I knew what to expect, so I got hold of a forged passport in good time and went underground. I lasted only until 1937, and then had to get out – Copenhagen, then on to Stockholm and exile for the rest of the Nazi period.
>
> As I saw it, we had to keep our small cadres in existence for the possibility of a revolutionary situation arising. Some day, Nazism would be beaten and there had to be something to put in its place. In 1935 I managed to recruit ex-members of the KPD for the SAP – risky perhaps, but worth doing. We kept our cadres small, collected information, sent it out of the country with our own frontier-runners. They brought in papers printed abroad – one of them was the Trotskyist

Unser Wort, which was produced in Prague. This was a big help for our discussions, as well as our distribution of written stuff. It was much safer than printing inside Germany – that sort of work is hard to keep secret.

We used cover names and changed these periodically, as an extra security measure. Walter Fabian and Erwin Bauer were two of the chaps who worked with me at the time. As we saw it, there was no hope of influencing the masses, the way that the White Rose group in Munich and the Red Orchestra lot in Berlin tried. It couldn't be done – it was too dangerous. We even had tests for people who wanted to join us – they would be given one difficult assignment to carry out, like taking material across the border into Czechoslovakia. They had to wait three months anyway before they could become members of a cell; then they were in. But in 1937 we ran into trouble. One of the youth cadres was infiltrated; it was led by a seventeen-year-old called 'Freddy' – I never knew his real name. He was caught, tortured and murdered by the Nazis. By then they had leads to other cadres. It was time for me to clear out. By that time I had run through three cover names, Lohse, Korting and Leonhard.

Willy Brandt? Yes, I met him in Berlin at the time. In fact, he gave me addresses in Norway, Denmark and Sweden when I had to get out. We went for a walk in the middle of Berlin, and I memorized them as we went along. People criticized him later on because he was not representing some formal concept of democracy in the Metro. What rubbish! They just don't know what resistance was about; we kept going in the only way possible.[28]

Another member of the resistance who knew Brandt at this time was Fritz Benke. Only nineteen when the Nazis came to power, he had taken an interest in politics from a much earlier age. At fourteen he was a member of a socialist youth group.[29] When the SJV was banned in 1933 he organized a cell of five young men and distributed illegal leaflets. His cell had to disperse in 1937, but he formed another during the war and in 1942 was busy chalking up anti-war slogans on the walls of public buildings. He went into hiding for the last months of the war. He met Brandt in SAP discussion groups during the summer of 1936, in the middle of Berlin or in the forests fringing its suburbs. Once they met outside the Camera cinema in Unter den Linden. On another occasion they discussed means of helping the widow of an SAP member who had committed suicide in gaol, jumping from an upper-storey window after being tortured by the Gestapo. There was a wretched sequel to their talk, which took place in the Tegelerwald, a forest on the north-west edge of Berlin – Benke tripped over a rock and broke his ankle. Brandt helped him to the nearest railway station and got him home.

SAP cadres in Berlin probably totalled under five hundred members at any one time.[30] Circumscribed as he was in his work, Brandt put in a certain amount of time at the Prussian State Library, studying contemporary history and the ideology, organization and policies of the Nazi regime. He had one especially awkward episode, when a Norwegian student decided to make friends. Not only did he ask altogether too many questions about Brandt's own supposed Norwegian antecedents as Gunnar Gaasland, but he turned out to be a red-hot Nazi into the bargain![31] Brandt succeeded in dodging this importunate 'fellow countryman'. On another occasion he recognized an old Lübeck acquaintance but did not dare to speak to him.

He left Berlin for Prague at the end of 1936, once again a nerve-racking business, then travelled to Brünn and Mährisch-Ostrau, then via Danzig to Oslo in January 1937. In March some notes of his were published by the *Marxistische Tribüne* under the title 'Aus der Organisation', 'From the organization'.[32] He expressed concern about the fate of German youth: the Nazis were making an all-out effort to capture them. This had to be countered, possibly by building up sports associations for anti-fascists. With factory workers Brandt's view was that more should be done to study their material grievances and get them rectified. This, he felt, was the right way to keep a critical or even hostile spirit towards the Nazis alive. In addition he recommended the careful utilization of shipping and tourism as links between the socialist underground and the outside world.

At the same time as this article was published he produced a report entitled 'Some Aspects of our Practical Work Without and Within'. His summing-up was clear-cut – 'The focal point of our entire work lies in the Reich.'[33] The SAP in exile must organize a central office for the collation of all information about the work of the underground in Germany – then all feasible ways of helping could be studied and developed. The SAP in exile should produce directives on political aims for distribution to the underground and should carry out a survey of views about events inside Germany from questions put to all approachable Germans travelling outside the borders of the Reich. His report had much to say about underground cadres. His main worry was that if left in isolation they would gradually wither. They had to be encouraged to seek discreet but productive contact with the workers in the factories and with young people. More imagination should be used in establishing and maintaining contact between the underground and the outside world; he suggested in particular the possibility of forging Nazi literature, brochures and the like, in order to slip in facts about the German situation. Another suggestion was that all Germans going to big football games and other sports meetings in foreign countries should be given leaflets and newspapers suitable for smuggling back into Germany. His report closed on a salutary note: there were no grounds for self-satisfaction, and a great deal of daily practical work remained to be done.

Six months before Brandt had returned to Oslo the Spanish Civil War broke out, leading to another important and only slightly less adventurous episode in his life. For Spain was shortly to be his destination.

War resulted from a balance of forces within the Spanish Republic that coincided with and encouraged the radicalization of attitudes on both sides. The Popular Front parties of the left were victorious in the 1936 elections. Yet, as one historian has pointed out,[34] the Popular Front polled only 4.3 million votes against their opponents' 4.4 million. And the Popular Front government, without a clear mandate from the Spanish people, allowed a campaign of violence to begin. On 16 June 1936 Gil Robles read out to the Cortes a list of outrages that he laid at the door of the Popular Front – 169 churches totally destroyed, 257 churches pillaged, 269 people killed and 1,879 wounded, 113 major strikes, 228 local strikes, 43 newspaper offices or printing presses attacked, 146 bomb explosions.[35] The Popular Front government were weak and radical; and the signs were that they were moving still further to the left – the socialists adopted the communist salute of the clenched fist, the communist red flag, communist phraseology. One unbiased view is that the Communist Party had become the key element in the Popular Front.[36]

On 18 July General Franco was flown from the Canary Islands to lead the military uprising against the Republican Government. Civil wars often start at a low pitch and only gradually develop real intensity. But the Spanish Civil War was exceptional in that hideous cruelties were committed early on by both sides. People who knew Spain believed that the Spaniards were incapable of fighting an organized war. In a sense this was true; but a three-and-a-half-year struggle lay ahead that would be characterized by terrible disorganization as well as terrible suffering.

The most operative fact about the war for German emigrants like Brandt was that Nazi Germany at once took a hand. A small armada of German Junkers 52 transport planes brought twenty thousand crack Spanish and Moorish troops to southern Spain from Morocco, Heinkel fighter aircraft arrived, the battleship *Deutschland* put in to Ceuta harbour. In November the Condor Legion was formed in Seville by German Luftwaffe personnel. German tanks were shipped to Spain too, and within a few months there were more than 6,500 Germans fighting on the Nationalist side. About a hundred German aircraft bombed undefended towns, culminating in the 'martyrdom of Guernica', the small Basque town that was pulverized in April 1937.[37] The Spanish people were not allowed to settle their own quarrels and their sufferings were hideously protracted. Nazi Germany, Fascist Italy to a lesser extent and the Soviet Union all used Spain as a battleground. Finally General Franco employed ultra-Fabian tactics to save manpower, avoid a *levée en masse* on either side of the lines and reduce material damage.

Opponents of Nazism like Brandt regarded Nazi intervention in Spain as an insolent challenge to the right of Spaniards to live their own lives. Brandt might have gone to Spain to fight had he not been so preoccupied with what was happening in Germany. Left-wing volunteers began to assemble in Albacete in October 1936 and the International Brigades were formed from them. Possibly as many as a hundred thousand foreigners signed up for service. Casualties were high,[38] so was the rate of desertion; by the spring of 1938 there may have been about thirty-five thousand left serving in the international brigades.

Although deeply interested in what was happening in Spain, Brandt went there only in February 1937 and then primarily as a correspondent of Norwegian and Swedish newspapers. He undertook to maintain contact with members of the SAP and other left-wing Germans fighting on the republican side. He had a tricky journey to Spain, as he was by now carrying the passport of Gunnar Gaasland. From Le Havre he was sent to Paris and had to wait several days for the official stamp needed to cross the Franco-Spanish frontier. He based himself in Barcelona. The SAP were closely allied with the POUM (Partito Obrero Unificada Marxista), the so-called United Marxist Party, who were probably farther to the left than the SAP, with links with the Trotskyists and the Anarcho-Syndicalists. They were the party of individualists and idealists, drawing such people into its ranks as the British novelist George Orwell, and the young British poet John Cornford. The centre of POUM strength was Catalonia and their headquarters were therefore in Barcelona.

Brandt had met members of the POUM first in May 1936 in Paris.[39] There was an air of extreme, even zany impracticality about them; their members talked incessantly about revolution as the only worthwhile end in itself; war was a 'revolutionary outbreak' that heralded the dawn of a new, Utopian society and had nothing to do with the defence of bourgeois democracy.[40]

They had little sympathy for the official socialist government that Franco and the Nationalists were determined to destroy, nor for the Moscow-steered official Communist Party, which they termed an 'anti-revolutionary force'.[41] They were irritated by being ignored by the military leadership. This was, however, understandable: because of their relatively small numbers they played no great role in the conduct and course of the war.

By autumn 1936 the Soviet Union was pouring arms into Spain and wanted its nominees in power. The POUM leaders were accordingly ejected from the Generalité or provincial government of Catalonia in December 1936. By early 1937 they were in greater trouble – for criticizing the rigged trials in Moscow, for calling Soviet Communism a 'bureaucratic regime' and for continually obstructing efforts to secure a unified political and military command. Brandt himself 'fell out with the revolutionaries, who seemed to have overshot the target, but I disagreed even more violently with those who sought to exploit the discipline which the military situation demanded by establishing a system of one-party rule'.[42] In his view the POUM had become stupidly sectarian and impractical, He tried to help by advising greater unity in order to get on with the battle to save Spanish democracy. He had learnt some Spanish at school and quickly picked up enough to be able to speak on public platforms.

Early in 1937 the POUM were being ruthlessly 'purged' everywhere outside Catalonia; May saw the real show-down in Barcelona, with a miniature civil war taking place inside Republican Spain. The POUM, in Brandt's own words, 'were persecuted, dragged before the courts, or even murdered by the Communists'.[43] Battles took place in the streets of Barcelona and early in June the party was declared illegal and, ridiculously, pro-fascist; forty members of the central committee were arrested. At the same time the Communists seized the opportunity to arrest a number of generals who had been too friendly with Largo Caballero, the former socialist prime minister; a number of Soviet political agents were sent home too, and their names vanished from Soviet history.

An earlier Spanish prime minister, Manuel Azana, used the phrase '*Sol y sombra* – light and shade – that is Spain!'[44] Political and military futilities should blind nobody to the blazing idealism and magnificent courage of the Spanish people. In Brandt's words: 'If I think back now on that spring and summer nearly thirty years ago, those unedifying squabbles and sordid intrigues have entirely faded into the background. . . . The image which remains most clearly of all in my mind is that of the proverbial pride of the Spanish people, their vitality, love for freedom and faith in the future, and the creative power which time and again would fight its way to the surface.'[45] George Orwell paid tribute to the heroism of the Spaniards who fought for the republic. It embodied a magnificent disregard of adverse odds: 'Everything was running short – boots, clothes, tobacco, soap, candles, matches, olive oil. Our uniforms were dropping to pieces, and many of the men had no boots, only rope-soled sandals. You came on piles of worn-out boots everywhere. Once we kept a dug-out fire burning for two hours mainly with boots, which are not bad fuel. . . .'[46]

So much for the *sol* of Manuel Azana. The dark side of the Civil War was shockingly apparent to Brandt. His particular nightmare was the decimation of independent-minded intellectuals by the Nationalists: 'In Franco's Spain teachers and academics are shot. In the province of Galicia 80 per cent of all primary teachers were put before the firing squad ... in the villages of other provinces 60 per cent of teachers, and 20 per cent ended up in prison. ... In the province of Granada there was a large contingent of intellectuals among the 23,000 executed.'[47] But the Republicans were accused of equal brutality – 'In Madrid,' according to one authority, 'to have voted against the Popular Front, attended church or worn a tie qualified anyone for a bullet in the neck, Russian style.'[48] Brandt discovered that revolutions 'are not romantic, but cruel and confused',[49] that the proclamation of high ideals is not enough – the dignity and compassion of the little man are traduced by an ignorant, self-seeking and potentially treacherous leadership. To him one external protagonist, Hitler, represented unqualified evil. The other, Stalin, wanted his kind of communist victory, which took no account of the wants of the Spanish people: 'The Comintern is determined to destroy all forces that refuse to obey its orders. It is for this reason that the whole international labour movement must rise against it.'[50] Brandt was denounced by the Communists as a Franco agent and Gestapo spy – after the war; the other side claimed he was a double-dyed Bolshevik of the international brigades.

Brandt left Spain after only four months, sadly disillusioned. His chief fear was that, should the republic survive, it would take the form of a Communist Party dictatorship (*'Spanien ist in einer Entwicklung zur kommunistischen Parteidiktatur'*).[51] At a British Independent Labour Party meeting in Letchworth in August he was deeply pessimistic about the POUM (so much so that one of his British hosts recalls that, after listening to him 'we began to realize that the communist leadership were a bunch of bloody scoundrels').[52] He had a reason to be. The POUM leaders were rounded up, gaoled, tried in October 1938 and returned to prison. Many were found there by Franco's victorious forces and imprisoned for a third term. The party was finished.

The Spanish Civil War left Brandt old in experience. He had been obliged to make a new home for himself at the age of nineteen in a foreign country. He had sought to evolve a political philosophy, only to see many of its premises shattered by the refusal of left-wing parties to co-operate. He had returned to Germany to work in the underground and boldly faced great danger. He had witnessed the heroism and the tragedy of the Spanish people. In 1935, when he was twenty-three, he heard that his grandfather, the only blood relation for whom he had a deep affection had committed suicide. His mother came to see him in Copenhagen, a half-way house betweeen Lübeck and Oslo. He remembers feeling much older already at that time. By the end of 1937 he was mature, thinking well ahead with judgement and instinct. War, world war, was in the offing, and with it would come a great deal more experience.

3

Empty Dreams

In 1938 Brandt was still only twenty-five, but with half a lifetime of experience behind him. In five years in exile he had achieved three things generally beyond the compass of other Germans. He had learnt to speak perfectly the language of the country of his choice, Norway. He had integrated to such an extent that he was accepted by the Norwegians as one of them. During these five years he spoke quite naturally of 'going home', when he meant Norway.[1] Finally, he had worked with great courage against the Nazis. In all three respects he had shown himself to be quite out of the normal run of German exiles.

Here was a young man with a singular gift for marshalling his thoughts and putting them down on paper with the same hard, logical clarity of his conversation. One fellow member of the SAP found him gay, humorous, always straightforward and – this was not everybody's view – instantly friendly:

> We were friends at once; before I met him, I had corres-
> ponded with him and got the impression of a tough, highly
> practical, matter-of-fact man, a go-getter. The reality was
> different: he was able to relax, loved a good laugh, had the gift
> of companionable silence too – one didn't need to babble with
> him. Not practical in little things though; he couldn't do any-
> thing with his hands, not even hammer in a nail or change an
> electric light bulb. He couldn't drive a car. As far as I know
> he's never learnt to drive to this day.[2]

A young British socialist found him

> ... a very attractive character, and not just because he was
> friendly and exceptionally good looking. He had a mixture of
> genuine shyness and forthright resolution which immediately
> appealed. He said what he thought, yet remained friendly in

36

spite of differences of opinion. I was to meet him later in life, and he was exactly the same man that he had always been. If he had one outstanding characteristic, I would say it was resolution – resolution to get things done and not to give up.[3]

Another friend in the SAP[4] remembered his readiness to help others. She and her husband fled from Nazi Germany to Holland, but were told to leave because they were not orthodox Social Democrats. They moved to Norway, contacted Brandt in Oslo. He took them in tow, introduced them to friends, found them somewhere to live. This was not an isolated act of kindness: later he looked after this married couple in Stockholm when the husband was very ill and paid the rent of their humble flat. They returned at the end of the war to Bremen, where he sent food parcels from Scandinavia – 'these are things that one can never forget about him'. He never forgot his friends.

He had an unresting urge to achieve something worth while, filling every minute of the day. But he was not obsessed with his work; he always found time for friends and he took exercise when he needed it. He had learnt to swim well, would learn to ski well too, walked fast and far, climbed mountains. At about the time when Gertrud Meyer left Norway in 1939 for the United States he fell in love, with Carlota Thorkildsen, a Norwegian girl working as secretary in a scientific institute. A little later they settled down together, with the intention of getting married soon. Then came the war. They put off marrying for the time being. This part of Brandt's personal life requires only brief treatment. He was forced to leave Norway for Sweden in June 1940 (see p. 47). Carlota was pregnant but did not follow him until spring 1941. They married in Stockholm; their daughter, Ninja, had been born in Oslo in October 1940. The marriage broke up in 1945 when Carlota and Ninja returned to Oslo. Their parting was dignified by mutual agreement and a readiness to remain on friendly terms.

Brandt has shown an extreme but understandable reticence to talk about his first marriage. His version,[5] briefly, was this: The parting in 1940 may have contributed towards putting things on the wrong footing. Carlota was unhappy over the thought that he would return to Germany after the war was over. The war years were hectic and disturbed – far worse for a young wife with a baby than for a husband who could at least bury himself in his work. Brandt was always tremendously independent and was never prepared to let himself become over-domesticated. Was Carlota, perhaps, possessive, as well as intelligent, sentient, lively? She was well-read and had a mind of her own. She may have felt that her place was in Oslo. At least the break left no serious ill feeling behind; and both have remained discreetly silent about their life together.

Meanwhile war had broken out. It seemed logical to Brandt that each fresh concession made to the Nazis would whet their appetite and encourage them to ask for more.[6] The concessions comprised a formidable list. In July 1933 the Vatican had signed a concordat with Nazi Germany. In January 1934 Hitler had been able to conclude a ten-year non-aggression pact with Poland, and in June 1935 the Naval Agreement with Britain. In the same year the plebiscite in the Saar had led to its return to Germany. In 1935 Hitler had reintroduced conscription, drawing only mild protests from the Versailles powers. In March 1936 he had marched his troops into the demilitarized Rhineland. Nazi Germany had scored a tremendous propaganda success with the 1936 Olympic Games in Berlin and in October had instituted the Rome-Berlin Axis with fascist Italy. Japan, the third bandit on the international stage, had joined the Axis in November. Racial and political persecution were now under way inside Germany and German armed intervention was taking place with brazen effrontery in Spain. In March 1938 Hitler had annexed Austria. In September 1938 had come the Munich Agreement, under which the German-speaking Sudetenland, with a population of three million, was handed over to Germany. This had paved the way for the dismemberment of Czechoslovakia, which Hitler was to invade in March 1939. He had begun to bring pressure to bear on Poland, stepping it up when that country's territorial integrity was explicitly guaranteed by Britain and France in April 1939. The Munich Agreement may have been a cowardly blunder, but in Britain the Labour and Liberal Opposition had fought all efforts to put the country's defences on to a sound footing, the Chamberlain peace policy was overwhelmingly popular and most Britons were not prepared to go to war unless goaded to absolute exasperation. The whole British press had acclaimed the Munich Agreement. Apposite judgements were those of Winston Churchill and Ernest Bevin, later Labour's foreign secretary. In Churchill's view: 'It is said that no one who approved of Munich should be allowed to hold office. To do that would be to cast a reflection upon the great majority of the nation at that time.'[7] Bevin was even blunter: 'If anyone asks me who was responsible for the British policy leading up to the war, I should as a Labour man myself make a confession and say – all of us.'[8]

A feeling of impotent isolation was increased by what was happening to the exiles themselves. Long before the Munich Agreement Czechoslovakia had ceased to be a safe haven. In the autumn of 1937 the Czech government had asked the SPD to stop all activities directed openly against Nazi Germany. The party's main base had become Paris, not a place for cohesive and constructive work in the last days of the politically corrupt and futile Third Republic. Its pungently decaying atmosphere had contributed to endemic quarrels, to suspicions, jealousies and even hatreds between rival factions of German exiles. Funds were short, too. In 1936 the *Zeitschrift für Sozialismus* had had to close down; in 1938 it had been the turn of *Sozialistische Aktion*. The SPD in exile concentrated on their *Deutschlandberichte*, reports on Germany, which appeared from 1936 onwards in English and French as well as German. But they had a decreasing impact on foreign opinion.

Brandt had been tireless in urging greater unity. In a letter of 27 December 1937 one finds him calling for a union of all German socialists with European socialist parties.[9] This would cure inbreeding and halt a leftward trend that would otherwise be exploited by the Communists. In a memorandum[10] he had called for co-operation with the Prague leaders, Otto Wels and Friedrich Stampfer. He wanted an increased effort to smuggle valuable news out of Germany – reports of the stepping-up of arms production, of the drive to get new autobahns built, of Nazi governmental pressure for longer working hours and shorter holidays, of increasing persecution of Jews and political opponents of the regime. In this memorandum he had admitted that news about dissatisfaction with the Nazi regime and its economic failures had to be taken with a pinch of salt. A letter of July 1939 sharply criticized the Communists for lack of accuracy.[11] The

Deutschland Information news service of the KPD was playing up the notion that a major revolt against the Nazis was under way. Nothing of the kind was happening; Brandt pointed out that there had not been a single known case of a Nazi party member being inducted into a socialist resistance cell. Of more relevance was the achievement of better work conditions and higher pay in some factories, a result of solidarity that was encouraged by the underground.

Brandt's SAP were ventilating the idea of a socialist concentration, instead of the Popular Front with the Communists. They were able at least to make a temporary alliance with the SPD in Paris. The Austrian socialists, too, were drawn into their discussion for a time. Brandt was active in youth affairs and tried to rally young Germans in exile under the banner of the Freie Deutsche Jugend (Free German Youth) or FDJ. Its aims were to have been to draw up a working programme and inform youth organizations in foreign countries about German preparations for war, the crimes committed by the Nazis, and the part played by the Hitler Youth.[12] The FDJ had held one conference near Paris, in July 1938. Thereafter its activities were few. Its title was annexed by the East German Communists after the Second World War.

As the war drew closer the rift between the German socialists and Communists had widened. One reason was growing doubt in the socialist camp over the intentions of the Soviet Union. A hint was passed out in summer 1939 by Walter Ulbricht, Moscow's German mouthpiece. He began talking of 'primitive antifascism', a phrase intended to convey disapproval of opposition to the Nazi regime that 'did not take account of the facts of the international situation'.[13] This line of talk was explained when the German and Soviet foreign ministers, Ribbentrop and Molotov, signed the Hitler-Stalin Pact on 23 August 1939. Britain's answer was a comprehensive mutual security pact with Poland on 25 August, but this did not deter Hitler. He ordered the invasion of Poland on 1 September and Britain and France, after brief but poignant hesitation, declared war on Germany on 3 September. Brandt's views were expressed in articles written for *Det 20 da arhundre*, the monthly of the Norwegian Socialist Party, in December 1939 and January 1940. By then the Soviet Union had helped to crush Poland, annexed the three Baltic states of Estonia, Latvia and Lithuania and attacked Finland. Brandt's opinions were caustic:

> Up until the end of August [1939] the German section of the Comintern was pushing out propaganda to the effect that if it came to the point, war should be waged against Germany, whilst simultaneously continuing to promise that a revolution in Germany was only a matter of time. Then the pact between Germany and Russia came and that silenced the German section of the Comintern. Profound disappointment was felt by those Communists who were left in Germany, and among those in exile confusion, whilst a few party secretaries actually managed to defend not only the pact which had made war against Poland possible for the German regime, but also the new Russian line which banished the word Fascism from the dictionary. . . .[14]

> The attitude of the socialist movement towards the Soviet Union today must be considered against this background. Relations have changed almost beyond recognition. It is hardly a novel situation to find the leaders of the Soviet Union in a state of outright war against the socialist movement. It has happened before. But today the whole movement is obliged to stand up and fight, and draw a clear dividing line between itself and the Soviet Union. It is not the socialist movement but the Soviet Union which has changed. It is not the socialist movement but the Soviet Union which has entered a pact of friendship with Nazism. It is the Soviet Union which stabbed Poland in the back and initiated the war against Finland.[15]

In Brandt's view Stalin had helped to strengthen 'reactionary anti-socialist and anti-working-class forces throughout the world'. Brandt's future policies towards the Soviet Union would always take account of what had happened in the past and be coloured by a healthy distaste and suspicion. Walter Ulbricht, on the other hand, found fulsome praise for the Soviet alliance with Nazi Germany on 9 February 1940 – the very day that the Soviet police returned thirty German Communists into the hands of the Gestapo. Virtually all died, the victims of Soviet *Realpolitik*.[16]

War heightened the sense of unreality and incipient nightmare for the German exiles. Isolated and cold-shouldered before, they were now almost totally forgotten. Prophecies of the disintegration of the regime had proved abysmally wrong. So had forecasts of increasing popular opposition in Germany. Retribution in the shape of thunderbolts from the western powers never came. Daily the German exiles awaited action by them. Instead the phoney war went on and on. For Brandt it was perhaps the most discouraging period since he had left Germany six years earlier. Contact with resistance groups inside Germany was fragmentary and unsatisfactory. Messages were carried in and out of Germany by Scandinavian and German seamen; the advice to the underground was to be more circumspect than ever.

He was more engaged at this time in Norwegian politics than before. He had become an associate member of the Norwegian Labour Party's youth organization, the AUF (*Arbeidernes Ungdomsfylking*), as early as 1933, and thus a member too of the Labour Party, the DNA (*Det Norske Arbeiderpartei*). One friend in the Norwegian Labour Party has this to say:

> Some of us were close friends, and he gained the confidence of our leaders. His friends at first were mainly on the left wing of the party, or in the independent left-wing students' association called *Mot Dag*. I remember my father, editor of the Labour Party paper in Christiansand, *Sörlandet*, telling me after he had met Brandt that he was the most intelligent German politician to whom he had talked since Karl Liebknecht. Brandt was an excellent lecturer and public speaker. He was already doing a very good job before the war for *Norsk Folkehjelp* and *Spaniahjelpen*, organizations which helped Spain and Finland during their wars.[17]

He was busy, too, with his writing. Apart from his journalism he was writing a book, *War Aims of the Great Powers*, published in 1940 in a Norwegian edition, and was collecting material for another book, a *History of the Youth International*. Most of the manuscript for the latter was lost during the war and the book was never published. He was writing political reports, too; those which survived show how wide-ranging his interests were. Thus early in 1940 he produced a study of Latvia under Soviet occupation,[18] a gruesome story of rule by the secret police, with factories shut down, wages compulsorily lowered and foreign trade cut off. Latvia was treated worse than Estonia or Lithuania, where fugitive attempts were made to woo the population. He also wrote a long and revealing memorandum on the Russo-Finnish War.[19] The Soviet Union had brought, as he saw it, unjustified pressure to bear on Finland to respect the 'security' of the city of Leningrad. Finland had thereupon offered to move the frontier 8 miles to the west. The Soviet response was to demand more concessions, provoke frontier incidents and set up a puppet regime in Tericki under Otto Kuusinen. When war broke out Finland at once accepted, while the Soviet Union rejected, the United State's offer of mediation. Finland accepted, and the Soviet Union rejected, the League of Nations' appeal for a cessation of hostilities. Brandt believed that Nazi Germany encouraged the Soviet attack on Finland to bring the Soviet Union into active conflict with the western powers.

Norway had declared her neutrality on 1 September 1939 and fully intended to maintain it. Opinion was in favour of the western powers, especially Britain, with whom the Norwegians felt a natural affinity. But the country, with a population of only three million, a tiny army and a tremendously long and indefensible seaboard, was in no position to make war. As a neutral she was of greater use to the western powers than as a combatant; her merchant marine was the fourth largest in the world. Only one small group, Vidkund Quisling's *Nasjonal Samling*, supported Nazi Germany. It claimed fifteen thousand active members yet never collected more than thirty thousand votes in elections. But her neutrality was precarious. The Germans sank neutral shipping – 150 vessels up to April 1940 – and German warships made illegal use of Norwegian territorial waters. In February 1940 the *Altmark*, an auxiliary vessel co-operating with the pocket battleship *Admiral Graf Spee*, was intercepted in the Joessing fjord by the British ship *Cossack*. The *Cossack* boarded her and took off three hundred British merchant seamen who were being taken to Germany as prisoners.

The invasion of Finland on 30 November 1939 put a further strain on Norwegian neutrality. The Norwegians were disgusted by the Soviet attack. They sent food, medical supplies and personnel. Norwegian volunteers fought in Finland and there were discreet soundings of the French and British governments to allow free passage for a joint expeditionary force to Narvik.

This would have cut off Germany's supply of Swedish iron ore and the Norwegians shrewdly suspected that Churchill was more interested in iron ore than in helping Finland.[20] In March 1940 Finland appealed for French and British military aid, but the Russo-Finnish War ended a few days later.

The Nazi government had already considered invading Norway. Full plans had been ready by the end of February. In an official directive Hitler gave three reasons – it would forestall British action, safeguard the iron ore supply via Narvik and give Germany vitally important submarine and air bases for use against Britain. On 8 April the British and French navies laid mines in sea lanes close to Norway's coast, to prevent the passage of 'contraband of war'. Norway protested, but on the night of 8–9 April the Nazi invasion began. The Norwegians fought bravely but the Germans gained a crucial advantage by capturing the port of Trondheim and the air base of Sola. Their object was to crush all resistance within forty-eight hours, capture the royal family and government and set up a provisional administration under German military control. The Norwegians were caught unawares. Their country had taken part in no war for 125 years. Their government was socialist and pacifist, and neutral. 'We were surprised and confused at first; later came indignation, and later still real hatred,' was one reaction.[21] 'We were frightened and very surprised. Even if we had no illusions about the aggressive policies of Hitler and the Nazis, we thought that the British fleet would smash the Germans, and that Hitler would have to pay this high price for a foolhardy action.'[22]

Brandt had been on holiday and returned to Oslo only four or five days before the invasion. Only a day or two earlier he had received his first author's copy of his book *War Aims of the Great Powers* and carried it proudly home, where Carlota had just become pregnant. A few weeks later the publisher, on the orders of the Gestapo, had to destroy the whole edition. On 8 April, addressing a meeting of German socialists, Brandt said that it was possible that a German invasion might come the very next day. After the meeting he told one friend the trouble should blow over – for Germany, the only important consideration was the shipment of iron ore and that would go on as long as Norway remained neutral.[23]

On the evening of 9 April a German ultimatum was broadcast

– all resistance was to end, all military installations to be handed over intact and radio and press put under German control. The king and the foreign minister, Professor Halvdan Koht, withdrew to Hamar, about 40 miles north-east of the capital, and were joined there by 146 out of the 150 members of the Storting – proof of their patriotism and attachment to the royal family. On 10 April they retreated again, to Elverum. Hitler's terms were repeated, and King Haakon agreed to abdicate if the Storting accepted them. They did not, and on 11 April the Luftwaffe launched murderously heavy bombing attacks on Elverum. Having failed to capture the king, the Nazis were intent on killing him. He could at this stage have sought refuge in Sweden. But Norway was still resisting and he was determined to stay in his country as long as possible. He moved north, where the Norwegian army joined forces with British units. But the brief British advance south was repulsed by the Germans on 22 April. King Haakon moved far to the north, to Tromsö, and with the Allies temporarily in control of Narvik put himself at the head of the Norwegian forces there and did not finally sail for Britain until 7 June. He went into exile only to maintain a government there and proclaim national resistance until Nazi Germany was defeated.

Norway had been given no warning. Her armed forces amounted to about sixteen thousand men, with seventy thousand available reservists; there were no armoured forces and the air force consisted of 120 planes in all.[24] The Germans used an estimated one hundred thousand troops in southern Norway, and had more than a thousand planes available. The picture is one of overwhelming German strength. Because of the veil of official security on the German side no clear picture of German losses emerges. But they may have been as high as sixty thousand men.[25] Their naval losses included ten destroyers and three cruisers, and two battle-cruisers and a pocket battleship were badly damaged.

Finally, there are the intensely moving words of King Haakon, broadcasting on 17 May 1940 from a 'place unknown': 'This dwelling place is ours and we love it for what it is, what it was and what it shall be; as love grows from the soil of our homes, there shall be a growth from the seed-corn of our love once more.'

45

Here was the authentic voice and spirit of Norway and its people.

When a country faces total defeat a terrifying aimlessness
descends on many people. At one moment there is much to fight
for; at the next, nothing discernible. For an exile living in a
country brought to this wretched state it must be at least as bad.
To give up must seem natural. Brandt toyed with the idea of
escaping to Sweden; on 11 April he was fairly close to the
Swedish frontier. Then he set off to the north for Lillehammer.
He knew that the *Norsk Folkehjelp*, the 'People's Aid' association, were setting up a temporary headquarters there. He felt that
his duty was to stay with the Norwegians who had given him his
second home. He found the People's Aid, moved with them, still
hoping that the British counter-attack from the North Sea ports
would succeed.

His position was perilous. He still carried only his 'stranger's
passport'. He was on the Nazi black list. He had failed to apply
for naturalization until 1939. It normally required at least five
years' residence in Norway and was never granted automatically.
On 1 May he found himself in a valley north of Andalsnes, with
British forces passing to the south on their way out of Norway.
The valley, the Sundalsdal, was blocked by German forces
advancing from Trondheim. There was talk of putting on skis,
climbing over the snow-covered mountains and making for
Sweden. But the frontier was 100 miles away; the idea was
shelved. He met, at this precise moment, an old friend from the
days of the Spanish Civil War. Paul René Gauguin was, like his
famous grandfather, a painter. Like Brandt he had gone to Spain
and they were together during the struggle in Barcelona between
the POUM, the Anarchists and the Communists. According to
Gauguin:

> Then we met again in the first days of May 1940 in Mittet-
> dalen, near Andalsnes, in Norway. I had landed up there with
> a fifty man strong improvised unit of the Norwegian Army. . . .
> I met, to my astonishment, Willy Brandt. We proposed that
> Willy should put on my uniform and let himself be taken
> prisoner with our unit. Willy spoke such good Norwegian that
> he couldn't attract attention. And so we arrived in the same

internment camp along with him, a school near Dovre. We were reasonably treated as prisoners of war, even allowed a degree of freedom to move around.[26]

Gauguin's clothes did not make a good fit; the trousers were too short and the jacket too roomy.[27] But they served their purpose; Brandt spent four weeks in Dovre. Prisoners could go to neighbouring farms and scrounge food. The German camp commandant was unco-operative only when they asked permission to fly the Norwegian flag at half-mast on 17 May, the national holiday. Gauguin was to appear in 1963 as a witness in a Copenhagen court, as a result of reports in newspapers that Brandt joined the Norwegian army during the war and fired on his own countrymen. Gauguin explained that Brandt was unarmed in Mittetdalen. The men of his own unit had got rid of their arms and were preparing to surrender. Yet the story that he fought against 'his own side' was to crop up time after time and produce a number of lawsuits.[28]

Brandt was released in June. He could not go home as the Gestapo would be watching the place. Carlota had moved to the Oslo suburb of Bygdö and was lodging with Dr Nicolas Stang and his wife Ragna. There they lay low, but not for long. German security was tightening up: house-to-house checks were beginning. Brandt, but not Carlota, moved to a wooden hut on the Oslo fjord belonging to a friend, Per Borgersen.[29] Here he lived a hermit's existence, broken only by the occasional visit from Borgersen and Carlota. Borgersen kept him informed of developments in Oslo; his advice was to escape into Sweden, and early in July Brandt decided to make the attempt. He had first to go into Oslo, say goodbye to Carlota, then take an early morning train to Kongsvinger, a dozen miles from the Swedish frontier, a railway junction and on one of the most obvious routes into Sweden. But there was no police-check on the train, although police and military were much in evidence round the railway station. From Kongsvinger he took the light railway to Björkelangen, only 5 miles from the frontier. Once again the journey passed without incident. At Björkelangen he left the railway and made his way to the farmhouse of Bolstad, which belonged to a captain in the Norwegian army, Ovo Gjedde. Gjedde and his wife gave him food and a guide who knew the terrain intimately and would bring him to within a few miles of the frontier.

Bolstad farm lies in uplands with pasturage and woods of fir and larch. The Germans patrolled the road to the farm from the railway and there were patrols on the frontier itself. Brandt and his guide made their way slowly and carefully in the gloaming. They saw no German frontier guards on the move; nor did Brandt see any after his guide left him. He crossed the frontier without knowing when he had reached Swedish soil – as so often in wild and hilly country, the frontier was not marked by posts or stones.[30] He walked on and went straight past a Swedish military post. There was a case for pushing on, farther into Sweden, but he was very anxious to give himself up to the Swedish police rather than be caught by them. Sweden had closed the frontier and Norwegians who tried to cross were unceremoniously returned to their own country. So he went back to the military post, reported himself there and explained that he was a political refugee from Germany. His explanation took some time: his Norwegian was so good that the Swedish police were at first convinced that he must be a Norwegian.

They took him next day to Charlottenberg for a lengthy interrogation. Luckily he knew a member of the Swedish parliament, August Spangberg. The police sent for him to bail Brandt out. First he spent a few days in a camp for internees at Baggä, then he was granted political asylum. In Stockholm he learnt, somewhat ironically, that his application for Norwegian citizenship had been approved. He learnt, too, that his name had been on the list of wanted persons that the Gestapo brought to Norway.

He settled down with ease in Stockholm, quickly learnt to speak Swedish and found plenty to do. His life in Sweden, as opposed to Norway, was – as he put it – only 'half Swedish'.[31] He lived largely in a Norwegian milieu. The Norwegian Labour Party had set up one of their two headquarters here – the other was, of course, in London. Political activity had to be discreet, for Sweden was determined to stay neutral. Apart from Norwegians Brandt saw much of fellow Germans in exile. He saw rather less of the Swedes, whom he found very different from the Norwegians. Norwegian reserve was natural and unaffected; Swedish reserve was a formal affair. Brandt has recalled their lack of conviviality – in the bars of Stockholm the Norwegians used to say: 'Now it's eleven o'clock – time for the Swedes to get out.'[32]*

He got down to work at once. He found a place to live, in the suburb of Hammarbyhöjden. There were political contacts to be taken up or re-established, with Norwegians, Germans and Swedes. He was commissioned to write a series of articles on the Norwegian campaign. These were expanded into a book, *Norwegens Freiheitskampf (Norway's Battle for Freedom)*, published in Hamburg in 1948, which served in turn as a basis for a two-volume study of wartime Norway. In addition he was making plans for launching the Swedish-Norwegian Press Agency, specializing in news from and about Norway. This office, in the Vasagatan, did not become a going concern until early in 1942.

In December 1940 he returned briefly to Oslo. He had two personal reasons for risking his neck when there was no apparent need. His daughter Ninja had been born in October and he wanted to see her. And there was the question of bringing Carlota and the child to Sweden. In addition, he wanted to make contact with friends in the Labour Party. He made his plans very carefully. There were by now recognized underground routes between Norway and Sweden. He travelled from Stockholm to Göteborg, then first by train and afterwards on foot to the frontier close to Halden. He picked up a guide on the Norwegian side of the frontier who led him through the night across a small stream and by careful detours round the eastern, landward side of Halden, then back into the town centre to the railway station. From there he took a train to Oslo. He carried forged papers but he never needed to use them.

He found Carlota and the baby well and made plans for them to come to Sweden in the following spring – they too had to find their way across the frontier, dangerously. He met members of the Norwegian Labour Party and learnt that the first stage of the German occupation had been uneventful. Kidglove treatment had been meted out for political purposes. After the shattering

* Brandt told the author that Norwegian reserve never affects the easy Norwegian informality. The Norwegians are very ready to use the familiar 'thou' in conversation. King Haakon once heard two of his officers talking in this way and asked: 'Does everybody say "thou"?' The officer in question answered: 'Why yes, Majesty, of course with the exception of thee and thy son.'

defeat of France, too, there had been a general feeling of hopelessness. Quisling had been busy mobilizing support for a policy of coexistence and the Storting, having returned to Oslo, was to offer to suspend the king's nominal authority. The Reich commissar, Josef Terboven, preferred to replace the Storting with an administrative council, which he instructed to ask King Haakon to abdicate. The king refused, stating in London that the council did not represent Norway. Hitler's dream of giving a 'Germanic' Norway its place in the 'new European order' was failing to materialize.[33] In December all judges of the Norwegian Supreme Court resigned, and resistance began in the schools and in the Church.

Brandt returned to Sweden by the same route as he had taken when entering Norway a few weeks earlier. Once again he crossed at night with a guide. Months later the Swedish police got wind of his previous movements, interrogated him and held him for several days in gaol in Stockholm. A charge of illegal political activity was dropped only after the intervention of the minister for social affairs, Gustav Möller.

Brandt did not see Norway again until the end of the war; so, a brief note on what happened there in the meantime. It is a story of simple heroism, backed by rugged courage and shrewd common sense. Resistance to occupation grew steadily; as Bishop Berggrav said: 'The soil may be occupied, but not the soul.'[34] School strikes began in 1940, with children as pickets and teachers flatly refusing to institute national socialist teaching. When a 'teachers' front' was set up by Quisling, twelve thousand out of fourteen thousand teachers refused to join and five hundred 'ringleaders' were shipped to Kirkenes in the far north, abused, overworked and half-starved. Over three hundred thousand parents wrote letters of protest to the Quisling administration.

In February 1941 the bishops asserted their unalterable belief in justice, truth and freedom of conscience, while calling on their flocks to avoid acts of violence and injustice.[35] They resolutely refused to collaborate with the German or Quisling administrations. So did the Norwegian press, and a total boycott of state-organized sport was instituted when it was taken over by Quisling. An underground press sprang up, stimulating resistance in the factories and public services. Close touch was maintained with Britain, through the famous 'Shetland bus' route – small boats sailed by night during the winter months, bringing back agents, radios and arms. This route was known to many thousands of Norwegians but never betrayed. The Norwegian resistance destroyed German armaments plant, lifted mines and assisted British raids. It operated a regular courier service across the Swedish frontier.

The Norwegians showed themselves to be a nation with guts and integrity. Brandt believed that the solidarity of Norwegian society was actually increased by German occupation.[36] In 1947 he estimated Norway's war losses as ten thousand, or one in every three hundred of the population. About forty thousand Norwegians were imprisoned by the Germans and nine thousand deported to Germany. Over fifty thousand sought refuge in Sweden.[37] When the Germans capitulated in 1945 the Norwegian secret military organization, Milorg, took over at once. The Norwegian navy and merchant marine continued through the whole war to serve the Allied cause, and five thousand Norwegian seamen died in Allied service, while one and a half million tons of Norwegian shipping were sunk by German action.

About forty thousand Norwegians joined Quisling's *Nasjonal Semling* and four thousand volunteers fought with the 'Norwegian legion' in the Soviet Union. But they constituted little more than 1 per cent of the population; Quisling's targets had been two hundred thousand party members and ten thousand volunteers.

Sweden was able to remain neutral and was desperately anxious to do so. But her attitude, up to 1943, caused deep resentment among Norwegians. In June 1940 she made an agreement with Germany under which iron ore would continue to travel to Narvik for further transport to German ports.[38] In 1941 she allowed the Engelbrecht division to pass through Swedish territory on its way to the Finnish front to fight against the Soviet Union. Transit arrangements for German troops continued up to August 1943. The Swedish government restricted deliveries to Norway of badly needed foodstuffs. Norwegian patriots were imprisoned as spies; newspapers in Sweden had issues banned or confiscated, to curry favour with the Germans.[39] The Swedish police force contained Nazis and anti-Semites, and was officiously

exact in keeping a tab on German exiles. They were not allowed
to carry out political 'propaganda'. Work camps were maintained
at Langmora and Smedsbö for 'suspicious' immigrants, and left-
wingers who had fought in Spain were held there. One revealing
incident was the vote, by 548 against 349, of the students of
Uppsala University in February 1939 against admitting refugee
intellectuals into Sweden – because they might deprive Swedes
of jobs.[40]

The Swedish attitude changed perceptibly after the German
defeats at Stalingrad and in North Africa. Norwegian exiles were
allowed to train in Sweden, as a potential part of a future liberation army. Norwegians and Germans in exile were latterly
allowed to take an active part in political life. On Sweden's side it
could be argued that 750 Jews – half of the Jewish community in
Norway – were granted political asylum. So were many Danish
Jews. But the best part of a thousand Norwegian Jews went into
concentration camps in Germany. Up to the autumn of 1941
Jews entering Sweden had to apply for a visa. A particularly
disgraceful case was that of the Austrian Jew, Robert Braun, who
was ejected after suffering gratuitous insults.[41]

In 1945 the Swedes sought to make amends by accepting
Danish and Norwegian prisoners of war and twelve thousand
Jews and Frenchmen from German concentration camps. But the
Swedish record, overall, was mixed. One book by Norwegian
authors says only: 'In the first years Swedish policy towards
Norway frequently seemed to err on the side of caution and
unfriendliness.'[42] Like the British, the Norwegians cultivate the
art of understatement.

Stockholm was, after London, the most important wartime centre
in Europe for left-wing exiles. Paris ceased to play any role after
the fall of France in 1940. Most of the SAP members fled to the
United States, a few to London. The London group created a
nucleus that was to return intact to Germany after the war. But
its members seemed sadly inactive during the war, epitomizing
Lewis Edinger's summing-up of exile politics – 'a tale of failure,
frustration, of shattered hopes and bitter strife'.[43]

Stockholm housed most of the 3,500 German exiles in
Sweden. According to Brandt[44] 2,700 were Jews and 800 political opponents of Hitler. 'Organized' German socialists numbered

250–300. There were about 100 ex-members of the KPD. At least 350 Germans belonged to a single locally based trade union – of importance since the Swedish trade unions were ready to recognize it and help its members. Yet another organization was the *Freier Deutscher-Kulturbund*, with 450 members. These four bodies organized joint appeals to the German nation not to take part in a 'people's war' against the Allied occupation, and to the Allies to grant a fair peace.

Among these groups the SAP were the smallest, with probably fewer than forty active members.[45] They maintained close links with the *Klub Osterreichischer Sozialisten*, the Austrian socialists led by Bruno Kreisky, who was to be Austrian chancellor in the 1970s. It was also associated with the Little International, the *Internationale Gruppe Demokratischer Sozialisten*. This embraced socialists from eleven principal countries – Sweden, Iceland, Denmark, Spain, Norway, Germany, France, Austria, Hungary, Poland and Czechoslovakia.[46] Its aims were to examine possibilities for peace, the future of Germany and Central Europe, future socialist co-operation on an international level, economic planning and the postwar re-creation of a Socialist International. Brandt acted as the honorary secretary of the group.

Perhaps Brandt's main achievement in the war years was his literary output. Six books were published by the firm of Albert Bonniers in Stockholm, two each in 1941 and 1943, one each in 1942 and 1945. Four dealt with the war in Norway and the German occupation. These four were published in the Norwegian language only.* The other two were on postwar aims and on guerrilla warfare. He also contributed chapters to at least three other books on wartime Norway. His writings on Norway were later condensed into the single volume *Norwegens Freiheitskampf*. His friend Ture Nerman helped with the editing of some of his books, including *Criminals and Other Germans*, published in 1946. This and *Guerrilla Warfare* (1942) were to be used years later by political opponents to show that he had advocated vicious

---

* The four books on Norway were: *Kriget i Norge* (The War in Norway) (Stockholm 1941); *Norge fortsätter kampen* (Norway Fights On) (Stockholm 1941); *Norges tredje krigsar* (Norway's Third Year of War) (Stockholm 1943); *Norges väg mot Friheten* (Norway's Road to Freedom) (Stockholm 1945).

guerrilla warfare against the German army, and had traduced his countrymen by classifying them, *en masse,* as criminals.[47] He had done nothing of the kind: *Guerrilla Warfare* was an objective analysis, and the other book dealt with war crimes affecting only a tiny percentage of the German people.

The sixty-three-page report that he helped to compile in 1944 on the postwar policy of German socialists is of special interest.[48] He outlined socialist aims in the context of a lost war. The victor nations, as Brandt saw it, would be more intimately involved in German affairs than after the First World War. The dismantling of German industry would be mooted (how right he was!), but should be resisted. Germany would have to make reparation for the untold damage caused by Hitler's armies. There could be no 'European solution' without the co-operation of both Britain and the Soviet Union, and a Germany prepared to carry through radical social reforms must seek good relations with both these countries. He visualized a socialist Germany rising out of the ashes of war and destruction – 'Conservatism has been badly compromised by its alliance with Hitler.'[49] Fair terms must be sought: 'A provisional democratic Government should not sign every document put before it by foreign powers.'[50] Finally, the German people must strive for national unity, not at all the same thing as nationalism.[51]

In 1944 he wrote another valuable book, *Nach dem Siege –* (*After Victory – the Discussion on War and Peace Aims*). It comprises a remarkable analysis of expected developments and reasonable aims. Brandt's conclusions show him to have been outstandingly well informed. Thus he believed that the Soviet Union was bound to swallow Eastern Poland, and 'push Poland to the west'.[52] The 'maximalist' demand of the Oder as Poland's western frontier would deprive nine million Germans of their homes.[53] He expected the Soviet Union to grab Bessarabia and the Bukovina from Roumania and he saw no prospect of the three little Baltic states recovering their independence.[54] The Soviet Union would reoccupy those areas that had been torn from Finland in the 1939–40 war and reconquered by the Finns with German aid. He even noted, with singular prescience, that Carpatho-Ruthenia, the most eastern province of Czechoslovakia, might 'become a subject for discussion' – even though the Soviet Union was that country's ally.[55] In the event it was annexed.

He pleaded for equitable common sense. At Teheran Stalin had undertaken to eliminate tyranny, slavery, suppression and intolerance – Brandt hoped that this was in earnest of the Soviet leader's true intentions.[56] A mass expulsion of Sudeten Germans from Czecho-Slovakia would, he felt, be a retrograde step,[57] and he urged the need to eliminate anti-Semitism. The Jews might feel bound to establish a state of their own.[58] He believed in a United States of Europe, including Britain;[59] the future creed for Europe must be that of interdependence. A useful economic step would be 'co-operation between the coal, iron and steel industries of the Ruhr, Lorraine, Belgium, Luxembourg and the Netherlands' – in fact, precisely those areas later brought into the Schuman Plan.[60] This would prepare the way for industrial cooperation on a broader scale. Once again he was right: the Schuman Plan was the forerunner of the Common Market. He argued in favour of 'militant humanism' and 'the welfare of the many, not the privileges of the few'.[61] He used evocative phrases such as mobilizing the 'underground army of freedom', and 'democracy can no longer be rationed'. There were frequent references to the dangers of Vansittartism – Sir Robert (later Lord) Vansittart, deeply distrusted the German people, thought of a seventy-five-year occupation of Germany, of all Germans being unteachable and of aggression being an integral part of the German character. While believing that the Nazis should be dealt with rigorously, Brandt felt that 'the crisis for democracy is universal, and fascism is not a purely German phenomenon'.[62]

These extracts give a picture of a remarkably mature mind. Of course nobody can be right all the time. Where the length of the war was concerned one finds him writing to Herbert George, in June 1941, saying it could not last more than another year.[63] In October 1942 he wrote to the same friend that the war could end in the very next month, or at the very latest in a year's time.[64] Jokingly he added: 'A weather-prophet here in Sweden has dreamt peace will break out on July 13, 1943.' It is of interest that, for security reasons, he wrote some of his letters to Herbert George in London in Norwegian. These were not always perfectly understood by George, who had left Norway for Britain in 1940 and who was not in the same class as Brandt as a linguist.

But the letters were revealing in one way: according to Norwegians who have read them, there was just one small grammatical mistake in eight long letters!

Some of his letters speak of personal affairs. Thus in June 1942: 'My wife and daughter Ninja came here a good year ago. The little one is just 20 months old and gives us a lot of pleasure. We're living a little way out of town in a nice, newly built house. I have nothing whatever to grumble about. Now and then one really has a bad conscience, about living so relatively normal a life and in so neutral a country.'[65] A year later Ninja is 'over two years old and talking a lot, mainly Swedish'.

An Austrian of whom Brandt saw much was Bruno Kreisky. Kreisky remembers Brandt best of all during this period for his unfailing good humour, his immense capacity for hard work and his steadfast belief in the impending defeat of the Nazi regime – unlike many social democrats who, up to Stalingrad, were thoroughly pessimistic.[66] He had a comical recollection too: on one occasion he and Brandt came out together from a meeting and hailed a taxi; it drew up alongside them but a somewhat tipsy Swedish sailor pushed his way into the taxi with a shout of: 'An honest Swedish sailor comes in front of you Nazi racketeers!' Brandt enjoyed the comedy of the situation.

One other letter of Brandt's, written in August 1943, gives a clear impression of what was in his heart:

While I have been in foreign countries, I have never tried to hide the fact that I'm a German; nor am I ashamed of it. I never hesitated about where I should go in 1933. I had been in Norway in 1931; I knew I could live there, and I wanted to. Norway has become truly my second home. In April 1940 I refused to leave Norway; I wanted to do my best for her, but sadly, there was so little that I could do. Yet my duty was to help Norway and repay my debt to her.

The Nazis took away my native country from me, and Hitler took away my German citizenship. Now I have lost my homeland twice. I intend to help them to restore themselves, as a free Norway and a democratic Germany. Today, too, there are Germans fighting against Nazism in Germany. They are my friends.[67]

He already knew of the attempts to organize effective resistance against Hitler in Germany itself. Long afterwards he was to say that he had expected the July 1944 attempt on Hitler's life: 'I knew it would come. I knew it had been postponed several times. I was afraid that my fellow countrymen wouldn't be able to organize. We have no tradition as far as operations of that kind are concerned. . . . I still think that change in 1944 could have meant a good deal, I mean apart from all the destruction during the last period of the war. It could have had a great influence on the whole set-up in Europe.'[68]

There were means, in Stockholm, of learning about what was happening in Germany. Friends of Brandt's, August and Irmgard Enderle, maintained contact with anti-Nazis in Bremen through German seamen.[69] They were in touch with active anti-Nazis in Oslo too, and Frau Enderle recalls valuable journeys to Germany by Norwegian women who were dedicated anti-Nazis. Brandt knew too of Karl Goerdeler, an opponent of Hitler who came to Stockholm in 1942 and 1943. In April 1942 Goerdeler met the Swedish banker Jakob Wallenberg and urged him to get in touch with Winston Churchill. He wanted a British assurance that Germany would get a fair peace if Hitler were overthrown. In May 1942 leading members of the German evangelical churches were in Stockholm, and were able to pass on lists of the key German opponents of Hitler to London.

Of more direct interest to Brandt were the visits to Stockholm early in 1944 of Theodor Steltzer and Adam Trott zu Solz. Steltzer brought a message from Julius Leber. Trott had to establish his identity with Brandt and his friends by telling Brandt a story about Lübeck that he would recognize. The only flaw was that Brandt did not recognize it, and it took Trott over an hour to establish his credentials![70] He wanted to know if Brandt would be ready to serve a new, non-Nazi government.[71] Brandt was deeply interested in Leber's participation in the plan to overthrow Hitler and much moved by the news of his execution on 5 January 1945. Later he wrote: 'The message of the dead man, more than anything else, prompted me to dedicate my life to the reconstruction of a new Germany, in the spirit of the man of the 20th July.'[72] He was referring to Leber's words: 'For so good and righteous a cause, the cost of one's own life is a fair price.'

A few months before the end of the war Brandt met the woman

who was to become his second wife. Rut Hansen came from Hamar, in Norway. She was married at the time that she met Brandt, to a railwayman, Ole Bergaust, who died a year later of tuberculosis. Bergaust had been a member of the Norwegian resistance. She has since said that she did notice Brandt soon after they met. He, too, was still married then – the divorce did not take place until 1947. Rut became a good friend; he was to marry her in 1948, in Berlin. She had been a journalist for a time and understood his work. More important, she had an instinctive understanding of his need for a considerable degree of independence.

The last days of the war found Brandt still in Stockholm. On 1 May 1945 he was about to address a meeting of social democratic groups when a note was handed to him, telling him that Hitler had committed suicide on the previous day. When he read this out there was – he recalls – no cheering, only a long silence. The sense of relief was too great to allow for rejoicing.

The day before Hitler's death Brandt had put through a telephone call to the Reich commissar in Oslo, Josef Terboven. His object was to find out if the large German army in Norway would surrender to the Allies; alternatively, whether it was planning a last-ditch resistance. Terboven answered the call, demanded to know the name of the caller, then put the receiver down. Obergruppenführer William Rediess of the SS came on the line. He worked immediately under Terboven; and he denied that any major change in the situation in Oslo was in prospect. Political prisoners, however, might be released, following negotiations between Count Bernadotte on behalf of the Swedish and International Red Cross, and Rediess's boss and titular head of the SS, Heinrich Himmler. He refused to say anything more. At least Brandt had the impression that a form of negotiation was under way and that his beloved Norway would be spared a pointless and hideously destructive battle to the death on her soil. Of the two principals in this strange telephone conversation, Brandt was to become German chancellor twenty-four years later. Rediess shot himself only a few days after he had answered the call.

4

Return to Germany

Brandt had come through the war sound of limb and with a wealth of experience behind him. Yet there was little to which he could at first look forward. He had none of the world's goods: in the war years he had inevitably spent as he earned. He had parted from his wife and small daughter. He had been deprived of German citizenship, and the nearest thing to home in Germany was the small flat in Lübeck where his mother lived with a step-father who was a comparative stranger to him. Once again he was very much alone.

The years in exile had taught him much. He had found, both in Norway and Sweden, a humanitarian, reflective sort of socialism, socialism in action.[1] The Swedish Socialist Party was in office from 1935 onwards. They created the first efficiently run welfare state in Europe. Brandt believed that social reform was an integral part of the Swedish way of life and political system.[2] Abstract aims like 'socialization' or 'state control' became less significant than the freedom, equality, welfare and security of the individual citizen. The subordination of political theory to practical achievement became a natural part of his thinking.

He went first to Norway, his own homeland as far as he had one. He arrived in Oslo on about 15 May 1945 and spent three weeks in Norway. In a letter to 'Theo' (the wartime code name of Ludwig Hacke, the former editor of an SPD newspaper in Saxony)[3] he described these weeks. There were old friends to find, views to exchange, knowledge of Norway's sufferings to be stored away and subsequently used. He loved Norway and was reminded, sharply and poignantly, of his love. There were some interesting thoughts in this letter to Theo. His own prewar Socialist Labour Party, the SAP, had 'in a practical sense' ceased to exist. Brandt did not think SAP members should simply join the SPD. For the SPD, too, had ceased to exist – at least in their old form. They had to regroup and reorganize their thinking. At the same time he opposed a sharp division between parties representing the working class.

At the beginning of July one finds him already circulating a report to friends in Stockholm and London about conditions in Norway.[4] The economic situation was grim; as we have seen, ten thousand Norwegians had died in the war; fifty thousand of Quisling's followers and suspected sympathizers had been arrested. Two factors helped: Norway's socialists were united and forward-looking, and the individual Norwegian was showing his traditional, ingrained common sense. About four hundred thousand Germans had been disarmed; more difficult had been the smoking out of the Gestapo and SS who, fortunately, were prepared to denounce each other to save their skins.

In Stockholm Brandt was busy helping the Swedish Aid Programme for Germany, a charitable undertaking that sent parcels to Germans, helped to return exiles home and organized holidays in Scandinavia for German children. In August he was writing to Jacob Walcher about the changing of Germany's eastern frontier. It was not vital to maintain the pre-1945 frontier but: 'I consider that the arrangement hit upon in the East is, in its present form, unreasonable.'[5] The frontier had been pushed west, to the Oder and Neisse rivers, resulting in the ejection of nine million Germans from their homes. He was worried, too, about the lack of co-operation between the working-class parties; but the most important problem was to prevent a third world war.

A letter to Herbert George was more revealing. He was worried that he might become 'too closely involved in Norwegian affairs'. After commenting on the admirable discipline of the Norwegians in rebuilding their country he went on: 'Now, I shall always feel intimately linked with Norway. But I have never forsaken the German working-class movement. It would be more comfortable today to withdraw to a Norwegian base. But I can't bring myself to make this decision. I want at least to make the attempt to give my help, so that the movement can be created afresh in Germany.'[6] This letter raised a crucial question: was he to remain a Norwegian citizen, or return to Germany, the country that had taken his citizenship from him? He was not going to decide in a hurry. The Oslo *Arbeiderbladet* wanted him to report the Nuremberg trials of the major German war criminals; so did the Norwegian Socialist Party press service. He decided to take a look at Germany once more, as a Norwegian journalist. He flew to Bremen via Copenhagen in October. There he found old friends of the 'emigration', August and Irmgard Enderle, who took him by car to Lübeck, 'where I was reunited with my mother after ten years. She and my stepfather had come through the war unscathed. . . . My mother and I had met for the last time in Copenhagen in 1935, and my stepfather had visited me in Oslo in 1937. When I was living in Berlin in 1936 I was naturally unable to let myself be seen in Lübeck; that would have been dangerous for all concerned.'[7]

He went on to Nuremberg and stayed there, but for a short break at Christmas, until February 1946. He witnessed the final abasement of the Nazi regime, with the spelling-out of the brutalities of the prisoners in the dock – Göring, the arrogant bully, Rosenberg, the daft racist, the vain and blustering Ribbentrop and the sadistic and sensual Streicher. He was depressed, if hardly surprised, by what he heard and saw: 'Prostrate Germany was like one of those horrible visions that sometimes overcome us on the verge between sleeping and waking . . . there nests in a remote nook of the brain the conviction that one is only dreaming, and that instantly the ghastly dream will disappear.'[8] The war-crimes trials, he felt, were necessary: 'Fascism was not a merc German phenomenon. But it received a special German stamp, and demonstrated in a terrible way to what evil purpose power can be abused in a highly developed country.'[9] He had certain criticisms of the trials: there was little recognition that some of the gravest crimes of the Nazis were committed against the German people; there was full Soviet participation in the international tribunal (and Brandt was very well aware of the crimes against humanity perpetrated by the Stalinist system); few German correspondents were allowed to attend the trials, yet it was the German people, above all, who needed to learn what had been done by the Nazis in their name.

There were bound to be flaws, of definition, method and of underlying morality. One legal expert present at the trials has listed some.[10] It is difficult to define 'military necessity' – where do the exigencies of warfare begin and end? It is even harder to define 'aggressive war' and allot responsibility. The absence of an international criminal court left complex interpretation to an *ad hoc* body which had to make the law as it went along. The Nuremberg trials did not produce a better world; mass murder went on. Yet in his summing-up: 'I have no regret that I spent a year of my life at Nuremberg helping to expose and punish the vile and cruel fomenters of hatred and violence between peoples and races. The lessons we spelled out were clear. Humanity ignores them at its peril.'[11] Another authority[12] has offered convincing reasons for believing the trials were successful. They were scrupulously fair. They helped to write the record of Nazi infamy for generations unborn and produced the necessary impetus for the assembling of witnesses and documentary evidence. The trials administered a salutary shock to the German people and gave them the chance of beginning to come to terms with their past.

Twenty-five years later Brandt, thinking back, had two reservations about Nuremberg.[13] Some so-called 'major' war criminals were unlucky: they were first into the dock and an example was bound to be made of them. Thus Albert Speer, who had seen the error of his ways, was given a twenty-year sentence – when hard-core Nazis were let off far more lightly later on. His second reservation concerned morality: war, as such, was bitter and brutal; could there be only one guilty party? At the time he felt that the trials had a moral worth; later, he was less sure.

In a book called *Verbrecher und andere Deutsche* (Criminals and other Germans), published in Oslo and Stockholm in 1946, he made it clear that 'Germany was bound to reap some of the racial hatred that the Nazis had sown'.[14] Apart from their uniquely perverted racism the Nazis made war deliberately, plundered occupied countries, enslaved their populations and trampled on human rights. No 'grown German' could evade his share of responsibility, although this was not identical with guilt.[15] In his view 'the worst Nazis were those who were already Nazis when Hitler came to power'.[16] But others were a danger to the new Germany – perhaps two million people who had served the Nazis and readily collaborated in wrong-doing. De-Nazification was a necessity, a 'political de-lousing'.[17] The young had to be protected, reoriented, emancipated from Nazi ideology. So, too, had Germans back from the wars, and Brandt was disturbed by their initial reactions. They were disgusted over the war being lost, violently anti-Russian and irresponsibly prepared to visualize another war, this time between the Soviet Union and the West.

Brandt took the unfashionable view that it would have been fatal if the Germans had been left to look after themselves in 1945 – there would have been a disintegration of society.[18] Allied administration achieved impressive results, and some mistakes, too. There was, as he saw it, no clear-cut Allied plan for Germany, not even for its western zones.[19] There was a tendency to pull down with one hand while propping up with the other. It was, he felt, a mistake to limit political activity – public opinion might otherwise have developed more quickly. But he praised the Allies for leaving much to local German authorities, providing the basic necessities of life and encouraging free expression.[20] He urged less preoccupation with political abstractions and more support for 'fundamental human values, rights and duties, for decency, truth, cleanliness and honesty'.

Verbrecher und andere Deutsche is full of acute observation and balanced opinion. He wanted the Germans to forget external, territorial losses and forge a more united, successful community. Frontiers were no longer sacrosanct.[21] Germany's future lay in the future of Europe; the vital need for the German people was not to ensure continuity but to make a fresh start. A real rift between the western powers and the Soviet Union was *not* to Germany's advantage: playing off East against West would pay no dividends. A last, apt observation: food was the problem that worried Germans most. He was right: in 1946 Germany faced a condition of near-starvation. A phrase currently used was that Germany had become a country where men lost all hope and women all sense of honour. Hunger and poverty were bad enough. The devastation reigning in major cities was worse. But behind lay a spiritual emptiness and demoralization that were worse still. Plenty of German émigrés who visited their homeland at this time turned tail and fled to the more welcoming climates of Britain, France and the New World.

In January 1946 Brandt met Erich Ollenhauer, an old friend who had spent the war years in London, and Kurt Schumacher, already marked out as the leader of the postwar Social Democratic Party. In Frankfurt he met Willi Richter, later chairman of the West German trade union congress, the *Deutsche*

Gewerkschaftsbund (DGB). His talks made it plain to him that he would be welcomed back to Germany by the Social Democrats.

He was worried by the East-West split in the working-class movement. In West Germany the Social Democrats were gradually reorganizing, with little initial help from the occupying powers. One social democratic group in Berlin, led by Otto Grotewohl, was bidding for the titular leadership. So was the so-called 'Bureau Schumacher' in Hanover. Social democratic groups in other parts of West Germany were jealous of their local authority. But in the Soviet zone the situation was very different. The Soviet government sent Walter Ulbricht and Wilhelm Pieck back from Moscow with cut-and-dried plans. These entailed creating 'popular' anti-fascist committees, gaining control of municipal administration, placing old-guard Communists at the head of police forces, educational authorities and personnel management, and 'steering' mayors who could be treated as figure-heads.

The Communist Party, KPD, was refounded in Berlin on 11 June 1945. It was under Ulbricht's control, with Pieck acting as father-figure, and the leading members were mainly from Ulbricht's Moscow group. Whereas other Communists had lost touch in the concentration camps or in 'bourgeois' western countries, the Moscow group were the apostles of up-dated Marxism-Leninism, Stalin's standard-bearers. Ulbricht's mission was to organize, not a German-Bolshevik revolution but the step-by-step transformation of an East German society already in process of disintegration, and the consolidation of a communist-controlled East German state. The first major step was the forced fusion, in April 1946, of the SPD and KPD of the Soviet zone. The Soviet zone branch of the SPD was drawn into the communist net – by a man, and by a stratagem. The man was Otto Grotewohl; the stratagem had been thought out in Moscow. It consisted of an all-out bid by the artificial working-class front to represent Germany's national interests under Soviet aegis. One slogan of the *Sozialistische Einheitspartei Deutschlands* or Socialist Unity Party (SED), which was the outcome of the SPD-KPD fusion, is illustrative: 'The Elbe and the Oder are no frontiers for the Unity Party.'[22] The Elbe was the dividing-line between East and West Germany; the Oder between Germany and Poland. Unreserved acceptance of the Oder boundary was later to become a communist article of faith. In rejecting it initially the

SED, under Soviet direction, were allowed to appeal to all German 'patriots' and pose for the time being as the spokesman of German nationalism. The party would in due course be ordered by Moscow to take exactly the opposite view. In January 1946 the SPD in the British and United States zones voted against fusion. In mid-February Kurt Schumacher, by now the acknowledged leader of the party in West Germany, came to Berlin for talks with Grotewohl. They led nowhere, for Grotewohl – whatever his unspoken doubts – was already committed to slavish acceptance of Moscow's orders. On 1 March Franz Neumann, the outstanding SPD leader in Berlin itself, secured backing for a party referendum. On 31 March 82 per cent voted against fusion with the KPD and on 21 April Schumacher was once again in the old capital, flinging down a challenge to the 'national Bolsheviks'.

At the SPD's first full-scale party conference, on 8 May in Hanover, Schumacher declared: 'The Social Democratic Party will be the decisive factor in Germany, or out of Germany will come nothing, and Europe will be the seat of trouble and decay.' He declaimed against the 'two real enemies, Moscow and Rome'. The SPD's embryonic programme included radical reform of the economic system, 'depoliticization' of police and civil service, reorientation of German youth, improvement of the food situation and a declaration of war on 'political Catholicism' and 'social restorationism'. Local elections in 1946 suggested that the party could win 45–50 per cent of the votes in a national election. But this first programme was strongly anti-clerical and basically Marxist in its social outlook. The party had picked up where they left off in 1933. The only additions to their philosophy were Schumacher's passionate hatred of Stalinist communism and the 'naïve trust in the victorious comrades of the British Labour Party'.[23]

Brandt attended the Hanover conference, but only as an observer. To Herbert George he wrote that the 'forced union' of SPD and KPD in the Soviet zone was a very serious development.[24] Artificially induced, it would set back the cause of working-class unity. A letter to Jacob Walcher – who favoured the fusion – was more explicit.[25] The SED had been created by undemocratic methods, by physical force in some places; there had been no free vote in the Soviet zone but only in Berlin; and their policies were merely a projection of those of the Soviet Union. They would be dominated by the 'communist apparatus'.

In this letter Brandt called for a clear-cut working-class programme, loyal co-operation with the occupation authorities, no illusions about a community of interest between the German working class and the Soviet Union, and all possible steps to be taken to improve the food situation. He was already channelling food parcels and books to party members whose selfless work for the SPD meant that they could not look after themselves. Later he wrote to Herbert George that 'Jim' – their wartime code name for Walcher – had gone over completely to the Moscow line.[26] As he saw it, German socialism would have to battle on two fronts, against capitalism and totalitarianism. But this did not mean 'aggressive anti-Bolshevism, which is regarded as good form in the United States'.

There was a plain hint in this letter that a return to Germany was now in the forefront of Brandt's mind. He wrote that he had not organized anything for himself. But offers had come.[27] One was from 'party friends' in Lübeck, 'who would very much like me to go there'; it was for him to become mayor. Brandt felt: 'I would be far and away too restricted there.'[28] There had in fact been three different offers to Brandt by this time. Lübeck's was a firm one, for the SPD were the strongest party there. The second offer came from the American-sponsored news agency, DENA, the third from the British-sponsored news agency, DPD, in Hamburg. He might have accepted this, and after an interview with the British supervisory board he returned to Oslo to think it over.

In September the Norwegian foreign minister, Halvard Lange, got in touch with Brandt. He wanted him to remain a Norwegian and proposed a variety of jobs. He could be Lange's head of press relations in the Foreign Ministry or press attaché in the Norwegian Embassy in Paris. Then Lange suggested that he should go to the Norwegian military mission in Berlin. In Brandt's own words: 'I did not take long to reply in the affirmative. But the formalities were not settled until the end of the year.'[29]

On 1 November 1946 Brandt sent a round robin to friends.[30] He explained that he had been a Norwegian citizen since 1940; the question of taking up German citizenship again was 'somewhat fictitious' at present. More relevant was 'where the individual can best serve the rebirth of Europe and, thus, German democracy too'. His attachment to German socialism would remain as strong as ever and he would review his position in due course. To Herbert George he wrote that his decision had been very difficult: he realized some German friends might be disappointed. But he had thought things over and believed his decision was right.

It looked surprising. A press attaché's post in the military mission of a small country like Norway might be a backwater. Admittedly he accepted for one year only – whereas the post in Paris would have entailed three years or more. He felt he would be 'at the centre of things' and able to keep Scandinavian opinion informed about Germany.[31] There may have been a deeper reason: he was never a man to hurry and he may have wanted time to think things over. As a press attaché in Berlin he could mark time while learning more about the German situation.

He travelled to Berlin at the end of 1946, in Norwegian uniform, a formality imposed on members of military missions. He was now thirty-three. Those who met him at this time have memories of a shy, slim young man, serious in expression and conversation, but ready to relax, make jokes and enjoy life.[32] He kept himself apart from the sleazier side of the Allied occupation – the fatuous *bonhomie* of the 'champagne Charlies', the heavy drinking of foreign journalists, the blatant racketeering on the booming black market. His usual attitude of wary reserve was heightened in Berlin: as an Allied official he had to keep his distance to some extent from his own German countrymen; as a German he studiously avoided the outbursts of anti-German feeling from the occupiers.

Berlin was a daunting place at this time. While Allied personnel contrived a hectic gaiety, the mass of Berliners lived in grinding poverty and in a city battered beyond recognition. Sixty per cent of the houses had been destroyed or badly damaged. Brandt called it 'a no-man's-land, on the edge of the world', and again, 'every little garden a graveyard, and above this, like an immovable cloud, the stink of putrefaction.'[33] The strange smell of the ruins, indeed, instantly impressed every newcomer, a compound of mildew, blocked drains and, doubtless, undiscovered corpses. There was 50 per cent unemployment; nine out of ten

67

were desperately hungry. Lacking coal or firewood, old people crawled from their homes to 'warm rooms' in communal buildings. There was a thriving black market in which the *Schieber* or profiteer was king. There were oases of feverish merriment, but the overall atmosphere was deep apathy and brooding melancholy, spiced by bitter mutual denunciation to disgusted Allied officials.

The winter of 1946–7 was one of the coldest in living memory, worse even than the 'black winter' of 1941–2. Brandt described it graphically:

> A new terror gripped the city; an icy cold. In the streets it attacked the people like a wild beast, drove them into their houses, but there they found no protection either. The windows had no panes, they were nailed up with planks and plasterboard. The walls and ceilings were full of cracks and holes – one covered them with paper and rags. People heated their rooms with benches from the public parks. . . . The old and sick froze to death in their beds by the hundreds. Within living memory Berlin had not experienced such a terrible winter.[34]

The food supply deteriorated. Yet the Berliners, once the shock of defeat was over, showed their traditional courage and good humour. The Berliner is a big city man, with wit which is broad and quick, great vitality and a ready friendliness. Sometimes cynical and coarse, cocky and cosmopolitan, his greatest attributes are a refusal to complain and an ingrained instinct for survival. His favourite saying is: *'Berlin bleibt doch Berlin'* – 'Berlin still stays Berlin'. Brandt wrote that the overwhelming majority stayed, against all the odds, 'decent'.[35] Living in Berlin

> . . . had a deep emotional effect on me and helped me to make up my mind what to do with myself. The question which had bothered me most was – had Germany enough vital strength left in her? The Berliners gave me the answer; and I found that same quality of endurance which the Norwegians had. The worst possible circumstances seemed to bring out the best in both, too. Conditions in Berlin, finally, reminded me of how much there was to be done for my country.[36]

One compensation was the presence of Rut. After the end of the war she was in the Norwegian Embassy in Stockholm and it was then that Brandt had really got to know her. She came to the Norwegian military mission in Berlin in April 1946. She had lost her father at the age of three, had had to earn a living at fifteen, first in a bakery, then as a seamstress, had worked for the Norwegian underground and had been arrested and spent some months in prison.[37] What impressed Brandt at once was that she was totally unaffected, totally natural.[38] She had a warm heart, was always ready to help an individual sufferer, was good with people generally. What he appreciated most was that she was companionable but undemanding. This dovetailed with his own deeply rooted desire for independence.

His work for the Norwegian military mission was not as rewarding as he had hoped. He wrote some useful reports, travelled much in West Germany, remained in touch with friends in the SPD. In his reports, however, he admitted that he was not able to 'reach' the German public,[39] and his contacts with German news media were inconclusive. In May 1947 he was writing to Herbert George praising the burgeoning political and cultural life in Berlin.[40] The thought must have been in his mind by then that he might join in it. Inge Scheflo, possibly his closest friend in Norway, knew that he was undergoing 'some sort of conflict of conscience'.[41] Scheflo had advised him to keep his Norwegian nationality, but felt that he could do more for Europe if he became a German again; he had much to offer both Germany and Europe. Herbert George, thinking instinctively, felt that he had 'never ceased to be a German'.[42] This was the view of Bruno Kreisky too: ideas and ambition could be realized only in some major field of endeavour. Germany was such a field; Norway was not.[43] Another old friend of the 'emigration', Frau Enderle, believed that he never lost his German 'being'.[44] She was full of admiration for his feat in belonging to Norway as well as to Germany: most emigrants had clung desperately to their German characteristics, or had shed them without finding any substitute.

On 7 November 1947 Brandt wrote to Halvard Lange to say that the SPD had pressed him to become their special representative in Berlin and that he had decided to accept this offer.[45] He found it hard to 'give up' Norway, was deeply grateful to her people, which political work in Germany would bring contact 'with all manner of men with whom I do not feel so much in common'. He went on:

It cannot be helped. The solution of the German problem will be dependent on decisions on an international political level. But there is much to be done inside Germany in the interests of Europe, democracy and peace. There are positive forces within the German people which will be able to make their mark on future developments.

You know I have no illusions. But I wish to try to help bring Germany back into Europe.... It is fairly certain that I shall suffer disappointment and perhaps more than that. I hope I shall face defeat if it comes with the feeling that I have done my duty. I shall carry with me all the good things I have experienced in Norway.... No artificial lines of demarcation can prevent me from feeling that I am a part of Norway. You can depend on me for the future.

To Herbert George he repeated that the SPD had offered him the Berlin post, but added that 'a number of so-called friends', former emigrants, had done their best to 'give a worm's eye view of me'.[46] They wanted to damage his reputation with the SPD leadership in Hanover. They failed, but their unfounded accusations were to be raked up years later.

Brandt took up his new post in February 1948. He renounced Norwegian, and reacquired German nationality. He retained his name of Willy Brandt, confirmed by due legal process in 1949. It was a momentous step: he gave up security in a country where he was happy and returned to one that was socially, morally, politically a jungle; bankrupt and bitterly hated by the outside world. Unlike most fellow emigrants he did not return to Germany out of a feeling of dependence. Years later he explained – he was needed more in a Germany that could go wrong, whereas Norway's future was assured. Berlin was the right place to make this new start for the question of Germany's future revolved around the old capital.[47]

He replaced Erich Brost, who went to Essen to found a new newspaper, the *Westdeutsche Allgemeine Zeitung*. Brost had come to Berlin in 1947 as the SPD's special representative. His main task was to maintain contact with the Berlin branch of the party and with the western Allies. He hardly knew Brandt,[48] but he knew his reputation, that of a young man with an old head on his shoulders. He had already had trouble with Schumacher, who behaved 'like a dictator' and was particularly truculent with the Americans. (When the American General Lucius Clay put his own plane at Schumacher's disposal the latter refused to thank him, as this would have been obsequious!) He proposed Brandt as his successor, believing he would stand up to the domineering Schumacher because he had 'real independence of character'. Not forceful but discerning, he picked on Brandt's key characteristic. If he had any doubt about him – 'really clever and not vain about it, patient, with a load of goodwill' – it was that he was slightly 'bohemian' and somewhat 'to the left' politically of Brost himself.

Brandt's new post was no bed of roses. There was the prickly, erratic personality of Schumacher, and prejudices against him because of his past. His difficulties with Schumacher were to last for several years; the prejudices against him have never been entirely overcome. He met Schumacher at several party conferences, listened to his jeremiads with respect and wrote to him on 23 December 1947 explaining his personal position and worries.[49] Schumacher had expressed his doubts to Brost about him; Brost had passed them on. They had to do with the fact that Brandt had left the SPD as a young man and joined the breakaway SAP and that he remained friends with Jacob Walcher, who had joined the SED. In his letter Brandt pointed out that the efforts of the SAP to secure a working-class front had 'been overtaken by events'. As for Walcher, he 'could not follow him along the path to the SED; I was a Social Democrat'. In the most striking passage of his letter he wrote: 'Let me declare to you unambiguously: I stand by the principles of democratic socialism in general and the policies of the German Social Democrats in particular. I reserve the right to work out my own views on any new issues that may arise. And I shall never agree in advance to every detailed formulation of policy, even if stamped by the leader of the party himself.' Strong stuff, it showed that Brost's belief that he would stand up to Schumacher was justified.

Schumacher was a Prussian, a bachelor whose personal fastidiousness may have contributed to an aggressiveness and excitability displayed in savage and vitriolic sarcasm.[50] His biographer, Lewis Edinger, wrote of his 'tortured body', his 'fanatical eyes' and 'jerky gestures'.[51] Allied officials found him truculent and touchy, and one American secretary of state, Dean Acheson, was frankly appalled by his bitterness.[52] He had lost an arm in the First World War and had spent much of the Nazi era in gaol. His sufferings may have unbalanced his character and he was already a very sick man when Brandt first met him. He was also in a desperate hurry: he did not have long to live and he believed that there was a tremendous amount to do. A furious impatience characterized everything he did or said. Sincere, courageous and honest, he was a dedicated socialist with a real hatred of injustice and privilege. One British minister who knew him well wrote of his 'moral passion and integrity'.[53] I myself found in him an engaging simplicity, a passionate belief in human dignity and freedom and an ability to expand in a warm-hearted and friendly way if he was aware of interest and sympathy.[54] He could relax, too: a British liaison officer recalled how at a beer and sausage party in Hanover Schumacher mounted a table and led the chorus of 'Here's a health unto His Majesty'.[55] But he seldom showed these sides of his character. He was obsessed by fears of political 'restoration', of the old, bad Germany coming to monstrous life again, of final and terrible retribution for a German nation contemptibly ready to surrender to greed, gain and power.

Brandt's relationship with this unpredictable and temperamental man was difficult.[56] He found Schumacher schizophrenic with members of his own party; he wanted them to be tough and independent, yet expected them to obey orders unquestioningly. He was ultra-patriotic, too – he told an American official: 'Never again will the Social Democrats be less nationalist than parties to the right.'[57] Brandt felt that his nationalism was designed to restore the self-confidence of the Germans. He certainly had a tonic effect on downcast and destitute refugees and returning soldiers. He also loathed rivals. Equally negative was his ignorance of the outside world. He had been isolated for the twelve years of the Nazi era; it contributed to his xenophobic distrust of foreigners – he loathed the French and Americans only slightly less than the Russians. But his forceful radicalism prevented German workers from accepting Stalinist communism, especially in industrialized areas suffering from unemployment, hunger and dismantling.[58] His heart was with the West, even though his head inspired opposition to steps needed to create friendship and understanding between the Germans and the western world.

The second obstacle to Brandt's work in Berlin was prejudice arising from his past. All returning exiles were blamed obscurely for having deserted their country in its hour of need. Brandt was believed to have fought for the Norwegian army against his own countrymen, to have denigrated 'good' Germans in his writings from Oslo and Stockholm and to have been too close to the Communists, perhaps even a communist agent – although while in Spain he had been branded by the Communists as a 'secret agent' of the Fascists! At the back of the campaign against him was a feeling of jealousy. He had been accepted by the Norwegians, by the Swedes too in some degree, had made his own way in life and been altogether too successful. In addition he was illegitimate, a social slur that he was never allowed to forget, and had changed his name 'mysteriously' while out of the country. In Berlin he was a mere newcomer and had played no part in the gallant struggle of the Berlin SPD to maintain its independence under communist pressure from 1945 to 1947. This had, indeed, been an epic. Working in dusty, ill-equipped little offices in the British sector, the SPD leaders presented a dauntless front to the communist challenge. The three who counted were Franz Neumann, the driving force, Otto Suhr, the titular figurehead, and Gustav Klingelhofer, philosopher and planner. For two years, until Ernst Reuter arrived early in 1947 from Turkey, this triumvirate dominated the Berlin SPD. Klingelhofer accepted Brandt without reservation; Suhr, too, after reflection; Neumann remained acutely suspicious, especially when he became Reuter's closest confidant.

A man of powerful physique and great personal courage, Neumann had been the spearhead of resistance to communist threats. When he made a speech at Weissensee, a Berlin suburb in the Soviet sector,[59] the Russians, determined to awe him, sent a score of officers to the meeting, who filled the whole front row. This made no impression. His speech was a rousing appeal for the independence and integrity of the SPD, the party that the Russians were elbowing out of existence. To Neumann it was galling that a newcomer like Brandt should play a part in the domestic politics of the SPD. In addition, Brandt stood to the right of centre in the party, while Neumann remained an ideological radical. Brandt believed in a *Volkspartei*, a party of the people; Neumann in an *Arbeiterpartei*, a party of the working class.[60]* Brandt has said that Neumann regarded himself as Schumacher's deputy in Berlin.[62] Brandt himself was instantly drawn to Reuter, and both Schumacher and Neumann regarded Reuter as a rival – Schumacher because Reuter had so different a temperament and approach to matters of policy, Neumann because Reuter quickly became the outstanding SPD leader in Berlin. Comparing Reuter with Schumacher, Brandt wrote: 'One could hardly imagine two men of greater contrast . . . on one side the man of fanatical will, completely absorbed in his ideas – on the other, the prototype of a humanist, who, never compromised in the pursuit of his ideals, also never forgets that all human toil is ephemeral.'[63] Where Schumacher stormed and protested against the Allies, Reuter sought to win their confidence. The 'little man in a beret' became as close to Brandt as any other man in his political life – 'he was young at heart and young in spirit. This made him a comrade. . . . We came from completely different social environments, but we travelled the same road; we had the same stars by which we steered our course.'

This is an unusually evocative passage in Brandt's usually factual writing. Reuter was an unusual man. An almost exact contemporary of Schumacher – he was just under sixty in 1947 – he too had served in the First World War. He had been taken prisoner by the Russians in 1916, joined the Volga German community after the Bolshevik Revolution and returned to Germany a Communist in 1919. He became disgusted with the stark crudities of the communist creed, joined the SPD and became mayor of Magdeburg and a member of the pre-1933 Reichstag. In 1932 he offered to bring his police to Berlin to prevent the

* Brandt's relations with Neumann include one comical vignette. In January 1948 Herbert George, by then in London, received a letter from Brandt about Neumann's budgerigar.[61] The bird was starving and needed a particular type of millet. Neumann had brought some from Stockholm but had none left. George procured the millet in London and sent it via Brandt to Neumann in Berlin. The budgerigar, one assumes, survived. This incident was typical of Brandt's invariable readiness to carry out small acts of kindness.

dissolution of the Prussian parliament by the Nazis. He was, inevitably, arrested by the Nazis when they came to power in 1933. Surprisingly, they released him in January 1934, and he emigrated to Turkey, where he worked as a schoolmaster and an official in the Ministry of Economics. Like so many Social Democrats, he had difficulty in getting back to Germany after the war. He arrived in Berlin in January 1947. He was given a job in the administration, looking after gas, water and electricity, and he made his presence felt.[64] The SPD mayor was Otto Ostrowski, unable to stand up to the pressure of the Russians, who were intent on controlling city services, the administration and the political parties. Ostrowski offered to resign in April and the SPD proposed Reuter as successor. As a 'lapsed' Communist he was unacceptable to the Russians. But on 24 June he was elected by eighty-nine votes to seventeen in the City Parliament. The Russians vetoed him – they claimed he had called the Soviet Union a 'nation of slaves' and an 'ant-heap of a state'.[65] In July the Soviet military governor, General Kotikow, declared that he could not become mayor. The western powers gave in; in theory the assent of all four occupying powers was necessary.

There was, for the moment, deadlock between the Russians and the three western powers. It was not the only matter on which there was disagreement. The Soviet Union wanted prior payment of $10,000 million of reparations out of current production from the whole of Germany, and proceeded to take about $500 million a year from the Soviet zone alone – this when the United States and Britain were importing $700 million worth of food into their zones. The Soviet aim was to reduce German living standards to the Soviet level and they refused to help draw up an economic programme for the whole of Germany. In addition, their aim was to 'democratize' Germany through the organization of a 'working-class front'. The refusal of the SPD in Berlin to co-operate was the first blow to this plan; the second was the lamentable failure of the Soviet-sponsored SED at the Berlin elections in October 1946. With the Russians in rigid control of two fifths of the city, the SED won only a fifth of the votes. The third blow occurred in February 1948, immediately after the successful Soviet coup in Czecho-Slovakia. The Russians had established complete communist control of the central trade union organization of the FDGB (*Freier Deutscher Gewerkschaftsbund*) in Berlin. This now split, and the Independent Trade Union Opposition (UGO) was formed in West Berlin. Two satellite political parties established by the Russians had also split – in each case separate West Berlin branches of the Christian Democratic and Liberal Democratic parties were set up.

What the Russians were doing in Germany was part of a pattern for the whole of Central Europe. Puppet communist regimes were installed in countries occupied by the Red Army, with control of the Ministries of the Interior, of Security, of Defence and of Information.[66] Small 'cadre' communist parties were expanded into mass organizations. Huge reparations were exacted from occupied countries. Genuine socialist parties were everywhere suppressed, by staged trials, concentration camps only relatively less terrible than those of the Nazis, persecution, torture and subversion.

The Soviet coup in Czechoslovakia convinced both Reuter and Brandt that Soviet encroachment in Berlin had to be resisted. In a speech to the Berlin SPD Brandt declared: 'The hope to be a bridge between East and West has collapsed. . . . Let's face the truth. Today bridges are not built but blown up.'[67] In the same month Marshal Sokolovsky, the Soviet military governor, told the four-power Allied Control Council that Berlin was a part of the Soviet zone. This was recognized as bluff by the western powers who, however, were not always united and were therefore slow to act. On 20 March Sokolovsky declared that the Allied Control Council had ceased to exist.

Already on 24 January a more sinister event had taken place. The Berlin–Bielefeld train, carrying British officials and 120 Germans, was held up by Soviet orders for eleven hours. On 30 March the Russians demanded the right to control personnel and their papers on all Allied trains to West Germany. On 1 April four Allied trains were turned back when Allied officers in charge refused the Russians permission to search them. Meanwhile the Russians had made all German vehicles passing in or out of Berlin carry passes countersigned by the Soviet authorities; this reduced goods traffic on the roads by 80 per cent in five weeks.[68] The Russians were removing at least one track from double-track railway lines and had organized a 'ring railway' round Berlin for Soviet zone trains. Early in April Soviet military posts on

76

roads were pushed up from two to three miles back from the border to the actual crossing-points, and a ban was imposed on food parcels from the Soviet zone to West Berlin.[69]

The Russians meant business, but the western powers were slow to react, at a time when the Russians were closing the Elbe road-bridge, ostensibly for repairs, and were forcing the British and Americans to withdraw their invaluable aid-stations on the Berlin–Helmstedt autobahn. The western powers regarded the creeping blockade as a side-show; their thoughts were on the reform of the German currency and the restoration of a sound economy. On 7 April 1948 the introduction of a new currency was forecast. This was the signal for the Berlin blockade to begin, although the full blockade by road, rail and canal became effective only on 10 July. Brandt avoided criticism of the western powers:

> It would not be fair to be over-critical, particularly when such a fine rescue operation for Berlin was mounted by the Western Powers. Maybe there were delays. . . . I would prefer to stress the positive aspects of the Blockade. First, it was a heroic episode in which the Allied pilots and the Berliners played the main roles. Then it brought about a feeling of real co-operation between the Berliners and the Allies. Those were grey, grim days; but our people showed their steadfastness, their courage, their dry humour and their basic decency.[70]

In the middle of June a message came from General Clay to say that an air-lift would be organized to supply the city. 'Reuter, I remember, pushed his spectacles up over his forehead and said, "I just don't believe it, but we've made our decision already – to stick it out".'[71] Later in June Brandt accompanied Reuter to United States headquarters and discussed plans in detail. Reuter was still sceptical about the air-lift, but in favour of General Clay's proposal (never implemented) to send a military convoy up the autobahn. Talk was of the blockade lasting possibly five to six weeks and Allied planes bringing in perhaps 500–700 tons of freight a day. In reality it lasted nearly one year and 1,736,000 tons were transported in 212,000 flights.

Brandt flew in and out of Berlin many times during the blockade. Men like himself and Reuter were liable to come back with their pockets filled with seed for flowers, or with gardening equipment in their briefcases. In Berlin what impressed Brandt most – apart from the endurance of the Berliners – was the way in which cultural life kept going. One special earlier memory was of the members of the Philharmonic Orchestra, on a bitter winter's evening, playing at the opera house in the Kantstrasse, wearing overcoats and mufflers.[72] These were hard times indeed. Food was very strictly rationed and much of it was depressing – powdered milk, dehydrated potatoes, with an invariable lack of fresh food. Fuel and light were strictly rationed too; Berliners took it in turns to get up or go to bed in the dark. Reuter coined the phrase: 'It's cold in Berlin, but colder in Siberia.' Public services ran only from 6 am to 6 pm; unemployment rose to over 150,000, or one in three of the working population. For airmen the danger was not to be underrated: 79 people lost their lives during the blockade, thirty-nine British, thirty-one American and nine German.

The blockade went on against a background of East-West diplomatic conflict. On 1 July the Soviet Union withdrew from the four-power Berlin *Kommandatura*; on 30 July the West Berlin police force was put under separate command from that of the Soviet nominee, Paul Markgraf. The city government was split and the political division of Berlin became absolute. The Berliners trusted their leaders. On 9 September 1948 Reuter told 350,000 of them in front of the ruins of the Reichstag that their independence and freedom depended on the western powers. Reuter, the 'little man in the beret', in his thick, almost glutinous accent, spoke straight from the heart, to thunderous applause from Berliners learning the hard way what democracy was all about – basically, the readiness of the individual to face up to hardship and danger in the interest of the community.

On 5 December 1948 new elections were held in West Berlin; Reuter became, at last, governing mayor of the city. The SPD vote rose from the 50 per cent of 1946 to over 64 per cent, and the party took 60 out of 98 occupied seats – the Christian Democrats won 21, the Liberal Democrats 17. Eighty-six per cent voted, on a cold and wintry day, the certainty of a grim winter ahead of them. This was the measure of their reinforced belief in themselves.

In July 1948 Reuter, with Brandt's backing, had begun enunciating his theory of a 'three-way policy' – progressing towards a West German state, resisting communist pressure on West Berlin, planning steps towards German reunification. Brandt had passed these thoughts on to the SPD executive in Hanover, an initiative that was not altogether to Schumacher's liking. Both Reuter and Brandt, again, wanted co-operation with the western powers, against Schumacher's avowed policy of forcing the maximum concessions out of them.[73] Reuter had forced one vote in the steering committee of the SPD but Schumacher had won by sixty-five votes to four, with eight abstentions,[74] a clear reflection of his predominance. Reuter had support in provincial branches, particularly in Hamburg and Bremen, but the central party apparatus remained unquestioningly loyal to Schumacher.

The Berliners concentrated on survival. Unemployment rocketed to nearly three hundred thousand, trade with the outside world ebbed to a trickle, and the city could not begin to share in West Germany's economic expansion after the reform of the currency. The blockade *was* having a real effect in a material sense, and the Russians had refused to budge during the exchange of notes and aide-mémoires in the summer of 1948. In the autumn they had vetoed United Nations proposals to resolve the Berlin question. A United Nations technical committee appointed by the Security Council in November got nowhere, but on 30 January 1949 Stalin, in a press interview, pointedly omitted mention of Berlin. A few days later negotiations began between United States and Soviet representatives at the United Nations and the blockade was actually ended by the New York Agreement of 4 May 1949. A Soviet order lifting all traffic and transport restrictions took effect from midnight on 12 May. Thus the blockade ended, after 322 days.

The Russians are inscrutable. But the signing of the Nato agreement by twelve nations in April 1949 may have been instrumental in their decision. This expanded the Brussels Defence Agreement of March 1948 signed by Britain, France and the three Benelux countries (Holland, Belgium and Luxembourg). The Brussels signatories were now joined by the United States, Canada, Denmark, Iceland, Italy, Norway and Portugal. The Nato agreement made it plain that the West would defend itself, even strengthen its defences, while Soviet pressure on

Berlin was maintained. The Soviet decision to relax pressure on Berlin was a reflex action to the West's show of determination. The Cold War had passed its peak. There is, indeed, a well-held view that the Soviet position was weaker than at any moment since 1945.[75] The West had shown that Berlin could be held, in spite of blockade. The Soviet zone, thanks to draconian dismantling of industry and reparations from current production, was declining economically. Soviet prestige was low and the Soviet Union still did not possess the atomic bomb. The morale of the West Berliners had strengthened and the French decided to merge their zone economically with the 'bizone' already created by the United States and Britain. The process of creating a West German state had not slowed down, and a federal constitution was in fact agreed by the parliamentary council in Bonn on 9 May 1949.

The Soviet feeling of weakness owed much to the underlying psychological uncertainty of mind of people who 'did not belong' in Central Europe. The British stationed one brigade in Hamburg; the Russians ringed Leipzig, a third of the size of Hamburg, with three divisions. The British Army of the Rhine was spread thinly over a zone that contained the industrial Ruhr; the Red Army, in a zone with a population of eighteen million, comprised thirty divisions. These divisions were aligned to deal with civil disturbance rather than to spearhead an attack on the West. All too often the West has been obsessed with its numerical inferiority *vis-à-vis* the Soviet Union. Yet the Russians, seeking refuge in numbers, have lacked *real* self-confidence. Reuter told one western journalist that the only road to German unity in liberty 'was incessant political warfare'.[76] Three things were needed – the West's proclaimed determination to liberate Eastern Europe from communist domination, systematic support for anti-communist forces there, and vigorous efforts to build a united, stable and prosperous Western Europe. This presupposed a stable West German state. Brandt felt that the western powers should have aimed at a more complete, more satisfactory agreement at the end of the blockade, and that this was a key moment for productive talks with the Russians.[77]

It seems clear, in retrospect, that the western powers were not geared to take the diplomatic offensive. Their natural leader, the United States, was a newcomer to the European scene. A telling

phrase to illustrate American insularity was coined at this time –
'the tendency of Americans to be so spellbound with their own
history as to wish to press other countries into the same
mould'.[78] France maintained a wary isolation. Britain was
terribly tired; the superb ability of Britain's embassies to gather
news and views, and to sift them, was often allowed to go to waste
in Whitehall.

Reuter and Brandt, again, were the foremost German protagonists of integration with the western world.[79] Prescience in this
respect has usually been ascribed to Konrad Adenauer, shortly to
become the first chancellor of the Federal German Republic. In
reality some of the Berlin SPD were a jump ahead. What happened on the doorstep was remote from Bonn. In the summer of
1948 the East German SED, following Tito-Yugoslavia's break
with Moscow, became an openly satellite and bolshevik party.
An East German 'People's Police' was organized, the precursor
of an East German army, in Russian service. Municipal administration, the press, the trade unions, education and the arts, every
facet of social existence was subordinated to rigorous communist
control. In a sense this was the Soviet gain out of the Berlin
blockade – the outside world became so preoccupied with the
city's struggle for existence that it did not notice what was happening beyond the city's boundaries. The Berlin SPD knew; their
leaders became correspondingly more realistic.

For Brandt the blockade was, more than anything else, a test in
human relationships. He had become closely attached to Reuter.
The two men were totally pragmatic, realizing that Germany's
problems would be solved by observation, understanding and
common sense. He was aware that 'my relations with
Schumacher were not as good as before. He had the impression
that I had become Reuter's man. Plotters and schemers, to be
found in every party organization, tried to create distrust between
us. They hoped to manoeuvre Reuter and myself into an open
conflict with the party leader.'[80] In the Berlin SPD he still faced
the animosity of Neumann and his friends. To them he was still
an intruder.

He was happily married by now and his first son, Peter, was
born in October 1948. It was a dark night, with winter stealthily
settling in on the blockaded city. Food and fuel to warm the

family home in the Trabenerstrasse were in short supply. So was electricity, and Peter was born by candlelight in a Berlin clinic. Brandt had little time for his family; he was working round the clock and one SPD member, Paul Hertz, said early in 1949 that he 'had the stuff in him to make a German Chancellor'.[81] If anyone took this statement seriously it was not Brandt himself. Determined, matter-of-fact, robust and confident, he had played a useful part in Berlin's struggle for survival; no more than that.

5

Rough Road to the Crest

Early in 1949 Willy Brandt made a speech, on the 'World Political Situation and the Tasks of the SPD', which gives a good indication of his ideas.[1]

First, the communist advance into Europe had been checked in 1948, by defending a free West Berlin. But real social progress – the true counter to communism – had not been achieved in postwar Germany. Nazism and war had led to the paralysis of basic social, economic and moral forces and nationalism was once again rising to the surface, thanks to 'the unbelievably short memories of some of our compatriots'. The task of the SPD was not to mark time but to lead; their duty was to the millions of simple, decent people who trusted the party. Finally, the freedom of Berlin must be maintained – 'If Berlin one day becomes a solid component of the Federal representative organs, there will no longer be an isolated Berlin question.' The survival of a free Berlin might prevent East Germany from being bolshevized, and there should be full co-operation with the western powers in the city. Berlin and Germany would be helped by the integration of Europe, or as much of Europe as possible. And whatever the problems, 'no situation is irredeemable. Only that nation is lost which admits that it is lost.'

These impeccable precepts embodied a pep talk that Berliners badly needed. The blockade was still on; the West was far away and the 'red tide', as Berliners called the communist world, eddied round the city. Evocative phrases were used like: 'Look across the Potsdamer Platz, and you can hear the ripples of the Volga.'[2] Cartoonists depicted the Berliner as a lone figure, coat collar turned up, hands deep in his pockets, gloom-patrolling down a street of ruins, trying to whistle some half-remembered tune, with the East wind howling in his ear, blowing all the way from Siberia. The hectic vitality of Berlin warred with a sense of

WILLY BRANDT

doom, yet at the same time blended with it. People woke up in the morning unable to face another day; the suicide rate became one of the highest in the world. Uncertainty of mind produced a rash of sexual assaults on children, a cult of astrology, transvestites and other perversions.³ The humdrum backcloth consisted of mass unemployment, lack of food and fuel and a temporary stop to all building and reconstruction work.

In May 1949 Brandt appealed to the SPD to move with the times. The party must offer true 'quality' of political thought and represent the national interest by initiating social reform. They had to remain realistic, but go on producing constructive ideas. Democratic socialism was not a cut-and-dried plan; it was a marriage of ideals with logical and desirable aims. If the SPD were to be the party of progress they had to set their sights at the right level for the right targets. He was deeply interested in the preparations in 1949 for the first federal elections. The federal German constitution was approved by the western powers on 12 May 1949. The *Länder* followed suit later in the month. The date chosen for the federal elections was 14 August 1949. Campaigning began towards the end of May.

West Berlin was not a part of the Federal Republic, in the fullest sense. Its citizens were represented in Bonn. But Berlin remained, technically, under four-power jurisdiction; West Berlin was subject to that of the three western powers, East Berlin to that of the Soviet Union. West Berlin sent eight delegates chosen by the City Parliament to the first federal parliament, the Bundestag, in Bonn. Their votes would not count in any operative parliamentary division. West Berlin was to become the twelfth *Land* in the West German *Bund,* or federation. Its status was anomalous, inevitably. The four powers remained responsible for Germany's future. Berlin was the one place where their responsibilities remained legally rooted, and the rights of the western powers helped to ensure that West Berlin, with more than two million inhabitants, was not swallowed up by a Soviet-sponsored East German state.

West Berlin, unlike the *Länder* of the Federal Republic, took no part in election campaigning. Meanwhile it underwent a partial transformation, a kind of preliminary face-lift. Food and consumer goods flowed in, plenty of the food coming from the Soviet zone in the shape of fruit and vegetables. One grievance among well-to-do Berliners was that the blockade ended too late to get their asparagus from Treuenbrietzen, thirty miles to the south. New clothes came in too, and quite suddenly, 'Cannes beach pyjamas, erratically intricate hair styles, and sandals, of red, green and fawn, many with ten-centimetre stilt-like cork heels or thin rubber Boogie-Woogie soles' appeared on the streets.[4] The first postwar luxury restaurants opened up; luxury goods arrived from the Soviet bloc, labelled 'for export' and unobtainable in the country of origin. Yet prosperity was only on the surface. Further down working-class families spent incomes of 300 marks (£20 or $80) a month on bare necessities. Old-age pensioners, with one third of this amount, were only just able to exist at all.

Brandt took part in the election campaign. He, like other SPD members, was appalled when the results were declared. Adenauer's Christian Democratic Party (CDU) emerged with 7·3 million votes, 400,000 more than the SPD, and with 139 seats in the Bundestag against the SPDs 131. Most of the remaining 132 members of the Bundestag belonged to right-wing parties ready to align themselves with the CDU but not with the SPD. Adenauer had made all the preparations for a CDU-led coalition, comprising CDU, Free Democrats (FDP) and the Lower Saxony German Party. The coalition had 208 seats out of 402 in the Bundestag, and could generally count on the support of another 30 to 40 members.

Brandt claimed that Adenauer and the CDU used Machiavellian tactics in the 1949 election.[5] They linked the SPD with ultra-strict controls – when Germans were trying to shake off the memories of sixteen years of a controlled economy. They assumed the guise of an ultra-respectable establishment, a sort of trustee of tradition. Their leaders branded the SPD as the stalking-horse of Bolshevism – with the implication of complicity in the Berlin blockade. Brandt's strictures were mild in comparison with the unbridled fury of Schumacher. He had been convinced that the SPD would win and, according to Adenauer, had carried out preliminary negotiations with the British High Commission over future policy.[6] Yet there were good reasons for the relative failure of the SPD. Their chief strongholds, Saxony and Thüringia, were in the Soviet zone. Berlin's built-in SPD majority did not count. The doctrines of the SPD, Marxist and anti-clerical, were outdated. Their economic ideas were confronted by the popular 'free market economy' of the CDUs economic wizard, Professor Ludwig Erhard. There was a traditional suspicion in the German middle class of the socialists, *die Sozis*, and the CDU were bound to find coalition partners where the SPD could find none. Finally, Adenauer had been underrated as too old – he was in his seventy-fourth year.

The 1949 elections were of crucial importance, for they set the pattern of politics for the next two decades. Adenauer seized his chance and, riding high on the wave of economic success, consolidated both his right-of-centre government and his heterogeneous Christian Democratic Party. He was to show a remarkable grasp of political management and his overall policy of economic retrenchment, step-by-step progress towards the restoration of German sovereignty and ever closer friendship with the western world fitted the aspirations of most Germans.

For Brandt, the SPD failure had two important consequences. Reuter remained in Berlin as mayor and Brandt turned down an offer by Schumacher to become SPD member of the Bundestag for Pinneberg, near Hamburg. Reuter's decision, incidentally, set an example followed by Max Brauer and Wilhelm Kaisen as heads of government in the city-states of Hamburg and Bremen, *Länder* in their own right. They joined Reuter in forming the *Bürgermeisterfraktion,* the mayoral clique that maintained a marked degree of independence from the SPD parliamentary party in Bonn. The second consequence of the 1949 elections for Brandt was his election by the Berlin SPD as one of its representatives in Bonn. Under the West German constitution Berlin, as we have seen, sent eight delegates, later increased to nineteen, to the Bundestag 'in an advisory capacity'.[7] The City Parliament in Berlin accepted this provision with an ill grace; indeed they demanded the inclusion of Berlin as the twelfth *Land* of the Federal Republic with full representation in the Bundestag. This demand was referred to the western commandants in Berlin; they, on the instructions of their governments, rejected it and even ordered that the eight Berliners for Bonn should not be elected by popular vote in Berlin but only by a vote in the City Parliament. The western powers were determined to maintain the special four-power status of Berlin.[8]

Adenauer agreed with the western powers. His critics suggested that his reason was to prevent Berlin from sending a strong contingent of fully entitled SPD members to the Bundestag. This may have been unfair. On 21 October he explained to the Bundestag that it was 'in the interests of Berlin herself' that provisions for the future inclusion of Berlin in the *Bund* should not be invoked.[9] This could be done 'as soon as the international situation permits', but for the present Berlin would only bring her laws into conformity with those of the Federal Republic.[10] As a sweetener Adenauer announced aid for Berlin, credits initially totalling 320 million marks. Berlin's special status has, in fact, been maintained ever since; so has the habit of the *Bund* of providing substantial financial help.

Brandt at the time agreed with Reuter that Berlin ought to become part of the Federal Republic. He later wrote: 'I supported him with all my strength. . . . West Berlin could only live if the Berliners participated in federal legislation and achieved a standard of living which the city could not provide out of its own means.'[11] He believed that the western powers could at the same time retain 'occupation rights'. Like Reuter he wanted the federal government in Berlin, at a time when the Russians were not keen to risk a new confrontation. This was unacceptable to the western powers, who were acutely conscious of the militarily strategic weakness of their position in the old Reich capital. Brandt did not press for Berlin's full inclusion in the *Bund* when he took his seat in the Bundestag, but he repeatedly proposed the transfer of federal government ministries to Berlin. There was a good case for the Ministry of All-German Affairs to be there; it was concerned with East German affairs and the issue of German unity. The minister, Jakob Kaiser, wanted Berlin as his headquarters; Adenauer opposed the idea – he regarded Kaiser as too independent and too progressive and wanted him under his eye, in Bonn. Brandt, in addition, emphasized that Berlin was not an economic liability but an asset to be developed; the Berliners did not want charity, but to stand on their own feet.[12]

For Brandt the chief value of membership of the Bundestag was experience of the workings of parliament and government. He joined in committee work, particularly foreign affairs. He took part in Bundestag debates. He met members of all parties and established friendly and productive relations, especially with Herbert Wehner, an ex-Communist who had been in exile with him in Sweden, and Fritz Erler, who had served in the Wehrmacht and became SPD spokesman on defence matters. For Wehner, Brandt developed respect and understanding, for Erler something more – according to one close friend, he may have stood 'a little in awe' of him.[13] Erler had incisiveness of intellect and strength of will, and another quality that Brandt shared, openness of mind in looking at problems and an ability to think them out without reference to established views and prejudices.

Brandt could have been link-man between Reuter in Berlin and Schumacher in Bonn. Reuter would have liked this. He was deeply disturbed by two aspects of Schumacher's leadership. Firstly, the tightly controlled, despotically ruled party *Apparat* was losing touch with supporters throughout the country. In Bonn it settled into its headquarters in the 'party barracks', an ivory tower for the functionaries under Schumacher, now more unapproachable as his health failed.[14] The SPD were earning their designation of 'the party of officials and employees'. At the party congress in Hamburg in 1950 only 4 per cent of the delegates were manual workers; 23 per cent were party functionaries and 53 per cent white-collar workers.[15] Loss of popular appeal was made brutally clear by the drop in membership: in 1947 it was 875,000, in 1949 736,000, in 1950 only 683,000. Many who left the party were under thirty years old. Many, again, must have been as disturbed as Reuter over the second, negative aspect of Schumacher's leadership – his total opposition to Adenauer's way of bringing the Federal Republic into Europe. Brandt admitted that opposition, for instance, to West German membership in the Council of Europe was purblind,[16] for young Germans were turning increasingly to European concepts of political, social and economic co-operation.

Brandt and his friends brought matters to a head over this question at the Hamburg party congress in May 1950. He appealed for a vote for entry, reserving the right of future criticism. But with nearly four hundred delegates present, only eleven supported him. Reuter, as a gesture of tact towards the party leadership, stayed away, but he asked Brandt to broach the European question in Bonn.[17] All Brandt learnt was that at least two thirds of the SPD parliamentarians were loyal, even submissive to Schumacher; his sheer force of character could still swing any vote in the SPD. In the view of one historian, this iron control was in the process of ruining the party.[18] This may have been an exaggeration. Brandt himself believes that Schumacher was gradually coming round to the view that the party needed new ideas and a new approach to the electorate.[19] Thus early in 1952 he wrote a foreword for the party's new action programme, indicating that socialist root principles could be married with forward-looking ideas. According to Brandt, too, he wanted SPD candidates in the 1953 elections from outside the ranks of traditional supporters; the best of the Hitler Youth generation, too young to understand what the Nazis were about and helpless to oppose them, should be attracted to the SPDs cause.

Yet Schumacher was failing to rethink policies clearly enough or soon enough. The electorate were unimpressed by pre-1933 socialist recipes – nationalization of industry, secularization of education, class warfare, a well-meant welfarism. The SPD leadership wrongly assumed that the German people were ready to surrender their volition to the state. Political success is the product of understanding between party and electorate; Schumacher thought a Marxist programme could be forced on to the electorate by an SPD who were becoming isolated and atrophied. The plain truth was that the Germans were anxious to work for themselves and, more surprisingly, to think for themselves.

One other issue disturbed relations between the SPD in Bonn and Berlin: West German rearmament. In July 1948 the Russians began arming a paramilitary People's Police, under one of Hitler's generals, Hermann Rentsch. This force was increased to 48,000 in the summer of 1949, and by early 1950 had its own artillery, tanks and reconnaissance aircraft. In the next two years the People's Police were doubled to a strength of over a hundred thousand and given new and formidable weapons, including Yak fighter aircraft. On 13 March 1950 the British government published detailed information about the People's Police, known as the *Vopos* (short for *Volkspolizei*). Adenauer accordingly asked the British high commissioner, General Sir Brian (later Lord) Robertson, if he could form and arm a similar federal police force. Robertson was agreeable.[20] On 16 March, indeed, Winston Churchill came out in favour of full-scale West German rearmament. He realized that there was an imbalance of conventional forces between East and West. A few weeks later General de Gaulle stated that West German rearmament was unavoidable, and early in August Churchill proposed that German contingents should be formed and attached to a European army. The United States, aware of the popular demand in Western Europe for lower defence expenditure, were ready to consider this; so, too, were the French – at least initially. But the British Foreign Office view was that Germans would play off East against West, the withdrawal of western Allied forces would be demanded, nationalistic elements in Germany would be encouraged and a new Franco-German hostility created, while most West Germans did not want to be rearmed.[21]

Schumacher was at first in some doubt. In Stuttgart, in September 1950, he declared: 'We are ready to bear arms once again if, with us, the Western Allies take over the same risk and same chance of warding off a Soviet attack, establishing themselves in the greatest possible strength on the Elbe.'[22] Schumacher changed his ideas very quickly when no such undertaking was forthcoming. But the Berlin SPD stuck to the view that a German defence contribution was reasonable, and a German government should go on seeking equal rights in the western alliance. Nato needed strengthening in any case at this stage; its fourteen divisions on German soil were utterly inadequate in the face of the 175 divisions of the Soviet Union and its satellites. The Berlin branch was more realistic than the party leadership.

Although commuting between Berlin and Bonn, Brandt was building his real career in Berlin. At the end of 1949 he had made a start in local politics, as party chairman in the borough of Wilmersdorf. He took over the party newspaper in Berlin, the *Sozialdemokrat*, which he renamed the *Stadtblatt*. As editor until the paper closed down in 1952, he wrote many of the leaders, which were couched in invariably moderate, cogent terms, with no particular grace of style but with an economy of words and short, simple sentences. There was no slavish adherence to the party line. Many of the leaders were written from Bonn. In July 1950 he was discreetly criticizing the SPD leadership in a commentary on the proposals of the Norwegian socialist, Torolf Elster, for a 'dogma-free socialism'.[23] Elster wanted increased personal freedom, enriched human existence, social security and social justice and higher living standards. He warned against over-centralization and rigid Marxist doctrine; Brandt – with Schumacher in mind – called his warnings 'modern and flexible'. In February 1951 he rejected all ideas of 'neutralizing' Germany between East and West – ideas fashionable in SPD circles in Bonn.[24] In April 1951 he was brave enough to compliment Adenauer for negotiating with the trade unions on workers' co-partnership in industry – a tribute to 'the enemy' which must have made Schumacher's hair stand on end.[25] Another editorial of concern to the SPD leadership was on rearmament.[26] He felt that 'unrealistic pacifism' was not the right riposte to the federal government's plans to rearm the Federal Republic – better to adopt a pragmatic attitude, analysing the situation as time went by. The federal government, of course, was often his target. In August 1950 he sharply criticized Adenauer for writing off Germany east of the Elbe;[27] in November 1950 for doing so little about German reunification.[28] In the same week he warned against concentrating on the 'little Europe' of France, Italy and part of Germany, leaving out Britain and Scandinavia.[29] He was ready, too, to strike a controversial note. Two examples – in January 1951 he stood out for an SPD-CDU coalition, in defiance of his own party;[30] in March he defended the United States high commissioner, John McCloy, for refusing to commute death sentences on certain German war criminals.[31]

The *Stadtblatt* provided a useful forum for his views, but hardly a career. It gave him a firmer footing in the Berlin branch of the SPD, where a struggle for power began before the 1949 elections, between Reuter, Brandt and their group and the traditionalists under Franz Neumann. A heated argument arose after the December 1950 Berlin city elections. The SPD vote had dropped from 64 to under 45 per cent, due to the Berlin economy not picking up fast enough – something for which Reuter's administration could hardly be blamed – and to disillusionment with the SPD opposition in Bonn. The CDU and FDP had secured, between them, 66 of 127 seats in the City Parliament, but their candidate for governing mayor, Dr Walter Schreiber, tied with Reuter with 62 votes each; by mutual agreement, Reuter remained mayor. The Neumann group wanted the SPD to go into opposition, and had the backing of Schumacher. But Reuter had his way; he argued that the Berlin situation was a special one and that as mayor he could secure adequate help for the city from Bonn.

In December 1950 Brandt became a member of the City Parliament and early in 1952 he ran against Neumann for the post of SPD chairman in Berlin. Neumann won, by 196 votes to 93; the majority accepted his argument that the SPD must keep its 'truly socialist profile',[32] and it did not dare to flout Schumacher's wishes. It was a disappointment for Brandt, who had allowed his candidature to go forward with the ready approval of Reuter.

A few weeks later Schumacher was dead. This is no place to write his obituary, but while he tried to delay the Federal Republic's integration into the western world and the recovery of sovereignty on terms acceptable to the western powers, he defended democracy, resisted the overtures and challenges of Communism and helped to give back Germans a sense of national dignity and pride. His unfortunate bequest to party and nation, however, was Erich Ollenhauer, his successor. Sincere and worthy, Ollenhauer was unimaginative and verbose, the accepted version of an SPD functionary, rotund and bespectacled, humdrum, uninspired. Predictably, he had the support of Schumacher's hand-picked party executive. He ran the party on a basis of consensus and compromise, surrounded by a bureaucratic, increasingly calcified old guard made up of dedicated officials like Wilhelm Mellies and Erwin Schoettle, the SPD legal expert, Adolf Arndt, Carlo Schmid, unkindly called the *Parade-Intellektueller* (literally, 'intellectual on show').[33] Seven lean years for the SPD under Schumacher were followed by seven leaner years under Ollenhauer.

Schumacher's death should have weakened the Neumann group in Berlin. It did, but not enough. Brandt ran again for the chairmanship of the SPD in May 1954. He was now a member of the executive of the SPD parliamentary party in Bonn. His years of exile were far behind him. He was well known and well liked. But Neumann beat him by 145 votes to 143. Brandt became deputy chairman, mainly to heal the rift between the reformers whom he led and the old guard under Neumann. The road to the top, in Berlin, was still barred to him.

In the meantime three quite different things had happened,

which need separate treatment. The first was the East German rising, in June 1953; the second, the death of Ernst Reuter, on 29 September 1953, of heart failure. Both were, for Brandt, traumatic events. Finally, there was the second defeat of the SPD in the 1953 federal elections.

The East German state had been created at the same time as the Federal Republic, not by free elections but by decree. It was dominated by the communist-controlled SED; other political parties were puppets. Economically, East Germany continued to be bled white by the Soviet Union. For this purpose: 'Workers were given collective wage agreements which reduced the trade unions to the status of an auxiliary arm of the Communist State; workers were set "production norms" on the Stakhanovite model and penalties prescribed for non-fulfilment; women were mobilized on a huge scale for industry; agricultural co-operatives were formed, to wrest a higher output from the mainly unfertile soil of East Germany.'[34] East Germany was a police state, lacking all basic human freedoms. It paid immense reparations to the Soviet Union and led a grey, grim existence under alien tyranny. Many sought refuge in the West. In 1949 129,000 left, in the next year 197,000 and 165,000 in 1951. The Iron Curtain frontier through the middle of Germany was sealed off on 1 June 1952. General Zaisser, minister of security, ordered the establishment of a 10-yard-wide forbidden zone along the frontier, a 500-yard wide controlled zone behind it and a 3-mile-wide zone prohibited to all normal traffic. Unauthorized persons in the controlled zone went to prison; those who set foot in the 10-yard-wide 'death-strip' were fired upon without warning.[35] The number of open roads running from East to West Germany was reduced from 227 to 50. Soviet interference with road traffic between Berlin and West Germany was stepped up. During the latter part of 1952 the East Germans sealed off 200 out of 277 streets between East and West Berlin and seized West Berliners' property and bank accounts in East Berlin. Political purges resulted in the SED expelling 150,000 members in 1951 alone.[36] Leaders too: in 1951 Paul Merker of the SED Central Committee, in 1952 Franz Dahlem, in 1953 Wilhelm Zaisser and Rudolf Herrnstadt. In 1953 the ministers of foreign affairs and food, Georg Dertinger and Karl Hamann, were sent to prison for fifteen and ten years respectively.

On 5 March 1953 Stalin died. On 10 March the Soviet government proposed discussion of a peace treaty with Germany and examination of conditions suitable for the creation of an all-German government. The western powers believed that this was an attempt to hold up the proposed Paris and Bonn agreements on West German sovereignty and participation in western defence, and retorted by demanding free, all-German elections. But the new Soviet leadership was worried by the German situation and sent a former political adviser in Germany, Vladimir Semeonov, to examine the possibility of a 'new course' in East Germany. Semeonov was recalled in April, but sent out again as Soviet High Commissioner at the end of May. On 9 June he reversed recent repressive measures – the tightening up of food rationing, confiscation of farms, persecution of independent tradesmen and undue restriction of travel, but not the most unpopular of all, the raising of work norms on which wages were based.

Soviet intentions have never been fully clarified. The Soviet leadership was in a state of disarray. Beria was about to make his bid for power. But the western powers felt that the Russians could have indicated good faith had they wanted to. In Bonn Adenauer was convinced of Soviet trickery. In Berlin Reuter urged Eisenhower to meet Malenkov, Stalin's temporary successor.[37] Two months later Winston Churchill was to make the same suggestion. In retrospect Brandt's feeling was that something positive might have been done:

> This could have been a key moment. We know rather more now than we did then; there was a real crisis in the Soviet leadership, the German question really was in the forefront of the Russians' minds; the Russians might have agreed to German reunification, with the Communist Party in a minority. But what then happened – the East German rising – actually set things back. There was still a chance for the western powers to demand negotiations over the *whole* of Berlin. As it happened, the sector boundaries were closed during the rising. Nothing could be, maybe, nothing in fact *was* done about it. In a way, this episode was a forerunner to the much later building of the Berlin Wall.[38]

The East German rising to which Brandt referred was a

94

spectacular, gallant and heart-rending affair. First of all, it was spontaneous; stories that it had been cunningly devised by the West Germans or the western powers were utterly false. It embraced virtually the whole of East Germany; in nearly three quarters of it martial law was proclaimed, and Soviet troops had to intervene brutally in every town with more than fifty thousand inhabitants save Plauen, in Saxony. It was a rising of the working class, not of a 'bourgeois' or military élite. The men marching through the streets of Berlin on 16 June 1953, and everywhere in East Germany next day, were workers, who asked for better working conditions but also for free elections and a secret ballot. Finally, the East Germans must have suspected that the western world would not lift a finger to help. This was, in fact, what happened. The twenty-five divisions of the Red Army, deployed to destroy German nationalists on the march, ground down working-class men who were unarmed and helpless in the face of Russian tanks.

It was all over quickly, and is in danger of being forgotten outside Germany. In 1974 one can only say that the western world is quick to forget anything that causes it embarrassment. The East German rising of 17 June 1953 did just that. The West decided, by automatic reflex, on a policy of inaction. There was no immediate diplomatic protest; western Allied military commandants behaved like tourists, going down to the sector boundaries and peering across them through field-glasses. The Russians decided that they did not protest about the brutal repression of the rising because they were either afraid or not sufficiently interested. This suggested that the western powers would no longer insist that everything that happened in Berlin was their responsibility, but would take the easy way out. The Russians were perfectly correct. Reuter's request for troops to be deployed on the sector boundaries was ignored; so was his proposal for talks with the Soviet commandant, General Dibrova. On 19 June Brandt wrote in the SPD paper, *Vorwärts*, that there could be no improvement in East Germany as long as Walter Ulbricht 'doesn't disappear'. He suggested that Bonn's all-German policy was 'too narrow-gauged'; there should be an effort to secure free elections in the whole of Berlin, as a model for the whole of Germany. German diplomacy should not remain passive. Later he recalled that on 1 July he appealed in the Bundestag for fresh efforts to secure a peace treaty and made it plain that all the occupying powers were doing too little in this respect.[39] He added: 'The events in the German east zone in 1953 were to become the precedent of the Hungarian tragedy three years later; a courageous uprising of the population, merciless intervention of the Soviets, stupor of the West.'

An estimated 4,000 East Germans had been arrested in East Berlin and 16,000 in the rest of East Germany; 30 were killed and 100 wounded in the streets of the single city of Leipzig; an estimated 40–50 death sentences were carried out after the rising ended, and dozens while it took place; most sinister of all, 7,000 East Germans simply 'disappeared'. The immediate political consequence was the military reinforcement that took place in East Germany; the Red Army was brought up to a strength of 400,000, with 7,500 tanks and armoured vehicles, 8,000 artillery weapons and 800 front-line planes, while the East German People's Army was given a standing strength of 190,000, with a reserve of 120,000 and 80,000 men in other paramilitary units.[40]

Ernst Reuter was already a sick man at the time of the East German rising. In the year before his death SPD policies had preoccupied him most. His influence had played a big part in the party congress at Dortmund in September 1952, when the demand for socialization was restricted to the coal and steel industries. His voice spoke in the final communiqué – 'We are separated from the Communists not merely by questions of fundamental policy but by the gaols and concentration camps of the Soviet Zone.'[41] He continued to appeal for realism in defence and foreign policies, for a real western initiative in the German question and for consideration of a 'national coalition' in Bonn that could help to mount such an initiative. He worked on – very much a stoic – almost to the end, which came suddenly at the end of September 1953. The Berliners placed lighted candles in their windows – a spontaneous gesture.[42] Brandt felt a sense of bitter loss; this was the first German since Julius Leber in pre-Nazi days who had inspired confidence and underlying affection and comradeship. Reuter had a great heart and a cool, logical brain. How much better it would have been for the SPD had he been its leader, in place of the brave but frantic Schumacher!

His death produced a difficult situation in Berlin. The SPD sombrely voted to leave the coalition government and were forced to go into opposition for the first time since 1947. This was a very difficult time for the city. The pressure from the Russians was off; as a result the feeling of embattled solidarity waned. But Berlin had an immense task of physical reconstruction, to build up trade with markets and sources of supply that were far away, to modernize industry and prune its swollen administrative bureaucracy. The new coalition and the governing mayor, Dr Walter Schreiber, showed lack of zeal and experience, reflected in the results of the December 1954 city elections. The SPD vote actually dropped, from 44.7 per cent to 44.5 per cent, but the joint CDU–FDP vote dropped still further, from 47·6 per cent to 43.2 per cent. Splinter parties of the Right siphoned off the residue, a sign of disenchantment and uncertainty of mind. Early in January the SPD formed a new coalition with the CDU. Otto Suhr became governing mayor, with Brandt President of the City Parliament. In effect this post was rather more important than that of the Speaker in a British parliament; Brandt was making his way in spite of the party hierarchy in Berlin.

In the meantime the 1953 federal elections had taken place. Although the SPD had just about held their own, the CDU vote had jumped from 31 per cent to 45 per cent. With small parties not represented in the Bundestag, because they had failed to capture 5 per cent of the vote, the CDU had an outright parliamentary majority – 244 out of 487 seats. This was a personal triumph for Adenauer and wherever he went during the campaign he was greeted by deliriously happy crowds. He claimed that he was 'seventy per cent of the Cabinet';[43] a great many West Germans agreed. Ludwig Erhard, as minister of economics, made a big contribution, but he had been given his head by Adenauer and credit for the impressive economic recovery of the past four years went to the chancellor too. He was the hero of the hour.

The West Germans felt the need to move out of isolation after the failure of the East German rising.[44] They mistrusted the SPD leadership, which were carrying on Schumacher's negative policies. His tortured features were still displayed on their election posters.[45] Ollenhauer hesitated to introduce new blood into the party management and during the next year both Brandt and

97

Fritz Erler failed to win places in the SPD executive. One historian wrote of the SPD management of 1954 that it 'lacks vision, imagination, and new ideas. It is intellectually narrow and smug; unaware of the challenge of the times, incapable of accepting it.'[46] The party made no appeal whatever to the middle class, to youth or to farmers. They ignored large sections of the community when they fought an election. Nor did they offer an interesting alternative policy to the government's; when they could have evolved a policy of social reform, they simply opposed steps to true international co-operation, European programmes to combat poverty at home and in developing countries. The SPD were bad losers. Ollenhauer talked of unfair electoral tactics and a plot to install a restorationist regime. Brandt himself perhaps too readily blamed the electorate, by calling the elections 'those of satiated content, or materialistic egoism'.[47]

Brandt and Reuter, before the latter died, moved towards a bi-partisan foreign policy. So did the West German trade unions. Their central body, the DGB, supported European integration, the Schuman Plan for a European coal and steel community and the general principle of co-operation with the western powers. In a speech of 12 June 1954 Brandt urged a security pact with the western powers in which effective defence measures would be married with a positive policy for German reunification.[48] The underlying thesis was that it did not help if the SPD offered only negative opposition to the federal government. The SPD was so little impressed by Brandt's arguments that in the elections to the executive of July 1954 he received barely half the votes given to Franz Neumann, 155 against 270. Brandt may have had, at the time, more impact on domestic than on foreign policies; the 1954 action programme added a preamble that the SPD 'does not represent the special interests of single groups', that 'Social Democracy has, from the party of the working class, become a party of the people', and that 'socialist ideas are not a substitute-religion'. These were very much Brandt's thoughts.[49]

Speeches during 1955 and 1956 show that he was much preoccupied by the failure of the western powers to do more than remain on the defensive over Berlin and German unity. His inquiring mind threw out ideas. In *Vorwärts* in April 1955[50] he stressed the importance of human relations: normalization of living conditions in East Berlin and East Germany should promote contact between East and West Germans. This thought, once boldly stated, has remained with him ever since. Speaking to the *Hochschule für Politik in Berlin*,[51] he warned against the evolution of a genus of East Berliner and West Berliner. He wanted conditions eased for East Germans travelling to West Germany. In December 1956 he was proposing the move to West Berlin of the federal ministries for Posts, Refugees and All-German Affairs.[52] He wanted a dialogue with the East German leaders, for he believed that West Germans had the better case to state. Speaking in Stockholm, he offered to join in public debate with the East German regime.[53] In October 1956 he called on the Soviet Union to give basic freedoms to its down-trodden satellite states.[54] Two days later he appealed for an end to Stalinist oppression in Central Europe; for East Germany he proposed a 'commission of experts' as an alternative to free elections and a democratic regime.[55] On 6 July 1956 he published a message of sympathy for the victims of the Posen riots in Poland. On 22 October he said in Berlin that developments in Poland were a reminder that Titoism and Gomulkaism existed in the East German SED too. His activity contrasted sharply with the mental attitudes of most of his countrymen, content to be good boys in the western camp, or of British and other diplomats, who let sleeping dogs lie.

In 1954 the Bonn and Paris agreements, on West German sovereignty and a West German contribution to the proposed European Defence Community (EDC), were signed. When the EDC collapsed into ruins, the Federal Republic was brought into Nato in 1955. This fitted Brandt's concepts but his forthright ideas were not generally accepted in the SPD. In January 1955 the party prescribed the *Paulskirche Manifesto* against rearmament in Frankfurt. Speeches were full of goodwill but unco-ordinated. It was all very well to preach the virtues of German reunification through negotiation as opposed to integration with the West. The SPD did not explain how East-West negotiation over German reunification could be set in motion. The Frankfurt manifesto fell flat.

In 1954 and 1955, and early in 1956, Brandt made some trips abroad. He was not, like the federal chancellor, Dr Adenauer, untravelled. These were the first journeys undertaken as a

representative of Berlin and of the SPD. In 1954 he was in the
United States along with three other members of his party, Fritz
Erler, Carlo Schmid and Günther Klein. The four gave
Americans a view of German socialists who thought prag-
matically and favoured full participation in the western world,
defence and all. Brandt and the others opposed the EDC – they
did not believe that a 'little European' army was what Europe
needed, nor that the peculiar rules laid down for it by suspicious
Frenchmen would make a real army at all. It was useful for
Americans to hear views that did not conform with the strict
pattern of party politics. Brandt's quick wit was displayed when
Shepard Stone, of the Ford Foundation, gave a party for the
SPD delegation and remarked at it that he wouldn't mind having
a free trip like theirs – over the length and breadth of America.
Brandt countered: 'For that, you would first have to lose a
war.'[56]

In 1955 he was in Belgrade, and in 1956 in old hunting-
grounds, Stockholm and Oslo. In the Scandinavian capitals there
were old friends to meet and some useful discussion of Europe's
problems. Belgrade was a more formative experience, a first real
view of Europe east of the Iron Curtain; he was impressed by the
vitality of the Yugoslavs, their readiness to go it alone after the
split with the Soviet Union, their trust in Tito. Yugoslavia was a
jungle of problems; what struck Brandt most was the courage and
determination of her people to get on with their lives and face a
future in almost as great isolation as the people of Berlin.

These travels apart, his life was mainly concerned with
developments in Berlin. As president of the City Parliament he
had much to do with the governing mayor, Otto Suhr, not a man
of original ideas, with a programme on straightforward, unambi-
tious lines – economic reconstruction, streamlining an inflated
administration, a *modus vivendi* with the Soviet authorities. Relations with the Russians were fair at this period, essentially
because this was how the Russians wanted them. Nikita
Khrushchev, now in charge in the Kremlin, settled for the *status
quo*, for the time being. Adenauer was invited to Moscow at the
end of 1955, Austria was given her State Treaty, tension between
the Soviet Union and Yugoslavia was relaxed. The basis of Soviet
policy in Germany was to build up the East German state,
crystallize the division of Germany, ignore West Berlin. History

has shown that when the Soviet Union relaxes pressure in some part of the world there is no counter-pressure from the West. Because this is so, Soviet pressure will in due course be resumed. The western powers were well pleased to sit back. As one historian wrote, the motto of British diplomacy had become: 'Anything for a quiet life.'[57]

Economic reconstruction, at any rate, was pushed ahead during this speciously promising thaw in East–West relations. By the end of 1956 unemployment was down from three hundred thousand to a hundred thousand; industrial production – Berlin was before the war the biggest centre of German industry outside the Ruhr – trebled between 1949 and 1956, and exports increased nearly five-fold; major housing projects were under way and the face of the city was gradually transformed. The Berliners benefited psychologically too: the courageous defiance of the early postwar years was replaced by settled confidence. They had learnt to live with geographical isolation and the ominous presence of twenty-five Red Army divisions encircling their city and cutting them off from the West. The city even became a joke-factory.* Yet what was happening in East Germany was the reverse of amusing. The 'cold revolution' was being pushed steadily ahead. Industrial workers were dragooned by the monolithic and inappropriately named Free German Trade Unions (FDGB), strikes were outlawed, farmers ground down by the system of compulsory delivery of products and by fear of collectivization of their land – a process pushed through to completion a few years later. Youth was mobilized under the banner of the monolithic Free German Youth (FDJ). A campaign began against the Christian Churches, with pagan 'youth-initiation' ceremonies taking the place of baptism; and the radio com-

* The Berliners make so many jokes that it may be invidious to pick out any. These are random specimens.

An old lady of Leipzig wrote to Walter Ulbricht to congratulate him on his birthday, adding: 'I wish you everything that the German people has been wishing you for years.' Next day she was arrested for incitement to murder.

A beggar who was cursing the East German communist regime was arrested by an East German policeman. Bystanders protested, and one of them said: 'Don't pay any attention to him; can't you see he's plumb crazy?' 'No, I can't,' said the policeman. 'He's talking much too good sense.'

Question: 'What is a tapeworm?' *Answer:* 'An elephant that lived too long in the Workers' and Farmers' Paradise.'

A 'normal harvest' in East Germany is one that is worse than last year's, but better than next year's.

mentator, Karl Edouard von Schnitzler, coined the slogans: 'God has left the Church' and 'To pray is not as useful as to think'.[58] Political purges continued, and about two hundred thousand East Germans fled each year to the West, with the clothes on their backs and a small suitcase in their hand. Berlin still offered a relatively easy road to freedom, by tram, metropolitan railway or even on foot across sector boundaries.

In 1955 East Germany gained the status of a nominally fully sovereign state, the German Democratic Republic (DDR). However illusory its sovereignty, it was becoming economically more viable – a prerequisite to survival. Ulbricht's first five-year plan, with targets deliberately set high, fell only 10 per cent short of them – 'Against the much publicized failures were a sixty-five per cent increase in lignite production – East Germany's main source of fuel – and the success of the so-called *'Schwerpunktprogramm'*, under which certain branches of industry were given priority. The progress of such firms as Leuna Chemicals, Schopkau Buna and Zeiss Optics was indisputable.'[59] The East German economy was being tied into that of Eastern Europe; as far back as 1949 the Soviet Union had organized the Council of Mutual Economic Aid (Comecon), designed to co-ordinate the economic policies of Soviet-bloc countries. The binding of the East German State into Comecon was as important to Soviet policy as its maintenance as the forward bastion of the Soviet defence system in Europe, under the Warsaw Pact that was the Soviet answer to Nato.

In 1956 East Berlin was officially declared capital of the DDR. The frustration of watching the division of Germany being consolidated was galling to a man like Brandt, and he urged in private that West Berlin should now be fully integrated politically into the Federal Republic and become its capital.[60] At least it needed to be proclaimed *Hauptstadt Berlin*, even if such a proclamation were not implemented. He was depressed by the failure of the western powers at this time to protest against continuous Soviet infringements of the city's four-power status.[61] This was being steadily eroded, and the division of the city made more absolute. Britain's former ambassador to Moscow, Sir William Hayter, has supplied an acute analysis of Soviet diplomacy. These were the cardinal elements: unlike the western powers, the Soviet Union operates in the diplomatic field unilaterally and 'on all levels',[62] knows what it wants, and sets out ruthlessly to get it; the Russians 'always negotiate for victory. It never occurs to them that the proper object of negotiation is not to defeat your opposite number, but to arrive at an agreement with him which will be mutually beneficial';[63] the Russians place no credence in the word of a 'bourgeois opponent', because of ingrained Soviet dependence on Machiavellian guile – 'Probably most people lie a bit, more or less, sooner or later; but few people lie as often and as freely as a Soviet official.'[64] Sir William realized that Soviet diplomacy suffered disadvantages. It possessed 'a certain clumsiness, amounting on occasion to an alienating brutality; an inability to inspire confidence in anyone; above all an almost total, perhaps incorrigible, lack of understanding of the real character, motives and feelings of the foreign countries and peoples with whom it has to deal'.[65] But the Russians made up for their hamhandedness by sheer persistence: 'The Russians are prepared to go on, at meeting after meeting, producing again and again proposals that the West had repeatedly declared to be unacceptable. But Soviet rejection of a Western plan is far too often thought to put it out of court. That is a mistake.'[66] Over the creeping destruction of Berlin's four-power status the western powers failed to make strong and continual protests; they assumed they would do no good and were therefore not worth making at all. This is not diplomacy but its negation.

Brandt was still much involved in the affairs of the SPD. One finds him outlining, in *Vorwärts*, guidelines for the next federal election campaign.[67] They were: social reform in the interests of social justice; a fair but modern economic policy; the development of a liberal way of life opposed to 'bureaucratic arrogance and reactionary cant'; persistent examination of the problem of German reunification.

The failure of the four-power Geneva Conference in 1955 had suggested very plainly that the Russians would not risk German reunification on acceptable terms. The permanent division of Germany into two states suited them; the possibility of a unified, communist Germany had become utterly remote. Western demands for free, all-German elections were rebuffed and the maximum efforts were made to build up the initially ramshackle East German state into a solid entity. As such, it would constitute a key piece in the mosaic of the Soviet Union's East European satellite empire. Remove one instrinsic piece of this mosaic and the whole of it could break up. The key pieces were Poland, Czecho-Slovakia, Hungary and East Germany. The surest way, in Russian eyes, of preserving this mosaic was to remove pressure on it, by securing the withdrawal of United States armed forces from Europe; without them Western Europe on its own could not pose any armed threat to the Soviet bloc. Military disengagement therefore became an important facet of Soviet diplomacy.

The SPD leadership, under Ollenhauer, was too unimaginative to understand this, or to grasp that the Russians wanted the continuing division of Germany, with the West German state weak and neutralized and the East German state permanently Communist and under Soviet direction. Ollenhauer and his friends began, in 1956, to ask for the withdrawal of the Federal Republic from Nato and of the DDR from the Warsaw Pact, with a four-power guarantee for a neutral and unified Germany. The SPD campaigned against the Conscription Bill, arguing that conscription would stiffen the Soviet attitude, harden-up East European satellite regimes, encourage American diplomatic inflexibility and destroy the chances of negotiating with post-Stalin Soviet leaders. Brandt was prepared to see the Conscription Bill modified or even abandoned. Erler favoured a small professional West German army, backed by a reserve. He believed that conscription would be unpopular, with reason; the Adenauer government believed this too and reduced the length of service in September 1956 from eighteen months to one year. The controversy, paradoxically, did Brandt more harm than Erler. At the Munich party congress of 1956 Erler was at last elected to the SPD executive; Brandt, yet again, was not. It seemed a thoroughly damaging blow to his party aspirations.

The outlet for his political ambitions was to prove to be Berlin. Suhr, the governing mayor, fell ill in October 1955. He was too ill to travel and the question of finding a successor became apparent. The most obvious candidate was Franz Neumann, still Chairman of the Berlin SPD and a member of the federal party executive. He remained unremittingly hostile to Brandt. One of his contemporaries heard him say at about this time: 'I may have to work with Brandt politically, but I can't stand him as a person.'[68] Neumann and the SPD Old Guard in Berlin continued to resent him as an interloper and he was painfully aware of this: 'I would have liked to have co-operated with him in the fullest sense of the word, to have talked over our political line and how to put it across. Ever since 1952 he had mobilized his followers against me. I tried to make my peace with him, but he was unforgiving. It made party work in Berlin difficult.'[69]

Neumann lacked what is vulgarly called star quality. In November 1956 an incident took place that showed him up in a poor light but brought out the best in Brandt. In many people's view it provided a tremendous boost to Brandt's reputation in Berlin itself, at a most crucial moment in his career. The incident was triggered off by the Hungarian rising against Moscow-controlled communist dictatorship. Like the East German rising of June 1953 it came, spontaneously, from below. A feeble effort was made by Soviet propaganda to show that the rising had been inspired by 'imperialist' machinations, especially in the shape of allegedly subversive broadcasts by Radio Free Europe, the American-backed corporation in Munich. This organization concentrated, with purpose and finesse, on beaming truthful news to the peoples of satellite Eastern Europe, telling them what was happening in their own countries, what the free world had to say about it and what was happening elsewhere in the world.

The Hungarian insurgents, whose leaders were socialists or even Communists, gained complete control in the capital, Budapest, by Sunday, 4 November 1956. The rising had, in fact, succeeded. But it could still be suppressed, and this is what began to happen when Soviet tanks rolled into Budapest that afternoon. The Berliners decided to demonstrate their feelings and on 5 November a hundred thousand of them streamed to the Schoeneberg Town Hall, the seat of the city's government. Ernst Lemmer, the Christian Democrat representative of the Federal Republic in Berlin, spoke of the gravity of the situation, but failed to move an audience that was seething with fury. Neumann did even worse; he was interrupted by whistling and organized choruses. Then a great cry arose, for 'action' and a march to the Brandenburg Gate, on the border of the Soviet sector.[70] Neumann's voice was completely drowned.

Brandt was not even billed to speak at the demonstration but he was attending it. He took Neumann's place, stated in clear and ringing tones his detestation of Red Army brutality but explained that a march on East Berlin would be dangerous and futile. Some set off for home, but thousands more were determined to march. Brandt climbed into an open police car armed with a loudspeaker and diverted the marching thousands from the Brandenburg Gate route to the Steinplatz, far removed from the waiting and heavily armed East German People's Police, and containing the usefully symbolic memorial to victims of dictatorship, Nazi and Communist alike. Here Brandt, now in sole command of the situation, addressed the huge crowd again, at greater length. He asked them to sing the song usually reserved for soldiers fallen in action – 'Ich hatt' einen Kameraden'. The meeting dispersed, but as the crowds turned for home a critical situation was developing on the Street of 17 June close to the Brandenburg Gate. Several thousand Berliners, mostly young people, marched there and tried to force their way through to the sector boundary. Their path was barred by West Berlin police and bitter fighting broke out. Red Army tanks took up their positions just inside the Soviet sector, guns at the ready. They had not hesitated to fire on the East Germans, 'their Germans', in June 1953; nor on the Hungarians only twenty-four hours before; they would have mown down West Berliners who, according to instructions, were the tools of western fascists and capitalists.

Brandt hurried to the spot and spoke yet again, explaining that Berliners must not play into the hands of the enemy. Once again he asked the crowd to sing 'Ich hatt' einen Kameraden'. Once again they obliged, with police and demonstrators joining in. But his task was still not quite over. In front of the Brandenburg Gate the West Berlin police had formed an effective cordon, and Russian and East German armed forces were a good 100 yards away, on the other side of the gate and screened from view. But a large crowd still milled round, hoping to launch some sort of assault. He spoke for the fourth time that evening, led the crowd back into the Tiergarten park and induced them once more to sing, this time the German national anthem. Later he was to remark drily: 'In political situations it is useful to remember that my countrymen are fond of singing.'[71]

He had won the admiration and respect of virtually every Berliner. It had been a family affair, for Rut had hardly left his side. He was later to pay a tribute to her for her simplicity, charm and ability to be herself.[72] Courage, too, was hers, a valuable attribute in a crisis like this one. Neumann was deeply hurt, by his own failure as much as by Brandt's success, and Herbert Wehner may have been right when he said that this incident turned rivalry into a fratricidal vendetta on Neumann's part.[73] It swung Berlin opinion over to Brandt's side and played a role in his being elected governing mayor of Berlin on 3 October 1957.

Suhr died on 30 August and Neumann's first thought was how to stop Brandt from succeeding him. He proposed Adolf Arndt, a worthy and upright lawyer, somewhat professorial and in poor health. In Bonn, Carlo Schmid told Arndt what he believed to be the background to Neumann's invitation; Arndt, appalled, withdrew at once. Instead the party committee in Berlin adopted Brandt as sole candidate, by twenty-four votes to thirteen. A final effort to foil Brandt, putting up a rival candidate, the popular mayor of the borough of Kreuzberg, Willi Kressmann, came to nothing; Kressmann withdrew. Neumann has since maintained that Brandt continued thereafter to pursue their quarrel and that he was responsible for Neumann's loss of his Berlin parliamentary seat in 1959 – he had lost his place on the SPD executive a year earlier.[74] This picture of a vindictive, power-hungry Brandt is unacceptable. One of his associates had this to say of him: 'He has always been a man of principle, and a human being much more than a politician. He has never had a lust for power, only a healthy ambition. If he had a weakness as a politician, it is that he lacks any streak of ruthlessness. In fact, he is rather too ready to see good in people.'[75] This tendency to see good in people sometimes helped, sometimes hindered him on the long, rough road to the crest on which he stood in October 1957. It is a trait that has stayed with him ever since.

6

Lord Mayor of Berlin

The governing mayor of West Berlin in 1957 was not yet forty-four years old, young in looks and manner, filled with a real sense of purpose, tremendous energy and a reasonable amount of ambition. He had emerged from the second rank of social democratic politicians, his party colleagues had finally accepted him as other than an interesting newcomer, and the rank and file began to see in him a future leader – perhaps of the nation as well as the party. One friend, Erich Brost, recalls that it was not long after Brandt took office that he picked him as a future chancellor.[1] He, Brandt and two or three others were sitting together one evening drinking a rough red wine – Brandt had a taste for the full and fruity wines of the Rhône. Brost told Brandt that his path would lead to Bonn; Brandt, preoccupied with the problems of the city and the threat currently being posed to it by the Soviet Union, was silent.

Friends and colleagues have picked out different characteristics in him. Dietrich Spangenberg, a friend since the early 1950s, saw in him the ideal, even epic team-leader – when he took up his post in Berlin he rallied the seriously divided SPD and 'he has been rallying his people together ever since'.[2] Spangenberg believed that Brandt was the only man who could have held the party together over the long period of electoral defeats and mental frustrations that it was to undergo. His deep loyalty to those who stood with him played a key part; sometimes loyalty went so far that he would not drop subordinates who were failing. He was instinctively shy and reserved, and one of his strongest points was his self-control; he was the reverse of the impulsive, dynamic Teutons of the Bismarckian and Nazi eras. Spangenberg noted, too, his refusal to pursue a *fronde* that he regarded as non-adult and a waste of time. His ability to concentrate deeply and un-interruptedly, for hours on end, was matched by a readiness to relax, think aloud with friends, exchange thoughts, above all listen and learn. He did not waste a moment of the day – even on holiday or out for a stroll on a working day his mind never idled. He thought pragmatically, not dogmatically.

Shepard Stone, his closest American friend, found his memory 'uncanny'.[3] He never forgot a single worthwhile thing that a friend said to him. All was stored away in a mind that was like a capacious and perfectly organized archive. He was a man of intriguingly varying moods.[4] He enjoyed companionship and long hours of discussion; yet he had an inner loneliness, an absolute need for being periodically left to himself.[5] Fluent in private conversation as well as public debate, he would sometimes lapse into inarticulate silence or monosyllabic response. He always found time for his friends; they meant a very great deal to him. Stone remembers how Brandt left a cabinet meeting to greet him, and Stone – in temporary awe of someone who had by then become head of government – addressed him by the polite form of 'you' in German, *Sie*, instead of the familiar *du*. Brandt smilingly countered with: 'Stop that nonsense – we're on *du* terms!'

Another American friend, General Barksdale Hamlett, United States Commandant in Berlin in 1957, was struck by his unflappable temperament: 'He is completely broad-gauge and I've never seen him when he wasn't perfectly at ease and able to meet the situation, no matter how much others were snipping at his coat-tails.'[6] The general admired him as 'honest and fair in all his dealings' but he agreed that he 'is a very complicated person'.

According to one of Brandt's colleagues in Berlin, Senator Otto Theuner: 'Willy was much more than just a good comrade; he would never leave a friend in the lurch; he would sooner drop or modify a political project than damage him.'[7] Theuner found him deeply sensitive about small things, but with nerves of steel in a crisis; and with a rare gift among German politicians, the ability to decentralize and let others get on with their jobs. For the Berliners, according to Theuner, 'he was "our Willy" and he always will be'. Another Berliner, Senator Rolf Schwedler, thought the cosmopolitan character of the Berliners a great help to him – they did not mind him having been an emigrant and 'semi-Norwegian'.[8] Brandt's quality that they treasured most was his ability to rise to the big occasion, as during the Hungarian uprising.

His work for Berlin was compared with that of Ernst Reuter in the Swiss paper *Die Tat* when he became governing mayor.[9] The writer believed that Brandt came out well in the comparison. His basic virtues were clarity and objectivity as a speaker, common sense and readiness to compromise as a political leader. He was non-doctrinaire and no hidebound 'man of the party'. The federal president, Professor Theodor Heuss, was quoted as having spoken of his 'intrepid energy'. The paper summed up that he was admirably qualified for his task – 'Berlin must be ruled, not just administered.'

As governing mayor of Berlin Brandt became, under the existing system, president of the Bundesrat, or federal upper house. As such he deputized for the federal president and came into increasing contact with political personalities. Two require special mention: Egon Bahr, who was to become his personal assistant in the city government and his closest political adviser, and Dr Konrad Adenauer, federal chancellor from 1949 to 1963.

Brandt has since turned to Bahr for ideas as a special confidant. Bahr was born in 1922 in Thuringia, the son of a schoolmaster, fought in the war and became a journalist after it ended. The Thüringians are regarded by fellow Germans as clever in a somewhat sly and introverted way and Bahr has some of the attributes of an *éminence grise*. A man who refused to bother about his own image, he had a flair for political planning and strategy. Some people regarded him as Machiavellian; others as a kind of political Sherlock Holmes, a master of deduction. He joined the SPD in 1957 and remained an independent journalist until 1960, when he took the post of head of Berlin's Press and Information Office. Brandt saw even earlier in him a man of truly independent character, with political genius and flexibility of political philosophy. Bahr would later play a vitally important part in the formulation of the SPD's and Brandt's own policy towards Eastern Europe.

Adenauer's role in Brandt's life was very different, that of a formidable political adversary who, in 1957, appeared to be in an unshakable position of power. Brandt first met him, fleetingly, in the Foreign Affairs Committee of the Bundestag in 1950; the chancellor warily made inquiries as to what kind of person Brandt was.[10] During the protracted debates on the Bonn and Paris treaties there was further contact; Adenauer was doubtless pleased that Brandt and some of the Berlin SPD were prepared to give a close and careful look at the treaties, though this was more as an opportunity for splitting the SPD than grounds for gratitude. A year or two later, when Adenauer was negotiating with the Soviet leaders, he had a slip of paper passed to Brandt in the Foreign Affairs Committee of the Bundestag, and on it: 'Bulganin is very interested in Berlin. He has asked me if Kempinski's still stands; he always ate well there in the past.' Brandt pushed across his written answer – 'And did you know if Kempinski's still stands?'[11] Brandt has since remarked that he has kept Adenauer's note, and his answer; if he sells them to Kempinski's (which indeed still stands, in Berlin's Kurfürstendamm), they may be framed and earn him a pretty penny.[12]

In May 1957 Adenauer had visited Berlin while Suhr was still governing mayor. Driving back to Tempelhof airport at the end of this visit Brandt had got in next to the chauffeur. Adenauer did not recognize the back of his head, and told Suhr he must stick it out in Berlin – he was badly needed there. Suhr, already a very sick man, replied that there was, fortunately, Willy Brandt available to take his place. Adenauer jumped at the chance of sowing a little discord among the Berlin SPD – 'I'll tell you what Herr Brandt wants; he wants *you* out of the way.' Then he suddenly spotted Brandt, only a foot or two away, in the front seat. 'Well, well,' he said, totally unabashed, 'what are you really interested in, Herr Brandt? We've just been having a chat about gardening and plant-culture.' Brandt, remembering that a 'friendly' biography of Adenauer, by Paul Weymar, had just been published, came back with: 'I'm interested in political biographies, Herr Bundeskanzler.' And Adenauer closed the incident rhetorically with, 'Now, whatever does *that* mean?'[13]

Later in the same year, now mayor of Berlin, Brandt visited Adenauer at his Rhöndorf home, a matter of near-royal command. The chancellor's usual searching stare at guests who had to climb the fifty-seven steps to the front door was wasted on Brandt, very fit after a holiday spent fishing and climbing mountains. Adenauer contented himself with a sly dig – 'You come from the East; what do you think of Tito?' As a Lübecker, Brandt was as much a westerner as Adenauer. A year later Adenauer was to slight him deliberately, when during a two-day visit to Berlin he put aside just one hour for talks with the City Senate and cancelled a private meeting with the mayor. The CDU press service issued a lame explanation of this obvious discourtesy, but Brandt would not be provoked and stated that he would not make a vendetta out of the incident.[14] Thereafter he studiously avoided a confrontation with Adenauer, shrewdly believing that the chancellor wanted a pretext for humbling a younger and less experienced opponent. In his view, Adenauer 'was a fox at all times. Latterly he lost his ability to grasp new ideas, but he did two good things for the German people. He and his curious Christian Democratic Union prevented a split between ex-Nazis and non-Nazis, and the formation of a dangerous right-wing party. And he gained time, while the situation stabilized itself – every year counted.'[15] This was a fair tribute to a redoubtable and relentless political foe.

As governing mayor Brandt's work centred on Berlin. But he was by now very much of a force in the Social Democratic Party, and this may be the best point to consider his role in it.

The SPD entered the 1957 federal elections with better prospects of success than at any time since 1949. Factors in the party's favour were the disappearance of the Communist Party (KPD), outlawed by the federal constitutional court in 1956, the unpopularity of conscription and the feeling that Adenauer, nearly eighty, must soon bow out. The SPD were now the sole legal representatives of the working class, opposed conscription with their *Ohne mich* ('Without me') slogan and were appealing for another effort to secure German reunification. This looked like a popular programme. But just below the surface were doubts. The party management was old, stale; and the 'Brandt group' of younger men had still not established itself in the central organization of the party.[16] This group wanted modernization and new blood in the party leadership, practical policies in place of dogmas, the abandonment of full-scale socialization of industry and readiness to look for coalition partners, even as a junior to the CDU in a new government. They asked for complete unity with the western alliance, full acceptance of a

German contribution to Nato and careful revision of all foreign-policy aims.[17]

Ollenhauer regarded many of these points as major heresies. Socialization of industry remained an article of faith for the unions and the SPD executive. He tried to compromise by asking for limited socialization, accompanied by a stiff anti-cartel law and an embryonic plan for giving shares in large industries to workers. This satisfied nobody. A guarded disapproval of conscription was maintained and SPD election posters depicted a significantly empty helmet, hanging on an upright rifle with its muzzle buried in the ground, and the caption: 'There is still time! Vote SPD!' The SPD wanted the banning of nuclear weapons on German soil and some indefinite form of neutralization as a *quid pro quo* for progress towards German reunification. Adenauer explained that the worst foreign policy is one based on a momentary mood and situation,[18] and went into battle preaching 'no experiments', no weakening of the western alliance, no neutralization and a sober reappraisal of the economic achievements of his party and government. He had the backing of industry, contributing 40 million marks, perhaps ten times the money available to the SPD.[19]

The outcome was a sweeping CDU victory. The SPD vote, indeed, went up from 29 to 32 per cent, its seats in the Bundestag from 151 to 169. Both the KPD and Gustav Heinemann's neutralist All-German People's Party (GVP) were defunct, and the increase in the SPD vote should have been greater. The CDU, which might have expected a cyclical swing against it, increased its vote from 44 to 50 per cent and its seats in the Bundestag from 244 to 270. Adenauer had consolidated his majority, based on a booming economy and a justified distrust of Soviet intentions in Europe. He was almost in a state of euphoria when, a few days later, the Soviet Union launched its first sputnik – 'I regarded this sputnik as a gift from Heaven, for otherwise the free world would have sunk even further into its twilight sleep.'[20]

For the SPD the failure in 1957 was crucial and should have been salutary. Since 1949 there had been a steady trend towards a two-party system, with the CDU moving ahead faster than the SPD. New thought and new blood were needed, but Ollenhauer was re-elected chairman of the SPD parliamentary party. It was difficult to demote a man so patently honest, hard-working and dedicated. At least he was given three new deputy chairmen – Carlo Schmid, Fritz Erler and Herbert Wehner. Schmid was well versed in the field of foreign policy. Erler was articulate and energetic, an admirable parliamentarian with a close personal understanding with Brandt. Wehner was a real driving force, tireless in political management and campaigning, with an alert and flexible mind. Three deputy chairmen of this calibre should have ensured a radical rethink of policies, especially as Brandt – at long last – beat Franz Neumann in the election to the chairmanship of the SPD in Berlin early in 1958. The forces of progress seemed to be in the ascendant.

Ollenhauer, at least, could not be accused of inaction. In the next year and a half the SPD indulged in a hectic bout of activity. Early in 1958 they launched their 'Fight against Atomic Death', to prevent nuclear proliferation and the stationing of nuclear weapons on German soil. Much play was made with the opposition to nuclear weapons of Dr Albert Schweitzer; huge SPD posters bore his picture and the famous doctor of Lambaréne sent Brandt – perhaps as a mark of appreciation – an elephant tusk. Brandt himself interpreted this gesture as a hint that he should be ready to show his teeth in defence of his city.[21] The SPD also gave a cautious welcome to the Rapacki Plan, the work of the Polish foreign minister, Adam Rapacki envisaging a nuclear-free zone in Central Europe. Nothing, as it happened, was to come of his plan; but American pressure for giving the Bundeswehr nuclear weapons was relaxed, then dropped completely.

In May 1958 the SPD party conference took place in Stuttgart and Brandt followed up his success in becoming *Land* chairman in Berlin by obtaining a place on the party executive. Speeches at the conference indicated a rethink of domestic policies. There was talk of the 'second industrial revolution' and a more modern approach to economic problems. Speaking on economic policy, Dr Heinrich Deist watered down the socialization of heavy industry; he asked for 'public corporation enterprises' in the coal and power industries, some state-run undertakings as a contribution to a mixed economy, help for middle-range and small industries and stiff anti-cartel legislation.

The seeds of reformist thought had been sown long before the

Stuttgart conference. Brandt paid tribute to the contribution of Schumacher, whose preface for the Dortmund action programme of 1952 called for re-examination of basic concepts.[22] Then at the Munich conference in 1956 a new emphasis was placed on industrial modernization and technology; the dead Schumacher had at last ceased to be an 'ideology substitute'.[23] After Stuttgart, Carlo Schmid argued that the SPD needed the option of an 'opening to the Right' – a section of the middle class must be won over. Brandt undoubtedly agreed with him, though he felt that there must be no sacrifice of basic principles.

The year 1959 was to be a key one in the formulation of SPD domestic policies. The crucial event was the Bad Godesberg party conference in November. Final preparations for the conference took place in July, when Ollenhauer decided that he would not stand as SPD candidate for the chancellorship in the 1961 federal elections. A successor was not named, but it was clear that Brandt might be in the running.[24] A commission was formed to decide on the candidature for the chancellorship and on party tactics. Its members were Ollenhauer, Brandt, Schmid, Erler, Deist, Zinn, the prime minister of *Land* Hesse, and Brauer, the prime minister of *Land* Hamburg. They were pragmatic, middle-of-the-road political thinkers, who believed in flexibility of mind and policy, in adaptation, renewal and progress. The problem that confronted these men was, as one historian bitterly put it, not to find a new ideological basis but to bring the SPD into line with the political philosophy of postwar Germany, and to rid themselves of their Marxist image.[25]

Brandt made his position clear in a speech to the Berlin SPD.[26] It was necessary, he said, to draw the appropriate lessons from electoral defeat. Basic principles must be maintained, but basic aims reviewed. Socialist theory must be synthesized with practical needs; there had to be clear thinking and speaking, without political jargon. The SPD must develop an inner-party democracy, in which members were emancipated from the control of functionaries. Here was the kind of talk the SPD needed; they had to abandon their apocalyptic attitude, foretelling the doom that Adenauer's rule would bring, their shadow-boxing with a neo-fascist outlaw who did not really exist and their posture of defenders of the 'poor', who were beginning to invest in Volkswagen cars, refrigerators, washing-machines and other 'bourgeois comforts'.

One authority[27] believes that Brandt came to terms, in a closely personal sense, with Herbert Wehner before the Bad Godesberg conference opened; that he needed support within the party apparatus; and that Wehner's special contribution was to reconcile old doctrine with the new image and new tactics of the SPD. This may well be true; Brandt and Wehner were to work together with a truly remarkable community of purpose after 1959. Brandt, however, had support in the SPD commission set up in July 1959, apart from Wehner's. Brauer and Zinn were elder statesmen who had become increasingly critical of sterile dogmas. Deist had shown his hand in Stuttgart and Carlo Schmid was on the side of compromise and progress. Erler was Brandt's obvious rival, but his health was just beginning to fail.

The party conference produced the 'Godesberg programme' of November 1959. Much of the thought that went into it had been evolved months, even years earlier; and the programme did not, after all, capture the hearts and minds of the German people and usher the SPD into power. But a new policy was approved at Bad Godesberg and, from then on, the fortunes of the SPD steadily, if unspectacularly, improved. The thoughts behind the programme were indicated by a member of the executive, Waldemar von Knoeringen, on 12 November.[28] The SPD would work out a scheme for curtailed public ownership, with 'public boards in the coal-mining, electrical power and nuclear power industries', but it was 'pointless to talk about public ownership of steel and chemicals, when no practicable plans exist for these industries'. Massive concessions were made to free enterprise and the SPD would sponsor 'free choice of consumer goods and services, free choice of a place to work, free initiative for employers ... free competition'. National wealth should be spread through the creation of government-controlled investment trusts and banks; industrial undertakings in government hands should not be denationalized. Social insurance should be buttressed by government grants, especially for the benefit of the economically weakest. There should be increased grants for education, sport, technical training and medical facilities for workers. The summing up of the *Manchester Guardian* correspondent to whom von Knoeringen spoke was: 'One thing is abundantly

clear. The Social Democrats are moving out of the realm of ideological thinking. Only practical programmes, they know, will win
votes today. And to help make a better German community they
must win political power.'

This was true; and Ollenhauer said it was utterly unrealistic to
insist on implementation of the political programmes of Karl
Marx and Friedrich Engels – the SPD would become a 'sect with
no political influence'. Wehner rammed the lesson home with an
appeal for an all-out effort to secure political power. The net
result of the conference was the emergence of the SPD as the
Fabian party of reform, with its creed a compound of Christian
ethics, a humanitarian way of life and shreds of classical
philosophy.[29] Its new pragmatism was encapsulated in the much-
quoted phrase of Schumacher – 'The problem is not just to have
been right in the past.' The liberal economic party programme
drawn up by Deist was approved by 324 votes to 16; a left-wing
measure calling for large-scale socialization collected only 89
votes. As a tailpiece to the conference, the party accepted the
principle of German participation in western defence, so under-
writing conscription. Opposition to the stationing of nuclear
weapons on German soil was now made dependent on force reductions on both sides in Germany and the creation of a
European zone of limited and controlled armaments.

At Godesberg the SPD rejected doctrinaire left-wing views.
They ceased to be exclusively the party of the workers: 'The
Social Democratic Party is a community of men holding different
beliefs and ideas. Their agreement is based on the moral
principles and political aims they have in common.'[30] They
ceased to be anti-clerical: 'A party is no longer regarded as a
church or counter-church. It is not a school of philosophers. It
does not feel obliged to explain the history of mankind.' They
ceased to be anti-capitalist, and they ceased finally to frighten
anybody any more. The old bogy of 'socialist revolution' was laid,
the days of the red flag and the raised fist of the embattled worker
were over. Marxist arrogance and omniscience were dropped.
They no longer claimed to create a new society, but to evolve an
optimum society by thought, plan, adjustment and compromise.

The programme was approved at what might look a surprising
moment in history. Bitter attacks were being made against the
ex-Nazi minister for refugees, Theodor Oberländer, and other

ex-Nazis in high office. Violent 'anti-leftist' propaganda was being whipped up by the publicist William S. Schlamm. Closer relations with the dictatorships of Spain and Portugal were under discussion. Here was plenty of grist for the radical mill. In addition, the left wing counter-attacked at Godesberg: voices were raised against any compromise with the socialist conscience.

Brandt played a notable part at Godesberg; one must go back in history to discover why he was in a position to do so. The principal reason was his success as governing mayor of Berlin. His predecessor, Suhr, had been forced by poor health to stay at home, and had thus been unable to 'sell' Berlin abroad. Brandt had reversed this situation. In 1958, his first year in office, he visited half a dozen countries, scoring a particular success in Britain. His directness of manner appealed to people there. His gift for saying the right thing, in an engagingly frank way, was in evidence, especially in Coventry, so badly bombed during the war. His address at the Royal Institute of International Affairs (Chatham House) was reprinted in *International Affairs* and gave this idea of his thinking on the Berlin and German questions. The free existence of West Berlin, he believed, depended on full co-operation with the western Allies; material reconstruction was making excellent progress and a free Berlin should be a 'uniting bond between the inhabitants of both sections of our disrupted land'.[31] Berlin had to remain 'a living bridge' between East and West, and 'the one to two million fellow citizens in the Eastern Sector belong to us; we refuse to be parted from them'.[32] There had to be 'a normalization in relations' and 'an open-door policy in human and cultural contacts'; and Berlin should promote this.[33] There was no isolated solution of the German question; it was clear that 'Germany will remain a danger-point as long as it is split along a line from Lübeck, through Helmstedt to Hof. Our struggle for self-determination is not our affair alone.'[34] Secret diplomacy could help, but the Soviet theory of two German states was a reality that had to be faced. The East German rising of 1953 and the Hungarian revolution of 1956 had shown that no military help could come from the West: 'Only one course now remains: an unflinching, stubborn struggle for a peaceful solution by political action.'[35] That involved a flexibility that had nothing to do with capitulation. What Brandt had to say in 1958 bore a remarkable similarity to what was to become, more than a decade later, his concept of a real *Ostpolitik*, or eastern policy.

In 1959 Brandt had spent even more time abroad than in the previous year. Berlin and its people needed the interest, understanding and support of the outside world. For never in history has the outpost of one kind of civilization had to battle so long to maintain its way of life; in comparison, the Great Siege of Malta passed in the twinkling of an eye.

In London he repeated his success of the previous year. A former Berliner, Max Grix, complimented him in a prescient letter on gaining the sympathy of Britons and urged him to come back soon.[36] In Stockholm the impact of his visit may have been reduced by Swedish preoccupation with neutrality – the mayor of East Berlin, Friedrich Ebert, had to be invited too. The Swedes had been impressed by an East German propaganda campaign delineating the Baltic as a 'sea of peace'.

In two visits to Paris in 1958 and 1959 he learnt much about French policy towards Germany. The Franco-German relationship was going through a crucial phase; federal chancellor Adenauer was seeking a settlement between the two countries; Brandt had no intention of intervening. He observed a studied discretion in his meeting with General de Gaulle in December 1958. The general's evocative diction was confusing: he referred continually to 'Prussia', but was really talking about the East German republic.[37]

His journeys produced an interview with Professor Heuss. The young governing mayor had been far afield and the old president had been ruminating. To his amazement, Brandt found himself receiving the Grand Cross of Merit of the Federal Republic, with star and sash, draped and pinned ceremoniously on him. Heuss had a gift for finding *le mot juste* – 'Herr Brandt,' he said, 'we can't very well send you off, naked, on your travels.'[38]

In Berlin he was quickly into his stride. Franz Neumann, indeed, made his final attempt to direct the policies of the Berlin SPD. He appealed for an ideological socialist line, total support for the SPD foreign policy formulated in Bonn and close control of the Berlin branch by party headquarters. Brandt disagreed, fundamentally, with these three aims. His opposition to dependence on ideology has already been analysed. He believed that the Berlin SPD must maintain a special view of foreign policy requirements, based on the special geographical position, tradition and outlook of the former capital city. This, alone, presupposed some independence from Bonn. Neumann's star was on the wane. Brandt had loyal and efficient deputies, Kurt Mattick and Jupp Braun, and a reasonably united party behind him. They were also a more youthful party than in West Germany; of the three hundred SPD conference delegates in Berlin in 1950 only forty-four remained eight years later. Finally, they were a politically active and prescient party, believing in new ideas and thorough discussion.

As a result the SPD had gone confidently into the Berlin elections of December 1958. As in Hamburg earlier in the year, they had campaigned without direction from Bonn headquarters and with a clear understanding of local needs. The result had been a most satisfying victory. The CDU's vote, indeed, had gone up from 30 to 37 per cent, but the SPD vote had gone up even more, from 44 to well over 52 per cent. The FDP's vote had dropped from 13 to 4 per cent, while the communist-steered Socialist Unity Party (the West Berlin branch of the East German ruling SED) had collected under 2 per cent – their worst showing yet. Brandt's election speeches had stressed the need for solidarity in the face of danger – that of a new Soviet squeeze on the city. The possibility of this had been plainly telegraphed by the Soviet leader, Nikita Khrushchev. One must briefly recapitulate the salient events leading up to this new threat to Berlin – the most serious since the blockade.

There had been a relatively placid diplomatic period after the Geneva foreign ministers' conference in the autumn of 1955. At that conference the western powers, the United States, Britain and France, had proposed agreements on European security and German reunification. The Soviet Union had dismissed the latter but aired its own ideas on a European security treaty, which would presuppose the continued division of Germany. A month earlier, in September, the Soviet Union had recognized East German sovereignty. The access routes of the western powers between Berlin and the Federal Republic, however, remained a Soviet prerogative 'pending the conclusion of an appropriate agreement'.[39] Notes continued to pass between the western powers and the Soviet Union, without anything being achieved.

Then, in April 1957, Bulganin, chairman of the Council of Ministers of the Soviet Union, had opened a correspondence with Harold Macmillan, then Britain's prime minister, lasting for over a year and continued by Khrushchev. The Soviet intention was that the *status quo* in Germany should be recognized within a European security agreement. In the summer of 1958 Khrushchev had begun toying with the idea of a summit conference. From Bonn Adenauer had urged the linking of any progress over European security with parallel progress on the question of German reunification. His allies had agreed, though Adenauer doubted Macmillan's sincerity. East–West diplomatic deadlock continued; but there was nothing unusual about that.

Then, on 10 November 1958, Khrushchev had attacked the western powers in a speech in Moscow in which he said that the Soviet Union was considering revising its attitude towards four-power control of Berlin and handing over its responsibilities to the East Germans. This would mean that the western powers would have in future to negotiate with East Berlin over all questions relating to Berlin. In notes of 27 November Khrushchev had expanded on this theme; apart from the transfer of Soviet authority, West Berlin should become a demilitarized free city within six months. During that time arrangements for the communications of the western powers would be unchanged. But failing agreement on Berlin's status, all Soviet powers would be handed over to the East Germans forthwith. In addition, the two German states should join in a confederation.

It was the time limit that came as a shock to the western powers. They had been lulled into a feeling of false security and the ultimatum was a horrid surprise. Yet the heavy Soviet stress on East German sovereignty was not new, while the Central Committee of the SED had proposed a 'confederation' of the two German states as early as January 1957. In March 1958 the deputy mayor of East Berlin had called for the 'normalization' of the situation in Berlin, and in July Walter Ulbricht had repeated this at the SED's fifth party congress, with claptrap about West Berlin being a spy centre and a hotbed of revanchists, militarists and imperialists. Khrushchev had included these accusations in his notes of 27 November.

The basic reason for the Soviet ultimatum was the weakness of its East German satellite. Up to 1958 roughly 2.3 million East

Germans had fled to the West, 15 per cent of the population. In 1956 and 1957 three quarters of those who left were aged fifteen to sixty-five, in fact working age. Only one in twenty was over sixty-five and therefore a ready-made pensioner.[40] Most East Germans left less because of persecution than because of the better life in the West. At the end of 1957 meat, fats and sugar were still rationed in East Germany, there was a chronic shortage of consumer goods and 'real wages' were low – an East German worker took 195 hours to earn a bicycle, against 88 for a West German, 65 hours to earn a pair of shoes, against 18. Steel and brown coal output doubled in five years – yet there were chronic shortages of fuel, electrical power and housing. The fact was that the East German economy was geared to the needs of the Soviet Union, within the framework of the so-called East European Common Market. The Soviet Union decreed that the East Germans should produce more coal, steel, chemicals and machinery but go without the comforts of life.

The Soviet Union had no intention of surrendering her stake in Germany. Since 1955 Soviet hopes of grabbing the whole of Germany had faded; a piece of cake was better than none at all and East Germany was of considerable value, a reservoir of technological skills, a useful source of industrial goods and uranium, potentially the strongest economic unit in the Soviet bloc, after the Soviet Union itself. It was a bastion of Soviet military power, with frontiers within sixty miles of the Rhine. Its independent existence suited Poland and Czecho-Slovakia, fearful of a powerful, unified Germany. And the East German state was stabilizing itself, in spite of repression and maladministration; talk of famine and revolution was unreal. 'The German Democratic Republic,' according to an SPD publication, 'has no legitimate future; it was quite literally "made in Moscow". It is an unnatural, fictitious state.'[41] It was indeed, but the Russians intended to preserve it.

The western powers had reacted to the Khrushchev ultimatum with a characteristic lack of urgency. They took more than a month to answer and produced no sort of diplomatic counter-offensive. This was the moment to point out that the whole of Berlin – not just its western sectors – came under four-power jurisdiction, that the East Germans had no right to proclaim the Soviet sector as their capital or march troops through it. The western powers could have suggested that a confederation should be based on the proportional representation of fifty million West Germans and only seventeen million East Germans.

At least the western powers remained cool. The SPD in West Germany regarded this as mere passiveness and hastily drafted its Germany Plan (*Deutschland-Plan*), a last effort to bring about German reunification. The plan proposed a 'zone of disengagement' – both parts of Germany, Poland, Czecho-Slovakia and Hungary; a reduction of foreign forces on German soil; a European Security Pact for states in the zone of disengagement; withdrawal of these states from military alliances; the maintenance of the existing status of West Berlin until a German peace treaty was signed. In addition there should be an all-German conference; joint German economic and other institutions; an all-German parliament; an electoral law, approved by referendum. The *Deutschland-Plan* looked well, on paper. But the western powers did not like it and neither they nor the West German government were informed or consulted. It was bound to fail and it was the last time that Ollenhauer gave a lead in foreign affairs.[42] By February 1959 the SPD were calling it only a 'working paper'. Yet the plan showed inventiveness that the western powers might have emulated, while its failure underlined the need for West Germans and the western powers to keep in step.

Brandt took a reserved view of the plan. He had no objection to offering the Russians a basis for negotiation. He had himself in January 1959 called on the Soviet commandant in Berlin, General Chamov, and discussed minor improvements for movement between the two parts of Berlin over glasses of vodka and Crimean 'champagne'. He said there had been 'tough talking'[43] and was not perturbed by caustic comments that the East German prime minister, Otto Grotewohl, had been caught in the Soviet net by drinking toasts with the Russians. Brandt's answer was: 'I don't need to get drawn into a discussion about whether one vodka more or less was handed out in Karlshorst.'[44] But the *Deutschland-Plan*, as he saw it, stood no chance when it ran so obviously counter to Soviet aims. He let the plan pass without comment and so lapse.

Khrushchev had given another turn of the screw with his note of 10 January 1959, when he called for a peace treaty between the two German states, and produced a draft agreement. Once again he had demanded the 'liquidation' of the occupation regime in West Berlin, and offered to examine proposals on converting West Berlin into a 'free city'. On 17 February he announced that if the western powers refused to sign a peace treaty with both German states the Soviet Union would sign one with the DDR – which Brandt called 'Khrushchev marrying himself'.[45] But from 21 February to 3 March Mr Macmillan was in Moscow and Khrushchev withdrew the six-month time limit for a settlement. On 19 March he publicly acknowledged the legal rights of the western powers and agreed to a foreign ministers' conference in Geneva on 11 May. The height of the crisis had passed. Mr Macmillan was, perhaps, given too little credit for his advocacy in Moscow.

The foreign ministers met in Geneva, where the Russians blocked a western four-stage peace plan – free elections and the unification of Berlin, the formation of an all-German committee to draft an electoral law, the formation of an all-German assembly and government and finally a peace settlement for the whole of Germany. Doggedly the Russians reverted to their proposal for a demilitarized 'free' West Berlin. The Geneva conference broke up temporarily, met again in mid-July but reached no conclusions. The Russians were stonewalling, for they had a new tactic, to use the East German government as front runner, producing a host of proposals ostensibly its own and designed to emphasize its 'sovereignty'. In a few months the East Germans made proposals for phased disarmament, total nuclear disarmament, a halt to overall rearmament, a non-aggression pact for the Baltic, a two-state confederation in Germany, and – the most obscure of all – the 'elimination of the danger of war on German territory'. In June 1960 the East German government sent out notes, protesting against alleged recruiting for the West German armed forces, the Bundeswehr, in West Berlin – at a time when the East Germans were staging military parades in the middle of Berlin in defiance of four-power agreements, and no soldier of the Bundeswehr had ever been seen in uniform in the western sectors! At the same time the East Germans raised tension by a threatening statement on the restriction of western aircraft to ridiculously low-flying heights and by displaying East German flags on railway stations in West Berlin – the *Stadtbahn* or metropolitan railway lines had remained under East German management. Behind all manoeuvres lay the Soviet intention of forcing recognition of the East German republic and sealing the division of Germany. But in the course of them the communist side scored only one minor point: at Geneva the East German as well as the West German state was allowed to contribute a delegation. The two delegations did not, admittedly, take an active part in the conference. They sat at neighbouring tables, and separately. Still, this was the nearest that the East Germans were to get to participation in a great-power conference up to the time of writing, 1973.

During this period of pressure on Berlin Brandt was firm and level-headed. As governing mayor he had two sets of problems: he had the city to look after; and he had to represent Berlin's views and interests in the field of international diplomacy. Fortunately domestic problems were being mastered. By the end of 1960 a hundred thousand new homes had been built in three years and West Berlin's income was rising by 10 per cent annually. The federal government was pumping 1,000 million marks a year into the economy. Unemployment was down to thirty thousand, trade flourished and imports and exports rose steeply. The cost of living was steady and in 1958 there were a million visitors. It was a place in which one ate cheaply, had an unrivalled choice of theatres and other places of entertainment and parked a car with case. The East German SED had to issue orders to members not to shop in West Berlin or attend the 'filmstar-gazing functions of the West Berlin Film Festival'.[46] Communist pinpricks caused little concern; thus tolls on barges using canals between Berlin and the West were met by the federal government. There were reserves of food and fuel sufficient for a six-month blockade, and this fact was well publicized.

Yet just below the surface lurked an element of fear and claustrophobia, and all the cocky confidence of the Berliners was needed to combat the feeling of isolation and apocalyptic destiny. According to one account in 1958:

The Berliners find it comparatively easy not to forget. At the end of the brilliantly lit Kurfürstendamm, surely the most garishly gay street in Europe, stands the shelled, sightless wreck of the Kaiser Wilhelm Gedaechtnis church, a grim, per-

manent monument to those bitter years. You need only take a
few steps away from a main thoroughfare to find the ruins
again. . . . In Berlin the night air still sometimes wafts the
curious, musty smell of the ruins – a fugitive reminder of the
days of destruction and defeat thirteen years ago.[47]

In his Christmas message Brandt laid a heavy emphasis on 'fortitude, self-reliance and a community of feeling with the West'.
Berliners needed to be reassured. Brandt's worry was that 'Berlin
would break up of itself'.[48] Pressure from Russians and East
Germans could sap confidence and lead, in turn, to a continuing
exodus from the city, which would have 'gradually sunk lower'.
The life of the city was its people; no amount of stockpiling of
essential supplies was a substitute, nor any number of Allied
guarantees. He was aware of defeatist talk in Germany and
abroad. A typical example: in 1950 Joseph Kennedy, father of
the future President of the United States, asked, 'What have we
gained by staying in Berlin? Everyone knows that we can be
pushed out the moment the Russians choose to push us out. Isn't
it better to get out now?'[49]

In 1960 there was one disturbing, if minor incident. On 16
September the *Manchester Guardian* published a plan for a strik-
ingly unrealistic 'solution' of the Berlin question: the people of
West Berlin, nearly two and a half million of them, should be
moved *en masse* to some convenient place just inside the borders
of the Federal Republic and a new capital city built there. The
plan was the work of the paper's defence correspondent, Leonard
Beaton. I was the same paper's German correspondent at the
time and decided, as a precaution, that the chancellor, Adenauer,
and the mayor of Berlin, Brandt, must be informed in advance.
The plan would attract comment and cause concern. Dr
Adenauer was informed through one of his advisers, and the
governing mayor in person a fortnight before the plan was
published. Brandt was shocked into silence when the plan was
explained to him.[50] I remarked that it must be 'something of a
surprise'. Brandt replied: 'Something of a surprise is certainly
not an over-statement.' He saw in the plan a negation of his hard
and courageous work. He expressed complete confidence in the
power of the western Allies to stay in Berlin, and in the city and
its people as a potential source of strength to the West. As long

as a free West Berlin existed there was hope of progress to freedom in the whole of communist Europe. This was far more important, in his view, than diplomatic pressures that arose out of Berlin's geographically and militarily exposed position. The West German and Berlin press, and other leading German politicians, voiced anger and disgust in less measured terms; there was some suspicion that the Beaton plan had been instigated by appeasers in the British Foreign Office.*

Brandt saw the Berlin question first and foremost in human terms. One phrase of his ran: 'Here one is not faced with problems of high policy; one deals with living people whom one can help.'[51] Yet human aspects and 'high policy' were inevitably interlinked. Sometimes, as he pointed out, the human factor has been called in to redress political shortcomings: 'When the Soviets tried to conquer Austria from within, when they hoped to take Berlin, it was not "capitalism" that defeated their plans, but the broad masses of the population under the leadership of the Social Democrats.'[52] Pressure on Berlin at the end of 1958 and the beginning of 1959 was essentially political; from August 1959 onwards interference with communications, triggered off by the holding of the federal presidential election in Berlin, was physical and personal. Brandt's part in both episodes was commendable. According to the former United States commandant in Berlin, General Barksdale Hamlett:

I remember well during my tenure as American Commandant in Berlin how Willy Brandt stood out during the very trying period after Khrushchev had made his threat to rout the Allies out of Berlin within six months. His reaction to this threat and his superb leadership of the citizens of the city during the six months when the Russians and their East German partners were causing all manner of disruptions of traffic into Berlin will always stand in my memory as the mark of a great man.[53]

The year 1960 was a relatively placid one for Berlin. Khrushchev had made up his mind not to pursue a major diplomatic confrontation with the West. His East German satellite was to have a

---

* A rhetorical question was posed by the newspaper *Bild Zeitung*. It asked what the editor of the *Manchester Guardian* would have to say if it were proposed to move the capital of the United Kingdom from London to Scotland. The writer was not to know that the editor was, in fact, a native of Glasgow.

chance of stabilizing its economy while the Russians and their East German tool, Walter Ulbricht, thought things over. Khrushchev's thoughts were turning to the task of overtaking the West in the economic field: it would be safer to bury western democracy in this way rather than risk a nuclear holocaust. By midsummer the SPD had to decide on their candidate for the federal chancellorship in the 1961 elections. After his failures in 1953 and 1957 the worthy but uninspiring Ollenhauer would not stand. Brandt was clearly in the running; this was his chance.

A year before Carlo Schmid still looked likely to succeed Ollenhauer. He was a gifted speaker, with a considerable grasp of constitutional law and a flair for foreign policy. Cultivated, charming, he lacked application and political killer-instinct and had little following among the rank and file of the party. Wehner had his eye on a managerial role. This able and astute man realized that the SPD's organization had to be put in order; from a high of 875,000 in 1947, SPD membership had sunk to its postwar low of 534,000 in 1959.[54] The Godesberg programme would bring in votes, but the sacrifice of socialist dogmas lost the party members. What the SPD needed was a candidate who could rekindle enthusiasm and restore confidence. Erler was not prepared to run; Zinn had become too parochially tied to Hesse. The SPD were short of flair and panache.

Brandt had played an important part in the framing of the Godesberg programme. One SPD stalwart, Fritz Sänger,[55] recalled how Brandt had helped to pilot through the first draft, had taken him aside afterwards and said, simply and directly, 'I believe that really has helped.' Even more important was his part in revising SPD foreign policy.[56] He induced the party management to accept the foreign policy of its Berlin branch, based on the realities of Germany's situation. These were its division into two states at the will of the Soviet Union, its vulnerability to Soviet pressure, its need of firm and powerful allies in order to maintain its independence and democratic freedoms and its interest in flexible, imaginative policies that alone could bring reunification nearer. He had another foreign policy card to play: on 17 June 1960 he appealed to all party leaders to put aside their differences and form a united front on questions of national importance. The Paris summit conference had collapsed a month earlier; his view was that only a 'big coalition' could frame a new all-German policy. On 27 June the leading columnist of *Die Welt*, Sebastian Haffner, wrote a piece called 'A Crown Prince from the Opposition', suggesting that Brandt was the logical successor to Adenauer as chancellor.

There was a final reason for Brandt's candidature. The SPD needed new blood and was in trouble with younger members. The Young Socialists (*Jungsozialisten*) were recruited from the under thirty-five age group and maintained a degree of independence from the party. The Socialist German Student Federation (SDS) was more loosely linked with the party. These two organizations were becoming increasingly radical, while the bulk of the party were moving away from Marxist habits of thought and speech. To the younger socialists Brandt's appeal lay in the fact that he was only forty-six, had an open and pragmatic mind and was already hinting at the possibility of East and West Germans' talking over their differences. To the rank and file of the SPD these things mattered less than that Brandt had real personality and was the antithesis of the fustian functionaries whom Ollenhauer had gathered round him.

There were anxious debates among the SPD leadership in June and July. Some concern was caused by a speech in Recklinghausen in which Brandt urged increased social and cultural contacts between East and West Germans.[57] Otherwise, he said, the two parts of Germany would lose all understanding of one another and 'would talk in two different languages'. He was thinking in terms of the 'small steps' that could bring the two Germanies closer together, but there was a dread among the SPD of making concessions to the East German regime, betraying the non-communist East German population and laying their party open to the charge of 'collaboration'. Few Germans reflected that increased contacts between East and West Germans were regarded by the Ulbricht regime as dangerous to its existence.

On 24 August 1960 the SPD executive decided that Brandt should be their candidate for the chancellorship. Almost simultaneously the East Berlin authorities announced the closing of the eastern sector to West Germans from 31 August to 4 September. Brandt had just paid a visit to the small, semi-suppressed East Berlin branch of the SPD. The East German restrictions may have been to some extent a reaction to that visit.[58] The East German regime, in any case, did not welcome the union, in one person, of governing mayor and chancellor-elect. Brandt was more dangerous than Adenauer because he knew and cared more about East Germany and her people.

His nomination was confirmed at the party conference in Hanover on 25 November 1960. He had paved the way for this in a speech at Bad Godesberg on 8 October at a Congress for the Younger Generation.[59] He had a little to say about Berlin but in the main the speech was an open appeal to German youth. He claimed that he understood the resentment of youth over its exclusion from policy-making, its rejection of dogmas, slogans and 'school solutions', its demand for realism, determination, imagination and mutual trust. He believed in reconciliation between youth and age; the SPD should therefore banish the practice of other parties, that of 'conducting a dialogue with themselves'. They realized that bureaucracy was ponderous and out of touch. They had much to offer youth, in particular the goal of a model state. This would show the communist world that the West was not 'old and satiated'.

At Hanover he accepted his nomination in a speech of even greater significance, which showed real independence of mind. Some authorities have believed that he was only a figurehead at this stage, a white hope put up to fight the dark powers of clericalist obscurantism and moneyed materialism.[60] The real power behind him, it has been suggested, was the triumvirate of Ollenhauer, still in charge of the party machine, the master-planner Wehner and the ubiquitous von Knoeringen, with Wehner the real power, drawing up election manifestos, planning election campaigns, determining broad strategy and day-to-day tactics. Brandt knew that this view was held in party circles. The key sentence in his Hanover speech, therefore, was: 'It is possibly not popular for me to say here and now that I cannot be the mere executor of the party, but must make every decision after careful consideration and on my own responsibility.'[61] Schumacher, of course, had never needed to say anything of this kind; Ollenhauer had never dared. Brandt was claiming independence, as candidate for the chancellorship and as a future chancellor.

For the rest he dealt briefly with publicity given to his change of name – it had been Willy Brandt for 'only twenty-eight years', but 'I have nothing to conceal'. The main points that he dealt with in the domestic field were the improvement of education, the development of individual skills, the replanning of urban areas and communications. He had more to say about foreign affairs. The military *status quo* had to be maintained in Europe, with flexible policies to overcome the political *status quo*. The Russians had to be watched with the greatest vigilance; Khrushchev had decided on peaceful competition, but the Soviet interpretation of coexistence was a situation in which 'pressure, blackmail and the destruction of all normal diplomatic and political usages' were legitimate weapons. There had to be a coherent policy towards East Germany – 'we must at last overcome our passiveness, and impinge spiritually and politically more strongly on the zone'. He wasted little time on Adenauer's policies, which he called 'this collection of incidentals' involving promises ranging 'from Nato to the mother-in-law'. But he condemned party sectarianism in a memorable passage that contrasted with Adenauer's denunciations of political opponents: 'We are all one family. Because of that our people must at last make peace with itself. I want to contribute to this end to the best of my ability. This, too, belongs to the new style which we want to introduce into German politics.' Here was the authentic voice of statesmanship.

Maybe the SPD wanted to give themselves a face-lift by adopting a vigorous, relatively young man as candidate for the chancellorship. At almost the same time John F. Kennedy was elected president of the United States at the age of only forty-three. The SPD would link the names of the two men in the coming election campaign – cash in, if you like, on Kennedy's charismatic personality and startling creativity of mind. Here, it was thought, was a more appealing tandem than the doddering duo of Adenauer and de Gaulle, leftovers from long ago. But the whole tenor of the Hanover party conference suggested a regained solidarity. The only note of disagreement came when Ollenhauer rejected nuclear weapons not only for the Bundeswehr but within the context of a fully armed western alliance. Brandt, Wehner and Carlo Schmid sat silent during the applause which followed.[62]

The federal election campaign of 1961 belongs to a later chapter. For the moment Brandt returned to Berlin where, in the summer of 1960, the storm clouds had again begun to gather. Adenauer, at this time continually announcing a worsening of the international situation that nobody else noticed, proposed – out of the blue – the holding of a West Berlin plebiscite, prior to the four-power summit conference in Paris. In Brandt's view this was a random idea, resulting from the chancellor's suspicion that the Americans and the Russians were becoming too friendly (Khrushchev had taken part in a cordial meeting with President Eisenhower at Camp David.) Adenauer, according to Brandt, had not thought his ideas out, had not consulted him as governing mayor and failed to understand that the Berlin population should not vote on matters reserved to the occupying powers.[63] Adenauer's proposal did have the effect of alerting the Americans. The secretary of state, Christian Herter, and other government spokesmen delivered tough speeches, stressing the need to reduce tension in Berlin, the dangers of a peace treaty between the Soviet Union and the DDR and the need for an all-German peace settlement.

In May 1960 Khrushchev torpedoed the Paris summit conference after the shooting-down of the American U2 spy-plane and refused subsequently to meet Eisenhower; the latter's intended visit to Moscow was cancelled. Apparently Khrushchev had suffered a diplomatic reverse due to the firmness, or immobility, of the western powers. But in reality the irresolution of the West had been exposed, morale in West Berlin was shaken and Khrushchev turned back to the problem of shoring up the tottering East German regime. In August he authorized an obvious probe by temporarily closing the Soviet sector of Berlin to West German citizens. On 8 September the East German authorities decreed that West German citizens must apply for visitors' permits to East Berlin. On 13 September they announced that they would not recognize federal passports issued to West Berliners as valid documents for journeys to the DDR. On 15 September they stated that the only valid document for West Berliners was the Berlin identity card – manifest interference in the internal affairs of West Berlin. Following western protests the situation calmed down. The British foreign secretary, Lord Home, assured the West German news agency, DPA, on 17 February: 'As far as we are concerned, there is no Berlin problem', a statement as ingenuous and as capable of misinterpretation as Macmillan's famous 'You've never had it so good' to the British people. Brandt, who had urged critical watch-

fulness of Soviet actions,[64] gave a heartening assurance to the
Berliners that he would not leave their city unless elected federal
chancellor.[65] The East–West German trade agreement had been
suspended on 1 January 1961, another sign of the worsening
political climate, but Brandt still advised 'technical contacts'
between the Berlin government and the DDR to reduce tension,
and 'small steps' to improve communication between the two
parts of Germany. Berlin, at any rate, was quiet and interest once
again shifted to the arena of international diplomacy.

Brandt met Kennedy in March 1961. Kennedy gave him a
warm welcome and he was instantly impressed by his knowledge
and matter-of-fact approach.[66] His views on the German
question had been something of a mystery. In 1957, in an article
in *Foreign Affairs,* he had warned against becoming 'lashed too
tightly' to a single man and party, Adenauer and the CDU.[67] He
wanted closer ties with the SPD. But in the early 1950s he had
shown pessimism about maintaining a balance of power in
Europe and advocated the strengthening of the United States'
own defences. He had shown a keen interest in disengagement.
Brandt found him interested in reducing tension in Europe and
aware of the dangers of Berlin's situation. But Brandt did most of
the talking, explaining the burgeoning bipartisan SPD–CDU
foreign policy, the economic progress in Berlin and nuances of
the Berlin question. Like Brandt, Kennedy was an excellent,
attentive and also retentive listener. Brandt said afterwards: 'The
destiny of the western world is in good hands.'

Kennedy had been anxious to hear what Brandt had to say,
since he was to meet Khrushchev in Vienna, on 3 and 4 June. For
Kennedy it was a dispiriting and disquieting experience, although
possibly salutary. Khrushchev was in his most overbearing mood.
His ebullience had sapped the patience of both Adenauer and
Macmillan, and actually made Adenauer's first foreign minister,
von Brentano, feel physically ill. Kennedy was suffering from
severe back trouble when he arrived in Vienna. Khrushchev, by
contrast, was on top of the world. In an aide-mémoire of 4 June
he fired out demands for an immediate peace conference, a time
limit of six months on bringing negotiations to a conclusion and
the creation of a free city of West Berlin – or he would sign a
separate peace treaty with the DDR and put Berlin's communications in East German hands. This aide-mémoire was published

only on 10 June by the Soviet news agency Tass. Five days later Ulbricht said in East Berlin that a free city of West Berlin would have to cease accepting East German refugees and close down radio or other forms of propaganda that perpetuated the spirit of the Cold War.

Kennedy said in a broadcast to the American people that his talks with Khrushchev were 'most sombre'. The Soviet government had reverted to its 1958-9 position and it looked as if intense diplomatic pressure would ensue. On 17 July the governments of the United States, France and Britain sent notes to Moscow rejecting the Soviet pretension to settle the Berlin problem unilaterally and reasserting their rights and responsibilities in Berlin. Kennedy backed up these notes in a 'Report to the Nation' of 25 July 1961. In it he said: 'Our presence in West Berlin, and our access thereto, cannot be ended by any act of the Soviet Government. . . . The immediate threat to free men is in West Berlin. But that isolated outpost is not an isolated problem. The threat is world-wide. . . . I hear it said that West Berlin is untenable. And so was Bastogne. And so, in fact, was Stalingrad. Any dangerous spot is tenable if men – brave men – will make it so.'[68] Kennedy has been criticized for comparing Berlin to Bastogne, when Berlin – defended by the equivalent of one effective division and surrounded by twenty-five Soviet and seven East German divisions – was militarily untenable.[69] The Allied forces in Berlin were never, of course, more than a tripwire. The name of Bastogne, however, was not ill chosen; holding it during the Nazi Ardennes offensive had been a morale-booster rather than a military decision. Kennedy, at all events, backed his words with actions. He announced increases in the armed forces of 217,000 men, additional appropriations of $3,247 million, an increase in the United States civil defence budget and the reactivation of ships and planes due for retirement. His 'Report to the Nation' concluded with a warning to the Russians not to send East German mercenaries into West Berlin – 'Gun battles are caused by outlaws, and not by officers of the peace.'[70]

All in all, Kennedy's actions were forceful and apposite. It has been suggested that he should have made some appropriate, statesmanlike move. But there was nothing of the kind that he could have done. The Russians were obsessed by the weaknesses but at the same time by the potential advantages of their position in Germany. They were prepared to give up nothing. Analysts of Soviet diplomacy have missed one paradox – the death of Stalin did not make negotiations with the Russians easier, save superficially. A single tyrant, in total control, can more readily make concessions than a consensus of tyrants, worried by their individual weaknesses and their need for prestige. Kennedy and his western partners were right to outface the Russians in 1961. But the latter really were worried over developments in their East German satellite. Things had gone from bad to worse. The population was falling at an alarming rate. The excess of live births over deaths was only eighty thousand a year. But a quarter of a million East Germans were leaving each year and only one in ten came back. The quarter of a million who left included an unduly high percentage of people badly needed by the East German state. In seven years up to mid-1961 the DDR lost an estimated five thousand doctors and dentists, eight hundred judges and lawyers, seventeen thousand teachers and twenty thousand engineers and technicians. At least 55 per cent of the East Germans who left were those basic elements of the so-called 'workers' and farmers' state'. This led to a continual shortage of labour, and a consequent inability of the technologically increasingly efficient East Germans to plan for the future. An incidental – of the two hundred thousand East Germans who fled to the West in 1960, 3,933 were members of the ruling and politically élite Socialist Unity Party.[71]

While a permanent labour shortage was being created, enough stabilization had taken place to show that the East German state could just be made viable. The farmers had been successfully collectivized in 1960 after a campaign of threats and browbeating. A campaign had begun to supply what official communist propaganda called 'the 1,001 small things that are missing', ranging from nail-scissors and drawing-pins to good quality clothing and household goods, fresh vegetables, motor-bicycles and the like. Not only was the economy on the upturn but East Germans were becoming reconciled to their form of 'people's democracy'. Most East German refugees admitted that they felt themselves to be Marxists and believed, however dimly, in the nationalization of the basic means of production.[72] A degree of pride in their achievements was becoming apparent; in August 1960 the president of the East German People's Chamber (*Volkskammer*), Dr

Johannes Dieckmann, told me: 'We had to rebuild our life from its very foundations and under the gravest difficulties. We suffered much more heavily than Western Germany under the burden of reparations. We had fewer resources. We received not one cent of Western financial aid. We have rebuilt by our own strength, and by that alone.'[73]

The East German leaders were even talking of producing a new type of human being, who would live by the twin principles of mutual and humanitarian aid and service to the State. This type would, they thought, be superior to the individualistic, ego-centric and fundamentally unsettled westerner.[74] This may sound utopian; but the East German state seemed manifestly worth preserving as a component of the Soviet-bloc mosaic. Yet its life-blood, in terms of human beings of working age, was draining away. It should have been obvious to the outside world that this made Soviet action in defence of the East German state unavoidable. That action meant, for Berlin, its third, perhaps most serious crisis since the end of the war.

7

The Wall in Berlin and the Elections in the West

The 1961 federal election campaign was the most unpleasant of postwar German history, chiefly because Konrad Adenauer and his CDU party fought it with no holds barred, aware that the SPD was mounting its first dangerous challenge since 1949. But one must return first to the situation in Berlin. This had become potentially explosive by July, with the stream of East German refugees into the city swelling into a torrent. The foundations of the East German state were shaking. Nobody realized this better than its ruler, Walter Ulbricht; he was bound to turn to his master, Khrushchev, for help.

Khrushchev had not been impressed by John Kennedy's showing in Vienna, nor by his 'Report to the Nation' of 25 July 1961. American critics of the report have since pointed out that Kennedy expressly gave guarantees to *West* Berlin and, by implication, was writing off *East* Berlin.* Here, it was argued, was an invitation to the Soviet Union to regard East Berlin as its own and to do what it wished with it. Khrushchev had at the same

---

* One of these critics was James O'Donnell, of the *Saturday Evening Post*. O'Donnell states that on the evening of 24 July he was having lunch at the Mayflower restaurant in Washington with the Sorensen brothers, two of President Kennedy's retinue of whizz-kids. Ted Sorensen produced the text of the president's 25 July 'Report to the Nation' and read out passages relating to Berlin. O'Donnell at once pointed out that the report wrote off East Berlin; he himself believed that this was being done deliberately, under pressure from the State Department, the Pentagon and Nato. The Sorensen brothers were surprised; they had imagined that Kennedy's report said all that needed to be said about Berlin.

O'Donnell took the matter up with other members of the Kennedy administration. He received neither sympathy nor credence. The late Senator Robert Kennedy produced the phrase: 'Jesus, Jim, we just can't be more German than the Germans themselves.' Kennedy's understanding, and that of James O'Donnell too, was that both Adenauer and Brandt had been consulted and had approved the giving of guarantees to West Berlin exclusively.

time been discouraged, by Kennedy's firm stance, from applying a new diplomatic and, possibly, physical squeeze on West Berlin. Yet the need for decisive action was obvious, and he may have been heartened by certain military factors. The United States army was below strength in Germany. Britain, having abandoned conscription, was in the same plight. French forces were always below strength and were now weakened by the generals' 'putsch' in Algeria. Nor would the western alliance, meaning the United States, use nuclear weapons in an emergency that fell short of actual war.

Khrushchev, like a gorilla who imagines himself threatened, ostentatiously flexed his muscles in public.[1] He halted the demobilization of Soviet ground forces, increased the military budget, staged a boastful display of new aircraft and resumed nuclear testing in the atmosphere. Such gestures, it might be held, were irrelevant where Berlin was concerned. The tiny Allied garrison of eleven thousand men was only a tripwire. The western Allies stood their ground, as firmly but unthinkingly as Harold's Saxon swordsmen at Hastings. The Berliners believed that their first duty was to display total composure and total confidence in the West.[2] They did just this, all too admirably.

Back in June Walter Ulbricht had made a revealing but unremarked statement at a press conference in East Berlin.[3] Answering a question as to whether there was a plan to divide East Berlin from West Berlin, he had said: 'I understand ... there are people in West Germany who want us to mobilize the building workers of the capital of the DDR, to erect a wall. I know nothing of any such intention. The building workers are building homes. ... Nobody intends building a wall.' The idea of a wall had not been broached by Ulbricht's questioner; yet there it was, mentioned twice, spontaneously. It had caused no comment. It should have been guessed that something was in the wind. Late in July there were unconfirmed reports of unusual movements of men and materials on Berlin's eastern borders. According to an American source: 'It became known in some quarters that large amounts of barbed wire and cement posts were being sent to Berlin. One officer of the US Mission in Berlin became so concerned over the prospects of the closing of the exit routes that he was thought by his colleagues to have an obsession. He was soon transferred. ...'[4] The supposition was that the materials coming into

Berlin were for closing exit routes to the West, from *West* Berlin. But another observer believed that the first information about building materials for Berlin was given on 10 August, allowing no time to work out why they were being sent in.[5]

A fair summing up was: 'Only a reliable intelligence report quickly transmitted and correctly evaluated to indicate a complete closing of the border could have brought the Allies together in time for convincing and concerted action. Such "hard" intelligence was lacking, even up to zero hour.'[6] Robert Lochner, head of the United States-sponsored radio network in West Berlin, Rias, said that no United States official had the faintest idea that a wall was about to be built through the middle of the city.[7]*

Brandt himself had no exact information. He had been worrying in a general sense about Berlin. On 12 July he had talks there with Adenauer, and a joint communiqué emphasized the right of the western powers to stay in Berlin, the inviolability of West Berlin's communications with the West, the need to maintain links between West Berlin and the Federal Republic and the right of self-determination of the people of Berlin.[8] The two men also discussed a proposal by Brandt for a fifty-two-nation peace conference on the German question, including all nations that had fought against Nazi Germany, and Adenauer's plan for a referendum for Berliners on the political conditions that they wanted. Adenauer was sharply opposed to the fifty-two nation

---

* I had personal experience of Allied ignorance as to what was going on in and around Berlin. On 30 July I wrote to a very senior member of the British Intelligence Staff in Berlin, expressing concern about a report that there was considerable movement on roads leading into East Berlin from both north and south. Since I was going on holiday I was anxious to know if this movement, mainly of goods packed in large lorries, had any significance. The British officer wrote back saying that there was nothing to worry about. His letter went on:

West Berlin is as confident as ever; Bank deposits are normal for the time of year; the Bourse is steady, and there isn't a room to be had in even the smallest pensions for the period of the Radio Exhibition later in the month. I believe the present crisis will end in anti-climax after the Federal elections – just as the 1958 one did after the French and Berlin elections. This is naturally my own theory and bears no resemblance to anyone else's ideas on the subject – *but I have a maddening habit of being right on most occasions*!

This letter was written on 3 August and reached me, by then on holiday, on 10 August. It suggests that the British authorities knew nothing at all at that stage about what was happening only a few miles away, on the outskirts of East Berlin.

conference; Brandt was not interested in a referendum, but it looked likely to take place around October.[9]

With his ingrained lack of interest in Berlin Adenauer was not the man to act at this crucial stage. Brandt certainly tried on his own account. Earlier in the year he had objected strongly to the Soviet refusal to include West Berlin in a new trade agreement with the Federal Republic; he felt that German-Russian trade talks should be broken off unless Berlin were included. A little later he had carried out soundings of possible technical contacts between the Berlin administration and the government of the DDR. At the end of July he told the Allied commandants that the East German regime could not afford to let the flow of refugees continue unchecked. According to one Allied official: 'We expected something drastic and Brandt thought that there might well be a mass outbreak from East to West Berlin of anything from 50,000 to 200,000 people.'[10] Brandt has since maintained that he had feared a new Berlin blockade earlier in the year, but that the Kennedy–Khrushchev meeting in Vienna averted this danger. He wanted the *whole* of Berlin discussed at an international conference, to give the West the diplomatic initiative. He sent Dr Günther Klein, Berlin's senator for federal affairs, to Bonn to propose this. But Adenauer's view was that all that was needed was to maintain the status of West Berlin. Brandt later commented: 'It is hard not to be bitter when one rereads this suggestion, and the answer to it.'[11] Brandt fretted over the attitude of Nato. At Oslo, in April, its Council had discussed only the 'three essentials': keeping Allied troops in West Berlin maintaining free access from the West and securing the liberties of the West Berliners. Brandt, once more, felt that ignoring East Berlin left the Soviet Union free to do as she wished with her part of the four-power city.

Brandt's prediction about a mass exodus of East Germans began, early in August, to come true. In the first eleven days of the month 16,000 arrived in West Berlin, nearly 1,500 a day. On 12 August the total was 2,400 the largest number ever on one day, in spite of increased East German security checks. At 5 pm on 12 August an East German resident told a West Berlin friend at the Düppel-Kleinmachnow crossing-point that the frontier there would be closed that night. At about 9 pm the Pan-American flight from Munich reported troop concentrations on the border of East Berlin. Then at 0.25 am on 13 August a West Berlin customs official on the Bernauerstrasse telephoned head-quarters to say that the border opposite him was being closed. Twelve minutes later Associated Press sent a news-flash – 'People's Police unrolling barbed wire along whole length of frontier between East and West Berlin.' At 1 am the East German press agency announced the closing of the border; this message was repeated by the East German radio at 3 am. A few minutes later People's Police detachments appeared at the Brandenburg Gate in the very heart of Berlin. Ramshackle bar-riers of timber and barbed wire were thrust into the gateway. Later the East German Council of Ministers issued a decree, justifying 'protective' measures to end 'subversive activities', including espionage and a 'regular slave traffic'. The Warsaw Pact powers declared the East German authorities empowered to take all measures for their own 'security'. Nothing was said about the real reason for them – the mass flight of East Germans from an oppressive and hated regime – but the building of the Berlin Wall was fairly under way. Only later would Ulbricht coin the phrase, the 'wall of peace'.

On 12 August Brandt was in Nuremberg, at the start of his whistle-stop election campaign. Speaking in the market square he said that the Soviet Union was 'preparing a stroke against our people'.[12] The East Germans 'are afraid that they are going to be immured in a gigantic gaol'. This language suggests that Brandt knew what would happen. But he was speaking in graphic terms only.[13] He was blamed in some quarters for Wilhelminian oratory and jingoism, as electioneering props.[14] His ignorance was illustrated by his movements: he took the night train for Kiel from Nuremberg and learnt of the building of the wall between Nuremberg and Hanover, where he left the train at 4 am and took the first available plane to Berlin. Cynics suggested that this dash to the scene of action was chiefly slick electioneering, but in fact nothing was more natural than that the mayor of Berlin should return to his post. After a quick visit to the wall he joined the Allied commandants, who met at 9 am. An official present found him 'grave but statesmanlike. He never demanded rash action from the protecting powers nor reproached us for lack of firmness.'[15] The same observer continued: 'After Willy Brandt had arrived to join our deliberations, we went on discussing for hours what effective practical counter-action we could launch. The fact is, we were all stupefied, and almost as much taken by surprise as everyone else.'

The Allied commandants had reason to be stupefied, for their ignorance was the product of a truly lamentable failure of both Allied and West German Intelligence. Suspicions that in fact they did know have never entirely disappeared;[16] Brandt has admitted that he has since heard that hints were passed out by the Russians to one of the three Allied military missions in Potsdam, and to the former United States commissioner in Germany, John McCloy, when visiting the Crimea earlier in the summer.[17]* Brandt has to this day no idea whether such hints were given by the Russians. Allied Intelligence should have followed up reports of unusual movements on East Berlin's outskirts. But the failure of West German Intelligence was even more striking. The West German secret service led by ex-General Gehlen was believed to be omniscient and ubiquitous. Certainly Gehlen's organization had agents in East Germany. Yet no warning came from it in August 1961, when thousands of tons of building materials were brought into East Berlin and massive reinforcements of People's Police were moved from provincial centres to the old Reich capital. Gehlen's failure was lamentable; it indicated a criminal negligence.

The myth of an infallible secret service chief should not go unchallenged. Nor should the equally misleading tale that Brandt encouraged the western powers to take military action. Brandt subsequently said: 'There could be no question of the western powers taking military action. Of course, one of the four powers was failing in its duties. But one could not carry out an occupation of the Soviet sector.'[18] Such an idea was never mooted, though one observer believed that the United States commandant wanted 'some show of force'.[19] An alleged CIA proposal, to send troops to remove the barbed wire and barricades, may have been considered.[20]

If military action was not feasible, strong diplomatic action certainly was. According to Brandt: 'I went to the commandants when I reached Berlin. I asked them to protest at once, and put

* McCloy has since assured Brandt that he was given no information of this kind while in the Soviet Union.

military patrols on the sector boundaries. The Allied protests should have been made in the capital cities of all Warsaw Pact countries, and the capitals of the four powers with responsibilities in Germany.'[21] But the commandants were ultra-cautious; they said they must first consult their governments, and they even took twenty-four hours to send military patrols to the sector boundaries. The on-the-spot protest to the Soviet commandant was not made until 15 August, and the western powers did not protest in Moscow until 17 August. Typically, this latter protest, which had taken four days to formulate, was contemptuously rejected by the Russians in under twenty-four hours. This diplomatic paralysis was inexcusable. Whether the still embryonic wall could have been knocked down at once is another matter – in a physical sense it was removable. But the Allied commandants should have driven straight to Soviet headquarters at Karlshorst and delivered their protest in the most forceful terms. The protests of the western governments should have been ready by the evening of 13 August. They had an unanswerable case: the East Germans were turning the sector boundary into a state frontier and using their armed forces in the city in direct contravention of four-power agreements. The protest of the commandants stated that 'not since the imposition of the Berlin blockade has there been such a flagrant violation of the four-power agreements concerning Berlin'. Not since the Berlin blockade had it taken the western representatives in Berlin so long to protest.

The performance of Adenauer and his government was equally hesitant. The chancellor was telephoned at 4.30 am at his home in Rhöndorf on 13 August, two hours before mass (it was a Sunday). He went to mass as usual and ignored an appeal from his minister for all-German affairs, Lemmer, to come to Berlin at once. On 14 August he merely spoke on television, saying there was no cause for alarm. On 15 August he resumed electioneering, as if nothing whatever had happened. In a speech at Regensburg, moreover, he produced a gem of tasteless indiscretion: 'If ever anyone has been treated with the greatest consideration by his political opponents, it is Herr Brandt, alias Frahm.' To taunt the governing mayor of Berlin, at his post and under heavy pressure, with the fortuitous fact of his illegitimate birth was monstrous. Brandt showed incredible restraint, contenting himself with: 'The old gentleman doesn't seem to grasp what's going on any more', and advising him to 'seek a peaceful evening to his life'. Only on 16 August did Adenauer address the Bundestag, calling the wall 'a declaration of bankruptcy on the part of the sixteen-year tyranny', and appealing for four-power negotiations on Berlin. In Berlin placards went up with unflattering cartoons of Adenauer and underneath, 'Where is the Chancellor? Is he playing *boccia*?' – an allusion to his addiction to this Italian version of bowls or *boules*. Not until 22 August did Adenauer go to Berlin, where he had a chilling reception. A few days later he told an astonished audience in Hagen that Khrushchev built the wall to help the SPD in the coming federal election.

Adenauer may have been politely discouraged from going to Berlin by the United States ambassador in Bonn, Dowling, on the obscure grounds that his presence would be embarrassing to the western powers.[22] This does not ring entirely true, since the Americans alone were prepared to do anything concrete. They sent a reinforcement of 1,500 men to their Berlin garrison, showed their few teeth in the city by moving tanks up to the sector boundary and sent General Lucius Clay, formerly military governor, as President Kennedy's special delegate to Berlin. Clay travelled on 19 August with Vice-President Lyndon B. Johnson and Adenauer asked to accompany them. Here, there can be no doubt, the Americans did refuse to take the chancellor along. Their reason may have been dissatisfaction with Adenauer in Berlin; his presence could militate against the success of the Johnson visit.

There were plenty of other ways for Adenauer to get to Berlin. Ten years later the former CDU deputy mayor of Berlin, Ferdinand Friedensburg, was asked whether the Adenauer government had failed Berlin at this critical moment. He answered: 'I certainly do think so. At that time events could have been influenced. Today we must pay for all this with considerable sacrifice.'[23] Brandt remarked that Adenauer, after waiting several days, told the polished but aggressive Soviet ambassador in Bonn, Andrei Smirnov, that for the common good, 'we must keep the peace'. A decent enough maxim, Brandt felt, but not appropriate for such an occasion![24]

While having no interest in useless recrimination, Brandt has since pointed out that even Ulbricht's 'orders' to the western garrisons were obeyed – they tacitly accepted the East German decision that they should enter East Berlin by, at first, three crossing-points only and, later, by only one, the notorious Checkpoint Charlie on the Friedrichstrasse. This was a blatant restriction of unlimited rights of access to all parts of Berlin for all four occupying powers.[25] But reports that Brandt told the commandants: 'You let yourselves be kicked in the backside by Ulbricht last night', on 13 August seem inaccurate.[26]

On 13 and 14 August Brandt spoke on Berlin radio, tersely and to the point. No one, he said, could think about federal elections at such a time. A kind of annexation had taken place in Berlin, in defiance of existing legal agreements; the rights of the western powers as well as those of the people of Berlin had been violated. So had the unity of Berlin: the sector boundary had been turned into a fortified state frontier. He urged a boycott of the Leipzig autumn fair and other East German functions. He believed that matters should not be allowed to rest with protests on paper. By the evening of 14 August any kind of physical action against the wall was vastly more difficult than thirty-six hours previously.

At a mass protest demonstration in front of the Schoeneberg Town Hall on 16 August Brandt said there would be no capitulation to East German aggression, but warned against rash individual actions that could lead to useless bloodshed. He told the crowd of nearly a quarter of a million that he would 'be happy if the federal chancellor would come to Berlin, if possible at once'. He appealed to the people of West Germany to show the greatest possible solidarity with Berlin, and to the East German police and armed forces not to allow themselves to be turned into scoundrels. He announced that he had sent a personal letter to President Kennedy. The letter had gone that morning.[27] It struck a critical note; the western powers had taken 'late and not very strong' action – whereas they had been much readier to protest in the past when mere military parades had been staged in the Soviet sector. The Berliners doubted the 'resolution' of the Allies. Brandt pointed out in discreet terms that western guarantees were being applied only to West Berlin, although their joint responsibility for Berlin and Germany as a whole had been called in question. The *New York Times* was to assert, much later, that Brandt had been very angry with the United States president and told Egon Bahr, 'Kennedy cooked our goose.'[28] Brandt's reference in his letter to mutual trust irritated Kennedy, whose alleged remark to Pierre Salinger, his press spokesman, was: 'I don't trust this man at all.' In Washington one observer claimed he heard Kennedy explode with anger, saying: 'That bastard in Berlin is trying to involve me in the upcoming German election.'[29] Western nerves were certainly badly frayed, but whatever Kennedy did in fact say can be offset by his addiction to rough language among his circle of advisers. This was all the more likely in a situation when he was so painfully aware of his impotence.

There were divisions of opinion among the western powers in Berlin. The British view was that they had no legal rights in the Soviet sector – this was incorrect, for the whole of Berlin was still legally a four-power responsibility. The French, too, were content to stand on their rights in West Berlin only. The Americans, according to one Allied officer, castigated the British for being 'yellow' and for readiness to cordon off the sector boundary to avoid incidents.[30] This, in turn, was unfair, for the British action dovetailed with Brandt's policy of avoiding a bloody confrontation between unarmed West Berliners and trigger-happy East German People's Police.

The morale of the West Berliners was only partially restored by the visit of Vice-President Johnson, accompanied by General Clay, on 19 August. The sight of this rough-hewn, impressively frontiersmanlike figure aroused huge enthusiasm among the Berliners, for whom Clay – with the profile of a distinguished Roman emperor – was already a hero since the days of the Berlin air-lift. Hundreds of thousands, many with tears in their eyes, turned out in the streets and cheered Johnson to the echo when he spoke at the Schoeneberg Town Hall. Flowers were hurled on to and over his car as he drove in from Tempelhof airfield; Johnson in return distributed ballpoint pens – a gesture inappropriately reminiscent of a carnival or advertising campaign. There was bathos, too, about Johnson's performance on 20 August, when he ordered a pair of shoes at one store and paid for a set of plates from the Berlin City Porcelain Works. The American urge to go shopping is well known, but this was perhaps not the right occasion – even as a 'business as usual' gesture. More apposite was Johnson's pledge of the lives, possessions and honour of the people of the United States in maintaining the freedom of West Berlin.

Among the western powers the Americans alone might have taken a real risk in August 1961 to restore the situation. Brandt went down on record as saying that while the western powers stood fast in West Berlin they tacitly accepted the loss of East Berlin, as a part of the Soviet 'orbit'.[31] He wrote this in 1963 and included the United States in his criticism; there was no emergency conference in the White House, even when the Red Army stood unchallenged at the Brandenburg Gate – 'With the Wall came the most effective effort so far to convince the Western Powers ... that there was no longer a Berlin Question, but only a West Berlin Question.'[32] The risk taken by the Russians in building the wall was minimized by western inaction. Much later Brandt outlined his thoughts in retrospect.[33] He had been worried, when the wall went up, by certain attitudes of mind in the western world. Thus Senator Fulbright suggested, two days before it went up, that a 'protective' action by the Communists might help to keep the peace. Fulbright thought the East German State could 'run dry' – as its citizens fled to the West. A section of the West German press had immediately called for action, and Brandt would later be accused in the Bild Zeitung of cowardice – its political commentator, Sebastian Haffner, wrote that the governing mayor of Berlin had to go. He had, Brandt argued, to find a constructive line of thought in this miserable situation. It was no use just complaining. The Wall was 'a monstrous absurdity'. But in August 1961 there was real danger of West Berlin citizens' marching to attack it. Brandt had to say, 'The Wall is there now, and cannot simply be overrun', and to think of steps to take, not to sweep the wall away – this quickly became impossible – but to make it 'permeable'. The physical presence of the wall may have been the launching-point of his future Ostpolitik, of bringing Germany together again by 'small steps'.

Among repercussions on federal election campaigning of the building of the Berlin Wall was a singularly futile letter to Brandt from the federal foreign minister, Heinrich von Brentano, who suggested that Brandt's letter to Kennedy placed the western powers under grievous pressure. The SPD in Bonn insisted that the German ambassador in Washington had been instructed to ask the president to ignore Brandt's letter. Brandt was accused of trying to improve his election chances by exploiting the Berlin situation. One unbiased view of Brandt's behaviour at the time was that of the political adviser to the British commandant, Geoffrey McDermott: 'He always resists the temptation to play the demagogue. It would have been easy for him to have whipped up emotions in Berlin at the time of the Wall but he preferred to follow a firm line, balanced between exaggerated hope and despair.'[34] McDermott added: 'I have seldom seen him get excited either in public or in private. He is a stimulating companion with a good tough sense of humour.' Indeed Brandt remained the calmest man on the centre of the stage in Berlin in August 1961.

The building of the Wall had a considerable effect on the people of West Berlin. They were not initially over-depressed; it had a stimulatory effect at first, as a target for demonstrators and an obstacle to be overcome by enterprising Berliners anxious to help East Germans to escape. A whole chapter of escapes began, many sensationally daring or clever. West Berliners dug tunnels into East Berlin and sent rescue squads through them. The East Germans escaped by other, multifarious means – swimming rivers and canals, crashing through road barriers in lorries, tractors and even railway trains, jumping from upper-storey windows on the sector boundaries, threading their way through the sewers, scaling and jumping the wall itself.

But the Wall kept growing. It was eventually to be 100 miles long, round the whole of West Berlin, with 238 watch-towers and 132 gun-emplacements. In its first 10 years of existence at least 64 people lost their lives on it, 48 shot down by the East German police. At least 100 more were seriously wounded; dozens may have been killed or wounded out of sight of West Berlin. Over 4,000 East Germans attempting to escape were seen, from West Berlin, being caught. An army of at least 20,000 East German police stood guard on the Wall, which quickly became a grim but incontrovertible fact. Brandt was realistic: 'There was no use whining. Nor any good trying to blow it up – we Germans are not good at that sort of thing. It was a part of world power politics. I have said – we must learn to live with the wall, not accepting, far less liking it. We had to plan to make it transparent, patiently and with care. It cannot be abolished; it has to be made, within a broader context, redundant.'[35] While General Clay remained in Berlin there were vague hopes of Allied counter-action. Clay may have considered using tanks to 'punch holes' in the Wall.[36] He sent tanks up to the Checkpoint Charlie crossing and on 23 October 1961 an armed American police escort raced into East Berlin to bring out the United States minister (from the embassy in Bonn), held by the East German People's Police for refusal to identify himself. Brandt considered that Clay's mission to Berlin helped psychologically: the Berliners were pleased to see him back.[37] Clay found Brandt fully co-operative, appreciative of the American role and a real leader at moments of crisis; he discounted reports of disagreements between him and Kennedy.[38] But Clay's position in Berlin was invidious; he had authority in the American sector, none whatever in the British or French. Acrimonious arguments contributed to his subsequent recall, in May 1962. The Berliners, at all events, still remember him with affection and admiration. He was given the freedom of the city and when leaving it paid a personal tribute: 'I did not need to be astonished by the wonderful performance of the Berliners. I didn't expect anything else of them.'[39]

Apart from alternating emotional exuberance and depression, the Berliners behaved well. But the Wall would, in time, subtly affect them. They lost a little of their old, buoyant optimism, of their ability to laugh at themselves, of the devil-may-care attitude of the surrounding communist world. Berliners loved the lime-light; apart from the gradually shrinking story of escapes, the limelight faded. Life became more mundane, a little less worth living.

The effect of the building of the Wall on the DDR was of long-term significance. In November 1961 an officer of the East German armed forces escaped to West Germany and his report was first published on 13 January 1962.[40] Ex-Major Siegfried Behr stated that all East German and Soviet military units in the DDR were alerted on 12 August 1961 and remained at full alert until 24 August. No leave was granted, all officers and men were instructed to go about their duties fully armed. Twenty-seven divisions, twenty Russian and seven East German, stood ready to put down the national uprising that was feared. Behr believed that only one East German officer in five was at that time a 'reliable Communist' and few of the rank and file would have readily marched against West Berlin or West Germany. Yet the Wall made any thought of a national uprising in the DDR illusory.

The East Germans who rose in 1953, like the Hungarians in 1956, visualized possible aid from the western world. Western failure to react when the Wall went up proved finally that no help could be expected in the future; the East Germans, after nearly thirty years of dictatorship of one form or another, decided to make the best of things under the Ulbricht regime. The correspondent of the *Neue Zürcher Zeitung*, Otto Frei, described what they had lost:

> Up to August 13, 1961 the East Berliners were half-free. They had of course, to work during the day in state-owned enterprises in an unfree society and were subject to an arbitrary legal system. But in the evening at the close of work, they came over to West Berlin to meet relatives and acquaintances, go to the movies or the theatre, stroll up the Kurfürstendamm, read Western newspapers. About eight million theater and movie tickets were sold each year in West Berlin to East Berliners. . . . About 60,000 people from the East came daily to West Berlin to work in factories and workshops. . . . For 13 years people could move fairly freely in both parts of the city and meet whenever they wished. Some 200,000 Germans from East Berlin and the Soviet Zone visited West Berlin every day. Berlin, despite political division, was still a special area.[41]

After the building of the Wall the East German authorities organized a disciplined communist society with purposeful unhurried ruthlessness. 'Socialization' of farmland and small business enterprises went ahead. The remnants of an independent spirit in the churches were unostentatiously suppressed. On 20 September 1961 the People's Chamber decreed massive 'voluntary' enlistment in the armed forces; there were two hundred thousand enlistments in three months, many of them far from voluntary. The Communist SED formed an organization, Worker's Fist, its slogans: 'The worker's fist smashes the snout of the militarist beast' and 'A clenched fist for the enemy; the enemy will lose his hair and teeth'. Strong-arm squads accosted citizens and, if they argued, beat them up. Aerials adjusted for West German television were ripped down.[42] There were numerous arrests and draconian prison sentences; in the next five years more than six thousand East Germans were gaoled for 'attempted flight from the Republic'.

Willy Brandt as a young school-boy and
In his teens

Ernst Reuter (centre) *and Willy Brandt* (immediately behind) sitting with the SPD faction in the German Senate in 1952

Brandt with HM the Queen in 1965, together with Chancellor Erhard (seated on the right), Minister Eric Mende (standing behind Erhard), Rut Brandt (third from left)

At a May Day rally, West Berlin Mayor Willy Brandt addressing three quarters of a million West Berliners in front of the old Reichstag building in 1960

With President John F. Kennedy in Berlin, 1963

Franco-German talks with (left to right) Georges Pompidou, Chancellor Kiesinger, President De Gaulle, Foreign Minister Brandt

With Konrad Adenauer in 1963

Signing the Russo-German non-aggression pact in Moscow in 1970: (left to right) Walter Scheel, Chancellor Brandt, Alexei Kosygin, Andrei Gromyko

On a visit to the Warsaw Ghetto memorial in 1971

In Oslo receiving the Nobel Peace Prize for 1971 from Mrs Aase Lionas

Brandt with novelist Günther Grass in 1972, who helped in his re-election campaign

On his way to vote in the West German Federal parliamentary elections, with his wife Rut and son Matthias, November 1972

The weight of communist propaganda told on the East Germans. Placards proclaimed: 'The measures of the government of the DDR have saved peace in Europe and the world', and the rumour was put about that the Americans, without reference to Adenauer, had approved of the building of the 'Wall of Peace'. Khrushchev paid a visit to its eastern side a year afterwards; well-trained communist choirs chanted *Freundschaft!* (Friendship!) rhythmically. One commentator wrote: 'Many people talk blithely of writing off Eastern Germany and its seventeen million inhabitants. It may, indeed, be deemed necessary. But ... it will be an act which the conscience of the Western world will hardly be able to forget.'[43] The western world, on the contrary, washed its hands of the people of East Germany without compunction.

The happiest man in East Germany was probably Walter Ulbricht. As Moscow's devoted servant – Ulbricht was for thirty years entitled to carry Soviet papers and 'loyalty' to East Germany came a bad second to loyalty to the Soviet Union – he was committed to a policy of economic competition with the West. The long chase to overtake West German living standards could now begin in earnest, with a stable labour force. The drain of labour to the West had been the greatest single hindrance to the first two East German 'economic plans'. For the Soviet Union, too, the Wall brought a feeling of real relief. The East German state could become a fully functioning part of the satellite system. Talk about the Wall being an abject confession of defeat was beside the point. Two thirds of the population of the Soviet bloc lived in the Soviet Union; any story could be sold to them. What was important about the Wall was not construction, but consequences.

Finally, the western powers. As so often in diplomatic confrontations between East and West, the latter have surrendered one position after another on the assumption that they were untenable. The East–West diplomatic confrontation, even with intervening episodes of détente, does and will continue; but the western philosophy remains defensive and instinctively hesitant. The building of the Berlin Wall taught western diplomats and governments nothing.

We must now return to the spring of 1961 and the prospect of the coming federal election in which Brandt was the SPD candidate for the chancellorship, the first put forward since 1949 with an outside chance of unseating that cruelly efficient old campaigner, Konrad Adenauer. For the first time the SPD were making a coherent effort to become a majority party, not based on sectional interest – that of a diminishing working class. In making this effort the party had problems. The communist vote could not be mobilized; it might be used for or against the SPD, or not at all. Middle-of-the-road voters were instinctively biased – that terrible, Nazi-framed phrase *die Sozis* implied instinctive rejection. For too long the SPD had despised anything 'bourgeois'. But the Federal German Republic was becoming ultra-bourgeois; so was a growing section of the electorate. Back in 1945 Kurt Schumacher had written of the need to bring craftsmen and tradesmen into the party, to give it a 'broad base'. But no one in the higher echelons of the SPD had done much about this. From 1949 the working-class vote was a declining factor; the 'establishment' sought to promote working-class voters into an 'affluence bracket' and sabotage the prospect of a viable opposition being created. Behind these problems lurked a nagging inferiority complex, engendered by twelve mainly fruitless years in opposition. The SPD had achieved something in Bonn, more in the *Länder*, but it was not easy to pinpoint successes and tot up a tally that the electorate would appreciate.

Adenauer had problems, too. He was not happy with the Kennedy administration in the United States, anxious to put out ideas, exotic, above all too youthful for his taste. He had lost ground as a result of the confusions of the presidential succession in 1959 – he had offered his own candidature, planned a kind of 'presidential democracy' to suit his own book, changed his mind and finally withdrawn his own proposal to kick himself upstairs. He had forfeited prestige and trust. Partly because of the presidential issue, he was embroiled in a vendetta with his deputy in party and government, Ludwig Erhard. This in turn led the Free Democratic coalition partner to set a term on his rentention of power: its chairman, Erich Mende, demanded in advance his retirement from the chancellorship within two years of the 1961 election.

Adenauer, then, felt conspicuously weaker than was generally known or supposed. His CDU accordingly reverted to personal vilification of Brandt. This smear campaign became almost the outstanding feature of the 1961 election. Participants picked on three facets of Brandt's past life. The first was his past political activities; the fact that he had been a socialist radical led to accusations that he was a communist agent. The second was his act of leaving Germany as an opponent of the Nazis, interpreted as cowardice or lack of patriotism. He was further accused of having donned Norwegian uniform to fight his fellow country-men or, in vague terms, of having worked against Germany. The third accusation was that his writings had been directed against Germany and her people – a variation on the theme of lack of patriotism. Mud-slingers alluded to his illegitimate birth. The campaign as a whole was designed to depict him as a shifty rene-gade.

As early as February 1961 Brandt had to take legal proceedings against Dr Hans Kapfinger, publisher of the *Passauer Neue Presse*, a right-wing paper circulating in Bavaria. It had run the whole gamut of libellous statements about Brandt, who him-self called the publisher a 'rotten character-assassin'. Kapfinger threatened counter-proceedings for libel; significantly, he instit-uted none. On 28 February the independent *Frankfurter Allgemeine Zeitung* noted that slander was freely used against Brandt. On the same day the French paper, *Le Monde*, observed that the smear campaign was being conducted by so-called 're-spectable' papers like the *Deutsche Zeitung*, but concluded that it would be counter-productive since it would disgust solid, sensible middle-class voters. This was mistaken: *Le Monde's* Bonn correspondent was honest and intellectual; he did not realize that the middle class was already suspicious of Brandt and all too ready to let its suspicions be fanned into flame.

On 15 February Franz-Josef Strauss, the 'favourite son' of the Bavarian branch of the CDU and strongly tipped as a future leader of party and government, used opprobrious terms in the 'outback' village of Vilshofen. He said: 'We have the right to ask Herr Brandt: What did you do *for twelve years* abroad? We know ourselves what we did inside Germany during that time!' Brandt, long before, had answered this loaded question. He said in November 1960: 'Least of all do I need to justify the fact that already in my youth I was a consistent enemy of the regime that brought us terror and war, and meant the worst possible national betrayal.' He had no case to answer; Strauss, by climbing on a bandwagon of vicious and spiteful propaganda, had, and still has. Thirteen years later, still a chancellor *manqué*, he has never explained his behaviour in the 1961 election campaign and has continued to pile insult upon insult.

On 1 March Brandt secured a court injunction restraining the *Deutsche Zeitung* from repeating unproven charges that he had sought to damage his people and his country while an emigrant in Norway. He pointed out that a Berlin court had found, in 1959, that there was no evidence to indicate that he had ever taken up arms against his native country. His legal counsel also mentioned that he had been deprived of his German citizenship in 1938 through an order signed my Dr Wilhelm Stuckart – who happened to have been the boss at that time of Dr Hans Globke, Dr Adenauer's right-hand man in the Federal Chancellery. This riposte was superfluous. No connection between Stuckart and Adenauer, via Globke, existed.

There was a certain irony in Adenauer appealing in the Bundestag on 8 March for a 'fair' election. His own party followers had already shown their hand. On the same day the Norwegian foreign minister, Halvard Lange, expressed astonishment over the attacks on Brandt. He exploded the idea that Brandt had ever ceased to feel himself a German; he had appointed him as press attaché in Berlin, with a civil not military role, and had been the first to accept his subsequent explanation that he wanted to help his own country, Germany, and work in the future as a German, in Berlin. Lange was ignored by the West German press. On 11 March Brandt wrote in the *Berliner Stimme* that the CDU were waging a campaign against him, based on 'hate, mistrust and slander'. On the same day Hans Kapfinger was served a court order to pay 30,000 marks (£2,700) to a named charity.[44] On 15 March *The Times* summed up neatly, saying that Brandt was 'accused' of three 'crimes' – being illegitimate, having spent the war years out of Germany and having once donned foreign uniform.[45] A week later the *Manchester Guardian* correspondent in Bonn suggested that the CDU had instructed its election campaign speakers to indicate that Brandt had been a 'traitor to his country'.[46] The CDU were also hinting, obscurely but nastily, that Brandt had nearly handed Berlin over to the Communists.

An article I wrote in the *Manchester Guardian* on 25 July indicated that character assassination had now been perfected – in 'a perfect essay in the art of political defamation'. This essay was described:

> The principal weapon being used against him ... continues to be oblique references to his emigration from Germany when Hitler came to power, his service with the Norwegian resistance during the war, and his return to Germany as a Norwegian newspaperman. The most damaging piece of literature is being circulated by the Essen publishing house, the Custos Verlag.
>
> This is a 28-page pamphlet entitled – What does Willy Brandt want? – produced by 'catholic journalists' who call themselves the 'Rheinische Gruppe' and are mainly right-wing members of the Christian Democratic Party. Their pamphlet is distributed free to households, and often goes to people with direct influence on public opinion. The pamphlet excuses other leading Social Democrats who were émigrés. At least, it points out, they did not swear an oath of allegiance to a foreign government. Men like Adenauer, the pamphlet continues, only fought against Hitler as temporarily disenfranchised Germans. But Willy Brandt's case was different; he became a citizen of a country at war with Germany.
>
> So different, indeed, that the pamphleteers compare Brandt with Walter Ulbricht, the Communist dictator of the East German Republic. Was Ulbricht, they ask, a German national hero, because he was an émigré in Moscow? Should Germans respect anyone who organized a German civil war, while in exile, in order to bring about the victory of communism in Germany? Willy Brandt is ingeniously linked with the Communist Cause by reference to his activities as a journalist in the Spanish Civil War.

The article concluded:

> The Federal Chancellor's own attitude towards his rival has been more guarded, but the cartoon which appeared recently in the *Westdeutsche Allgemeine Zeitung* may have been appropriate. This was entitled 'Solidarity in Berlin', and it showed Adenauer patting Brandt on the back with his left

hand. In his right hand is a crooked stick which he is using to
try to trip Brandt, while at the same time catching him a hefty
kick on the knee-cap.... Brandt is not kicking back. That,
certainly, is a fair commentary.[47]

At the end of July a Custos Verlag pamphlet, with a circulation
of 220,000, was confiscated. Another Custos pamphlet directed
against Wehner because he had once belonged to the Communist
Party, was confiscated on 17 August. But the weevils of the
smear campaign tried again; the anti-Brandt pamphlet was re-
published with a circulation of 38,000, and twenty-two 'offending
passages' cut out. A leading member of the CSU, Richard Jaeger,
even compared Brandt with Hitler – for the ludicrous but
deliberately damaging reason that Hitler had changed his name
from Schiklgruber, just as Brandt had changed his from
Frahm.[48] This sort of nonsense should have been self-defeating.
Sad to relate, it had a considerable appeal; it was still too soon
for someone who had played a real part in opposing Hitler to
emerge in the very forefront of German politics.

For Brandt the smear campaign made the 1961 election night-
marish. Libels could not be totally ignored, for the public
reaction would be that there was something in what was being
said. Yet to overreact was equally mistaken. The most maddening
aspect was that there was so much to get on with; his election
campaign was a hectic, uphill battle against the odds. Adenauer
and the CDU were totally confident of victory. The party
congress in April in Cologne proclaimed a feeling of certainty,
based on steady and often spectacular economic achievement and
complete solidarity with the western alliance. The SPD's modified domestic and foreign policies were contemptuously dismissed as a feeble attempt at imitation. Brandt battled along with
vigour and courage. At an SPD congress in Bad Godesberg on
15 and 16 April he pledged his commitment to the seventeen
million people of East Germany – they could not be divorced
from the German nation as a whole and the DDR had no claim to
be regarded as a fully-fledged state. At an extraordinary party conference in Bonn on 28 April he announced the guidelines of SPD
policy – support of Nato, full confidence in the Bundeswehr,
increased European integration, more property owners and
higher living standards. This might sound a bit mundane and

obvious; but what a change from ten years previously! Then the SPD opposed the Adenauer policy of full co-operation within the western alliance, rejected the 'free market' economics of Ludwig Erhard and short-sightedly concentrated on representing the interests of a diminishing working class. The SPD were going into the 1961 election with their eyes open, not blinkered.

Brandt turned his especial attention to the industrial Ruhr, for the CDU had launched a powerful drive in that area, which they called the 'frontal attack on the red town halls'. In the local elections in the spring of 1961 the CDU raised their vote from 38 to 45 per cent, capturing even the traditional 'communist citadel' of Solingen. The SPD vote dropped from 44 to 41 per cent. Asked beforehand whether he would regard the local elections as a trial run for the federal elections, Brandt answered smartly: 'Depends how they turn out.'[49] In May he proposed a television confrontation with Adenauer, who turned the idea down flat. Television cameras are relentless: the contrast between the firm, forceful features of the forty-seven-year-old Brandt and his own wrinkled, antediluvian face would have been disastrous. He was worried by the image being built up of Brandt as a 'German John Kennedy'. The two men had obvious points in common – youth, vitality, readiness to move with the times, interest in social progress. Kennedy was an immensely popular figure in Europe. The CDU managers were infuriated by the thought of Brandt cashing in on his charisma.

In the face of a real challenge Adenauer's election tactics were impeccable. The CDU assured the German people that they could rely on their father-figure, counting the blessings he had brought them. The economy was in good order; the Federal Republic was a trusted member of the western alliance; election slogans warned 'No experiments!' and 'Remember Hungary!'; meetings were held out of doors, catching crowds of people on their way home from work. Security, stability, prosperity and strong government were things that the CDU could safely promise; their governments had produced them in the past. Added to all this, the party had plenty of money to spend; one estimate was a total of 35 million marks for electioneering.[50]

In July Brandt was still optimistic. In an interview with the *Atlantic Monthly* he radiated confidence and good sense.[51] What sort of socialism was he offering to the electorate? His answer: A socialism that searches for solutions, no Pied Piper's music to catch votes, no mirage of a welfare state. How could he improve on Adenauer's foreign policy? By producing more constructive ideas for a western alliance that must be kept stable and united. Already he had a surprisingly comprehensive idea of an *Ostpolitik*: the Federal Republic should try to build up relations with the Soviet Union and its satellites based on facts and not on dogma. Such relations should be continuously explored and should not stagnate. Exploration, he thought, implies counter-pressure; stagnation means resignation to the *status quo*. His eastern policy would be more imaginative and adventurous than that of Adenauer, who was content to consolidate behind the Iron Curtain frontier and was frankly uneasy about diplomatic exploration beyond it. Yet Adenauer's purely defensive policy may have been more attuned to the mood of the electorate, working zealously, enjoying the good things of life, not inclined to look beyond their own noses. One of Brandt's close associates, thinking back, believes that lack of political ruthlessness told against him. He did not go all out for what he wanted, but operated on a basis of careful and penetrating reflection. 'The election campaign as a result was not a simple matter for him . . . he wanted to remain himself.'[52] This refusal to pose as a dynamic miracle-man appealed to some, but not to a majority of voters. Used to being looked after, they still preferred the octogenarian oracle.

A helpful shot in the arm was President Kennedy's statement that Brandt was 'worth supporting'. How could a United States administration do this? The answer was, by being neutral. 'Well, that will be something new for us,' Brandt remarked.[53] United States administrations had never concealed their preference for the CDU in the past.

The odds, up to August, were heavily on a sweeping CDU victory. The smear campaign had damaged Brandt while Adenauer was on the top of his form. The electorate were used to Adenauer teams and their aura of confident, almost smug satisfaction. Middle-of-the-road voters still regarded a vote given to the SPD as a vote thrown away, for the SPD had no potential coalition allies, while as long as Adenauer remained a 'big' coalition of CDU and SPD seemed unthinkable. Then came the Berlin wall. It need not have benefited Brandt, for Germans were reminded of their dependence on their western allies and Adenauer. Their need for reassurance was reinforced when Khrushchev, on 31 August, attacked the Federal Government and announced the resumption of Soviet nuclear bomb-tests. The CDU at once produced an election poster showing a furious Krushchev with fist upraised, the caption 'Now we all know – Krushchev demands Adenauer's downfall!', and the opposite rallying cry – 'In this threatening hour the German people stands solidly behind Konrad Adenauer. The German people will give Khrushchev the right answer on 17 September!' But Adenauer's subsequent performance – his failure to go to Berlin at once, his oblique reference to Brandt's illegitimate birth, his absurd statement that Khrushchev built the Wall to help the SPD – lost him support. The German electorate may have been somewhat thick-skinned but this sort of talk was childishly spiteful. When Brandt addressed a crowd of thirty thousand in Dortmund on 8 September there was an impressive demonstration of solidarity with Berlin. Public opinion polls showed the SPD catching up; four days before the election an Emnid poll gave them 39 per cent against the CDU's 44. Rumours were rife that the FDP leadership was tired of serving under Adenauer (there was truth in this) and that Erhard would be chancellor after the election. Adenauer's riposte was to state unequivocally at a press conference on 15 September that he had no intention of retiring.

The elections took place on 17 September. The result was a disappointment for Brandt, but something of a shock for Adenauer. The SPD vote rose from 31.8 to 36.3 per cent, with 190 seats in the Bundestag in place of 169. The CDU lost nearly three quarters of a million voters – their share fell from 50.1 to 45.2 per cent, their Bundestag seats from 270 to 241. They lost, more importantly, an absolute majority in Parliament, which Adenauer regarded as a personal affront. The FDP under the energetic and resourceful Erich Mende did best of all, raising their vote from 8 to 12 per cent and their Bundestag seats from 43 to 67. They had reasserted themselves as very much a third force in West German politics.

Brandt had done well, but why had he not done even better? The CDU held a big advantage in power and skill in the pure mechanics of electioneering; they had more money, better propaganda and administration; they had studied American election tactics and tightened up their finances; they had made full use of all of their good speakers, whereas some of the big men of the provinces in the SPD stayed out of the fight. The electorate liked Brandt's youthfulness, charm of manner, easy informality and ability to get on with all sections of the community. But the average German still set a high premium on experience and authority, Adenauer's attributes. Then there was the impressive list of CDU achievements. One much-used SPD poster urged: 'Build more homes, instead of barracks.' But the third Adenauer government had averaged over half a million new homes a year – more than in any other country in Europe. The SPD declaimed against rising prices; the CDU could show that the cost of living had risen by only 13 per cent in a decade, against 35 per cent in Britain, more in France. Real wages had risen by 32 per cent in Germany during the same period, against only 7 per cent in Britain and 5 per cent in Sweden, while the most obvious have-nots, the old-age pensioners, were placated by a new and progressive Pensions Act eight months before the elections. SPD warnings about the dangers of increased unemployment – a few years before Ollenhauer had talked of a potential seven million unemployed – could be easily laughed off. Six million new jobs had been created in the last decade.

The 1961 elections were won and lost on domestic issues and there was nothing much that Brandt could do about them. It remained to be seen how Adenauer could restore his personal position. Perhaps unwisely, Brandt proposed an all-party government of 'national concentration', and repeated this on 22 September, arguing a state of national emergency.[54] He wanted an all-out political campaign to bring German reunification nearer. Brandt had a meeting with Adenauer on 25 September over which a veil of secrecy was drawn. This was exactly what Adenauer wanted. He was keenly aware that Erich Mende, now cast in the role of king-maker, intended to depose him and offer the FDP participation in a new coalition if Erhard became chancellor. Brandt's honest belief in an all-party coalition played into Adenauer's hands. In the political horse-trading that now took place the SPD quickly became expendable. The FDP would not serve under Brandt, for fear of losing its financial support from the German Confederation of Industry, and its leaders dreaded a big 'black-red' coalition, leaving them in impotent isolation. Mende had to modify his terms to the CDU; even so, he negotiated toughly and forced a bargain. Adenauer was induced, under pressure, to give him a letter promising to retire from the chancellorship in about two years' time, well before the 1965 elections. Mende and Adenauer's right-hand man in the parliamentary party of the CDU, Heinrich Krone, were the only people besides Adenauer to receive copies of this letter.[55] Mende undertook to stay silent for at least one year, and kept his promise; the FDP executive was given the gist of the agreement and not the letter.[56] In addition Adenauer dropped his foreign minister, von Brentano, at the insistence of the FDP. On 7 November Adenauer was re-elected chancellor; on 14 November the CDU–FDP coalition took office.

Brandt returned to Berlin. Before the election he had promised the Berliners that he would leave them only to become federal chancellor, and thus be in a position to safeguard their interests. There was plenty to do in Berlin. As one observer put it: 'Suddenly, as West Germany was running over with economic activity, the half-empty barrel that was Berlin started to fill. The city was not far from catching up with West Germany when it was struck by the economic calamity of the Wall.'[57] Seven per cent of West Berlin's labour force vanished overnight, the tough, hard-working *Grenzänger* – 'frontier-crossers' – from East Berlin. Economic growth was to drop to an annual rate of about 1 per cent; export orders fell in a few months by 18 per cent. There was danger of a drift of population to West Germany, where there were six unfilled jobs for every person unemployed. West Berlin's population statistics were unpromising, too – 1,363 women for every 1,000 men, young males tending to emigrate, the birth-rate sinking and more than 18 per cent of the population over sixty-five years old – against only 10.5 per cent in West Germany.

Karl Schiller, senator for economics, estimated that fifteen thousand people of working age had to be attracted each year to West Berlin, or the city would relapse into an economic, political and psychological defensive.[58] Massive investment was needed. With more labour and capital West Berlin would do more than survive: it would prosper. Everything possible was done to help.

Income tax was cut – for some income brackets to 30 per cent below West German rates. Cash bonuses were paid to low-income workers. Special credit facilities were granted to refugees and to small businesses. There were special marriage allowances and reductions of turnover tax. Big credits were made available to exporters. Schiller wanted more trade with East Germany, running at 1,800 million marks' worth in 1961. But trade with West Germany was far more vital, with a volume of 19,000 million marks a year. Berlin, Schiller said appositely, had moved from being 'a show-case to being a test-case'. During August and September 1961 the net outflow from West Berlin had averaged 1,100 people a week. In October it had dropped to 800 and by December to 550. The year showed a net inflow of over 5,000 people, but this was due to the huge number of East Germans escaping to West Berlin before the Wall went up. Brandt offered young West Germans settling in West Berlin a down-payment of 100 marks in their first month and 50 marks in each of the next two months. If unmarried they would get free journeys twice a year to their homes; if married and parted from wife or husband, four free journeys. Plane fares from Berlin to West Germany were reduced by 30 per cent; the difference between the old and new fare was paid by the Bonn government. Brandt announced large-scale building projects – 85 million marks for the city auto-bahn and underground railway, 25 million marks for the two universities. The housing programme was stepped up from 20,000 to 25,000 new homes a year. Federal grants were raised from 2,000 million to more than 2,500 million marks to maintain West Berlin as a viable outpost of the western world. A pattern of aid was set that has been maintained ever since.

There were physical as well as economic stresses. Brandt has said that August 1962, when a young man, Peter Fechter, was shot at the Wall and left to die by the People's Police, was in a physical sense almost more dangerous than August 1961.[59] The West Berliners were easily goaded into demonstrative action, stoning East German guards along the Wall or Red Army vehicles bringing relief guards to the Soviet war memorial in the British sector. Allied protests against the barbaric inhumanity of the East Germans, who shot to kill, had no effect and this increased the Berliners' rage. Yet Brandt had to reduce the risk of purposeless bloodshed. West German police had to use truncheons and water-cannon to stop unorganized mobs from storming the Wall. To keep order while maintaining morale was supremely difficult. But nine months after the Wall went up Brandt was able to say: 'West Berlin can live with the "*status quo* minus", as I call the situation that exists since communication with East Berlin was cut off. It has proved its ability to look the Wall in the face as an ugly fact of life, and carry on.'[60]

It would require chapters to describe the physical atavism of the Wall. In course of time there were to be 210 squat, ugly and sinister watch-towers overlooking it, manned by trigger-happy East German robots. Great sections of central Berlin were reduced to ordered wildernesses. Checkpoint Charlie, sole crossing-point for Allied personnel, was a weird sight, with armoured vehicles often confronting each other across fifty yards of 'slalom' barriers, aptly suggesting an obstacle race against death for the motorized East German escaper. Grotesquely, flowerbeds were laid out in the 'death strip' on the eastern side of the Wall, with nothing bigger than begonias, so as to leave a field of fire. Alsatian dog patrols moved along the Wall; dogs were trained to attack, if necessary, East German soldiers and officers. Indeed 23,000 men and officers of the People's Police deserted to the West between 1949 and 1967 – earning this force the sobriquet of 'the world's most unreliable army'.[61]

Political pressure on Berlin, at least, was eased. The Wall made further Soviet pressure on West Berlin superfluous. In a speech to the Twenty-Second Congress of the Communist Party in Moscow, on 17 October 1961, Khrushchev had withdrawn the time-limit that he had imposed for settlement of the Berlin question. A peace treaty, he said, need not now be signed before 31 December 1961. The Sino – Soviet dispute was taking shape and there were meetings between representatives of the Soviet and United States governments early in 1962. It suited the Russian book to relax pressure on Berlin and simply sidetrack western protests. Soviet diplomacy was entering a defensive phase in Germany, but only much later would Adenauer begin to wonder whether there should not have been a coherent attempt to talk to the Russians and talk sense into them.[62]

At the end of 1961 Brandt was again urging the holding of a conference, this time a four-power summit in Berlin. This could focus world attention on the monstrous nature of the Wall, and he wanted western pressure to secure renewed contact between East and West Berliners. He thought, too, that four-power responsibility for the whole city should be reasserted. Logical and legitimate western demands should be tabled continually. This could help to evolve a 'political will to win on the Western side'.[63]

In the summer of 1962 he gave cautious support to the American plan for an international authority to supervise West Berlin's communications with West Germany. Adenauer and Ulbricht both opposed it, but Brandt's view was that a written guarantee of West Berlin's communications would be a major gain. Ulbricht was instantly agitated; his aim was to assert East German sovereignty and control communications through East German territory. Once again, a potentially promising western diplomatic initiative died still-born.

In January 1963 Brandt had a chance of taking the initiative personally. Khrushchev was attending an SED congress in East Berlin. On 17 January Brandt authorized Egon Bahr to propose to a Soviet embassy official in Berlin that he and Khrushchev should meet. He wanted to explain that a constructive German policy would be preferable for the Soviet Union to shoring up indefinitely a bankrupt and unpopular East German regime. Beria believed this in 1953; so probably, did Semeonov. But within a hour of Bahr's mission Brandt's CDU deputy mayor, Franz Amrehn, declared that the CDU would leave the Berlin coalition government if Brandt called on Khrushchev. Brandt drew back. He felt that he could not put the coalition at risk. This may have been a mistake. As it happened, the coalition broke up anyway, and there were new Berlin elections on 17 February.

The elections were a brilliant success for the SPD and for Brandt personally. The party's vote rose from 52 to 62 per cent. That of the CDU dropped for the first time since 1948, from 37 to 28 per cent. Brandt was identified with the faith, firmness and endurance that have kept the Berliners' liberties intact. The cancelled interview with Khrushchev evidently told in his favour. He formed a new government with the FDP, although he did not need their help, and he earned the nickname of 'Willy the Winner' from American journalists. His success in Berlin, moreover, was one of many by the SPD: in ten *Land* elections after the 1961 federal elections, their vote rose by 1.6 million, that of the CDU by only half a million. In these ten elections the SPD outstripped the CDU as the strongest single party overall.

During the three years preceding the 1963 Berlin elections Brandt had spent much time representing the city abroad. In Israel in November 1960 he called for the establishment of normal diplomatic relations between the two countries. In Tel Aviv he said: 'A German who speaks in Israel has to be aware of the terrible burden of the past. I am aware of this burden.... Please believe me, that responsible people in my country have tried to learn their lesson and base their actual and future work upon the lessons of history.... I think we are not permitted to forget in order to make it easier for others to forgive.' The *Jerusalem Post* called his speech 'courageous'.[64] In spite of scattered protests – no German was welcome in Israel – the visit was a success.

In April 1962 he was in Britain; here too there were some hostile demonstrations, though not to do with Brandt as a person. On his return to Berlin he noted that the 'shadows of the past' had not entirely disappeared; he asked responsible Germans whether enough was being done to improve Anglo-German relations. Driving round London in an official car he made a different kind of observation – he would have liked to travel on top of a bus again, and really see London.[65]

Of a very different nature was his visit to the United States in October 1962. He made two speeches at Harvard University, 'not an institution known for pro-Germanism',[66] where he received repeated standing ovations in a packed auditorium. He denounced the 'Wall of shame' in Berlin and spoke of the 'ordeal of co-existence'. He had no illusions about Soviet policies: 'Peaceful co-existence, Soviet style, means the militant pursuit of Soviet aims.' He classified Khrushchev's three basic aims as avoidance of nuclear war, weakening the western alliance and attracting uncommitted nations into the Soviet orbit. The answer to Soviet diplomacy was diplomatic initiative and offensive; this was the only way to hold one's ground.[67] In Washington he had talks with President Kennedy. He told the president that Germans would not accept the division of their country; the desire for reunification lived on. A changed world situation could change the Soviet Union's German policy; in the meantime he wanted small steps to improve the situation locally. And the younger generation in Germany would feel increasingly entitled to ask for what they felt was their due; they had no guilt complex, since they grew up after the Nazi regime had been swept out of existence.[68]

A few days after Brandt returned to Berlin came the Cuba crisis. He recognized the danger of the Soviet Union salving its pride through reprisals on West Berlin. But he believed that Kennedy was right to force the Russians to dismantle their missile bases on Cuba, and he said so forcefully. Relations with Kennedy were on a sound footing; they remained excellent until the president's death.

8

Marking Time

Most men and women go through difficult periods in their lives, often in middle age and marked by a lack of confidence and waning of ambitions. There are no rules about such things, not even probabilities. In 1963 Brandt was just fifty years old. He had come a very long way, with concentrated effort and plenty of setbacks. Crude and vicious smear campaigns had a cumulative effect, and had gone on ever since he returned from exile. The shock of his federal election defeat in 1961 may have had a delayed impact and there was still backbiting within the SPD. All of this was depressing and he was always a man who worried deeply about his country's future. The Wall showed that the German question was as far as ever from being solved. Finally, he was feeling his age – probably for the first time in his life. According to a long-serving member of his staff,[1] he had been suffering a 'cyclical low' in personal morale for some time. This happened every few months: it seemed as if he took mental stock of himself and what he was doing and was depressed by his own critical assessment of his achievement. That there were ups and downs in his career was not necessarily relevant, for he always rose to a real challenge. He was – still is – vastly self-critical, and he has always been deeply depressed when people round him have let him down. When disappointed he has always sought to avoid nursing a grudge, and simply put the person in question out of his mind. This, too, requires an effort which has, in turn, cost something.

He has always been an extremely robust man. He eats well, and drinks what he feels like drinking. He has simple tastes – a thick soup, with a bit of sausage in it, potato-cakes, a dish of pork and sauerkraut – although he appreciates good cooking and interesting dishes too. He has always drunk plenty of beer, and sometimes needs something stronger. Journalism induces drinking – part of the process of filling in long hours of waiting, of strain or of hard work at times of the day and night when most people can relax. Brandt has never ceased, basically, to be a journalist and a worrier, to keep his eyes open and his ear cocked, to live every moment with awareness and interest in using his brain. The journalist eats and drinks on a pattern that the average citizen might regard as singular, because he needs to keep his mind at work.

One high-ranking Allied official in Berlin,[2] who knew Brandt well when the Wall was built, noted that he 'worked long hours, took little or no physical exercise, at times drank too much beer, and when I last saw him, was putting on too much weight. This physical deterioration did not seem to detract from his intellectual ability.'* Brandt's former secretary[3] would have contested a deterioration and regarded it as 'absurd' that his eating and drinking habits earned him a spate of perverse or purely bucolic criticism, even disparaging nicknames. But she was aware that he was going through a difficult period, was chronically and not just 'cyclically' depressed and had developed a degree of claustrophobia. He had a hatred of feeling fenced in, and refused treatment prescribed by his doctor because he did not want to feel dependent.† A close and lasting friend put it this way – 'There were difficult years all right. The waning of confidence in himself may have given him compulsive habits – but only for a time. He shook them off when he had to; he never really lost the capacity to discipline himself.'[4]

One close friend thought that his nadir was in 1964. He was talking much at that time of the transience of life – 'The big men all die off too quickly.'[5] Friedrich Ebert was a case in point; leading the German nation at the age of forty-eight, dead at fifty-four. Brandt's ambition, the same friend believed, was draining

---

* I had several personal interviews with Brandt at this time. I well remember his formidable appetite and his capacity for holding his alcohol. I cannot remember Brandt for one moment losing his mental concentration and not being able to answer every sort of question with total clarity and certainty.
† The treatment that had been prescribed was twice-weekly massage. Brandt had a horror of anyone fussing about him, and he probably regarded this advice of his doctor as absolutely superfluous.
  Nor was he ever ready to report sick. One of his staff in Berlin, Frau Tilli Pensel, remembers him moving through the corridors of the town hall with an expression of restrained suffering on his face. She, in a womanly way, insisted on finding out what was wrong. He had a carbuncle between the shoulder-blades, but did not intend to tell anybody. (Frau Tilli Pensel in a letter to the author.)

away. He kept repeating: 'I've got as far as I shall ever get.' Younger men would come to the fore and way should be made for them. His former secretary thought 1965 was the low point; he seemed to discard the high hopes that had been the basis for an immensely energetic life.[6] Moments of silence stretched into minutes; he brooded, though he never inflicted his troubles on others. Those who did not know him imagined that these silences indicated that he was surly, or at least 'strange'.

Yet he never lost his gift for being periodically forthcoming and an excellent companion. He was much helped by Rut, whom one Allied commandant regarded as a 'gay, vivacious and charming woman' who, however, 'in true German style kept very much in the background'.[7] Another Allied commandant found him invariably easy and friendly, with an iron self-control, at his best on informal occasions such as an evening stag-party.[8] The American ambassador in Bonn, George McGhee, called him 'a tower of strength during this period which was terminated by his departure for Bonn'.[9] Brandt, even in these difficult years, 'epitomized both for the people of Berlin, and the world, the determination of the city to survive Russian pressures; in my judgement he made a greater contribution than any other single German towards this end'. McGhee picked out his capacity for endurance as his outstanding asset; indeed he needed it, even though it was not a time of violent or dangerous pressure on Berlin and its mayor.

Finally, a tribute from a man who was to become Britain's prime minister. Harold Wilson met him in Berlin a year after the Wall went up, while visiting with a Labour Party delegation. He found him 'superb in dealing with our questions and a good deal more eloquent in the English language than some of my own team. All of our people fell for him – Nye Bevan had when he had first won an election in Berlin. It was nice to find Victor Yates, a militant pacifist, proposing the vote of thanks to Brandt on this occasion – the theme, the Wall is an outrage and an act of violence.'[10] Wilson set much store on Brandt's self-restraint, a quality that Anglo-Saxons perhaps value above any other – 'He achieves much by never banging the table and by speaking quietly. He had the gift of exercising power, at his ease; and he showed in Berlin that he had no intention of being a softie.'

Rut did most to bring her husband through these difficult years. She had an aptitude for keeping his feet on the ground and thinking in terms of people and their feelings.[11] She was proud of him; when the magazine *Quick* asked what she learnt from him she answered: 'Patience and tolerance, plenty of tolerance.'[12] She recognized Willy's periodic need to be alone; as a Norwegian she understood this ingrained male sense of independence more easily than a German housewife. She may have understood, too, what one political associate meant when he said: 'You can love your family very much, without being what is called a family man.'[13]

Brandt, at about this time, was beginning to have some trouble with his elder son, Peter. By 1964, at fifteen years old, Peter had a mind of his own. He was a lank, serious youth, who had out-grown his strength and may have felt combative as a result. Fifty years ago a boy had to be a socialist before he was twenty-one, whatever he became afterwards; today he tends to search for ideals within the 'new left'. Peter was radical and youthfully uncharitable; the magazine *Quick* described him as 'lefty and inhibited'. Probably he suffered from having a father in the public eye; he was inclined all the more to seek different views of his own. The differences with his earnest elder son were, as Brandt saw it, exaggerated – 'Apart from an initial lack of patience on my part, we have got on well together. And he's a very good student into the bargain. He never had anything to do with the tendencies to violence of the student revolt. His political views lie to the left of those that I held in my left-wing socialist youth. He thinks social democracy inadequate, and although we get on well in a personal sense, we've given up trying to convince one another politically.'[14] He once said, in reference to Peter: 'It's often harder to convince your own son than a politician.'[15] Nothing so very strange about that; it is a common experience among parents today. Brandt has pointed out that he himself, as a young man, was no pillar of the establishment. Anyway, 'You must let young people rebel sometimes – otherwise they are never going to settle down.'[16]

Peter finished well at university, became engaged to a pastor's daughter and by 1968 was very much 'back in the family fold'.[17] He never lacked humour either – when very young he asked his father why he 'didn't have a proper job, like other fathers'.[18]

Brandt's relations with his two years younger second son, Lars, have always been excellent, and with the youngest boy, Matthias, affectionate and gay. Oddly, Peter and Lars have nothing of their parents' strong features and robustly handsome good looks; Matthias as a child was the dead spit of his father, with the same vigour and ease of manner.

One or two of Brandt's remarks about family life are illustrative. 'One is not to respect the arguments and convictions of one's son the less, simply because he is young', is typical.[19] So, too: 'To be in opposition is a privilege which no one should deny to youth.' On another occasion he was more conservative: 'The democratization of the family still doesn't mean that the question of who is the father of the family is put to the vote.' He could philosophize, too – 'Youth is not a merit; seniority isn't either. My own experience suggests that youth is a credit balance, which becomes smaller every day.'

Brandt suffered no lasting harm from this difficult period. For one thing there was too much work, and work which he enjoyed and knew was worth while. It had so many facets:

> The first interesting thing about it was that it brought me into touch with major foreign policy issues, every day of the week. Then it associated me with public needs and public feeling. And one could see the results of one's efforts actually taking shape – Berlin has been really down and out, and the struggle all the way back up the hill was very visible.[20]

> Let me give you an example of the sort of thing which made the job of governing mayor exciting. Herbert Karajan, the leader of the Berlin Philharmonic Orchestra, arrived at my home one Sunday morning. He explained he could only hold the orchestra together if a new philharmonic hall was built, worthy of their work. I told him this would take a bit of time. He agreed, but – if his chaps knew that the hall was being built, they would stay on. Well, it was done; it *had* to be done. It was worth doing, anyway.

The United States government and American institutions were prepared to help Berlin. Consultations with Brandt's friend Shepard Stone resulted in the Ford Foundation channelling millions of dollars into the cultural life of the city. American money helped to reconstruct the Academy of Arts and when the

United States ambassador in Bonn, David Bruce, told him there was a handsome sum available to equip a hospital, Brandt knew that this offer must not be turned down – 'The hospital cost ten times as much as the sum which our good American friends produced at the outset. But what did that matter? American help got the whole project going; Berlin got a hospital. That was what counted.'[21]

There was occasionally time to relax, and Brandt relaxed best alone, with a rod and line, having a swim or with a good book to read. The job of mayor of Berlin entailed a terrible amount of 'representational' activity. Rut drew a very firm line below what she considered social – even a dinner at the home of one of the Allied commandants was to her a business occasion.[22] Yet Brandt and Rut could enjoy themselves at an official occasion too. Shepard Stone recalls a Berlin press ball where there was considerable gaiety. It was helped by Stone giving ten out of the twenty tickets that he had bought for the tombola to Rut, as a small return to his charming hostess. With one of them she won the first prize, a new Volkswagen car! Was it appropriate for the 'first lady' of Berlin to keep it? With great good sense Rut decided it was; she kept the new Volkswagen and gave her old one away.[23]

The greatest strain of all, according to Brandt, was 'to have to talk to people all the time, sort out their problems, encourage them by giving them a picture which often had to be a little better than was really the case. I used to say to my friends – each year I am five years older. One of them, Rolf Schwedler, asked: What's to happen to your family, if you drop dead? I had to make a joke of that, but I'm not sure he meant it that way.'[24]

Certainly he was able to see the results of his work since 1957. A couple of years after the Wall was built, the *Manchester Guardian* had this to say:

Under the inspiring leadership of the Governing Mayor, Willy Brandt, Berlin is changing its face with the ingenuous facility of a debutante. The great gaps in the Kurfürstendamm have almost all been filled, with new hotels, office-blocks and flats. Schloss Charlottenburg has been restored to its pristine splendour. The Dahlem picture gallery is being rehoused in the new National Gallery in the Tiergarten. The Reichstag has

risen out of the ruins to which it was reduced by the Nazis. . . .
There are to be major extensions to the Free University and
the Technical University, a new City Library and a new 'cultural centre' close to the scarred and charred Potsdamer Platz.
New stretches are being added to Berlin's unique feature, the
City Autobahn, a dual carriageway network with a planned
length of 62 miles. . . . Roughly 20,000 new homes are being
built each year and the housing problems of a city which was
nearly 50 per cent destroyed during the war will be solved in
the next decade. . . . There will be nothing like a slum left in
West Berlin by 1975.[25]

There were, in the summer of 1963, two vitally important events
in Brandt's life. One was the visit to Berlin of President Kennedy
on 26 June, after three days in Cologne and Bonn as Adenauer's
guest. This visit probably ranks as the most impressive exercise in
morale-boosting in history. The prelude to it was uninspiring.
Kennedy had become increasingly aware of the need to shore up
the Allied position in West Berlin. When the Soviet foreign
minister, Gromyko, offered the West the same rights as they
would have in any 'foreign country' in October 1961, Kennedy
reputedly riposted with: 'You have offered to trade us an apple
for an orchard.'[26] In Bonn the president found Adenauer
uninterested in Berlin, and the Chancellor's speech of welcome at
dinner did not mention the division of Germany. Nor was
Kennedy impressed by Adenauer's warning that Brandt and his
friends were not reliable – that once in power they might 'do a
deal with the Russians'.[27] In private talks with Brandt, Kennedy
found agreement on policy aims and on the need to firm up the
western alliance, with the United States playing an even bigger
role than before.*

Kennedy's Berlin visit was dramatic. Wherever he went he was
greeted by huge, wildly cheering crowds and he found the right
words for them. The climax was the vast demonstration in front of
the Schoeneberg town hall. Kennedy could not begin speaking
for nearly five minutes, so great was the tumult of cheering. But

---

* Kennedy was to mention to Brandt the fact that Adenauer had warned him
against the SPD and the party's candidate for the chancellorship. Brandt's
answer to Kennedy was: 'Don't take that too badly. If you only knew how many
Americans the old gentleman has already warned me against!' (Heli Ihlefeld,
Willy Brandt. Anekdotisch [Munich 1968] p. 67).

the end of his speech brought possibly the greatest crescendo in the city's history, when he said: 'All free people, wherever they may live, are citizens of this city of West Berlin, and because of that I am proud as a free man to be able to say: *"Ich bin ein Berliner".'* Brandt too received a big reception, but Adenauer cut a restrained, even sorry figure. The Berliners had not forgiven him his poor performance in 1961, when the Wall went up.

Five months later Kennedy was dead. In a personal message to Brandt his brother, Robert, wrote, 'He loved Berlin.' In Brandt's view,[28] Kennedy did much to shake Europeans out of their apathy. His policy of Atlantic partnership and dynamic search for peace were far preferable to the alternatives – inaction, or a relapse into cold war. Brandt felt that the philosophy of the 'new frontier' set a limit on self-satisfaction, the inner enemy of the western world. Kennedy, in his view, instituted a third round in East–West relations; the fourth lay ahead, in which there would have to be a diplomatic follow-up to the co-existence that Kennedy accepted.

Kennedy was mourned in Berlin with deep and sincere grief. Yet at least one prominent American observer felt that the president did not fully appreciate the nature of the Berlin problem.[29] Nor should one forget that American–German relations went through difficult times during Kennedy's first two years in office. There were disagreements over arms policy, over offset arrangements to cover the foreign exchange costs of Allied forces in Germany, over American pledges of support. Adenauer lamented the dead secretary of state, John Foster Dulles, and in Bonn the whizz-kids among Kennedy's advisers were distrusted as opportunists and intellectual gymnasts.

One of Kennedy's principal services to Europe was to encourage untiring re-examination of foreign policies. Those of the western powers had become atrophied and defensive. British diplomacy withdrew into a hedgehog position, of defending Allied rights in Berlin, access to it and the freedom and viability of West Berlin.[30] In Bonn, Adenauer fell back on his 'ten-finger system'.[31] His 'western policy' comprised European integration, friendship with France and the United States and loyalty to Nato. His eastern policy consisted of four-power responsibility for Germany, the empty dogma of 'reunification in freedom', the Hallstein Doctrine, which implied no relations with states recognizing the DDR and rejection of any diplomatic initiative in Central Europe. The result of this static defence was that 'the gulf between the two parts of Germany is steadily widening, not just because the fences are getting higher and the minefields deadlier. Politically, socially and economically, the German Democratic Republic and the Federal Republic are growing further apart. . . . With every year the outlook for German reunification appears dimmer.'[32]

Brandt had already considered a new, constructive approach to the problems posed by Germany's division between two world blocs. So had others, among them Dr Gerhard Schroeder, the CDU foreign minister in Adenauer's 1961 cabinet. Schroeder was preaching a 'foreign policy of the possible'[33] – entailing reappraisal of existing policies, close co-operation with the Federal Republic's western partners, persistent pressure for better living conditions for the East Germans and explaining the virtues of this to the Soviet Union. All this was sound enough and Schroeder claimed that there was a wide measure of agreement with the SPD opposition and that the time could be ripe for a bipartisan foreign policy.[34] Schroeder's sound and forthright views must have worried Adenauer, unused to his foreign minister speaking his own mind. The chancellor remained obsessed by the fear of being accused of selling the pass to the Communists, and related this fear to party politics. The combination he feared was that of the SPD, FDP, the refugee vote and Christian trade unionists. The danger of losing a trick to the poker-faced Russians was such that he preferred not to play a card at all. He was afraid of offending his western partners and reawakening their dread of a second Rapallo. The Rapallo Treaty of April 1922 between Germany and the Soviet Union had become closely associated in the minds of western statesmen with the Hitler–Stalin Pact of August 1939.[35] Rapallo had, in theory, given the Weimar Republic the chance of playing off East against West. However unreal such a possibility was in the 1960s, Adenauer wanted at all costs to avoid arousing western suspicion.

Brandt was less inhibited; he had discussed new lines of thought with his closest adviser in Berlin, Egon Bahr. His own views would continue to be astonishingly consistent. According to one historian, the most important of them were the maintenance

of a strong western alliance, an assured position within it for the
Federal Republic and a maximum American contribution to it;
the improvement of relations with Eastern Europe, including the
Soviet Union; and readiness to negotiate with the Soviet Union
and even the DDR, while never renouncing the German right of
self-determination.[36] Brandt had no illusions about the Soviet
interpretation of co-existence, which was 'not peaceful but
militant'.

Bahr agreed to act as front-runner, an unusual role. One SPD
man who knew Bahr at the time found him 'inhibited,
melancholy, not at all sure of himself – save in his thinking'.[37] In
a conference organized by the Evangelical Academy at Tutzing
on 15 July 1963, Bahr enunciated the new version of *Wandel
durch Annäherung* – roughly, change by means of mutual
approach. He couched it in theoretical terms, but his meaning
was plain – the German question could not be solved by a single,
sudden agreement, but only as part of a slow process of East–
West rapprochement. The Soviet Union held the key to agreement, which could come only by means of small steps. The
Soviet Union would not allow East Germany to be 'torn away';
East Germany could be 'transformed' only with Soviet approval.
The East German state's political development, Bahr went on,
lagged behind that of countries like Poland and Hungary.
Ulbricht clung to power, not in spite of being the 'last Stalinist'
but because of it. Because the Red Army intervened, the East
German rising of 1953 actually consolidated Ulbricht's regime.
And since the Soviet Union bolstered up that regime, it would
have to be treated as a negotiating partner. This did not mean *de
jure* recognition – Bahr pointed out that the United States and
communist China had negotiated without recognition of Peking.
Nor was recognition of the DDR implied when a West German
citizen paid the toll on the autobahn, when a West Berlin policeman failed to return fire across the Wall or when a West German
representative negotiated the terms of a new trade agreement.
The chief task, Bahr considered, was to ease conditions of life for
the East Germans. Any improvement would help to relax
tension; any raising of living standards would be positive. For
tension strengthened Ulbricht's hand, and crisis forced the Soviet
Union to intervene. The policy of *Wandel durch Annäherung*

alone offered a straight but narrow road, to be trod with self-confidence but without illusions.

Brandt himself wrote: 'To normalize relations between Germany and the Soviet Union is, under these [existing] circumstances, one of the most difficult tasks imaginable.'[38] The Soviet Union had to accept that it was better to enjoy reasonable relations with seventy million Germans than 'to have a few friends, who only pretend to represent seventeen million Germans'.[39] A key to the realization of worthwhile co-existence was that the whole western alliance understood what part it had to play. He foresaw, as he put it in his own speech in Tutzing, 'no ideological co-existence, but only ideological confrontation'.[40] There would continue to be 'an equilibrium of fear' and a situation of 'no war, but no peace'. He went on: 'The problem is to stabilize the *status quo* in a military sense, in order to secure the necessary freedom of manoeuvre for the political conquest of the *status quo*.' It was necessary to overcome 'immobility' and 'ideological trench warfare'.

Brandt further developed this theme in speeches at Scarborough and Washington, where he addressed Americans for Democratic Action. At Scarborough he pointed out that military détente was useful, but the elimination of root causes of political tension was more important. The Soviet Union had to be convinced, by a unified western alliance, that a real change lay in its own interest. Nor should one regard this task as insuperable and therefore not worth embarking upon – the Soviet Union was itself subject to the processes of change, and 'the grandchildren of Khrushchev may possibly still call themselves communists, but in practice be nothing of the kind'. In Washington he made it plain that the pursuit of détente did not mean abandoning basic principles; the most fundamental were human rights and the collective self-determination of the community.

Détente, in the view of Brandt and Bahr, was not a 'soft' or supine policy. It offered a better chance of victory on the political battlefield than mere inaction. Brandt's phrase, 'better small steps than big leaps,'[41] indicated persistent effort to secure change. This was complementary to Schroeder's 'policy of the possible'. Adenauer, due to retire in October 1963, had begun to talk about working to help the East Germans, while one of his most promising lieutenants, Rainer Barzel, coined the phrase 'change through activation'. CDU views on an all-German policy were not stagnating, but they were becoming more sharply divided. Schroeder and his supporters wanted a policy of movement; Strauss and the so-called 'Gaullist' wing favoured a passive West German role while the western alliance planned to 'Europeanize' the German question. In spite of his incredible staying-power, Adenauer was just too old to embark on a new eastern policy. Years before, in 1953, he had told Ollenhauer that his work would be done only when 'a settlement is reached with the East which will fit into the over-all framework of my policies'.[42] In 1963 the reins were slipping from his hands and the risks involved in proclaiming a new policy seemed too great. The electorate had been fed on dogmas for too long, and a majority of the CDU preferred the prospect of isolating the DDR. Yet ironically, a DDR that felt itself isolated would become increasingly dependent on the Soviet Union.

The replacement of Adenauer by Erhard brought no real change in CDU foreign policy.* The Strauss faction remained adamant that close relations with satellite regimes in Eastern Europe were pointless, as long as they slavishly supported Moscow's German policy. Strauss and another right-winger, Baron von Guttenberg, insisted that the Federal Republic's true allies in Eastern Europe were its downtrodden peoples, not its rulers – although it was not clear how the Federal Republic should establish contact with the former. The Erhard government was hamstrung by internal division in the CDU, by Adenauer's malicious sniping at his former minister of economics, by social malaise and growing economic difficulties. Erhard did not feel strong enough to take a major initiative, which even a 'policy of small steps' entailed. Much was being written about the advent of 'polycentrism' – the East European satellites, supposedly, were developing minds of their own. There was a comfortable theory that the Federal Republic need only sit

---

* Adenauer's departure produced a note of comedy when he visited Berlin on 10 October to say goodbye to the city. In a valedictory speech Brandt made pointed reference to Adenauer's failure to come to Berlin when the Wall went up -- 'At one particular moment we really did miss the federal chancellor.' Adenauer had not the slightest intention of expressing regret, let alone of admitting himself to have been in the wrong. So in his answer he claimed that the notes he had made during Brandt's speech were illegible; as a result he made no reference whatever to the content of the speech!

and watch a process of fragmentation, relying on its economic strength and commercial connections with Eastern Europe to encourage the momentum of change.

Brandt was at least able to take a limited initiative. For more than two years the people of West and East Berlin had been totally cut off from one another. Friends and neighbours were torn apart. So were families, and even newly-weds who had not yet bought a home found themselves on opposite sides of the Wall. So did courting couples. The building of the Wall made it impossible for West Berliners to set foot in East Berlin, while East Berliners had only the option of risking their lives in order to get into West Berlin, knowing they could never return to their homes. On the evening of 5 December 1963, Brandt received a letter from the government of the DDR, suggesting that a form of limited and restricted *Laissez-passer* for West Berliners might be introduced. Brandt acted with the despatch that the Western allies could well have emulated. He informed the Federal Government on the same day; the Allied commandants received his memorandum on 6 December. Brandt sent his representative, Dr Leopold, to East Berlin on the afternoon of 6 December. There were talks between Berlin, Bonn and representatives of the western powers on 7, 9 and 10 December. They cleared the way for further negotiations between East and West Berlin, which ended on 17 December. The upshot was an agreement under which West Berliners were allowed visits to East Berlin over Christmas, which the East Germans limited to eighteen days. During that time 1,200,000 visits were paid to East Berlin by West Berliners. A quarter of a million West Berliners made at least one trip.[43]

Brandt pointed out that thousands of East Germans from outside Berlin had flocked into the city during the eighteen-day period of grace. Nor did the agreement damage Berlin's status, or imply surrender to a false ideal of co-existence; it opened the way for similar ones in the immediate future, although not a real breakthrough to détente. The East German regime would continue to insist on its own recognition as a prerequisite to more far-reaching concessions; no West German government was prepared to grant this for the time being. Nor did the West Berliners favour it: in a public opinion poll in January 1964 79 per cent said they would reject a new pass-agreement if it entailed recognition of the DDR, while only 8 per cent would have accorded recognition. Yet nine out of ten wanted further agreements negotiated. The East German regime would make no further concession; in 1964 for instance, it rejected even a limited exchange of newspapers between the two German states. The Ulbricht regime still regarded the truthful written word as a deadly enemy. One small achievement in the field of inner-German détente at this period was the ransoming of eight hundred political prisoners from East Germany in 1964 for a sum of money that has never been specified. Another 1,800 East German political prisoners were ransomed in 1965–6.

There were at least signs of the beginnings of détente in relations between the Federal Republic and East European satellites other than the DDR. The Federal Republic established trade missions with Poland, Hungary and Roumania in 1963, with Bulgaria in 1964. But the western powers had no clear idea what they wanted from détente and were not prepared to give it sufficient backing. In his last years in office Adenauer had sometimes spoken of the need to make Nato a unified organism, with a political as well as military content. But Nato remained weakest where it needed to be strongest, on the ground in Europe, especially in Germany. In 1950 Nato's land forces in Europe were planned to total seventy to eighty divisions. By 1953 its land forces were visualized only as a shield of thirty divisions. In reality its strength fell far short of even this modest target, although the Soviet Union and its satellites mustered 150 to 200 divisions for a European war. One founder of Nato, Paul Henri Spaak, remarked 'There was something moving, but also something almost pitiful in this alliance between countries which had emerged exhausted from a ruthless war.'[44]

By 1963 Nato was losing impetus and sense of purpose. As one commentator put it: 'If an alliance is to prosper, its strength *as an alliance* should grow. This is demonstrably not so with Nato.'[45] The Alliance failed to decide on joint control of nuclear weapons, size of conventional forces or joint weapons production. In addition, France was deliberately obstructing unity of action, while Britain failed to give a lead in Europe – an essential requisite if President Kennedy's idea of 'twin pillars' of Nato in Europe and America were to be realized. Nato's failure to build a truly effective military alliance has continued ever since. The same commentator saw the organization three years later as 'tormented, bewildered, even bemused'.[46] In a badly needed critique he wrote that Nato ministers met in Brussels to find out if Nato actually existed. All sense of direction and volition had gone. De Gaulle was dismantling the alliance, while the British foreign secretary 'cut an invisible figure'. Nato was becoming palpably second-rate: 'They are all nice men, Mr Rusk, Mr Stewart and the rest. But they are appallingly dull. They have been reading the briefs of their officials so long that the grey print has entered their souls.' This criticism was amply justified. Nato continued to exist only because there was no alternative.

Thoughts about Nato are relevant to the story of postwar Germany and Willy Brandt's part in it. The foreign policy that the SPD was developing towards Eastern Europe, under Brandt's guidance, was inextricably linked with the consolidation of the western alliance. A German initiative in the East–West confrontation had to be approved, understood and backed by the Nato powers. Brandt understood this and remained totally committed to Nato. The discreet pursuit of détente was no contradiction.

In December 1963 Erich Ollenhauer died; he had served the SPD with immense dedication but little flair. In January 1964 Brandt was nominated his successor as party chairman, in addition to being its candidate for the chancellorship in the 1965 elections. He could consolidate his shadow cabinet – two notable additions were Karl Schiller, soon to become federal minister of economics, and Helmut Schmidt, replacing Erler as the party's defence expert – and work out policies and tactics for the 1965 elections. Elections in 1964 in several *Länder* showed a swing to the SPD; at last the SPD looked as if they might break through the 'political sound barrier'[47] of a 40 per cent share of the national poll.

In 1964 and 1965 Brandt covered the length and breadth of the country, explaining the SPD's role. His case was that the party had borne the brunt of the spiritual struggle of the workers against communist doctrine; had worked out how a modern industrial society should function; had played a signficant part in the *Länder;* had spearheaded the struggle for Berlin; finally, had worked hard and with success in parliamentary opposition in Bonn. They did not need to be ashamed of their record. In one speech after another he showed his knowledge of social problems. He was acutely aware of the need for better communications and town planning, of problems of noise and pollution, the overall environmental scene and the last remnants of the problem – in West Germany's affluent society – of poverty. What had to be done was to develop the assets of the nation, the abilities and skills of its citizens, its towns and villages and its countryside. The Federal Republic had become a model state, not based on sleepy welfarism and material comfort but on a true sense of values in life. Brandt believed that the party could lead sixty million inhabitants of the free part of Germany into the last quarter of this century.

He spelled this out at the Karlsruhe party conference of the SPD in November 1964. In his concluding speech he spoke of his hopes for the 1965 elections. Victory was not yet sure; but the SPD had a real chance of winning – 'that depends today very largely on us'. He referred to Herbert Wehner as the 'many-cylindered motor of our party'; he would deal with every question of organization. In spite of his rough edges, Wehner had won his way to the hearts of many German socialists. Bringing the record of achievement up to date, Brandt pointed out that the SPD had collaborated in the ratification of the nuclear test-ban treaty, had secured the preamble to the Franco–German Treaty of Friendship in 1963 and played the principal part in promoting the creation of German missions in East European countries and in negotiating two 'pass agreements' for Berlin in 1963 and 1964. On the pass agreements Brandt's view was: 'Alleviations for human beings are no substitute for a far-reaching all-German policy. But by helping people, one is helping the nation.'[48] Some weeks later he repeated his all-German precept: 'Small steps are better than big words.'[49]

The second 'pass agreement', of 23 September 1964, was a useful lead-up to the Karlsruhe party conference. The 1963 agreement had enabled West Berliners to cross into East Berlin during an eighteen-day period; the 1964 agreement provided for authorized crossing at Christmas 1964 and at Easter and Whitsun 1965. In addition East German old-age pensioners could visit West Berlin for several weeks at a time – Walter Ulbricht could spare them from the DDR's overstretched and undergeared economy. West Berlin's own output doubled between 1961 and 1965. Huge contributions were made by the Federal Republic and the United States. There were grants to major electrical industries, Siemens, Borsig, AEG and Telefunken; money was poured into the consumer goods industries; cultural aid extended from new libraries and concert halls to the impressive 'student village' of the Free University; a children's air-lift operated to the North Sea coast and the mountains of West Germany. The hardihood of the Berliners, and the imagination of their government, ensured that these projects prospered.

Berlin's appearance changed: 'Nature has covered the ashes with flowers. Trees have grown tall in the Tiergarten. The Trümmerberg (literally, rubble hill) is green with pine and shrub. People have rebuilt stone on stone, so that by their works they might redeem and remake a place where children can play and young men can learn to live in hope and dignity.'[50] Berlin was moving steadily ahead and its governing mayor and the SPD took a lion's share of the credit. The only discordant note was struck by the students. There were strikes on the campus of the Free University and leftist proposals for a 'synthesis' between the East and West German political and social systems. Like their fellows at other universities, these students held radical, if largely unfledged views. In isolated, embattled Berlin they seemed oddly out of place.

The Erhard government and the CDU were girding themselves for the 1965 federal elections. The portly, cigar-puffing and comfortably friendly Erhard was making a generally good impression on the electorate. Adenauer's iron control had been replaced by rule by cabinet consensus. It seemed to work well enough. Erhard's strength lay in his fundamental decency, readiness to compromise, outward-looking economic philosophy, the excellent relations that he and Gerhard Schroeder established with the Anglo-Saxon nations and his ability to decentralize. Erhard's weaknesses were an ingenuous approach to foreign affairs, surprising sensitivity to criticism[51] and a total lack of political killer-instinct. Yet he could show real strength of purpose – he informed de Gaulle in July 1964 that he placed the highest value on America's friendship, and managed in November

1964 to reduce the exorbitantly high grain prices fixed by the Common Market Six.

Erhard suffered from his so-called allies. De Gaulle was in the process of taking France out of Nato, sniping continually at the Americans and barring Britain's way into Europe. Adenauer's performance was worse: he made slighting remarks about Erhard to all and sundry, criticized him vitriolicly in newspaper interviews and snubbed him in the Bundestag. There were other clouds on the horizon for Erhard: the right-wingers in the CDU were growing unco-operative, his FDP coalition partners were worried by the 'lethal embrace' of so eminently liberal a chancellor and the leader of the Bavarian branch of the CDU, Franz-Josef Strauss, sulked like Achilles in his tents, following his disgrace at the end of 1962 for his murky part in the persecution of the weekly *Der Spiegel*.

The public remained impressed by Erhard's *bonhomie*, unruffled calm, and the atmosphere of bourgeois prosperity that he radiated. Yet Willy Brandt went into the 1965 election campaign with high hopes. He believed that the SPD had, at last, the right programme to become the strongest single party and an unexpendable partner in the next government coalition.[52] The programme was drawn up at the party conference in Karlsruhe in November 1964. In foreign policy it supported the Atlantic Alliance, further European integration, the Franco–German Treaty, even closer friendship with Britain and Italy, reappraisal of East–West relations. In domestic policy the SPD 'thoroughly approved' the social market economy of successive CDU governments and private property rights. In 1949 they were the legatee of 'logical' Marxism, including class warfare, control of the basic means of production and government by and for the proletariat. Now, in 1964, they adopted the middle-of-the-road economic philosophy developed under Adenauer's unseeing eye and Erhard's inspired direction.

The Karlsruhe programme threw out useful social ideas, more equitable division of property, savings for the lower income groups, 'mixed' investment companies in which these workers' savings could be employed, better working conditions in factories that were already the most modern in Europe, phased educational reform, special aid for old-age pensioners and young marrieds and attention to the problems of the environment. None of this could be faulted; nor could such economic precepts as the maintenance of stable prices, balanced incomes and full employment. A tail-piece to the Karlsruhe programme drew attention to weaknesses in the Bundeswehr and proposed remedies. A socialist party discerning on such matters is, indeed, singularly enlightened.

The framers of the Karlsruhe programme – chief among them Willy Brandt and Herbert Wehner – showed courage and prescience. Brandt recognized that an economic system that functions successfully must not be disrupted. It required prescience to rely on honesty and common sense. The SPD went into the 1965 elections as a politically mature and adult party. In the late autumn of 1964 they were ahead in the public opinion polls for the first time in postwar history. By April 1965 the polls disagreed: Emnid showed the SPD ahead, Allensbach the CDU. The polls also showed how ill-informed the electorate was: 65 per cent did not know what the basic law of the federal constitution was, 35 per cent had never heard of the CSU (Christian Social Union) Bavarian Branch of the CDU and 41 per cent did not realize that the SPD had radically revised its former Marxist programme. Still, the polls had their own impact; Rainer Barzel, one of the most promising younger CDU leaders, began by May to talk about the possibility of a big coalition with the SPD. Another factor in the SPD's favour was the agreement at the beginning of 1965 to limit election expenses. The SPD and FDP were not to spend more than £1,335,000, while the CDU could spend up to £1,100,000 and their CSU Bavarian branch up to £356,000. The preponderant power of the purse, hitherto on the CDU's side, had at least been curtailed.

Early in 1965 an unusual sort of political ally appeared on Brandt's side in the shape of the novelist Günther Grass, author of *The Tin Drum, Dog Years* and other bestsellers. Grass launched his literary friends, including Heinrich Böll and Rolf Hochhuth, into the fray with such slogans as 'The job of a citizen is to keep his mouth open', and 'I live and pay taxes in Germany and not on Parnassus'. He organized his own election tour on Brandt's behalf, charging entrance fees as an entertainer, collecting 29,000 people at his meetings and over 14,000 marks from them. Witty, irreverent and the declared enemy of the CDU establishment, Grass paraded his panache and his banana moustache to some effect. But he and his friends were a trifle too exotic for the sober electorate. Erhard's counter-attacks were superfluous. On 10 July he said in Düsseldorf: 'I must call these poets by their name; duffers and Philistines who dare to pass judgement on things they simply don't understand.'[53]

The average voter probably agreed with Erhard. Nor was he flattered by Hochhuth comparing the German worker with the slaves who built the pyramids. The German worker had a much better opinion of himself than that. There was an element of gimmickry about Brandt's campaign, too. The SPD mobilized eighteen young writers in Berlin who drafted speeches and coined slogans for a 'nominal' payment of $2½ an hour in what became known as 'Willy's campaign office'.[54] Berlin cabaret performers – in the van, Günther Neumann and the *Insulaner* – appeared on Brandt's platform. So did, incongruously, the French singer, Sacha Distel. Party workers 'spontaneously' presented Brandt with symbolic gifts – a Ruhr miner's lamp, a bricklayer's tools and, in one place, a less obviously symbolic live chicken.[55] The *Guardian's* Bonn correspondent thought that Brandt had been projected as 'the poor man's Kennedy'.[56] The French paper, *Le Monde*, called him '*Spartacus embourgeoisé*'.[57] Such criticisms affected the German voter less than the widely publicized fact that Brandt's sixteen-year-old son, Peter, had signed a communist-sponsored manifesto attacking American policy in Vietnam. Peter withdrew his signature at the end of August, but the damage had been done.

The political tide ebbed and flowed. In June the SPD vote in the Saar elections rose by 10 per cent and in local elections in August in North Rhine-Westphalia the SPD beat the CDU for the first time, with 46 against 43 per cent. The statistical picture seemed to favour the SPD; one London newspaper pointed out that in the previous four years the SPD had gained one and a half million voters in *Land* and local elections, while the CDU had lost two and a half million.[58] *The Times* forecast a swing to the SPD. In previous elections there had been some external threat – the East German rising in 1953, the Hungarian and Middle East crises only recently over in 1957, the Berlin Wall just built in 1961. But in 1965 – nothing of the kind![59] Just a year earlier the correspondent of the *Atlantic Monthly* flatly forecast a different result – 'The Christian Democrats will emerge stronger than ever at the 1965 Federal Election.'[60] His reasons – that the German economic miracle was more solidly based than the booms in France and Italy, and the establishment gave the German public the three things it most desired: order, prosperity, security.

Brandt was an immensely active campaigner. The London *Observer* described his style – 'Willy Brandt stands very straight before his audiences. His legs are planted apart, he wears a dark raincoat and a tightly wound dark scarf, and a little briefcase is tucked under his arm. He radiates strong authority but also some mystery; he is no television star, but the "man from headquarters".'[61] *The Times* found him 'youthful, handsome, hail-fellow-well-met and fired by boundless energy'.[62] His audiences were more sluggish than he wished, though they occasionally rose to his direct but always rational speeches. At one station on a whistle-stop tour a supporter asked him to autograph a 20-mark note, then told the crowd: 'I'll never cash this as long as I live.'

In an interview with the *New York Times* he laid a heavy emphasis on a German peace settlement – he was prepared to start a dialogue with the Soviet Union if there were parallel four-power negotiations, he would consider reciprocal troop reductions in Europe, and he thought even an 'Austrian solution' for Germany possible, giving freedom, unity and neutrality.[63] He hinted at the need for an all-party government to promote a settlement and he urged political awareness – the Federal Republic was 'a giant economically, but politically a dwarf'. In one speech after another he repeated his demand for a German peace treaty and criticized the CDU for diplomatic immobility.

Certain factors were telling against Brandt. CDU propaganda depicted the SPD and the British Labour Party as political twins. Much was made of Labour's record of failure in office. At Dortmund on 8 August Erhard spoke of a law of nature that socialist government in large European countries brought increased risks for the national economy and currency. More important was the part played in the campaign by ex-chancellor Adenauer. While not for a moment burying the hatchet in his feud with Erhard, Adenauer ignored him and turned his fire on the SPD. He was still a more effective campaigner than any other German politician, drawing huge crowds and captivating them with his subtle mingling of flattery, irony and self-congratulation.

A major difficulty for the SPD was that of producing obvious alternatives to the main points of the CDU programme. The most-used CDU slogan was *'Unsere Sicherheit'*, our security. The SPD produced *'Sicher ist sicher – darum SPD'* ('Sure is sure – therefore SPD'). This was not inventive. Brandt was worried by the number of don't knows disclosed by opinion polls; these were people who thought most of all about security. And what could be more secure than Erhard, the sturdy 'locomotive' pulling the CDU bandwagon along? The SPD talked of a better road to prosperity, but prosperity was already very much there. Unemployment was down to under 100,000; there were 730,000 vacant jobs. Exports were 10 per cent up on the 1964 figures and hourly earnings were up by $11\frac{1}{2}$ per cent. There were 1,300,000 foreign workers in the country to do the dirty jobs and Erhard's election message was that 'only a combination of proven economic genius and the diligence of the German people can guarantee continued prosperity'.[64] Erhard boasted of his role in rescuing the pound sterling and underlined the woes of the people of Britain under a socialist regime.

Brandt questioned CDU insistence on no experiments: 'The antithesis of "no experiments" is not "experiments at all cost", but "no dread of experiments". This is the guiding principle of our policy.'[65] True enough, but the electorate was unimpressed. The popular image of the SPD, moreover, was unexciting. Years earlier Brandt had told his old Norwegian friend, Martin Tranmäl, that the SPD had become respectable, and Tranmäl countered with 'too respectable'.[66] What most Germans saw in the SPD was a party without profile, with a distinct family resemblance to the CDU but without its record of solid achievement. Brandt was himself to say to Sweden's prime minister, Tage Erlander, that perhaps the party was 'too boring'.[67] Then there was the vicious slander campaign against Brandt. Placards carried the words: 'We shall not vote for traitors to our country' – a reference to his supposed service against Nazi Germany in Norwegian uniform. During the summer he had to bring legal proceedings against Lothar Brenner, a journalist who claimed that he had betrayed Germany. He had to pursue seemingly unending libel actions against Dr Kapfinger, the Passau publisher, against the Catholic weekly's *Bild Post* and the Custos publishing house in Essen. The old, stale, untrue stories were trotted out – that he had 'deserted' his country and people, fought against them, fired on fellow Germans, reviled decent German citizens in the hour of defeat. The *Frankfurter Rundschau* published one cartoon that showed him being ordered out of Germany by Nazi officialdom and, below, being castigated as an 'emigrant' by federal officialdom in the shape of exactly the same man, behind the same desk, only having shed his swastika armband.

On 18 September 1965 Brandt said in Lübeck that his party were a 'chest's breadth in front'. The next day the West Germans went to the polls; Günther Grass was pelted with rotten fruit and his flat was set on fire. This may have been an omen, for the CDU emerged as an easy victor. Their vote was up from 14.4 to 15.5 million, although their seats in the Bundestag increased from 242 to only 245. Their share of the poll was up from 45.3 to 47.6 per cent. The SPD too, had gained, with 39.3 against 36.2 per cent, 202 against 190 Bundestag seats and a vote of 12.8 million against 11.4 million. But it was not enough: all that could be said was that the CDU had failed to get an overall majority in the Bundestag. The balance was still held by the FDP with 49 seats, enough to form a coalition with either main party.

Brandt did not try to conceal his disappointment. In a newspaper interview he said 'I don't intend to talk round the point. The SPD has not achieved its election target.'[68] He was disgusted with the smear tactics used against him and he announced his return to Berlin, hinting that he might retire completely from federal German politics. A severe internal crisis for the SPD and a possible change of leadership were predicted. The public opinion pollsters had boobed – they had shown the two big parties running neck and neck at the end. Members of the intelligentsia who sought to strike an honest blow for progress had made no impact on the electorate, and were now all the more ready to denounce it for its servility. Finally, Adenauer was incensed by Erhard's personal success and by the CDU doing better than under his own leadership four years earlier. Years later Brandt gave this summing-up of the 1965 elections:

Of course, we had hoped to do better than in 1961; but not vastly better. Although Adenauer was no longer leading the other side, Erhard was very popular and his popularity was actually increasing at the time of the election. In his own field of action he had not put a foot wrong; he was on the crest of the wave and his real difficulties were to come later.

We gained three per cent more of the vote. That was not too bad. For me personally the worst thing was the truly depressing way in which the campaign was fought. It was far, far worse than in 1961. This was why I did say I would go back to Berlin, maybe leave Federal politics. I wanted to stay on, however, as SPD chairman. But I began to wonder if I was the right person to lead in an election campaign – was I a liability to my party? This was why I said at the time that I did not want to run as candidate for the Chancellorship again.[69]

There was a tendency at this time to write off Brandt as nothing more than an able, industrious and popular mayor of Berlin. One historian, writing just after the 1965 elections, said:

Herr Brandt, who looks like becoming a German Stevenson rather than a German Kennedy, has decided not to lead the SPD at a third election. He has decided that his period of emigration – ruthlessly attacked by the CDU – will for ever be held against him. . . . Herr Brandt's defeat is a personal tragedy for a man who has done more to sustain his country's honour than the entire Federal Cabinet.

For all Brandt's smooth talking, his statesman's hat, savoir-faire and American-style organization he remains, in his person if not in his policies, in the tradition of good old social democracy; a man of humble origin who as a very young man was fired by ideals rather than merely by ambition, a young man who could no doubt have made his peace with Nazism but who preferred the precarious existence of an emigrant.[70]

These passages had the authentic ring of a political obituary.

So Brandt returned to Berlin to lick his wounds. Since 1961 he had led in two elections and the SPD vote had risen 3 per cent in each, from a base of 33 to 39 per cent. He has since admitted that he could scarcely have hoped to put his party on top during these four years; but he made a coalition with the FDP a statistical possibility and he induced leading members of the CDU, including the president of the Bundestag, Eugen Gerstenmaier, to discuss seriously the prospect of a 'big' coalition of the two main parties.[71] He and Wehner created a good electoral team and an election programme that was down to earth and progressive. After the defeat Wehner said that he had turned the party's 'unguarded flank', foreign policy, into one that was safely protected.[72] From now on foreign policy concepts were to remain entirely consistent. The West was to be strengthened and unified in order to check Soviet expansionism. This, in turn, meant the fullest degree of American involvement in Europe. The Federal Republic had to play a full part in the western economic and military system. The German right of self-determination must not be surrendered, but relations with Eastern Europe could be explored and improved and there could be a readjustment of East–West all-German relations by negotiation.

The CDU/FDP coalition in Bonn settled down again under Erhard in an atmosphere in which contentment was limited by the first forebodings of approaching economic recession. Brandt had two preoccupations – the organization of the party and administering Berlin. For the next months he was to spend less time in Bonn than at any stage during the previous decade. The SPD were overcome by a mood of lethargy after the election failure and the party conference in Dortmund in June 1966 was expected to pass quietly. Instead, the radicals attacked the 'bourgeois' tendencies of the leadership and warned against a breach between party and trade unions Brandt rose to the occasion; there was a wave of new confidence and sense of purpose, and he was re-elected chairman by an overwhelming 324 out of 326 votes. This was the biggest ever vote of confidence in an SPD chairman, and it was followed up by a striking SPD success in the North Rhine-Westphalia *Land* elections in July. This result later had important consequences on the federal level, for it showed very plainly that the SPD was moving ahead again after the set-back in the 1965 elections.

Berlin presented no new problems, but Brandt had to take the reins firmly in his hands again, after an enforced absence due to electioneering, and he had to reassess Berlin's position and potential in the light of a changing international situation. This was not an easy task.

In the first place, West Berlin was managing to become more normal, in a material sense. According to one contemporary account: 'Today, Berlin's fashion-houses set the pace for West Germany; Berlin is the centre of the nation's food-processing, printing and electrical industries. The complex of the Siemens electrical combine has become the biggest single concentration of industry in Germany.'[73] The city's exports had quadrupled in under ten years; in a decade and a half, 280,000 new homes had been built; more than one hundred thousand West Germans had come to Berlin to live and work; the Reichstag had risen from the ruins.

More important, West Berlin was under less pressure than before. One ocular symptom might be regarded as negative; the Wall itself had been 'modernized', with lawns and flower-beds and with the regime offering prizes for 'new look' blueprints, in a competition entitled *moderne Grenze* – up-to date frontiers. Rubble and rusty barbed wire were tidied away, machine-gun posts camouflaged, and the People's Police were instructed to make routine patrols with aggressive Alsatian dogs look like pleasant promenades to give 'the people's own Fido' his fun and exercise.

Since the Christmas 1964 pass-agreements a million visits were being made by West Berliners to East Berlin at Easter, Whitsun and Christmas, and about three hundred thousand East German old-age pensioners had holidayed in the West. The DDR continued to release political prisoners for whom ransoms were paid. In January 1966 the DDR sent a delegation to Bonn from its newly formed Council for All-German Affairs, with a six-point plan that included mutual recognition of both German states, disarmament and a normalization of East–West German relations. The *Atlantic Monthly* forecast that the DDR's communist regime would survive the departure from the political stage of the septuagenarian Walter Ulbricht and would continue to operate under 'his two ablest lieutenants, fifty-three-year-old Socialist Unity Party chieftain Erich Honecker and fifty-one-year-old administrator Willi Stoph'.[74] The East German regime, miserable thing though it was, no longer felt under grievous pressure; its standard reflex action, to apply pressure against West Berlin, was no longer necessary.

Could limited and somewhat indefinite 'normalization' be exploited? Brandt would have liked to do so. On 12 October 1966 he crossed into East Berlin for five hours of talks with the Soviet ambassador to the DDR, Abrassimov. The talks could not produced concrete results, but they enhanced Brandt's prestige. A chief reason for western diplomatic failure *vis-à-vis* the Soviet Union has been an ingrained inferiority complex. Adenauer suffered from this; Brandt showed that it was utterly unecessary. The meeting with Abrassimov still constituted a severe test. It had to be justified to the government in Bonn, which automatically distrusted any approach to the Russians, and to the people of Berlin, who had more grounds for apprehension. The meeting followed a period of acute strain for Brandt. On 23 October 1966, a Sunday, he became suddenly very seriously ill. He was coughing badly, began to choke and had what West German newspapers wrongly described as a heart attack. His heart, however, was entirely sound. In his own words, this is what happened:

> The feeling of choking merged into a sensation that I was suffocating. It appears I went blue in the face; I was unconscious for a time – just how long I don't know, as I was alone in the house but for our housekeeper. She couldn't know how long either, when she found me. The doctors looked me over carefully afterwards; they couldn't find anything organically wrong, and there never has been a real explanation of what happened. I've said more than once that I think I know now what dying must be like and what the phrase 'between life and death' may mean.[75]

This curious seizure was the result of cumulative strain, spread over a considerable period. Throughout his life Willy Brandt has driven himself hard, and more than once there have been signs of intense strain having a delayed effect. He himself believes that it could be significant that this period of strain coincided with his having just passed the age of fifty: men, unlike women, have no clearly defined menopause, but they may suddenly feel their age and require to readjust.[76] This may even be beneficial – as Brandt put it: 'One may be able better to canalize one's energies, focus one's aims, become more effective than before. In a sense one may change gear, and so travel farther without needing to travel so fast. Passing a physical prime may produce mental deterioration; it doesn't need to.' In his view what happened brought a loss of sheer ambition, but not of sense of purpose. It could even have helped him to redefine his objectives.[77] Was he, in mechanical terminology, able to move into a controlled over-drive? Did his experience help to develop a more settled philosophy of political life and clear his mind for the major decisions ahead? If so, his experience was timely; important decisions had to be made within weeks.

The reason was that the Erhard government was in trouble. Four days after Brandt's brief illness the FDP left the government. They had done the same thing in the past. This time they were alarmed by looming economic recession and wanted no share of responsibility. And the good-natured and liberal chancellor was, as FDP leaders saw it, killing their party by kindness. Why should voters support the FDP when the CDU was led by a man who embodied bourgeois virtues and free-wheeling economic policies?

By the late autumn there were nearly seven hundred thousand unemployed. In comparison with the economic situation in, say, Britain, that of West Germany was healthy. But the German view of recession differed from that in other European countries. A British or a French government became worried when exports stagnated. German economists were already deeply concerned when the actual rate of growth of exports slackened. Erhard hesitated between investment incentives and minimal financial controls, and confidence in him was shaken. Yet his troubles were not economic only. Right-wing nationalism was again coming to the boil. There were plenty of unrepentant ex-Nazis left in Germany. Most of them probably respected Adenauer for his impressive and massive authority, but Erhard was a different matter, politically easy-going and modest. In 1966 a new National Democratic Party emerged as a real potential force in German politics, particularly in mainly Protestant North Germany. Their target was 'weak' government in Bonn and they collected nearly 8 per cent of the votes in the Hesse *Land* elections. They were equally successful in the Bavarian elections a little later. The new party denounced Brandt as 'the Norwegian' and Wehner as 'the traitor'. One party spokesman declared: 'As for Herr Brandt, I sat beside him on the same school bench. He may have changed his name – and his nationality – but not his nature.'[78] Brandt was less worried by personal attacks than by the new party's electoral successes. There had been, so far, only a minor economic recession; what would happen in a real economic crisis? Hesse and

Bavaria, moreover, were very different *Länder* politically; yet the new party obtained a foothold in both.[79] (In fact there was a core of unrepentant ex-Nazis in both *Länder* too.) They were even more of a worry to Erhard. His government was blamed for their appearance on the political scene; and the CDU, not the SPD, stood to lose votes to it.

On 2 November Erhard told the CDU executive that he would resign if an alternative government could be formed. On 10 November the SPD urged inter-party talks on a change of chancellor. Shortly afterwards Brandt had a long talk with Adenauer, the first since they had spent a whole day together at Adenauer's holiday home in October 1962. Adenauer was certain that Erhard must go; he envisaged a new approach to the Soviet Union – for mistakes had been made in the past in Bonn's eastern policy.[80] Inter-party consultations lasted a fortnight. Their outcome was a 'big' coalition between CDU and SPD, with the personable Kurt-Georg Kiesinger, the CDU prime minister in *Land* Baden-Württemberg, as chancellor, and Willy Brandt as foreign minister. Brandt was at first dubious about a 'big' coalition; Wehner was in favour. Even after the terms of the coalition were agreed, in principle, on 26 November, the SPD had to make their own decision. They approved only after earnest and at times heated debate.

The decision had been a difficult one for Brandt. It meant leaving Berlin.

I had been governing mayor for very nearly ten years; that's a long time. And I had acted on Suhr's behalf for about two years before that, when he was still in the job but very ill. Of course, I had to be ready to leave Berlin in 1961 and again in 1965, when I ran for the chancellorship. But what a break really means becomes clear only when it does, in fact, happen. At least, I would have no mental reservations; that's not my way.

For Rut, it was worse than for me. She had built up a whole circle of friends in Berlin. She was able to see with her own eyes what one could do for the city, and she was proud of that. We had a real home life there, too; we were really happy in Berlin.

Of course, I did say years earlier that I would leave Berlin only for Bonn, to become chancellor – because as chancellor I could do more for Berlin than as governing mayor. But in 1961 and 1965 I could not envisage any other job in Bonn than that of chancellor; nothing else was open to me. And I was thinking of the pride of the Berliners. I thought of that again in 1966, and I believed then that taking the post of foreign minister was still the right decision.[81]

He discussed two ideas of his own with his friends. The first was taking the minor post of minister for cultural affairs, the second that he should stay in Berlin, but back the new government. The advice of his friends was strongly in favour of his becoming foreign minister.[82] The SPD executive agreed.

Bonn would offer a parochial life, with no cultural milieu to compare with Berlin's wide choice of theatre, music, art and literary circles. In Bonn the politician is continuously under observation, something repellent to a man of Brandt's independent character. Bonn is an inflated hick-town of endless political tittle-tattle, intrigue and suspicion. It's climate is equally unhealthy thanks to its airlessness, the very antithesis of '*Berliner Luft*'. Brandt's own thought about the place was: '*Ein bisschen Falschheit ist in Bonn auch immer dabei*' – roughly, 'there's always a touch of duplicity about Bonn'.[83] In spirit it was a long, long way farther off than Berlin from his native Lübeck or his adopted Norway. He went there with mixed feelings.

9

The Evolution of an *Ostpolitik*

The leaders of the two parties which formed the 'big' coalition in December 1966 began their task with misgivings. The CDU had gone resolutely into the federal elections little more than a year earlier, determined to keep Erhard as chancellor and the Free Democrats as coalition partners. They had succeeded in both objectives. The relative failure of the second Erhard administration came as a shock to their pride and confidence.

Adenauer had imbued his followers with a distrust of German social democracy that had become ingrained and almost pathological. The progressives in the CDU had generally been kept out of his cabinet. He believed that German socialism was, and would remain, unacceptable and dangerous. For the CDU in 1966 there seemed to be grave risks in taking the arch-enemy into partnership. The right wing of the party, led by Franz-Josef Strauss, remained highly and vocally critical. For Brandt, too, there were risks in bringing the SPD into the government as junior partner. The trade unions were suspicious; the 'new left' was frankly appalled. The lifting of the ban on the Communist Party was already being mooted – in fact it re-formed in 1968 as the Deutsche Kommunistiche Partei (DKP) – and there was a danger of SPD left-wingers shifting their allegiance to a party that continued to preach Marxism, class warfare and workers' rights. The only alternative for disillusioned left-wingers was to go into extra-parliamentary opposition, accepting a kind of genteel anarchy. Brandt was jokingly to remark that extra-parliamentary opposition – APO in the German abbreviation – was more like OPA, the German child's abbreviation of Grandpa.[1]

More serious for Brandt was that a section of liberal-left intellectual opinion was offended by what it regarded as an immoral pact with the CDU establishment. Other critics maintained that the SPD, as junior partner in the coalition, were doomed from the outset; every success would be exploited by the CDU, every failure laid at the door of the SPD.[2] Less credibly, one critic stated: 'Since Schumacher's death German Social Democracy has renounced an independent foreign policy. The concept that a strong party could function as a political opposition sank with Schumacher into the grave.'[3] Schumacher had, in fact, died in 1952 and the SPD had continued to constitute a numerically strengthening opposition for the next fourteen years. Brandt had to compete with a 'no surrender' element in his own party, and an 'all or nothing' complex that Schumacher had once engendered.

Reasoned criticism came from a leading liberal, Ralf Dahrendorf. He saw the big coalition as the apogee of negative conservatism – the CDU conservative in a hidebound way as a result of ruling too long, the SPD conservative because they were afraid of losing the chance to govern.[4] Dahrendorf wanted sweeping social and administrative reform; student participation in university affairs; the end of the system of 'interrogatory arrest'; curtailment of bureaucratic controls; a more equitable system of personal taxation; even the calling by its right name of the DDR. He complained bitterly of stagnation and decay, the consequences of an exaggerated demand for security, which was 'no more than the security of the trapped rabbit'.[5] Meanwhile outspoken complaints came from Günther Grass and other intellectuals who had fought so valiantly for the SPD in the election campaign of 1965. They tried very hard to avoid criticism of Brandt, for accepting the coalition and the posts of foreign minister and vice-chancellor. They liked him, believed in him. Instead they vented their scorn and anger on the new chancellor, Kurt-Georg Kiesinger. The thought of an ex-Nazi becoming chancellor twenty years after the end of the Nazi era was utterly repugnant; this was the worst kind of restorationism and a betrayal of Germany's future. There were gloomy prophecies of the demolition of German democracy,[6] and of the final stultification of a German electorate that no longer knew by whom it was governed.

Whatever the objections of liberals, intellectuals and 'new left' opposition within the SPD to the coalition, they died still-born – it was 'like a firework', and had only a short and colourful life.[7] The truth was that the SPD, as a party, were hungry for an overdue share in political power in Bonn. Then there was the personality of Kiesinger himself. He was likely to prove an awkward running-mate for Brandt. He had elegance and much superficial charm, but some found him egotistical and vain. He had a streak of political ruthlessness and some of the characteristics of the political climber and trimmer. The Nazis had recruited him because of his popularity, ability and obviously Aryan good looks. The same thing had happened to Brandt's predecessor as foreign minister, Gerhard Schroeder. But there was one all-important difference: Schroeder had left the Nazi Party, Kiesinger had not. The latter represented the most orthodox and least lethal type of the *Mitläufer*, the fellow-traveller who did not believe in Nazism at all but time-served until the Nazi era ended. Those *Mitläufer* who joined the party under threat, or out of ignorance, could be held to be less disagreeable. Kiesinger, in Brandt's words, was a politician who 'was always on the look-out for a four-leaf clover'.[8] He hoped for a lucky break, regarded it as no more than his due. He was an opportunist, with likes and dislikes but no political philosophy. He could argue that he was doing something necessary by leading this coalition. The right answer was that there were better men to do this, chief among them Schroeder. At least Kiesinger was an efficient party manager and chancellor. By October 1967 one cartoonist[9] had the 'footballers', Kiesinger and Brandt, barging each other off the 'big coalition football'. Two years later the smooth functioning of the coalition provoked very different comment on the eve of new federal elections. The *Nürnberger Nachrichten* showed Kiesinger and Brandt slanging each other over the heads of a bewildered audience, then sitting down together and chorusing: 'Well, you made a proper hash of me at the meeting.'[10] The *Frankfurter Allgemeine* had the two getting out of the coalition limousine, donning boxing-gloves and explaining, 'We've got something to settle now, but let's get back in again afterwards.'[11] The coalition had, in fact, survived and there had been a fair degree of give-and-take between the two partners. This may indeed have been its outstanding achievement.

Brandt's comment on his association with Kiesinger was that, apart from the nation's need of a coalition at that time, there had to be some 'element of honesty' in the collaboration of an ex-Nazi chancellor and an anti-Nazi vice-chancellor. His own reason for waiving scruples: the SPD executive had carefully considered, in 1958, SPD participation in a coalition government led by Kiesinger, in *Land* Baden-Württemberg. The executive, with the approval of its chairman, Ollenhauer, decided then that Kiesinger's membership of the Nazi Party was no barrier to co-operation.[12]

One reason for the solidity of the coalition was the strong and effective SPD contingent in the cabinet. Apart from Brandt there were eight SPD ministers, five in important posts. Herbert Wehner was minister for all-German affairs; in this job he could produce a powerful back-up for Brandt's efforts to develop East–West relations. Karl Schiller became minister of economics, where he set out to create a new compromise between long-term planning and Erhard's 'free-market' economics. George Leber brought a strong personality to the Ministry of Communications. Gustav Heinemann, a CDU member of Adenauer's first cabinet who had resigned in protest against rearmament, formed his own party and finally joined the SPD, was minister of justice. Finally, Carlo Schmid with his finesse and *savoir faire* was an ideal link with the *Länder* as minister for Bundesrat affairs.

One deprecatory notice of Brandt's appointment suggested that the post 'sounds more important than it is. In the nineteenth and first decade of the twentieth centuries, Foreign Ministers helped make foreign policy. Nowadays it would be hard to find a Prime Minister who does not run his own foreign policy, and a foreign minister who is more than a messenger boy or public relations officer. Brandt is congenial, a good dinner companion, popular with Western statesmen. As a PRO he will be admirable.'[13] Certainly Adenauer had treated his foreign minister of long standing, von Brentano, as little more than a privileged employee, while Schroeder's more independent role as foreign minister owed much to Erhard's readiness to decentralize. Brandt did not want to raise the prestige of his office simply for its own sake; he had a foreign policy to offer as well. As he put it: 'Anyone with a sense of history will not lightly pass over the fact that a man of my persuasion should become German foreign minister.'[14] It was a tremendous opportunity to put the SPD squarely on to the map of federal politics.

He worked at high pressure from the outset. According to one adviser he rarely left the Foreign Office in the Koblenzer Strasse before ten at night and even then he habitually took away a big bundle of papers. Yet they were always signed and in perfect order when he arrived at his office the next morning.[15] The professional diplomats of the Foreign Office were amazed by the speed with which he mastered intricate briefs. He had the diplomat's greatest asset, an intuitive understanding of people as well as problems. He had other assets, too. In spite of his humble origins he was much more a man of the world than, for instance, Adenauer.[16] While Adenauer had hardly been abroad before the age of seventy Brandt was well travelled and felt at home in a dozen capital cities. He knew how their inhabitants thought and behaved. He had a deep feeling for historical event and development; he wanted to 'live history', playing his own part to the full.[17] He was extremely well read where recent and contemporary history was concerned and sought inspiration in the stories of other German statesmen – Bismarck, Rathenau, Stresemann, even Adenauer. A minor, but valuable asset was that, in Dr Günther Struwe he found a speech-writer attuned to his mood and method. Struwe came from Holstein, the part of Germany to which Lübeck belonged after it ceased to be a 'free city'. He spoke the same dialect (*Platt*) as Brandt; this was an intimate bond. He was keenly aware of Brandt's sense of destiny, backed by the conviction that there was a great deal for him to do.[18] He enjoyed working for a boss who treated his whole staff as a team. Another adviser considered that where unity of purpose was concerned Brandt's tenure of office was the finest hour of the German foreign service.[19]

One final asset: Brandt did not allow his becoming foreign minister to change his way of life. He moved into 12 Kiefernweg, on the Venusberg hill, a well-appointed house with a large garden. It was a real home, used little for official entertaining. There was a family atmosphere, with all three boys often at home and a number of family pets. Brandt's study was tucked away in an attic, and a bed was made up there if he was working late. He retained his ability to relax and to live simply. He showed an invariable, undemanding moderation; he never expected red-carpet treatment, asked little for himself and as minister ate the same simple canteen meals as his staff.[20]

The late Robert Kennedy said that he could not get used to a

Brandt not at his post in Berlin – he would call him 'governing foreign minister'.[21] The joke was apt, as Brandt intended to be more than a functional foreign minister. He had clear-cut ideas on foreign policy and he was convinced that Germans must initiate thought and not leave everything to the western Allies. His phrase was: 'The world, whether we like it or not, does not have the feeling that it owes us something.'[22]

His main preoccupation was relations with Eastern Europe; indeed it was the hope of developing a cohesive *Ostpolitik* that had helped to induce him to accept the coalition and a key role in it.[23] On 6 December 1966, taking over from Schroeder, he emphasized the unavoidable need for reconciliation and co-operation with Eastern Europe. Realistically he added: 'And that will be a long road.' With typical generosity he paid a tribute to his predecessor, now minister of defence.[24] Eight days later, at a Nato meeting in Paris, he expanded this theme: there had to be a step-by-step progress towards East–West understanding – in particular, better relations with Czechoslovakia and Poland, countries that had suffered so bitterly and undeservedly from Nazi aggression and brutality. The Czechs should know that the Federal Republic rejected the 1938 Munich agreement, and the Poles that the question of Germany's eastern frontier could be regulated, but only in free agreement with Bonn. His government, in the interests of détente, backed agreement on nuclear arms control and mutual force reductions in Central Europe. Nor was Bonn losing interest in a 'Western policy'; Brandt reminded his listeners that he strongly favoured expansion of the Common Market, by including Britain and other Efta countries. On 24 January 1967 he spoke to the Council of Europe in Strasbourg, urging increased technical, cultural, economic, scientific and, 'where possible', political collaboration with Eastern Europe. Détente, he went on, involved no preconditions; it was not a magic word, nor an end in itself. 'Inner-German' contact should develop so that 'the two parts of our country' should not grow farther apart. But, he admitted, the East German regime had shown no signs of helping over détente. At least the division of Germany would become less painful if a peaceful co-existence were achieved.

In the meantime the first breakthrough in relations with Eastern Europe had taken place. On 31 January 1967 the Federal

Republic established diplomatic relations with Roumania when its foreign minister, Cornelis Manescu, came to Bonn. This was not entirely a surprise: Roumania was moving out of line with Moscow and the Ceausescu government was determined to promote Roumania's own political and economic interests. The country had no common frontier with Germany, no quarrel with the Federal Republic and an aversion to Comecon, the so-called East European Common Market. Brandt did not want to exploit this diplomatic success as he feared a reflex action of alarm on the part of the DDR and the Soviet Union. In fact the DDR at once signed treaties of friendship with Poland, Czechoslovakia, Hungary and Bulgaria – a palpable attempt to isolate Bucharest. These treaties, Brandt explained, 'do not bar the initiation of diplomatic relations with us, but mean a postponement of the course of normalization'.[25] He referred, discreetly, to diplomatic relations with Roumania as being only a useful step.[26] He noted the absence of friendly gestures from Moscow, Warsaw or East Berlin; of the DDR leaders he remarked that the 'most zealous' would produce a substitute for the word 'German', if they could discover one. He made a special plea to the Poles who, he felt, knew that no nation can be kept divided for ever. As regards East–West relations, the view was gaining ground that Europe belonged together, historically and where the future existence of the whole continent was concerned. He repeated his appeal to Poland to the newspaper *Mann in der Zeit* in April.[27] He said that the German people understood better than ever before the Polish nation's desire and need to live within secure frontiers. But he would not embark on a policy of 'renunciation'; he wanted to save as much of Germany as possible for the German people. This did not mean rejection of realities or imply an attempt to isolate the DDR. That would arouse acute suspicion in Warsaw and Prague. Nothing could be done in a hurry. In June he re-emphasized this.[28] Two thoughts – 'Europe cannot be built up at one stroke', and 'The time of grand enterprises is past'.

On 2 July came a radio interview.[29] His chief concern where the German question was concerned, he explained, was 'to make the lives of people more bearable, as long as the division of Germany exists'. This entailed 'talking to those who exercise the real power and belong to the administration'. As far as European security and unsolved all-German problems were concerned this meant Moscow; for inner-German questions of communication, trade and cultural affairs it meant East Berlin. There was no way round these facts. His government, Brandt went on, sought 'regulated coexistence'. This meant a *modus vivendi*, excluding legal and political differences that had to stay unsettled. There could be no miracle and his friends abroad understood this – he mentioned in particular the three western powers with responsibilities in Germany, the Scandinavian countries and Japan. (His recent Scandinavian tour had taken in Denmark, Finland, Sweden, Norway and Iceland.) The East German regime, he said, seemed intent on isolating itself. Ulbricht's last speech had been 'ninety-nine per cent crass propaganda against the Federal Republic'. Nor had there been any direct answer to a letter written in April, proposing talks on sixteen points of mutual interest. Instead there was a DDR campaign in which East Germans wrote to the communist press declaiming against that letter from Bonn – which had never been published and whose contents they had never seen! At least the East German prime minister, Willi Stoph, had – after this fanfare of propaganda – said on 25 June that he would give it his attention.

Brandt was neither surprised nor disappointed by the East German performance as it was entirely predictable. Stoph had indeed sent a letter in May proposing 'normalization' of relations. In his case not people but prestige mattered; he demanded full recognition of the DDR by Bonn, the establishment of diplomatic relations and acceptance of the inter-zonal boundary as a state frontier. He had other demands – for the federal government to drop its claim to represent the whole German people, for West Berlin to be completely detached from the Federal Republic, for both German states to join the United Nations. There was only a dialogue of the deaf between the two German governments. Yet a dialogue it was; it was entirely unusual for the two governments to communicate at all.

By 1967 Ulbricht had still not created a 'second German nationality' in the DDR. West Germany, with a population three times greater, considerable wealth and democratic freedoms, continued to be a magnet to the seventeen million East Germans. Ulbricht was still hated and feared, in spite of East German schoolchildren being taught fairy-tales about him saving Red Riding-Hood from the capitalist wolf.[30] Early in 1967 he still did not feel strong enough to proclaim permanent East German independence. At the seventh congress of the Socialist Unity Party in April he declared that Marxism-Leninism recognized the need for a unified Germany – Marx, Engels and Liebknecht had been the 'best patriots' and German unity had been destroyed by imperialist machinations, in defiance of the wishes of the German working class. German unity could be reforged on the basis of the achievements of the DDR, whose socialist structure should extend to the whole of Germany. This was so much claptrap. The Soviet bloc conference that took place in Karlovy Vary in the summer of 1967 underlined the Soviet intention of keeping Germany divided and maintaining the *status quo* in Central Europe. The Soviet Union's 'European front' was to be shut down, while limited expansion could be achieved in the Middle East and Eastern Mediterranean and heightened vigilance observed in the smouldering ideological dispute with China. Ulbricht could be relied upon to dovetail DDR with Soviet policies – this did not preclude him appealing for help, as at the building of the Berlin Wall. Ulbricht was ready to pay only lip-service to the ideal of German unity since this would mean the destruction of the East German system, which was utterly unacceptable to the Soviet Union.

Brandt's *Ostpolitik* took these facts fully into account. But Brandt, too, had inhibitions; the philosophy of his *Ostpolitik* could not yet be divulged in full. It was impossible to explain that German reunification was for the time being totally unattainable, an empty dogma, a creed that people accepted as an act of faith. The West Germans would not face such an unpleasant fact; that would have been a betrayal of the seventeen million East Germans. They could accept closer relations with Eastern Europe and a détente that might even apply to the DDR only if the unity and self-determination of the whole German people continued to be asserted. Suspicions about détente were illustrated by political cartoons in which Brandt was the main target. The critical *Die Welt* showed him as a mouse emerging from his hole and saying to a gigantic Soviet cat: 'Now can you hear me?'[31] The CSU *Bayern Kurier* had Brandt throwing food out of a barrel labelled 'Concessions' to Ulbricht, the shark, with the caption, 'If we feed him regularly, perhaps he will turn into a harmless carp.'[32] And the *Donau Kurier* portrayed the foreign minister banging a tennis ball hopefully against the concrete wall of the Iron Curtain.[33] The cartoonists knew that Brandt's *Ostpolitik* had the full backing of the chancellor so the *Nürnberger Zeitung* placed Kiesinger and Brandt under a tree in the Garden of Eden, with the DDR snake holding a letter from Willi Stoph in its mouth.[34] The *Münchener Merkur* showed them walking a tightrope labelled 'coalition policy' and fighting off bees that emerged from the hive of 'recognition' – of the DDR.[35]

The *Ostpolitik* of the coalition was supported by Kiesinger and the CDU in spite of the doubts that were sometimes expressed by the Bavarian branch of the party and isolated right-wingers. On 13 December 1966 Kiesinger had said that he would include the problem of Germany's division in overall negotiations on disarmament and security – German unity was no longer a precondition for East–West negotiation. In March 1967 he had told the Bundestag that the German people had an irrevocable right to live together in one state, but the present objective was to secure a 'peace order' in Europe. On 12 April he had told them that détente should extend to both parts of Germany; 'inner-German' détente was part of a European détente. He had made no mention of the old dogma, asserted by Adenauer, that moves to settle East–West differences must be accompanied by parallel progress towards German reunification.

A year later Kiesinger made two statements that showed that deadlock over détente in no way modified his belief in it. In the CDU paper *Rheinische Post* he offered mutual renunciation of force to the Soviet Union, 'including the other part of Germany', the DDR.[36] Renunciation of force, he pointed out, could be a theme offered to Stoph, without a formal recognition of the DDR. Then on *Südwestfunk* he claimed that 75 per cent of the West Germans had declared 'in favour of our peace policy', in an instant poll. The German question as a whole need not be solved prior to the pursuit of a 'peace policy', but was intimately connected with the whole process that was being unfolded.[37]

Since the coalition ended, a legend has evolved that the CDU was from the first opposed to Brandt's *Ostpolitik*, but what Kiesinger said in 1967 and 1968 shows that this was not the case. No foreign minister could pursue a policy of his own against the wishes of the federal chancellor and the senior partner in the two-party coalition. Brandt's *Ostpolitik* was discussed at great length in the federal cabinet and approved there. Three out of its four main guidelines had, by 1968, been fully accepted. They were the inclusion of the DDR in the process of détente, mutual renunciation of force with all East European states and the policy of 'small steps' to improve the lot of the seventeen million East Germans. The fourth guideline concerned the outdated and academic yet still controversial question of existing frontiers in Central Europe. This, too, had been aired in the federal cabinet. If no decision had been reached this was due less to differences between the CDU and SPD than to a shared feeling that recognition of the Oder–Neisse Line as Germany's eastern frontier might boost the radical right-wing vote. The neo-Nazi National Democratic Party was a real force and pessimists were predicting over 5 per cent of the vote for them in the 1969 federal elections and forty to fifty members in the next Bundestag. Kiesinger said as much to the journal *Der Stern* on 23 October 1967.

Finally, one should not forget that Kiesinger regarded himself as the executor of Adenauer's policy of firm friendship with France. Brandt's very first appearance outside his own country as foreign minister had been at the Nato Council meeting in Paris on 14 December 1966. His explanation of *Ostpolitik* had been well received and the French press had seen a truly promising 'new start' in German policy towards Eastern Europe. Calling on General de Gaulle, Brandt found unreserved approval – the General had been the first prominent West European statesman to recognize the Oder–Neisse line, as early as 1959. Brandt capped their interview with a jest – it was a pleasant irony that a social democratic foreign minister could take the 'German Gaullists' in hand, so that they would not make trouble for the General.[38] The 'German Gaullists', led by von Guttenberg, were the foremost opponents of *Ostpolitik*.

In August 1967 Brandt wrote explicitly: 'We do not make our policy of détente dependent on progress over the German question.'[39] Once again he made it plain he was not for 'peace at any price'. Productive détente, he explained, was being blocked by the East Germans, the Russians and the Warsaw Pact bloc as a whole. The East German regime denied basic freedoms to its subjects, unaware that the more freedom was granted the more recognition and approval would be shown by the outside world. The Soviet Union, for its part, attacked only two members of the western alliance, the United States and the Federal Republic. This merely made détente more difficult. The Warsaw Pact states had shown at the Karlovy Vary conference that they still hoped to disrupt and destroy Nato. Brandt made it clear that Nato would last as long as the Warsaw Pact. Two months later, at the Free University of West Berlin, he boldly stated: 'I am enough of a realist to know that the self-determination of the German people does not stand on the agenda of practical policies.'[40] But he held out an olive branch to the Soviet Union. This was the hundredth anniversary of the birth of Rathenau, the German foreign minister who concluded the Treaty of Rapallo in 1922 with the Soviet Union. Brandt emphasized that this was a 'natural occurrence', an overdue end to a treaty-less situation. The implication was obvious: if it had taken three years for Germany and the Soviet Union to reach agreement after the First World War, how much more overdue was agreement twenty-two years after the Second World War?

Did Brandt expect quick results from his *Ostpolitik*? The indications are that he did not. Continuous warnings, to the effect that small steps only were feasible, suggest that he never fixed his sights too high. Yet in due course it did show useful results. The establishment of diplomatic relations with Roumania was followed by talks between Brandt and Roumanian leaders in August 1967. Agreement was reached on closer economic and cultural links. In the summer agreement was reached with Czechoslovakia, too, on the exchange of trade delegations and goods and payments arrangements. Then in February 1968 permanent trade missions were established, with consular capactiy. And in 1968 diplomatic relations, broken off in 1957, were re-established with Yugoslavia. There were soundings of the Hungarian and Bulgarian governments; nothing concrete came of them. In Brandt's words: 'These governments thought it correct, or timely, to take into account the demands of East Berlin and of others. We respected their position, and made it clear that we would work together to improve *de facto* relations within the framework of what was possible.'[41] Meanwhile he made a positive effort to reassure the Soviet Union in February 1968. A memorandum expressed readiness to move towards 'détente and a closening of relations between both parts of Germany'. A new phrase was coined – the two parts of Germany were not to regard one another as 'abroad'. From this phrase sprang the concept of two German states, but one German nation, subsequently Brandt's definition of the *status quo* in Germany.

Progress in relations with the Soviet bloc did not mean that he neglected the 'western policy' that was a necessary coefficient of *Ostpolitik*. Immediate objectives were the expansion of the Common Market of the Six and the further strengthening of Nato, but he had to move with care. Adenauer had made no effort to help Britain into the Common Market. Erhard repeatedly stated that Britain must become a member, but secured no action. Brandt felt that Britain could best be helped by tact and firmness in private discussion, not by declamatory statements in public. He set out to help from the moment he became foreign minister. In February 1967, for instance, he was among the first to acclaim Harold Wilson's declaration, on behalf of the British government and the Labour Party, to back the political and economic aims of the European Community.[42] In April he stated in London that Anglo-German relations had never been better and again applauded Labour's decision to seek entry into the Common Market; a British entry, he said, would be as much in Germany's interest as in Britain's. Cool, unemotional and realistic, he gave the firm impression that he would give Britain quiet behind-the-scenes backing. He denied that the European Community was 'a citadel for us to burrow into and entrench ourselves against the world around us. The Europe of the Six and an expanded Western Europe as well must not stand against its neighbours; it must attract, not repel them. It must be open, not shut off.'[43] But he had to play his hand carefully. In October he told the Bundestag that Common Market decisions had to be unanimous; France insisted on this. A month later General de Gaulle stated that France was not prepared to negotiate on a British entry. Brandt was in a quandary; France was ready to make 'special arrangements' for Britain and it was a moot point whether these could usefully bridge an interval, or whether the French looked on them as a stratagem for postponing negotiations indefinitely.

In December he was again in Britain, for talks with Harold Wilson and his foreign secretary, George Brown, at Chequers. The British view was that there must be a clear-cut decision on whether negotiations for entry could take place – Britain did not want special arrangements that France would cite as making entry into the Common Market superfluous; she preferred to activate Western European Union as a forum in which European problems could be discussed. Brandt gave the British government his support, possibly with misgivings; the French claimed that Britain was using WEU as a 'back door into Europe' and boycotted meetings. The activation of WEU turned out to be a barren exercise in oblique diplomacy.

In the Bundestag Brandt repeated his reason for wanting Britain in the Common Market. Her entry would pave the way for membership of the other applicants, Norway, Denmark and Ireland; it would take the European community out of a phase of stagnation; she would be an asset in her own right. He concluded: 'Our own interest, which it is up to us to represent, and our understanding of the state of European interests, obliges us to speak a clear language and urge our French neighbours not to make things too difficult for themselves and others.' When the Common Market's Council of Ministers met in Brussels on 19 December to consider the British application he urged negotiations with Britain. All in vain: France once again blocked them. For Brandt the only consolation was that Britain did not withdraw her application for membership. At a dinner in Luxembourg on 18 January 1968 he recalled Winston Churchill's Zurich appeal in 1946 to unify Europe. He went on: 'And now Britain is knocking on the gate of the European Economic Community. As a European I ask myself, somewhat bewildered, why Great Britain must knock. Did she not prove, in Europe's darkest hours, that she belonged to it? I was in Scandinavia, others were in London, others still were listening-in to London – but at that time we all knew that Great Britain stood for, and suffered for, and was consuming herself for freedom. Gratitude may not be a political characteristic, but forgetfulness scarcely befits us either.'

The British government was grateful to Brandt and aware that he had to tread with caution. George Brown's predecessor at the Foreign Office, Mr Michael Stewart, had this to say:

He just could not afford to be too valiant a spokesman of Britain's needs and interests; he had to reckon with the danger of a head-on collision with the French. So the West Germans played around for a time with the idea of some suitable trade arrangement in place of British membership in the Common Market. Of course we couldn't accept this – not unless a trade arrangement was explicitly understood by the Six as well as ourselves to be a stage on the road to full membership. We rejected any substitute for that, and we were right to do so. I believe Brandt came to understand that.

I think Brandt decided that the right way of helping us was for the Federal Republic to seek a more equal voice with France in the affairs of the Common Market, then put our case – in a down-to-earth way. He had no dreams about an ideal form of European political unity. He was purely pragmatic and practical about what could be done for Europe. He was helped by the 1968 student riots in France – they actually began while Brandt and I were having talks. They made the West Germans realize they need not be quite so dutiful to the French – de Gaulle's regime was not, after all, omnipotent. German self-confidence *vis-à-vis* France rose as a result. This was something quite different from that terrible and disgusting German contempt in the past for the French, and it was all to the good – this was the right time for the Germans to stand up for themselves, especially with so sensible and civilized a man as Brandt to represent them.[44]

George Brown's opinion of Brandt was equally favourable. He was 'one of the most likeable people I have ever met – courageous, honest, gay at times, totally lacking in pomposity. He has a remarkably clear mind and he thinks his problems through. I admire him in every way. Of course, he doesn't suffer fools gladly and he has his "favourites". Perhaps he depends a bit too much on a small, closed circle – but that's his affair.'[45] Brown had no doubt that Brandt had helped as much as he could over Britain's application to join the Common Market – 'not like Kiesinger. Kiesinger had his own line to Paris; he could be weak and stubborn at the same time, and he was desperately afraid of breaching the Adenauer legacy of a Franco-German *entente*. Willy was quite different. Short of breaking up the coalition government in Bonn, he went just about as far as he could to help us in. In particular, he co-operated over using Western European Union as a vehicle for airing our views and explaining our problems. That helped too.'[46] In his book *In My Way* Brown called Brandt 'my favourite European politician' and went on:

> Brandt has done things which require physical, mental and moral courage to an extent which few men could sustain. He inherited a German Social Democratic Party with very out-dated traditional thinking, and requiring super-human energy and understanding to reform and revive. Like others, he had little in the way of natural advantages with which to do it. He was, of course, lucky in his colleagues but even so it was Brandt who saw the way through, not only to leading the Social Democratic Party to victory but towards uniting Europe. He is a man of shining courage – doing things which to everybody else it seemed impossible to ask a German politician to undertake. Thanks to Willy's courage and imagination, Germany may yet bring about the beginnings of a genuine détente between East and West.[47]

Michael Stewart, George Brown and their prime minister, Harold Wilson, too,[48] all realized their debt of gratitude to Brandt for his quiet, unspectacular but effective help to Britain. It bore fruit at a later date. The other principal plank in Brandt's western policy was the consolidation of Nato as Western Europe's defensive shield. It was fashionable about this time among left-wing German intellectuals to denounce Nato for discouraging political emancipation in Western Europe, and for embodying a policy of strength that was a latter-day replica of discarded American strategies of 'roll-back' and 'containment' of the communist world.[49] Left-wingers found plenty to criticize besides in Nato. Its demands entailed the spending of money that could have been used for worthy social ends. It had, it was argued, become superfluous; its forces in Europe were no more than a trip-wire and the only deterrent to Soviet attack on Western Europe (although left-wing intellectuals remained quiet about this) was the American nuclear response.

Brandt had no sympathy with left-wing critics. He has set out his own views about Nato with crystal clarity:

> The North Atlantic Treaty Organisation is first and foremost an effective defence alliance. It prevents potential opponents from being tempted to exert political pressure on any one of

the allies through military force. But constant effort is required to maintain this defensive strength in the face of constantly advancing technical development. We realise that the commitment in Europe is a great burden on the United States. . . . I am afraid that the time for any significant lightening of the United States' burden has not yet come. . . .[50]

NATO and a policy of détente are not mutually exclusive. On the contrary, the existence of NATO – that is, its political weight and its readiness to defend our territory against all attacks – has shown that a policy of tensions and crises is of no avail. The weakening of NATO would reduce the possibility of a détente and lessen its effectiveness. The military deterrent has ensured the peace of Europe. . . . Military security and détente do not contradict, but supplement each other. Without the firm support of the alliance we cannot carry on any policy of détente. Similarly the political objective of the alliance will not be realised without an East–West détente.[51]

The political purpose of Nato, according to Brandt, was 'to bring about a just and enduring peace-order in Europe in conjunction with appropriate guarantees of security'.[52] He saw it as a potentially constructive organization as well as the defensive shield of a militarily weak Western Europe. The Soviet Union was the strongest land power in time of peace that had ever existed. In 1968 it had two million men under arms, with 140 divisions at full or nearly full strength. For use in Central Europe there were 75 Soviet divisions, 20 of them in the DDR, and 3,700 aircraft. Other communist-bloc states contributed another 60 divisions. Against this were 22 Nato divisions, some under strength. The Red Army could be expected, in the event of war, to reach the Rhine in around sixty hours.[53] In addition to the United States' nuclear deterrent, admittedly, Nato had 7,000 nuclear tactical weapons in Western Europe, which in theory could deter the Russians from overrunning West Germany. But these nuclear tactical weapons could be destroyed before they became effective by shots from the Soviet Union's great arsenal of over 700 medium-range nuclear rockets.[54] Europe had to be prepared to make sacrifices for a defence policy of her own, or even for a roughly equal voice to that of the United States. Détente would increase contact between Europeans and loosen the Soviet

Union's grip on her satellites. But a strong Nato was a pre-requisite for successful détente – 'Without sufficient military strength a policy of détente is mere provocation'; and: 'A Europe protected by the USA alone must resign herself to being treated as a political object by the two super-powers.' This was Brandt's own philosophy of European defence.

In the military circumstances prevailing in 1968 – and the balance of military power in Europe has changed little since then – talk of mutual force reductions seemed unrealistic. Yet this was proposed by Dr Erich Mende, the leader of the sole opposition party in the Bundestag, the FDP.[55] Nor was he alone: at the Nato Council meeting in Reykjavik in June 1968 there was acceptance in principle of 'balanced' force reductions in Europe, while the United States and Britain decided to redeploy 35,000 and 6,000 troops respectively – recalling them from West Germany but keeping them theoretically on call for Nato's use. In 1968 it was not only left-wing intellectuals who wanted a thinning-out of western armed forces, which were already piti-fully thin on the ground.

The events of 1968 were to remind the western alliance of its weakness. On 5 January the Stalinist leader, Antonin Novotny, was replaced by the liberal Alexander Dubček as First Secretary of the Czech Communist Party. Economic, social and legal reforms followed, press censorship was relaxed, Czech citizens were allowed into western countries as tourists, economic aid was sought from the West, and a new government was installed in Prague. On 10 June, incidentally, Dubček appealed for a normalization of relations with the Federal Republic. In July Czech intellectuals signed and published a manifesto calling for a new reformed socialism, leading to the introduction of democratic freedoms. The Soviet government was alarmed, particularly as there had been student riots in Warsaw in March. On 21 August the Red Army invaded Czechoslovakia and occupied the country and the Soviet government forced the Czechs to reintroduce press censorship and restore hard-liners to the administration. During the next year most measures of the Dubček government were revoked.

The western powers did nothing for the Czech people. It is arguable that nothing concrete could have been done, but feeble and futile protests only confirmed the Soviet Union's belief that

it was free to consolidate its military occupation of Czechoslovakia and repress her people. The Soviet Union was even
emboldened to proclaim the 'Brezhnev doctrine' of the unlimited
right of interference of super-powers in countries regarded,
arbitrarily, to be in their spheres of influence. Claims that Soviet
intervention in Czechoslovakia demonstrated the bankruptcy of
the communist world were wide of the mark. The Red Army
drove into Prague because the Soviet leadership believed that the
disciplining of the Czechs was not merely necessary but unavoidable. Soviet diplomats explained that Czechoslovakia was an
integral part of the mosaic of communist-bloc countries in
Europe. Take out one vital part of the mosaic and the pattern of
Soviet control is shattered.[56] For the Soviet leadership the loss of
Czechoslovakia meant an exposed southern as well as western
flank for the vulnerable DDR, encouragement for breakaway
elements in Hungary and Roumania, a bad example to Poland. It
would put the whole satellite empire at risk. The western powers
could have sent their observers to Prague, called at once for an *ad
hoc* United Nations mission to the Czech capital and indicated
readiness to make Czechoslovakia a test case at the United
Nations General Assembly and Security Council. They could
have bombarded the Soviet government with memoranda, on
behalf of individual Czechs, or groups, or the legitimate government that was being ruthlessly suppressed. They could have
invoked economic sanctions, for moral rather than economic
effect.

Brandt at least did what he could. As Russian troops were
actually on their way to Prague on 20 August he made a statement on the situation – not in his capacity of foreign minister but
as chairman of the Social Democratic Party. This gave him more
chance of saying what he wanted. He condemned Soviet aggression without reservation and remarked that East German armed
forces were taking part in the invasion of Czechoslovakia –
playing the same jackal's part as Mussolini in the invasion of
France in 1940. He pointed out that the Soviet aggression
damaged all efforts to promote détente in Europe and work for a
new peace order. He contemptuously rejected accusations that
the Federal Republic had intended to interfere in Czech affairs.
Returning to the question of the DDR's intervention, he branded
the Ulbricht regime as the emblem of all that was retrograde and

obscurantist in the Soviet bloc and he apologized to the Czech people for East German participation in what amounted to a second Munich. In a radio interview a few days later[57] he said that the Soviet rulers feared the 'democratization' of the Czech form of socialism; it was Czech workers, farmers, tradesmen and even honest members of the Czech Communist Party who were under Soviet pressure, and he paid a tribute to people 'who have not had it easy in the past' but who were showing courage and determination. He concluded by appealing for western strength and preparedness. In one speech after another thereafter he returned to the situation in Czechoslovakia. He pointed out that the military balance in Central Europe had been adversely affected; both the disposition of Nato forces in Southern Germany and the western early-warning system were involved. He linked the Soviet military presence in Czechoslovakia with increased Soviet naval activity in the Eastern Mediterranean.[58] He explained that whereas the military situation, in global terms, had not significantly altered, the Soviet military presence in Czechoslovakia produced special problems for the Federal Republic and a reminder of the need for the protection of Nato.

The Soviet invasion forced Brandt to put his *Ostpolitik* on ice for the next year. There were already mutterings within the coalition; right-wing members of the CDU were claiming that a policy of 'movement' merely encouraged the division of Germany and consolidation of the DDR, without improving inter-German relations or the terms of existence of the seventeen million East Germans. Kiesinger was increasingly beset by doubts and there were reports of Brandt having threatened his resignation at a cabinet meeting.[59] But in spite of irritation and frustration Brandt did not consider jettisoning his *Ostpolitik*. Only the timing of his plans changed; for the moment, the Soviet Union was intent on holding down Czechoslovakia, discouraging Roumania from over-dramatic deviation and Poland from over-eager self-expression, and stabilizing the DDR. While this was the situation it was no use talking to the Soviet leadership.

To some extent an empty year lay ahead for Brandt. True, his successor as mayor of Berlin, Klaus Schütz, visited the Poznan (Posen) Fair in June 1969, coming away with the impression that

Polish opinion towards the Federal Republic was softening and that the Poles could be reassured about the inviolability of their Oder–Neisse line western frontier. True, there was some loosening-up on movement in and out of the DDR. According to one authority 1.5 million East Germans, almost all old-age pensioners, were allowed to visit West Germany in 1968 and 1.26 million West Germans visited the DDR. Some work was done on nuclear-arms control during this period and the Federal Republic took part in discussing a nuclear non-proliferation treaty in Geneva. Brandt's attitude was that it was absurd for the Federal Republic to seek nuclear status, since its governments had consistently renounced the right to produce or own nuclear weapons. The West German interest was restricted to the use of nuclear energy for purely peaceful purposes, phased nuclear disarmament, along with mutual force reductions and, possibly, the creation of a European zone of reduced military confrontation.[60] As a non-nuclear power the Federal Republic, while agreeing that the nuclear club should not increase its membership, sought reassurance that existing members should show their sense of responsibility. Measures discussed were the banning of all nuclear tests, the running-down of nuclear weapon stockpiles and the limitation of all strategic weapons and their uses. In Geneva Brandt remarked pointedly that dangers to humanity came from big powers, not from small ones. But he favoured German approval of a non-proliferation treaty, although it had to be postponed until after the federal elections.

Like Brandt's *Ostpolitik*, the British application to join the Common Market remained on the agenda, without anything concrete happening. In June 1968 the Gaullists had won the French elections and de Gaulle – that inveterate opponent of British membership – looked anchored in power for years to come. In February France boycotted Western European Union meetings. But in April de Gaulle resigned from the presidency, after a surprise defeat in the national referendum, and in August the new president, Georges Pompidou, devalued the franc. With France's position weakened an all-out attempt to secure agreement from the Six for Britain's application seemed on the cards. But the West German elections were due to take place in September and any German initiative would have to wait until they were over. And Kiesinger was lukewarm and increasingly anxious not to offend the pro-French right wing of the CDU.

Of Kiesinger one historian said: 'He has the ability to say something today and water it down tomorrow, so that nothing remains of it.'[61] Whereas the British prime minister, Harold Wilson, found Brandt helpful after a visit to Paris in July 1969,[62] he considered even earlier that Kiesinger was cautious to a degree in supporting Britain – 'We became increasingly convinced that he would never be prepared to press to the point of annoying General de Gaulle his undoubted conviction that Britain must be admitted to the Six.'[63] Nor did the General's fall help, for the West German election campaign was already under way and the wily Kiesinger had no intention of stirring up strife in his own party.

Part of Brandt's time, inevitably, had to be spent on party affairs. His outstanding party statement during the time that he was foreign minister came at the end of the Bad Godesberg party conference on 13 November 1967. He justified the existence of the coalition on the grounds that effective government had broken down under Erhard – the super-luxury, chrome and automatic-controls limousine had got stuck in the mud. The coalition was a good working arrangement – not a love-match, nor marriage under duress. It was an alliance of two equally entitled partners; the SPD were not being turned into a plaything of politics. Nor had they joined the government in a smug, self-satisfied spirit; they were aware of the problems confronting the country. Again he denied that joining the coalition had brought a showdown with the trade unions. He said that the two main dangers in 1966 had been economic recession and the growth of political radicalism; they were not caused by the coalition. The neo-Nazi National Democratic Party won successes in the Hesse and Bavarian elections *before* the coalition government was formed. The SPD minister of economics, Karl Schiller, had at once taken measures to stabilize the economy. The SPD had inherited troubles arising from the previous government's shortcomings. They had gone into the coalition from patriotic motives and to exercise influence in office. Partnership with the CDU in no way inhibited the SPD in their quest for social progress. Pensions were to be raised by 30 per cent by 1971, unemployment pay was to be increased and the social services would be expanded, and government grants for cultural and scientific research had already doubled. The SPD would continue to work for the creation of a truly modern society, based on social justice and the good of the whole community. They would pay special attention to the problems of German youth.

Years later Brandt was to say that risks of the SPD deteriorating in office were outweighed by the advantages of sharing in government.[64] The party gained invaluable experience and took their proper place in the public eye – their ministers became widely known and appreciated. He believed that the coalition had introduced a more flexible foreign policy, prevented an economic recession and combated political extremism, on the whole successfully. Admittedly the NPD reached its peak in 1968, with almost 10 per cent in *Land* Baden-Württemberg, traditionally the least radical and most 'sensible' corner of the Federal Republic, famed for the 'Swabian peaceability' of its inhabitants. A 'big' coalition, Brandt agreed, should never rule for too long, or its critics would go into unproductive extra-parliamentary opposition.[65] Some SPD members were quickly impatient and one hit Brandt on the head with his umbrella at the 1968 party conference in Nuremberg. Asked if he was hurt, Brandt answered, 'No, he only hit me on principle.'[66]

Federal elections in West Germany normally take place every four years; presidential elections every five. For the first time since 1949 these two elections coincided in 1969. In March the candidates for president were Gerhard Schroeder, of the CDU, and Gustav Heinemann, of the SPD. The election, as usual, took place in the Bundesversammlung, a composite body of over a thousand delegates. It was hard to visualize a better choice than Schroeder, outstandingly successful in successive governments, as minister of the interior, foreign minister and, finally, minister of defence. He had the personality, presence, integrity and vision for the job. Heinemann was impressive too, a reformer, humanist and experienced politician with close connections with the evangelical churches. Much depended on the Free Democratic members of the Bundesversammlung. In the past most of them would have voted for the CDU candidate. Nor had they any quarrel with Schroeder. But after two close but indecisive votes their new leader, Walter Scheel, brought his party over to Heinemann's side.* Even so the vote was only 512 to 506 in his favour.

Heinemann, as it happened, did not make an auspicious start. When sworn-in as president on 1 July he declaimed against pressure groups, big industry and their political lobbies and called for more democracy and social reform. Federal presidents are meant to steer well clear of party political issues, even though Heinemann spoke in general terms. But his election with Scheel's help meant that the FDP had at last broken away from its role of uneasy satellite of the CDU. Brandt had talks with Scheel at this time. Scheel was in favour of a future left-of-centre coalition government – provided election results made this feasible. For him there was one paramount consideration: a future SPD–FDP coalition would need a sufficient parliamentary majority for him to convince the right-wingers in his party and retain their support. The FDP was still fairly evenly divided among the left-liberals who supported Scheel's preference for the SPD and the right-wing conservatives with an ingrained distaste for everything socialist. In each *Land* the FDP had a differing political colour. The progressives were strong in Baden-Württemberg, Hamburg and Bavaria; the conservatives in parts of the Rhineland and Hesse.

Scheel genuinely believed in social reform and regarded Brandt's pragmatic and rational socialism as acceptable. He wanted greater authority emanating from parliament and less dependence on pressure groups in the CDU establishment. Finally, he was ambitious and realized that he had a better chance of personal success in alliance with the Social Democrats than with a CDU leadership that might have accepted Adenauer's assessment of him as a lightweight. For Brandt a key consideration was whether Scheel was strong enough to keep his party together. There were doubts, so the SPD had to keep their options open up to the last moment.

* According to the former chairman of the FDP, Erich Mende, there were two operative votes, in internal session, by the 83 members of the party taking part in the presidential election. In the first, 57 voted for Heinemann, 23 for Schroeder and 2 abstained, with 1 absent. In the second, 78 voted for Heinemann and 5 for Schroeder. Mende maintains that this was due to the announcement, before the second vote, that an electoral law – intended to produce direct suffrage and so certain to eliminate the FDP as a parliamentary party – would be dropped by the SPD if the FDP voted solidly for Heinemann. He says that this announcement was approved by Brandt personally. (Erich Mende, *Die FDP* [Stuttgart 1972], p. 100.)

As a result the 1969 election campaign took place in a minor key. The CDU and SPD found it difficult to attack one another as ex-partners. The FDP had to observe considerable discretion. Three years in lonely opposition in the Bundestag had been enervating; the right-wing vote had drifted to the CDU or even to the NPD. Wehner said that the FDP were 'shrinking to a healthy size', but this was not how their leaders saw it – the FDP vote might fall below the 5 per cent mark, thus excluding the party from the Bundestag.

This low-profile election suited Brandt, with his instinctive moderation. In an early statement he said: 'I hope that the SPD will succeed in showing themselves even more clearly than hitherto to be the party of solid progress and of necessary democratic reform.'[67] When being officially adopted in March as the SPD candidate for the chancellorship he announced that he wanted 'to be the chancellor of internal reforms', and he gently reminded listeners that the Germans 'have not completed our democracy; we've just begun it'.[68] Asked what the 'big' coalition had lacked, he answered: 'There were practically no jokes about it.'[69] He circulated instructions to eschew polemics and announced that he was not interested in hitting below the belt; nor would he be influenced by his opponents' style of fighting.[70]

Germans of independent political views complained that there was too little to choose between the two principal parties. The SPD laid greater stress on *Ostpolitik* and expanding the Common Market. They were ready to sign the nuclear non-proliferation treaty and more interested than the CDU in the third world. They had more advanced ideas on educational reform and Brandt took a leaf out of Harold Wilson's book in stressing technological development and scientific research. He depicted the SPD as a modern party, enlightened, open-minded, progressive. The CDU were frankly embarrassed by his tactics; they would have preferred a tough, hard-hitting campaign and were increasingly apprehensive about FDP intentions. Kiesinger decided to direct his fire on the SPD's minister of economics, Karl Schiller. This was unwise, for Schiller was credited with being almost as great a financial wizard as Erhard. Kiesinger's doubts about the *Ostpolitik* that he had countenanced and even encouraged were growing. Words like 'capitulation' and 'sell-out' began to appear in his speeches and he tried to make capital out of Brandt's readiness to accept the nuclear non-proliferation treaty. The CDU said the usual things about security, prosperity and ordered progress, but with less authority and confidence than four years earlier.

Less than a fortnight before the elections Brandt gave an interview to the weekly *Der Spiegel*.[71] He made it clear that he did not visualize the continuation of the coalition after the elections; he did not see room in the next government for a 'Foreign Minister Brandt'. Kiesinger reverted to Adenauer's outdated castigations of the SPD as irresponsible and undependable. In a television confrontation Brandt coldly reproved him for trying to wreck the good name of a democratic party with every chance of forming the next government. Kiesinger, incensed, disagreed vociferously, and one newspaper considered that this fierce altercation had sounded the death-knell of the coalition.[72]

Voting took place on 27 September. It was clear early on that the FDP were doing very badly and the NPD much worse. The latter would obviously not return members to the Bundestag and there was a danger that the FDP would not either. In that event the CDU would have an overall majority in the Bundestag. The FDP scraped home, but with 5.8 per cent of the poll against 9.5 per cent in 1965 and only 30 seats against 49. The CDU vote dropped from 47.6 to 46.1 per cent; that of the SPD rose from 39.3 to 42.7 per cent, with seats up from 202 to 224 – only 18 less than the CDU. Brandt telephoned Scheel and just before midnight confronted the television cameras. His message was that the SPD and the FDP would form the next government, with a parliamentary majority of only twelve but the utmost confidence that they would represent the German people's wishes and satisfy their needs. Brandt remarked semi-jokingly to journalists: 'Hitler has now finally lost the war!'[73] In his heart he meant that the party was at last in power that had never compromised with Nazism and had no part in the 'restorationist' character of post-war Germany. The federal president spoke – again unguardedly, but with obvious joy – of 'a caesura in the history of Germany'.[74] President Nixon, learning only that the CDU had emerged as the strongest single party, sent a premature message of congratulations to Kiesinger, unwisely published. Brandt was later to remark to the *New York Times*'s correspondent in Bonn: 'To err is human, the more so at that distance.'[75] Some wit noted that the Americans came out worst of all: they had studiously cultivated the CDU for twenty years and had virtually no links with the SPD.

Later, too, Brandt was to say that he had been so sure of winning the day that he had signed a sheaf of greetings cards beforehand.[76] His first thought had been not to be sentimental.[77] His next was more apposite: he had not let the people down who trusted him through thick and thin when he began for a moment to lose heart. This would be the first government led by the SPD since that of Herman Mueller, thirty-nine years before.

The result of the election – even more, the political outcome of the slight swing to the left – was a real shock to the CDU. There were recriminations, talk of ousting Kiesinger from the leadership and clear indications that Franz-Josef Strauss wanted a position of greater independence for his CSU Bavarian branch of the party. The right wing *Bayern Kurier* published a cartoon of a gloomy little cabinet, entitled 'mini coalition facing maxi problems'.[78] Independent papers were not exactly optimistic about prospects either. The *Frankfurter Rundschau* visualized the new government as a punch-bag, with Kiesinger and Strauss trying out their fists on it.[79] The *Süddeutsche Zeitung* had Brandt standing on a plank, with Walter Scheel leaping from a height on to the other end in order to shoot him into the chancellor's seat of office.[80] Scheel, incidentally, was from now on the chief target for the wit of conservative cartoonists, who showed him as a runty, dwarfish figure, sometimes ludicrously attired as a prince or standing on stilts to give the illusion of normal political stature.

On 21 October Brandt was elected chancellor by 251 Bundestag votes against 235. He had three more votes than the 248 that was exactly half of the Bundestag. His comment was: 'Anyway, 300 per cent of Adenauer's majority.'[81] (The latter's own vote had given him a majority of one after the first Bundestag elections of 1949.) When the votes had been counted Kiesinger was the picture of restrained misery and Strauss refused to wish the new chancellor luck on behalf of the CSU. Brandt had always shown himself a conspicuously more chivalrous loser.

Within twenty-four hours Brandt was able to announce the names of his ministers – a record in the short history of the Bonn parliament. On 28 October he made his statement of government policy. The *Ostpolitik* already instituted by the coalition would be pushed ahead. But there would be no recognition of the DDR and although two German states existed their relationship would be of a special nature. The economy would be stabilized, but not allowed to stagnate, under a system of 'functionally efficient market economy' – a phrase that must surely have made stalwarts of the Marxist past turn in their graves! Private property would be better spread, social benefits increased, reforms worked out in the realms of justice, education and taxation. Close attention would be given to bringing Britain and other applicants into the Common Market, and Brandt implied that there was nothing new even in proposals to enter into early negotiations with the Soviet Union and Poland. His statement of government policy was the reverse of dramatic or sensational: it was sober, factual, objective. He had more to say in a book, *Hundert Jahre Deutschland*, published at about the time of the federal election. He told readers that the division of Germany was the consequence, not the cause, of the division of Europe; the German question could not be solved in isolation. It was no longer any use demanding progress towards reunification as a condition for improving East–West relations – this was plain from the time that the coalition was formed in 1966.[82] Germans, he wrote, must look at the story of Germany's past and learn its lessons without emotion. The 'policy of the sword' had failed to give her a place in the sun; the legend of *Deutschland über alles* was a thing of the past.

Much later he was to say that he would probably not have tried again to become chancellor had he failed in 1969.[83] He would have taken over the leadership of the official opposition in the Bundestag and thought things out from there. He would have had to decide whether he was the right man to win the votes the SPD needed, and the right man to hold the party together. As things turned out he did not have to resolve these problems. He moved into the chancellor's offices in the Palais Schaumburg, allegedly saying: 'Throw the windows open and let some fresh air in – but we can leave the windows intact.'[84] He left intact, and in its place, too, the portrait of Konrad Adenauer, hanging in the hall. A mark of respect? Or a tribute to the continuity he desired? More likely a tribute to, and a mark of, his own tolerant good sense.

10

Framing a Foreign Policy

As federal chancellor Willy Brandt would govern a Federal
Republic of sixty-two million inhabitants, the heir of the united
Germany of 1871 to 1945. He had won his post in the teeth of
tremendous difficulties. A Bonn policeman told me one month
after he became chancellor that his appointment was impossible.
The reasons? He had betrayed his fatherland in wartime, and had
fathered a son who was a Communist. In the past Germans had
long but muddled memories, and small minds. Prejudice against
him when he became chancellor was immense: four years later a
considerable hard core remained. One British newspaper, the
Daily Mirror, acclaimed him, when he was appointed foreign
minister in 1966, as 'a German with clean hands'. Large sections
of the German population remained unalterably opposed to
admitting this.

Brandt had managed, against all the odds, to ferry the SPD
with him into a position of power. His party's popularity lagged
behind his own and popular prejudices against them were greater
than personal ones against himself. For twenty years the SPD, in
the eyes of an overwhelming majority of Germans, were not fit to
govern. Brandt's selection as their candidate for the chancellorship in 1961 was the first stage in the process of changing their
fusty, somewhat dilapidated image. The *Sozis* were still associated in the public mind with the Marxist gospel, as traduced by
Joseph Stalin and others. They were somehow dangerous. Few
Germans understood that the 1959 Godesberg programme really
was a turning-point in SPD thinking – a calculated compromise
with a capitalist society that was astonishingly resilient. It had
become axiomatic to regard the SPD as the Opposition, able to
do useful work but not an alternative government.

How was Brandt able to do so much for himself and his party?
The reasons lie very much in his own character. His instinct for

compromise played a big part in the framing of the Godesberg Programme and in every subsequent concession made in the interests of the nation. Other leading SPD men had the same instinct for compromise – one thinks, for instance, of Carlo Schmid, Erler, von Knoeringen. But they never convinced the party rank and file. Brandt did; it was a particular virtue of his that he never ceased to be able to speak, from the heart, to the so-called 'common man'. Sheer persistence was an even greater factor in his success. Superficially his life story has all the appearance of fore-ordained success, yet few politicians have had more setbacks or more obstacles to overcome. Time after time he was rejected by his own party; twice he was rejected by a proportion of the electorate big enough to suggest that he could never become chancellor. He never gave up.

He had the same gift as Adenauer, that of setting himself objectives, then concentrating his energies on achieving them. He gave his party a facelift and his government the basic elements of a new policy towards Eastern Europe. Like Adenauer, he learnt how to govern a nation by first governing a great municipality. And there was a big political and diplomatic content in the role of mayor of Berlin. But his most priceless asset was that of canalizing and utilizing to the full his own buoyant energy and his necessarily limited yet in no way circumscribed abilities. His record is reminiscent of the biblical parable of the talents of silver: he who buries or hoards his personal talents fails to fulfil himself. The ultimate secret of his success lay in his ability to exploit his fabulous memory, personal charm, understanding of others, his keenly analytical mind and uncanny ability to switch his thoughts at will to a new topic and concentrate utterly upon it. Genius is given to few, but this ability to mobilize and deploy one's assets is an excellent substitute.

Brandt organized his cabinet of fifteen members in record time – as we have seen, the list was published one day after his election as chancellor in the Bundestag. Four of them were of immediate importance: Walter Scheel, foreign minister; Karl Schiller, minister of economics; Helmut Schmidt, minister of defence; and Horst Ehmke, minister without portfolio and Brandt's personal aide in the federal chancellery. Adenauer had unjustly called Scheel, now fifty years old, a 'lightweight', probably because of an innate suspicion of his motives.[1] Now he was one of only three FDP cabinet ministers. A non-party man, Hans Leussink, became minister for technology, while the rest belonged to the SPD. Scheel had shown an interest in alliance with the SPD as far back as 1953, when he was partly instrumental in tumbling the CDU government of *Land* North Rhine-Westphalia. He was a modest but progressive liberal, with a charm that some found superficial but an ability to make friends. One commentator called him 'a man to go tiger-shooting with',[2] an allusion to his good humour – an attribute of Rhinelanders – and strong nerves. He was viciously lampooned by CDU supporters, bitterly resentful of the part he had played, first in securing the election of Gustav Heinemann as president and then that of Willy Brandt as chancellor. A favourite joke was: 'Is it important, or shall we send Walter Scheel?'[3] Elegant, engaging, witty, Scheel's main tasks were to be the execution of Brandt's *Ostpolitik* and holding together an FDP that observers believed must fall apart as a result of its unnatural alliance with the SPD.

Karl Schiller, fifty-eight years old, had served as minister of economics in the 1966–9 coalition. Stiff, professorial, a technocrat by disposition, he was the SPD's answer to Erhard, a hard-headed, thoroughly competent economist. Oddly, this dry, formal man with so little charm was popular with the voters – the Germans still tend to venerate omniscience in the field of economics. Yet in spite of long service as an SPD senator in both Hamburg and Berlin he had no real following in the party. Confronted by the worldwide problem of inflation, he was to show himself to be less than a wizard. He was also to display tetchiness with his colleagues. The former British prime minister, Harold Wilson, found him tiresome, with an irritating prolixity and a continual harping on the 'inner certainty' of his personal views.[4]

Helmut Schmidt was the opposite of the introverted Schiller. Able, vigorous and adaptable, he earned himself the nickname of '*Schnauze*', literally 'snout' but implying a bold, even brash assertiveness. Only fifty in 1969, he had risen to the rank of first lieutenant in the artillery towards the end of the war. An aggressive, colourful speaker, he had a strong following in the SPD but a hard row to hoe as minister of defence. The Bundeswehr was becoming rather too much of a 'citizen army', as he found when he had to prescribe hairnets rather than have hair cut to a military length.

Finally, Horst Ehmke, forty-two years old and a bundle of energy, was to become the Figaro of the new government, an indefatigable link-man between the Chancellery and the outside world. Brandt's choice of this former professor of law at Freiburg University, with a caustic, sometimes earthy wit and a gift for repartee, no respecter of persons and a politician down to his fingertips, was significant in one particular respect. Adenauer ruled through a Chancellery staff who served him and did not communicate with cabinet, Bundestag and party. Brandt exactly reversed this: he kept the Chancellery closely in touch with political institutions that mattered, above all with individual ministries.

There was plenty of talent elsewhere in the cabinet. The SPD establishment was represented by the minister of finance, Alex Moeller, a successful businessman, by the trade unionist Georg Leber, in charge of transport, and by Egon Franke, a self-made man whose Ministry for All-German Affairs was renamed the ministry for Internal German Relations. Two younger SPD leaders were the minister of justice, Gerhard Jahn, and the baby of the team, Erhard Eppler, thirty-nine years old, teacher, social scientist, a friend of federal president Heinemann and now in charge of development aid.

The two notable omissions were those of Wehner, now leader of the SPD Parliamentary Party, deputy chairman and in charge of party organization, and Erich Mende, Scheel's predecessor as leader of the FDP. For Brandt, Mende was too much of a conservative. Yet he would have made a good minister of the interior, and it will remain an open question whether some gesture should not have been made to the right wing of the FDP. But there were simply not enough cabinet posts to go round, and Brandt's philosophy favoured the elimination of unnecessary portfolios. Mende and two of his supporters in the Bundestag would, as it happened, leave the FDP early in the history of the new coalition and seek a political home with the CDU.

For the rest, Brandt's cabinet was distinguished by its quota of intellectuals – four out of fifteen ministers – and by its youth: the average age of its members was exactly fifty. One man outside the cabinet whose earlier appointment deserves mention was the new mayor of Berlin, Klaus Schütz. He had taken this post in October 1967, after a year as Brandt's secretary of state in the Foreign Office. He was a war veteran with a crippled arm, a rather shy man, but a deep thinker who played a formative part in the evolution of the SPD's *Ostpolitik*. He had nailed his colours to the mast in a speech made in March 1969 to the *Land* association (*Landsmannschaft*) of the lost province of Silesia, when he urged a cool appraisal of territorial questions. In June 1969 he had visited Poland and on his return had stated that the prewar situation east of the Oder-Neisse line could never be restored – in the simplest terms, a man who travelled from Berlin to Warsaw crossed first the DDR and then the Polish frontier over the river Oder. These were hard facts.

Two other features of Brandt's government deserve mention. Firstly its takeover from the CDU was admirably unassertive. A cartoon in the *Süddeutsche Zeitung* depicted Brandt, in white tie and tails, making an uproarious entrance into the federal box of the political theatre, turfing out an amazed Kiesinger and a sour-faced Strauss with: 'You're sitting in our seat!'[5] In fact the SPD takeover was discreet. Madame de Staël noted modesty as a German trait in 1804, along with readiness to learn from foreigners. After the brash assertiveness of the Empire and the Nazi era Adenauer imposed restraint; to Brandt restraint was second nature. The second feature of the Brandt government was popularity with intellectuals. The dramatist Rolf Hochhuth declared: '21 October 1969 is the day fullest of hopes for democracy in Germany since 8 May 1945,'[6] while Günther Grass believed in Brandt 'because he doesn't travel with illusions in his suitcase',[7] and Erich Maria Remarque gained from him 'a real sense of security'.[8] *Die Zeit*, the most thoughtful newspaper in Germany, pronounced: 'The Federal Republic has, for the first time since Adenauer, a chancellor once more.'[9]

But it was not only the intellectuals who supported him: the actress Marlene Dietrich discovered in Brandt the 'symbol of a new Germany',[10] while this letter came from and eight-year-old boy: 'Dear Federal Chancellor Brandt, because the CDU is so cheeky and often talks rubbish, I'm sending you and your wife a bar of chocolate.'[11] One young man[12] from the former CDU stronghold of Münster gave the following reasons why Brandt was the right man to lead his country: because he had lived abroad he knew what the outside world thought of Germany and the Germans; because he had lived in countries with a strong and long democratic tradition he had learned modesty and tolerance. Brandt was the reverse of a demagogue; nor did he oversimplify, like Adenauer. Finally, he realized that policies had to do with people, and with their creative thoughts. Here was promise of the long overdue reconciliation between the politicians and the intellectuals, taking the latter from the fastnesses of their ivory towers and the former out of the slough of materialism.

Brandt settled into the Palais Schaumburg with unassuming ease; neither its ambiance nor the tasks facing him daunted him the least. No ghosts of Adenauer and his faithful band of advisers stalked its corridors or the broad walks of the garden. For a man born illegitimate in a Lübeck back street, this ability to be instantly at home was not the least impressive of Brandt's achievements.

He told David Binder, of the *New York Times*, shortly after becoming chancellor that he 'would be the Chancellor of domestic reforms. There will be a lot of domestic policy-making. . . . Our position is to overcome the distinction between subjects and the powers-that-be, to create co-responsibility in society.'[13] In a material sense his government would seek to reduce the discrepancies between income-groups, with a farm labourer earning £50 a month, an industrial worker three times that and the boss anything from twenty to forty times as much. In foreign affairs, Binder wrote: 'The Brandt administration will offer East Germany a treaty to renounce the use of force between the two German states and to recognize the inviolability of each other's borders as well as the territorial integrity of the two states.' Where doubts about his *Ostpolitik* were concerned Brandt was reassuring: he agreed with Wehner that Germany was too big a country to play no role in the balance of power but too small to impose a balance on the countries round her, and he promised not to attempt social democratic 'infiltration' or penetration of Eastern Europe – the Soviet invasion of Czecho-Slovakia showed this would be fatal. Prophetically, Binder pointed out: 'Brandt knows . . . that his administration, with its narrow, twelve-vote majority in the Bundestag, must produce popular results fast, if his coalition with the Free Democrats is to hold on to power.' There were at least three waverers among the thirty FDP members of the Bundestag; another three could bring the government down. Yet Brandt radiated confidence; he told Binder that the Federal Republic would be 'a loyal ally, but not a comfortable government', and that he would 'be Chancellor of a liberated Germany, not a conquered Germany'. Binder observed that Brandt's attention was sometimes switched off, 'his gaze wanders into what one might imagine as Nordic mists'. That, certainly, is one of Brandt's habits, but moments of apparent abstraction are, for him, moments of deeper than usual reflection. The Germany that he was called upon to lead offered much upon which to reflect, beneath the façade of busy prosperity and confidence.

In his book *The Future of Germany*, Professor Karl Jaspers claimed that German parliamentary democracy had not rooted itself: 'All Germans participants in their state? No, most are still subjects of the state rather than participants in it. Every four years they choose between lists placed before them, but they do not really know what they are choosing. They have to bow – first to the party proposals, then to authorities that claim to exercise powers conferred by the electorate.'[14] Jaspers was alarmed by the enigmatic nature of the present-day German – every first look at him induced the same questions as to who he really was, what he was really thinking about, whether he could be trusted. Jaspers's nightmare was the faceless German citizen in the mindless German state.

In more prosaic terms Professor Kurt Sontheimer expressed the same fears: 'The unpolitical tradition is the continuation of the submissive way of thinking towards the state, which continued into the period of democracy.'[15] Two failures were the neglect of communication between government and people, and the people's lack of any share in the running of society.[16] Society, again, was curiously unformed: 'The political form of organization of German democracy has, as it were, been superimposed on the social institutions of the country. It is a modern roof over a house whose foundations and living rooms are made from bricks of another age.'[17] Out of this political hybrid came, in his view, a basic sense of insecurity amounting to a 'cartel of fear' and a desperate preoccupation with day-to-day life.

Writers made illuminating comments in a series of articles published by the *Atlantic Monthly* of Boston.[18] Irving Kristol thought that Germans opted after 1945 to be 'something else', rather than develop themselves; they wanted to be western, or European, or cosmopolitan; but 'the Germans are left with their history and their identity; and they have no idea what to do with them'. Midge Dexter found them still obsessed with the Nazi past: 'Most would, and did, respond to mention of the Nazis with extreme irritation, self-pity, claims of innocence, attacks on the sins of others, references to their sufferings during the war; and the young, of course, by announcing the year of their birth.' Stanley Kaufmann was totally pessimistic – to him, the contemporary German was 'a legatee and a doomed man'. These writers found most hope in German youth and intellectuals. The intellectuals were readiest to analyse the past, the young people to come to terms with it. If the intellectuals were obsessively critical and the young corrosively cynical, these were natural reactions to the restorationist society of the Adenauer era. Yet the overall picture painted by these writers was a bleak one. One is reminded of the poem that Berthold Brecht left unpublished during his lifetime:

> The new ages do not begin at once,
> My grandfather already lived in the new age,
> My nephew will probably still live in the old one.
> The new meat is eaten with the old forks;
> The old stupidities come from the new antennae.
> Wisdom was handed from mouth to mouth.

Whatever his thoughts about the psychological inhibitions of the German people, Brandt saw to it that his government got down to work with gusto. His team worked harmoniously together; if it had to work hard, there was time for laughter.[19] One newspaper[20] thought the atmosphere of the cabinet that of an English club – relaxed and sometimes merry. Ministers called one another by their Christian names, in 'the jolliest clique, which ever ruled on the Rhine'. This was high praise; Adenauer's cabinets had operated smoothly and efficiently, Erhard's owed much to his paternalistic warmth and Kiesinger exercised his suave charm adroitly. Brandt relied on a man-to-man relationship with ministers, on a feeling of shared trust and a surprising degree of decentralization of authority. He was always ready to listen patiently to his ministers, although he liked them at cabinet meetings to give short and precise accounts of problems and actions. His cardinal rule for these meetings was that there was no hard-and-fast routine. On one point he was a stickler: he definitely required his own briefs for weekly cabinet meetings two days beforehand. If they were not ready in time he was angry.[21]

The first important action of Brandt's government was to re-peg the exchange rate of the Deutschmark. On 24 October it was revalued, upwards, first by 6.5 per cent, finally by 8.5 per cent. The undervaluation of the mark had become a matter of serious concern to the Federal Republic's neighbours. West German exports were running at £14,000 million a year, against imports of only £12,000 million; undervaluation of the mark enhanced this imbalance, with an adverse effect on the currencies of commercial competitors – even including the United States. Any unilateral change in the exchange rate of the mark scares Germans, however unjustifiably. The Gadarene career of the mark in the early 1920s, its slow slide during the world economic depression and the almost total worthlessness of the Reichsmark from 1945 to 1948 provided Germans with haunting if confused memories. Brandt's government was only partially successful in explaining that revaluation meant cheaper imports that would stem price increases and limit inflation. To most Germans, changing the mark's face value amounted to monkeying about with the currency.

Then there was the task of bringing Britain into the European Economic Community. Brandt believed that the entry of Britain and the Scandinavian countries would give the Common Market a new stimulus, propelling it over a hump caused by French insistence on a position of special power, by quarrels over agricultural policies and by inward-looking exclusiveness. He had to play his hand carefully. Too open or forceful a sponsorship of Britain's entry could have been counter-productive. Masters of diplomatic technique, the French would have launched another blocking campaign to prevent her entry. French objections had to be overcome gradually and there were times when Brandt even appeared to be treading with too much care. According to one

British statesman,[22] Dr Joseph Luns, the Dutch foreign minister, once bitterly reproached Brandt in a Brussels hotel for not stating Britain's case with greater force. Yet Luns later paid this tribute to Brandt's determination and tact: 'The very subtle and effective ways in which he managed to convince President Pompidou that it would be in France's interest – in view of the changed realities of power – to have Britain in, were particularly instrumental in persuading the French Government to take positive action.'[23] Luns played a big part himself in promoting Britain's case, by direct and challenging methods. Unlike Brandt, he did not need to set at risk a Treaty of Friendship and Co-operation with France.

According to Britain's prime minister,[24] Brandt's loyalty and understanding over the Common Market issue were invaluable and were rendered the more effective by his openness, friendliness and discretion. Brandt never forgot that the western alliance had to be strengthened – this, and not an independent approach to the Soviet bloc, was the basis of his *Ostpolitik*.[25] The expansion of the EEC would certainly help. At the inaugural session of the EEC summit at The Hague on 1 December 1969 Brandt called for immediate acceptance, in principle, of the applications for entry of Britain, Ireland, Norway and Denmark, and for detailed negotiations to begin early in the New Year. Close and enduring relations should also be developed with other Efta countries like Austria, Switzerland and Sweden. He argued that delays in expanding the EEC had hindered the integration of the Six. Its expansion would enable Europe to compete with the super-powers and develop East–West relations. It would allow a greater contribution to be made to the developing countries and be a spur to European youth. He used the phrase: 'Without England and the other applicant states, Europe will not become what it should and can become.'

Brandt's speech, forthright and full of common sense, played a considerable part in winning the day; there was a unanimous decision in favour of opening negotiations with the applicants for EEC membership. Two days later Brandt told the Bundestag that Europe would 'take a courageous step forwards' and thus avert a dangerous crisis. A protracted period of doubt and dissension had ended. With typical tact, he paid a special tribute to President Pompidou – 'without him and his brave attitude, we would have been wrecked. The course and outcome of the conference were a splendid proof of Franco–German friendship.' The gratitude of the British Labour Government to Brandt was unbounded.*

Approval of negotiations was only a first step. Brandt trod with care in Paris in January 1970. Preliminary discussions would, he suggested, be completed by mid-1970 and the conditions created for full-scale negotiations.[26] He regarded Franco–German relations less as a priority – in view of an impending British entry into Europe – than as exemplary: Franco–German friendship provided a basis for West European unification and all-European co-operation. Speaking at a banquet, he again thanked Pompidou for the part he had played at The Hague. In London in March he spoke to the Foreign Press Association and at a dinner given by Harold Wilson. He called the conference at The Hague 'the most important foreign policy event in my Government's terms of office; it overcame European stagnation'.[27] Answering Mr Wilson at the dinner, he said that he looked forward to the closest co-operation with the British government and Labour Party, working in mutual loyalty to their European partners and confident that the decisions at The Hague were a 'victory for reason'.[28] During his visit he was given an honorary doctorate at Oxford University, the first German statesman to receive this honour for 150 years.

The first budget of the Brandt government began to take shape in January 1970, when cuts in spending were announced that eventually totalled 2,000 million marks (£250 million). The budget was finally approved on 9 July. Its provisions give a picture of the government's overall domestic programme.

In their search for social justice the SPD were bound to help pensioners. Retirement pensions were raised by 5 per cent, pensions for war wounded and war widows by 16 per cent and 25 per cent respectively. Sickness benefits were increased by 9.3 per

* Brandt's own opinion, as expressed to the author, was that Britain and the Six stood to gain in equal measure from Britain's entry into the EEC. No major continental country has had a deep-rooted and persistent democratic tradition; thus British representative institutions could serve as valuable models for a Europe only today in process of achieving political stability. He believed that British membership of the EEC would pave the way for closer cultural and social relations with Europe. One of his pet projects is the creation of a standing European Youth Conference as an adjunct to the EEC. Plainly European youth, currently going through a phase of frustration, requires fresh outlets.

cent and pensioners ceased to pay a 2 per cent health insurance contribution. Tax-free allowances for children were raised across the board; for example, one million families could now claim an allowance for the second child, against three hundred thousand families previously. There was a new fund of 100 million marks for handicapped children. Under a law for the creation of property for workers, a married worker would normally keep up to 95 per cent of his pay, and graded tax remission for married wage-earners applied up to a wage of 48,000 marks (£6,400) – indicating the staggering prosperity of the Federal Republic. Increased allowances were given for retraining and advanced training and for refugees from the DDR. Expenditure on education and scientific research was to increase by 300 per cent between 1970 and 1974. There was to be ten years' obligatory schooling, thirty thousand more places would be created in schools and an extra 1,000 million marks allocated for new school buildings. There were to be five thousand new scholarships for graduates, costing an estimated 50 million marks a year; this number was to be quadrupled by 1974.

It was proposed to create 44,000 new jobs, paying particular attention to West Berlin and backward areas close to the inter-zonal frontier. The budget for social housing was raised by 36 per cent, for communications by 14 per cent. The long-term communications programme foresaw 28,000 kilometres of new or converted motorway being built by 1985, with a real effort to bring goods traffic back to the railways. A 'federal reserve' of ten million tons of crude oil was to be created, and campaigns against noise and pollution were outlined.[29] Hard on the heels of the budget came increased federal grants for sport, a town-planning law and – a totally different kind of measure – reduction of the voting age to eighteen, giving an additional two and a half million young people the vote.

These figures give the barest outline of SPD domestic policy. Then there was foreign policy. Brandt had plainly forecast his intention of making a special German contribution to the improvement of East–West relations. He had indicated his targets – the Soviet Union, Poland and the DDR. From the moment that he took office this task became the most important and immediate in his spectrum. It remained so for the next two and a half years.

A year before coming to power he had written: 'There is a threefold aim in our policy on the East: improved relations with the Soviet Union, normal relations with the East European states, and a *modus vivendi* between the two parts of Germany.'[30] In May 1969 he had said in Hamburg that the East–West confrontation in Europe should be ended by strengthening the western alliance first, then by developing East–West relations and paving the way to the creation of a 'European peace-order'.[31] In June he had made it clear that the development of East–West relations must be a constructive process and must on no account involve mere appeasement.[32] A European Security Conference should involve no preconditions, should be carefully prepared, should be attended by the United States and Canada as Nato powers, and should be held only when there were reasonable prospects of success. This was the formula laid down by the Nato Council of Ministers and Brandt accepted it unequivocally. In the Bundestag on 30 October he restated his readiness to negotiate with the DDR 'on a basis of equality and without discrimination'. But his government would not treat the DDR as a foreign power; a special relationship should exist between the two German states. Three days later he gave an important interview to the weekly, *Der Stern*;[33] he was ready to meet Walter Ulbricht or Willi Stoph, to negotiate with the DDR, the Soviet Union and Poland and to 'put frontier questions on a normal footing'. To extraneous questions he gave frank answers: he wanted to stay in office 'for more than four years', and to reform the Chancellery; and he agreed that his appointment of Horst Ehmke as 'Chancellery minister' had worried SPD leaders who thought that a 'deputy-chancellor' had been created.

There followed interviews with the *Stuttgarter Nachrichten* and *Westfälische Rundschau*. Brandt told the former that a *modus vivendi* with the DDR would enable the East Germans 'to live better'.[34] But the improvement of relations with Eastern Europe would be a difficult business. The negotiations ahead would be tough. To the *Westfälische Rundschau* he pointed out that the DDR would merely create a smokescreen by insisting on a state treaty between the two Germanies; what was needed was practical arrangements that were mutually beneficial.[35] He summed up his arguments for a new *Ostpolitik* in his 'Report on the State of the Nation' to the Bundestag on 14 January 1970. He believed that a moment of truth had arrived; patriotism must be based on what was attainable, to maintain freedom in parts of Germany already enjoying it, settle problems peacefully, nurture human rights for all Germans. In Germany as a whole one must move gradually from juxtaposition to a co-operative 'togetherness'. There could be talks about Berlin, to safeguard West Berlin's communications, increase contact between the two halves of the city and relax tension locally. Limited concessions could bring more trust and understanding, greater security, a more lasting peace. Limited détente should in no way affect the rights and responsibilities of the western powers in Germany, nor the integrity of Nato.

Preparations for a first meeting between Brandt and the East German Prime Minister, Willi Stoph, were already under way. On 25 February 1970 Brandt told the Bundestag that his government had fulfilled its pledge to prepare talks with the Soviet Union and Poland, and 'not to avoid' them with the DDR. He denied that any sell-out of German interests was contemplated; the Bundestag, including the Opposition, had been kept fully informed of government aims and plans. Willi Stoph had, in fact, already invited Brandt to meet him. The invitation had reached Bonn on 11 February. *Der Spiegel* remarked: 'What had for twenty years been either a nightmare or wishful thinking for Germans has entered the realms of reality.'[36] On 8 March Brandt wrote to Stoph suggesting a meeting-place, and agreement was reached on 12 March on the Thuringian town of Erfurt. Oddly, Stoph had made an unwitting concession to historical symbolism: Erfurt was just about the most central place in prewar Germany. The meeting was fixed for 19 March.

In an interview with the *Süddeutsche Zeitung* Brandt was starkly realistic. He expected Stoph to be 'a difficult partner in a dialogue', since he was a man with inflexible views, who masked his personal feelings behind his arguments – in fact, a deliberately faceless man, although Brandt was too discreet to say so. For the meeting, Brandt set his sights low; he hoped that it would break the ice and lead to a second encounter, and that 'confrontation would be replaced by co-operation and communication'. He had the full support of cabinet and coalition, limited understanding from the CDU and the benevolent interest of the Soviet Union. He would not go to Erfurt with a 'Brandt plan' in his pocket, nor was he interested in winning a prestige victory.

Brandt and delegation travelled by special train. The arrival at Erfurt was at 9.26 am and Stoph, when welcoming him on the platform, scored as he saw it a first trick with the words: 'I welcome you in the German Democratic Republic. I am glad that you accepted my invitation.' Brandt's readiness to meet him long before his invitation went out was conveniently glossed over. According to one bystander[37] Stoph's face wore a glassy expression of assumed uprightness, preluding a papal pronunciamento. Brandt answered in a natural voice: 'I hope for a good success.' The two men sized one another up with quick, close glances. Stoph then led Brandt across a full hundred square yards of red carpet – an outlandishly 'democratic' touch – to the portals of the station, adorned with the bannered slogan 'The DDR is the German State of Peace and Socialism'.

The talks took place in the Erfurter Hof hotel, opposite the station. As the two men walked there members of the large crowd broke through the police cordon, shouting 'Willy! Willy!'. Jokingly, Brandt remarked to Stoph: 'Do they mean Willy, with a "y" [himself], or Willi, with an "i" [Stoph]?' There was no recorded answer; there didn't need to be. When the delegations disappeared into the hotel the crowd formed up outside, chanting 'Willy *Brandt*! Willy *Brandt*!'. Then Conrad Ahlers, Brandt's press chief, showed himself at an open window on the second floor. The tumult below increased, with 'Willy Brandt to the window! We want to see him!'. When he came there was a great wave of cheering, to the acute embarrassment of the heavily armed People's Policemen outside. The ovation even shook Brandt; he smiled, nodded, spread his hands a little deprecatingly. He had not dimly expected a hero's welcome. An article in *Der Stern*[38] forecast nothing of the kind. A *Stern* reporter had spent the day in East Berlin, assessing reactions to the planned Erfurt encounter. Answers were vague or discouraging, like 'nothing will come out of it', or 'I'm not interested in politics anyway'. East German officials told the reporter that it was high time the Federal Republic recognized East German sovereignty and stopped blackening the name of the DDR in the outside world. Hence Brandt's astonishment, and controlled emotion.

The East German authorities, typically, took immediate counter-action. Reinforcements of People's Police hurried up, pushed the crowds back from the hotel and hustled those who argued out of the station square. A girls' choir paraded singing 'Demand to Willy Brandt, the DDR will be recognized'. When, late in the evening, the meeting ended the station square had been systematically packed with the usual East German rent-a-mob, prompted by official cheerleaders. Stoph's principal speech at the meeting was broadcast word for word, but not a line of Brandt's answering speech was heard.

In his principal speech Stoph was tetchy, at times almost insulting. East German peace initiatives had been rebuffed by the Federal Republic, which had 'tried to reverse the results of the Second World War, by accelerated rearmament and by trying to undermine the DDR'. West German policies had been formulated 'for two decades by the forces of restoration and revenge under the leadership of the CDU-CSU'. These anti-DDR policies had failed and the logical thing to do was to establish normal and full diplomatic relations between the two German states. Stoph called upon the Federal Republic to do this, and to recognize all existing territorial frontiers in Europe. He accused the West German Ministry of Defence of having planned attacks 'against socialist countries, in particular against the DDR, its towns, its villages and its citizens'. East Germany had, in some mysterious way, been 'occupied' by the Nazis – 'we socialists have always consistently fought against fascism and war'. Stoph extolled the 'democratic achievements' of the DDR, its 'free self-determination' and democratic constitution; and he claimed that his state had been robbed of 100,000 million marks by West German political sabotage and economic sanctions. Then a threat: 'We socialists are interested in the victory of socialism in all countries, including the Federal Republic, which would make possible at a later date a reunification based on democracy and socialism.' He concluded by demanding recognition of the sovereignty of the DDR, the establishment of normal diplomatic relations between the two German states and their acceptance into the United Nations.

Brandt had to endure gibes, moralizing, repetition and sheer length in this predictably useless speech, and still produce a sensible reply. His answer was to the point: the German nation still existed (proof had been provided by the East Germans in the station square!). But the German state had been divided by war and postwar East–West confrontation – 'We cannot simply undo this division. But we can try to modify the effects of partition.' In addition: 'We must not make it impossible for the German people to decide, in free self-determination, how they will live together.' He preferred to 'proceed from the continuing and living reality of a German nation', rather than from territorial division. He laid down six salient principles:

1 Both states must preserve the unity of the German nation. The two states were 'not foreign to one another'.

2 The principles of international law remained applicable – respect for territorial integrity, peaceful means to settle disputes, the exclusion of all forms of discrimination.

3 Force should not be used to change the social structure of either German state.

4 There should be neighbourly co-operation, over a broad field.

5 The rights and responsibilities of the four powers in Germany as a whole, and Berlin in particular, must be respected.

6 So should the efforts of the four powers to improve the situation in and around Berlin.

He asked that both German states should relieve the human suffering caused by Germany's division. He gave two examples: children should be reunited with their parents and engaged couples enabled to marry. He avoided accusations; he could have added that the Berlin Wall caused bitter suffering, that the East German police ruthlessly shot down would-be escapers and that the only people whom the East German regime willingly allowed to 'go west' were old-age pensioners who cost public money to keep them alive.

The East Germans had organized an agenda for the Erfurt meeting that reduced straight talking to a minimum. The midday banquet was a long-drawn-out affair of five courses. A post-prandial session was wasted answering points made in the morning's speeches. Brandt resolutely rejected the absurd accusation that he was planning armed attack on the DDR, saying caustically: 'We cannot pay anything more for the consequences of the social order you have installed.' The early evening was spent in a visit to the near-by concentration camp of Buchenwald. This has been maintained as a memorial of communist martyrdom under the Nazis. The DDR official guides have a well-rehearsed patter, dealing with the sufferings of Ernst Thälmann and other Communists, and it is hard to discover from them what happened to Jews, socialists, foreign workers and the handful of British prisoners who died there. Once again, East German officialdom portrays the camp as a symbol of 'foreign', Nazi 'occupation' of this decent, democratic part of Germany. Brandt laid a wreath at the memorial to the dead of Buchenwald, but his visit was a strain. His hosts played the new East German national anthem as a reminder of the division of Germany, while he wanted to think of Buchenwald as a real link, forged by shared suffering, between the Germanies past and present.[39]

An evening session was taken up agreeing a second Stoph-Brandt meeting. This took longer than seemed humanly possible, but there is not much that is human about the East German regime. Eventually a meeting was fixed for 21 May in Kassel in West Germany. This was included in the joint communiqúe, containing nothing else but verbiage.

There was a typical East German scene when Brandt's special train stood for twelve minutes in Erfurt station before pulling out. Stoph and his foreign minister, Otto Winzer, paraded up and down the platform like stuffed dummies, with Brandt looking out of the window, waiting to say goodbye. Brandt asked his entourage – 'Who do you suppose looks after things here?' The answer was: 'DDR Protocol'.[40] A moment later the train pulled out, Stoph and Winzer came to life and uttered words treasured up but little-meant – 'Good journey' and *'Auf Wiedersehen'*. Brandt's own summing-up was: 'A long day, quite an experience and a necessary part of our political life.' Later he said, 'At least Stoph and I agreed on one thing – that another war should never be started from German soil.'

The next day, 20 March, Brandt made a statement to the Bundestag. He summed things up in one short sentence – 'The journey to Erfurt was right, it was necessary and it was useful.' He was not disheartened by Stoph's glum insistence on full recognition of the DDR and he believed his visit underlined the reality of the single German nation. Subjects that could be discussed at Kassel were the regulation of East–West German relations, the improvement of communications between the two states and the elimination of discrimination in foreign relations. In the Bundestag the chief CDU spokesman, Rainer Barzel, delved deep to find grounds for complaint. They included Brandt's alleged failure to answer Stoph's attacks on Adenauer, Strauss and Schroeder, or protest against the lack of freedom in the DDR. But he expressed genuine concern too:

> Do we see it correctly, that the Federal Government is on the way to recognizing the Oder–Neisse Line; to taking up special relations with the DDR, relations that contain some evidence of recognition; to entering into new commitments towards the Soviet Union; and that the Federal Government's perspective is to have two German states become members of the United Nations Organization? Do we see this correctly? Of counter-concessions, of European beginnings, of protection for minorities, of open borders and of free traffic for people, information and opinion – of these things we see nothing.

The absence of counter-concessions, as the CDU saw it, justified their future objections to the whole of Brandt's *Ostpolitik*.

Stoph spoke to the rubber-stamp East German People's Chamber on 21 March. He repeated time-worn accusations that the Federal Republic intended to absorb the DDR and that it still claimed to represent the people of the DDR – Brandt had explicitly renounced any such claim. A psychosis of revenge still existed in West Germany and West Berlin 'stood on the soil of the DDR'.

The prospects for the second Brandt-Stoph meeting were not bright. Brandt had in the meantime paid visits to the United States and to Norway and had taken pains to explain the aims of his *Ostpolitik*. At the SPD conferences in Saarbrücken on 13 May he said there was no question of hoisting the white flag in a regulation of all-German relations. The topic of *Ostpolitik* took second place here – more time was spent on the burgeoning revolt of the SPD youth, the *Jungsozialisten*, nicknamed '*Jusos*'. They wanted a radical domestic programme, the weakening of ties with the United States and Nato, outright condemnation of the Vietnam War. By listening courteously Brandt drew their fire.

Later he remarked ironically that few young people who sang the 'Internationale' nowadays, knew more than the first part of the first verse.[41] Saarbrücken produced a resounding vote of confidence in Brandt; he was re-elected party chairman by 318 out of 331 votes.

The Kassel meeting, after Erfurt, was bound to be an anticlimax. The novelty had gone and predictability was increased; Stoph had laid down the hard line that he was unlikely to forsake. Whereas East Germans in Erfurt had demonstrated their gratitude to Brandt for coming, nothing so spontaneous could be expected in Kassel. To the great mass of West Germans Stoph was head of an illegal and tyrannical government, who had sold his national birthright to the Kremlin, an insensate, inhuman communist zombie. The West German Communist Party, of course, organized artificial demonstrations. The extreme rightwing National Democratic Party counter-demonstrated, merely giving Stoph a useful grievance to exploit. Conrad Ahlers, Brandt's official spokesman, said on 20 May that the talks were viewed with a healthy scepticism.

They took place on 21 May in the Schloss Hotel, a mile from Kassel railway station. Stoph arrived with a rigidly restricted brief and, therefore, with nothing to lose. He immediately took the offensive, in unprecedented fashion – he interrupted Brandt before the latter had spoken the first two sentences of his opening speech, read out an 'explanatory statement' accusing the Federal Republic of claiming authority in internal East German affairs and declaimed against 'neo-Nazi elements' that had demonstrated against his delegation. His object was to reduce the effect of Brandt's opening speech; he knew it could contain proposals that he did not want to answer.

These proposals were under twenty headings, their aim an overall agreement to regulate relations between the two German states. The six principles that Brandt had laid down in Erfurt were included. In addition he proposed increased movement between the two German states, with eventual complete freedom of movement; the reunion of members of the same families; co-operation over posts, telephones, information, culture, education and the environment; an expansion of trade; and the exchange of chargés d'affaires. He also supported membership in international organizations for both German states and guaranteed that neither state should negotiate on behalf of the other, or claim to represent it.

Brandt had a clear idea of the kind of agreement that could be reached between the two states; Stoph pretended to have none at all. He trotted out familiar accusations: the Federal Republic would not recognize the consequences of the war, was persisting in revanchist policies, still had not recognized existing frontiers and had not even declared the 1938 Munich Agreement null and void. He demanded full recognition of the DDR's sovereignty and ignored Brandt's twenty-point proposals. In the afternoon he did not answer Brandt's request that he should publish the Bundeswehr plans for an invasion of the DDR, which he claimed were in his possession. It is not possible to call a robot's bluff. The only moment of light relief was supplied by Brandt himself, when seeing off Stoph and Winzer. Winzer was a very small man and Brandt told Stoph: 'Hold on to that foreign minister of yours, or you'll lose him!'

Brandt's critics considered him naïve to suppose that Stoph could be talked round, but he refused to be discouraged; he reaffirmed that the road to worthwhile agreement with the DDR would be long and difficult, but must be trod with great patience. Agreement with the DDR was not isolated from other developments in East–West relations; getting sense out of the East German leaders was only one aspect of *Ostpolitik*. Movement towards agreement with either the Soviet Union or Poland would, he believed, react on the East German attitude. The converse might be equally true, but East Germans, less secure than Russians or Poles, were least likely to join in a real initiative.

Negotiations with both the Soviet Union and Poland were already under way. Early in the year there had been talks with the Soviet Union on an exchange of technical and scientific information and an agreement on the delivery of 1.2 million tons of steel tubes in return for 4,000 million marks worth of Siberian natural gas. Preliminary soundings for a state treaty with the Soviet Union were conducted by Egon Bahr. Early in 1970 he had warned: 'We cannot recoup the last twenty years in the next two months.'[42] In fact he returned only two days after the Kassel meeting with the news that the Soviet Union would join in formal negotiations on a treaty involving the mutual renunciation of force. Here was a minor but significant breakthrough. Brandt felt that a non-aggression treaty with the Soviet Union was possible, and would react on both the Polish and East German governments. Nor had his show of patience and goodwill in his meetings with Stoph been wasted, since Moscow and Warsaw had been impressed by it.

Brandt tried to explain to the Bundestag on 27 May why CDU spokesmen, before the Kassel meeting, were wrong to assume that it could only be a fiasco or a miraculous success. The DDR leaders would go on saying their piece and dragging their feet. However heavy the going at Erfurt and Kassel, the meetings constituted preliminary work that was unavoidable; drudgery was sometimes required in diplomacy. He was able to explain himself more cogently in a statement of policy on 17 June, the anniversary of the 1953 East German rising. His *Ostpolitik*, he explained, was based on the strength and continuity of the western alliance and would grow from the settlement of differences with Germany's eastern neighbours. The Federal Republic would not forsake the doctrine of self-determination within a European 'peace order'. It would uphold the rights of the four powers in Germany, and would not therefore recognize the division of Germany 'under international law'. His summing up was: 'We aim at concrete détente with all [states] in central Europe, and against none. This requires bilateral discussions with all those [states] responsible, that is with the governments in Moscow, Warsaw, Prague and East Berlin.' His government would pursue its chosen path 'without haste, but also without hesitation', and would willingly accept responsibility for its actions, believing in its own evaluation of what could be achieved.

Speaking on the BBC some months later, Brandt made it plain that he had no inhibitions about seeking agreements with communist countries. He told his interviewer, Lord Chalfont, that he did not visualize the communist world 'developing towards western democracy', but there were four or five interesting new trends within the Soviet Union. The end of Stalinism had opened the way to change. This did not mean that a West German government could gaily embark on a policy of *rapprochement* with the Soviet bloc; every move had to be discussed fully with the Federal Republic's western partners. This close consultation helped to crystallize western policies –

thus 'creating a framework within which some of the German problems might come closer to a solution'.[43]

Brandt was always aware of the risks involved in his *Ostpolitik*. The basic Soviet aim of world domination has not changed; Khrushchev's successors intend 'burying' the democratic western world, albeit by peaceful means. The Soviet determination to hold on to every advance-post in Europe had not weakened, as Soviet intervention in Czechoslovakia and the 'Brezhnev doctrine' of defined spheres of influence showed. A *sine qua non* for a successful *Ostpolitik* was the staunch and imaginative support of the western alliance. In addition, Brandt has had to reckon with the impatience and uncertainty of mind of the Germans themselves, and with the threat that a future CDU government would reverse his policies and destroy his work.

Still, the Soviet Union was showing a keen interest in détente, for purely selfish purposes. One well-held view is: 'The shots fired on the Ussuri [in January 1969 between the Chinese and Russian armies] were the starting signals for Moscow's new détente initiative towards the West, particularly towards the Federal Republic.'[44] Two months after Ussuri the Warsaw Pact countries declared in Budapest that the era of European confrontation should end; and in October 1969 the Pact's foreign ministers proposed at Prague multilateral agreements on the renunciation of force and closer East–West economic and technological ties. Soviet satellite states were suffering from the strain imposed by East–West hostility in the heart of Europe. In particular the stability of the northern tier of Poland Czechoslovakia and the DDR was badly shaken by the Prague rebellion of 1968. Restoration of stability could be helped by détente; this was the majority view. The DDR remained the satellite least interested in détente, because of lingering fears of its leaders that their power would be weakened by closer links with the West. Only in July 1970 did Walter Ulbricht admit, in a speech in Rostock, that the two German states could reach agreement on a basis short of full diplomatic recognition of the DDR.

One writer, Bernhard Leverenz, has explained that the Soviet interpretation of détente is not the same as the western. He quotes the statement in April 1965 of the Soviet diplomat, P.N. Fedoseyev, that peaceful co-existence between states did not imply peaceful co-existence between 'socialism' and capitalism.

Between the two, a bitter economic, political and ideological battle must continue; 'Socialism' had to win this battle, and could do so without war.[45] Another writer, Georg Bruderer, believed that the Soviet Union recognized three types of conflict with the free world – armed conflict, economic warfare and ideological warfare. She did not want an ideological truce between socialism and capitalism; the ideological struggle was permanent.[46]

The Soviet Union foresaw a possible military advantage from détente, the thinning out and eventual withdrawal of American forces from Europe. American disillusionment had resulted from the disastrous Vietnam War, western lack of gratitude, the balance of payments problem and the old isolationism. Any thinning out of American forces in Europe would be welcome to the Soviet Union and total withdrawal could spell the end of Nato as an effective military counterweight. The Warsaw Pact could afford to dissolve itself as a reciprocal gesture, for its component states are allied with one another in a network of bilateral treaties. The first was signed between Roumania and Hungary in January 1948; there have been twenty more thereafter.

Brandt had a useful card of his own to play. He insisted on an amelioration of the Berlin situation, in particular a written agreement on the city's communications with the West – something that the western powers had never been able to obtain. The formula that Brandt devised, and the western powers accepted, was a neat one; the Federal Republic would go ahead with negotiating and signing treaties with the Soviet Union and Poland, but four-power talks on Berlin would have to achieve satisfactory results *before* the two treaties could be ratified by the Bundestag. The Soviet Union, Brandt realized, would refuse openly to link a non-aggression treaty with the Federal Republic with a practical agreement over West Berlin. But his formula was an appropriate diplomatic device; material gains over Berlin would outweigh whatever concessions were made in the treaties with the Soviet Union and Poland and the package would promote peaceful co-existence founded on facts.

Progress in the negotiations with the Soviet Union was swift and the Russo-German treaty was signed on 12 August 1970. The two countries mutually renounced the use of force against each other. They accepted the 'map of Europe' as it stood and undertook to respect the territorial integrity of all European states. This did not involve West German recognition of the DDR according to international law, nor have any bearing on four-power rights in Berlin. The Soviet Union waived its right of intervention, as a victor nation, in the affairs of the Federal Republic – a right that existed only on paper since four-power rule ended in 1948. By signing the treaty the Soviet Union tacitly jettisoned her image of the Federal Republic as a militarist, fascist, revanchist state. For twenty-one years the Federal Republic had been a tailor-made bogeyman. The ideological war against its 'capitalist' regime would continue, but in a minor key.

Brandt was pleased with the treaty, although when initialling it he produced a typical understatement – 'It's just – business'.[47] At a press conference in Moscow he pointed out that it would have an impact on West German relations with other Warsaw Pact states and opened the road for arrangements with the DDR and four-power agreement over Berlin. Back in Bonn, he said that one of the first results should be progress in September towards agreement with Poland. His chief cause for satisfaction, of course, was the knowledge that the Soviet Union would join at once in talks on Berlin with the western powers, but for obvious reasons he could not make too much of this.

Critics in the West have pointed out that Brandt formally recognized the *status quo* of the Soviet Union's East European empire, accepted frontiers to which the Soviet Union had no legal right and encouraged Soviet hopes for a European security conference that would be exploited in order to reduce the American military commitment in Europe.[48] Yet there was plenty of behind-the-scenes opposition to the treaty in the Soviet Union itself. According to one western diplomat in Moscow the following arguments were used:

1 Berlin would, as a result of four-power agreement, cease to be a convenient 'pressure-point', exploited at will by the Soviet Union in the past.

2 The DDR regime would be placed in a difficult position. Concessions might weaken the regime. (This did, indeed, happen, when Ulbricht had to resign his post of chairman of the ruling Socialist Unity Party in May 1971.)

3 Since the Americans would eventually pull out of Europe

anyway, it would be simpler to wait than seek an 'equalization' that involved making concessions over Berlin.

4 By signing a treaty with the Federal Republic, the Soviet Union was manoeuvred into encouraging a Polish–West German treaty too. Yet this would make Poland less dependent on Soviet protection.

5 Peaceful co-existence would set the Soviet satellite empire at risk. The mildest wind of change was a peril to states as shaky as Czechoslovakia or as staunchly nationalist as Poland.[49]

The advisability of signing a treaty with the Soviet Union could be endlessly debated. It gave a little to both sides, and had a minor symbolic value. Its usefulness depended primarily on whether it helped to promote four-power agreement over Berlin. Brandt staked on it doing so; he was right.

Meanwhile negotiations with Poland were pushed ahead. Brandt had offered talks in November 1969 and a favourable reply came a month later. The first round began in February 1970, in Warsaw, between Dr G. F. Duckwitz and the deputy foreign minister of Poland, Josef Winiewicz. Trade talks began in Bonn at the same time. Winiewicz made one important point clear: his government dropped its demand for West German recognition of the DDR as a precondition to any Polish–West German agreement. For Poland the negotiations now had one main objective – West German recognition of the Oder–Neisse Line as Poland's western frontier.

The Polish regime of Vladislav Gomulka and Josef Cyrankiewicz had several reasons for wanting agreement over frontiers with West Germany. (The DDR had, of course, recognized the Oder–Neisse Line as the 'frontier of peace' twenty years earlier.) The Nazi occupation of Poland had left a residue of fear of German strength. There was fear, too, of the Soviet Union doing a deal with the Federal Republic over Poland's head, and awareness of dependence on the Soviet Union as long as the Oder–Neisse Line frontier was not recognized. Poland wanted to expand economic and technological contact with the West and break down the hard dividing-line between Eastern and Western Europe – the alternative was increasing economic isolation from Western Europe, with its huge economic potential. One could detect, too, Polish impatience with the East Germans – a phrase used by one Polish diplomat was: 'They are the Germans we don't like, while the West Germans are those we don't have to like.' There was a feeling in Poland that Brandt was a man who could be trusted, and that his government was one with which one could do business. To many Poles Brandt represented the 'new' Germany in a way that no previous West German chancellor had done. Poles have never ceased to wonder at the way in which the outside world forgets the bitterness and despair of their suffering under Nazi tyranny. They gave Brandt, as an opponent of Nazism, much greater credit than did some of his allies and many of his own countrymen.

For Brandt, recognition of the Oder–Neisse Line involved a major political risk and demanded high courage. No other West German had dared to antagonize millions of refugees from eastern territories in the Federal Republic. Refugee associations, the *Landsmannschaften*, would not have hesitated to blacken the reputation of the politician or wreck the prospects of the political party that accepted the Oder–Neisse Line. Now responsible people, especially in the press, were at last pointing out that East and West Prussia, Silesia and Pomerania were irretrievably lost, that acceptance of realities was not an act of political cowardice. But even in the ranks of the SPD there were refugees with strong feelings; they could, logically, point out that the Potsdam Agreement gave Poland only temporary administration over areas whose future would be decided in a final peace settlement.

Brandt would have liked a treaty that, like that with the Soviet Union, proclaimed a mutual renunciation of force, that absorbed the frontier question as painlessly as possible, settled the future of the hundred to two hundred thousand 'ethnic Germans' in Poland who might want to be repatriated and normalized overall relations in a decent and dignified way. The Poles went all out for recognition of the Oder–Neisse Line. A satisfactory fourth session of talks took place in late June; the Polish–West German treaty might be ready by September. Paradoxically, this timetable was set back by the signing of the Russo–German treaty in August; it concluded fairly explicit West German recognition of the Oder–Neisse Line. As a western diplomat[50] in Warsaw put it: 'The Poles felt that they had been beaten to the post, by having their frontier settled by Big Brother. Now they reckoned that their own negotiating position was circumscribed. They could not ask for more explicit recognition of the Oder–Neisse Line than Moscow had already obtained.'

Poland still stood to gain much by the unequivocal recognition of the frontier. The greater part of the old German provinces had not been Polish since the Middle Ages, and then only temporarily. East Prussia had never been Polish. These essentially German areas by 1970 contributed 30 per cent of gross national output, 40 per cent of electrical power, 50 per cent of Poland's grain and 40 per cent of her potatoes. Final confirmation of Polish ownership of these resources was coming just thirty years after Hitler's proclamation that 'Poland as a state has ceased to exist', when the West German successor-state was in a material sense the most powerful country in Europe. It was hardly surprising that the West German–Polish talks were pushed to a successful conclusion by the end of November 1970. Brandt travelled to Warsaw on 6 December to sign a treaty that he believed was an historic act, parallel to the reconciliation with France a decade earlier.[51]

The treaty did two things for Gomulka – who had made it clear that it would set the seal on his political career.[52] It established that the Oder–Neisse Line was Poland's western frontier, and that Poland's frontiers were inviolable and could not be changed by force. The word 'recognition' was carefully omitted, for the Federal Republic was constitutionally unable to recognize boundaries not its own (the Polish boundary was, of course, between Poland and the DDR). The reservation was made that this treaty should not be an obstacle to the terms of a final all-German peace settlement. The Poles took some persuading before accepting these formulations. At one stage, the chief West German negotiator, Dr Duckwitz, told Winiewicz: 'We are playing our cards in the open; you can trust us. More important, Brandt really wants peace with Poland, and you can trust *him*.'[53] The Poles, volatile but always receptive, understood; they banked, rightly, on Brandt's solid goodwill.

The treaty was signed on 7 December. In a message to the people of the Federal Republic Brandt heavily underscored the appalling sufferings inflicted on Poland by the Nazis. He said: 'Names like Auschwitz will be in the minds of both nations for a long time to come and will remind us that Hell on earth is possible. . . . I therefore say, to subscribe to this treaty, to reconciliation, to peace, is to accept German history in its entirety.'

Paying a visit to the Warsaw ghetto, to lay a wreath at the memorial to the Jews slaughtered there, Brandt spontaneously knelt for a moment, in that great empty space in which and round which not a single Jewish family lives any more. It was a totally unrehearsed gesture; not one of his entourage expected it.[54] Later he said: 'I did not plan it, and I'm not ashamed of it.'[55] The Poles, as one western diplomat observed, 'sat up and took notice; they realized Brandt was someone unusual'. They may have been slightly embarrassed too: anti-Semitism was rife in Poland before ever the Nazis set foot in the country, and did not end during a postwar period in which the Jewish population had sunk to little more than twenty thousand. It may have hurt that Brandt was capable of 'an act of shattering simplicity'.[56]

The West German press took an adult line on the treaty with Poland – it was necessary but painful, like the drawing of a decayed tooth. It was a reminder of bitterness, wrongdoing and suffering. It gave Germany nothing, for the repatriation of Germans still living in Poland was not a part of the treaty. It opened, just opened, a window on a future in which Germans and Poles could be friends – it could not, in itself, signify a warm-hearted, impulsive gesture of reconciliation. Past history is not repaired by calculated strokes of the pen.

There were dissenting voices. Axel Springer, the biggest newspaper-owner in Germany, wrote in *Die Welt* that Brandt had made his peace with the Polish regime but not with the Polish people.[57] An 'act of pessimism' had betrayed the rights of the refugees and cemented the division of Germany. Springer, maligned for his expertise and material success, was convinced that the Soviet Union had never called off the cold war but was waging it with new tactics. This is a point of view that should not be lightly dismissed. The *Neu Zürcher Zeitung*, that reliable yardstick of observant Swiss thinking, had already written that Brandt was making concessions 'free of charge',[58] and that his *Ostpolitik* originated from the failure of the western powers to take proper action when the Berlin wall went up in 1961.

The Polish regime, it may be noted in passing, did not benefit from the German treaty. Within a fortnight it was overthrown, after a violent and dramatic upheaval caused by price inflation and wage cuts. The new national-communist regime was ready to accept the treaty. It remains a milestone, both in Brandt's career and in the post-1945 history of Germany.

By the end of 1970, then, Brandt had achieved two major foreign policy objectives, the treaties with the Soviet Union and Poland. The four-power negotiations over Berlin were making steady progress. A new picture of relations with Eastern Europe was emerging. He had, perhaps, gained a greater reputation outside than in Germany. His *Ostpolitik* had been matched by his key role in opening the way to the expansion of the Common Market. The outside world was aware of his potential.

Battle for Survival

In December 1970 Brandt received the freedom of the city of Berlin and in his speech of thanks he promised to do everything possible to secure a settlement for Berlin – this was, he said, the supreme test case for his government and his foreign policy. At about the same time the question of the freedom of his native city of Lübeck arose, but parochial and party politics blocked a decision. There were 49 city councillors; 25 were SPD, 23 CDU and 1 FDP. A majority wanted Brandt to have the freedom of the city – perhaps on the anniversary of his becoming chancellor. But CDU councillors argued that he had done too little for Lübeck and should be in office for three years before they made a decision.[1] The SPD councillors were unwilling to force a decision then and there – Brandt indeed asked them not to press the matter – and it was reached only on 16 December 1971.

He received the freedom of Lübeck on 29 February 1972. He was the first man to gain this honour since the writer, Thomas Mann, in 1955 – an even more controversial choice, for it took the indecisive councillors of Lübeck thirty-five meetings to reach agreement, only three months before Mann's death. As a freeman of Lübeck Brandt found himself in strange company. Apart from Bismarck there had been three pillars of the old, imperial order so inimical to Brandt – von Moltke, von Waldersee and von Hindenburg – and four Nazi leaders, Hitler himself, Hermann Göring, Wilhelm Frick and Alfred Rosenberg. The latters' names had been struck off the roll of Lübeck's freemen in 1946; one may note that Hitler became a freeman on All Fools' Day 1933, after exactly sixty days in power. Brandt, by contrast, had to wait two years and four months. The celebrations passed off harmoniously and he took the opportunity of visiting the grave of his mother, who had died in 1969.

The CDU councillors of Lübeck might have continued their

rearguard action save that Brandt had in the meantime received the Nobel Peace Prize. The five-member Nobel Committee of the Norwegian Parliament had voted unanimously for Brandt, out of thirty-nine candidates, on 20 October 1971. The official citation noted that he 'had taken concrete initiatives leading to the relaxation of tension'. Those mentioned were the pacts with the Soviet Union and Poland, the signature of the nuclear non-proliferation treaty and his efforts 'to secure for the people of West Berlin the fundamental rights of personal security and full freedom of movement'.

Brandt was surprised by the award. That his name had been put forward was, of course, known; but he had favoured the nomination of Jean Monnet, 'father' of the Common Market.[2] His first reaction was of guarded deprecation; he said that the honour 'applies to all of us together', meaning ministers and party leaders who backed his *Ostpolitik*. Reactions elsewhere were mixed. In Britain *The Times* appealed for 'a wide and warm welcome' and called Brandt 'a man who has pursued laudable aims with vigour and intelligence ... a good German, a good European, a good citizen of the world'.[3] The *Daily Telegraph* called the award 'a massive interference in West German politics' and suggested, presumably with tongue in cheek, that 'Mr Brezhnev, despite his earlier activities in Czechoslovakia, has every reason to feel aggrieved at not being bracketed equal with Herr Brandt as a harbinger of peace'.[4] The *Guardian* summed up the views of many people when it called this award 'a prize for courage' – Brandt had shown immense pertinacity and had stood up to a barrage of criticism and sneers at home. The contents of secret papers were leaked to the press, he had been depicted as being 'soft on communism', lampooned and libelled. Yet he went on making the cardinal point that 'whatever one thinks of communism as practised in Eastern Europe and the Soviet Union, the vast majority of the middle and older generations there have suffered more death and destruction because of Germans than of Communists. For a German Chancellor to look so fearlessly back as well as forward surely deserves a prize.'[5]

Receiving the award on 10 December 1971 in Oslo, Brandt said he accepted 'on behalf also of those who are helping and have helped me' in the quest for peace. It was a difficult quest; one letter had reminded him of the story of the Red Indian boy asking his father as they came out of the cinema, 'Do we never win?'. Brandt recalled that Alfred Nobel allegedly said he wanted 'to help dreamers, who find it hard to succeed in life'. He added: 'Well, it's not for me to judge whether the Nobel Committee has made the right choice, but this much should be known; I can hardly afford political dreams at present, and I've no wish yet to give up my work.' At Oslo University he said that a good German could not be a nationalist today. He must belong to Europe, for only in Europe could Germany refind herself and refashion her history. For Europe co-existence had become the basis of her very existence, the sole chance of survival. The story of Berlin showed this. Protests had not helped the city; the Wall stayed, communications remained under threat, the rift through the middle of Germany grew deeper, political poker changed nothing. Europe had to create an atmosphere of mutual trust and make a real beginning in economic, technical and cultural co-operation. In the military field there could be a 'conference on security, co-operation and force reductions'. This was the first time that Brandt had expressed himself with such clarity on this last question.

Awards apart, Brandt was nominated the 'man of the year' by *Time Magazine* in January 1971. The announcement coincided with reports of threats to his life from crackpots and cowards. The normal rate after he became chancellor was forty a month. In November 1970 it soared to over a hundred. In January 1971 there was a reported plot to assassinate him while on a short holiday in Kenya; in February another to kidnap him on a country stroll near Bonn. Yet personal security was something about which he worried little. He refused to move into the 'Chancellor's bungalow', in the grounds of the Palais Schaumburg, preferring the seclusion and better air of the Venusberg. He was determined to keep his official and personal life separate.

The strains of office were having some outward effect by early 1971. He drove himself hard; indeed he has never rid himself of the feeling that life is too short to get everything done.[6] He sometimes brooded on official occasions, he looked superficially fatigued – there were more lines on his face and he laughed and smiled less readily.[7] His own recipes for the near-exhaustion of any head of government were to sleep it out whenever necessary, to relax by reading books in peace[8] and to take holidays in the fjords and mountains of Norway – far from fashionable resorts. He was paying more attention to his health; regular check-ups had become the rule. One magazine made a study of the hours that he was keeping:[9] in a four-week period he spent 152 hours in the Chancellery and was at home for exactly half the evenings; he spent 11 hours during this period in planes and 59 hours on SPD party work; he was leading a more sedentary life than when foreign minister – during a four-week period in that post he had spent only 42 hours in the Foreign Office, 20 hours in planes and was far more often abroad. But as chancellor he was working even harder than before.*

In his 'Report on the State of the Nation' of January 1971 Brandt concentrated on foreign affairs. He grouped his objectives under six headings. The German people's right of self-determination would be upheld. So would the reality of a single German nation. A written agreement would be sought with the DDR, on the basis of the twenty points put to Stoph at Kassel. The legal status of Berlin would be maintained and a satisfactory conclusion of the four-power Berlin talks would enable the German–Soviet treaty of August 1970 to be ratified. Finally, the treaty with

---

* *Jasmin*, the magazine in question, noted some of the idiosyncrasies of his daily life. He rose at about 7.30 am, dressed quickly and with a certain eagerness to get started on the day. Sometimes he swam in his private pool before breakfast. He glanced through some of the day's papers at breakfast, usually *Die Welt*, the *Süddeutsche Zeitung*, the *Frankfurter Allgemeine Zeitung* and the *Bild Zeitung*. He always greeted his chauffeur, his security guards and his office staff with an easy informality. His chauffeur brought him the day's news survey compiled by the Federal Press Office and he looked through this during the quarter of an hour's drive from the Venusberg to the Palais Schaumburg – under Brandt's orders, official drivers observed the speed limit, in contrast to the habit of Adenauer and some of his ministers of deliberately exceeding it.

A cardinal rule was to clear his desk before going home at about 6.30 pm. This was one facet of his passion for tidiness. Like Erhard, he used green ink when marking official papers, and he had long ago developed a curious trick of playing with three matches while reports were read out to him – in his case, an aid to concentration. While Adenauer used to conduct his guests to the front door of the Palais Schaumburg, Brandt's attentiveness generally took the form of helping them on with their coats. The staff of the Chancellery was increased by about 100, to around 350, soon after Brandt became chancellor.

Poland would also be submitted to the Bundestag 'in the same political context'.

Brandt's targets were the early conclusion of the four-power talks on Berlin, followed by Bundestag ratification of the treaties with the Soviet Union and Poland. This could break the deadlock with the DDR. Further ahead lay the possibility of treaties with Czechoslovakia, Hungary and Bulgaria – thus rounding off the Federal Republic's relations with the Soviet bloc. Brandt was doubtless doubly keen to complete the main part of this process by the end of 1971; completion of his principal foreign policy aims during the first half of his four-year term of office would enable him to turn his attention fully to domestic affairs during the second half. His timetable was not precisely calculated but this sort of plan made good sense. Elections are usually won on domestic issues; the government needed a margin of time for reforms and improvements to bite before the federal elections due in 1973.

Three factors invalidated this timetable. First, the CDU Opposition decided to destroy his *Ostpolitik*, root and branch. Their leaders decided that it was both dangerous and unpopular – on the latter score they were mistaken. The Soviet bloc could not forget that the CDU were the strongest single party in the Bundestag, with every chance of winning the next federal elections. Rather naturally, East European interest in promoting Brandt's *Ostpolitik* for its own sake waned. The Soviet Union began to attach increasing importance to a European security conference, as the next stage in détente. In the second place, the DDR had even less interest than before in a practical agreement between the two German states. For the Soviet Union was now less keen to give the DDR regime a push, and it had required Soviet pressure to induce Stoph to meet Brandt at Erfurt and Kassel. For a time it had looked as if DDR propaganda would have to concentrate on the United States as the enemy. Now East Berlin could argue that West German revanchism, militarism, imperialism and the rest were still not dead – they lived on in the utterances of Barzel, Strauss and other CDU leaders. And these people might, in next to no time, be ruling the Federal Republic. Here was a ready-made pretext for the DDR to relapse into truculent diplomatic immobility. Finally, the four-power agreement on Berlin took a terribly long time, most of 1971 in fact.

Bundestag ratification of the treaties with the Soviet Union and Poland had to be put back to 1972. In addition ratification became more difficult. What looked at the outset like routine evolved into a life-and-death struggle for the Brandt government, with what had been a small majority in the Bundestag crumbling away to nothing. And the final signature of the Berlin agreement had, in its turn, to wait on Bundestag ratification of the treaties.

The four-power talks on Berlin were bound to be protracted. The western powers were asking for a written guarantee of the city's communications with West Germany – something that the Russians did not grant in the protocols signed in London in 1944, or at the Potsdam Conference, or again at the end of the blockade in 1949. In addition the western powers wanted the easing of conditions in Berlin, with increased personal movement between West and East Berlin. For their part the Russians wanted the West German presence in Berlin to be curtailed and a Soviet consulate-general to be established in West Berlin. They were not prepared to discuss Berlin as a whole – even though it was a four-power responsibility – and they had no intention of having the Berlin Wall removed. The viability of the DDR still depended on its maintenance.

A western draft was produced in February 1971, a Soviet draft in March. In May the seventy-seven-year-old Ulbricht resigned as first secretary of the East German Socialist Unity Party. By August the end was in sight and the four powers signed the agreement on 3 September. It represented a fair compromise, with a balance of advantage to the West. This was because of Article A of Part 2 of the agreement. It read:

> The Government of the USSR declares that transit traffic by road, rail and waterways through the territory of the German Democratic Republic of civilian persons and goods between the Western sectors of Berlin and the Federal Republic of Germany will be unimpeded; that such traffic will be facilitated so as to take place in the most simple and expeditious manner; and that it will receive preferential treatment.

In addition the Soviet Union undertook not to seek to change 'the situation in the area' unilaterally, and recognized ties between West Berlin and the Federal Republic. It also declared that 'communications between the Western sectors of Berlin and areas bordering on these sectors, and those areas of the German Democratic Republic which do not border on these sectors, will be improved. Permanent residents of the Western sectors will be able to travel to and visit such areas for compassionate, family, religious, cultural or commercial reasons, or as tourists, under conditions comparable to those applying to other persons entering these areas.'

The Soviet Union secured its consulate-general in West Berlin and an undertaking that plenary parliamentary sessions would not be held in the city; nor would the 'federal assembly' (*Bundesversammlung*) assemble in West Berlin to elect a federal president. Of significance too were provisions under which the Federal Republic could perform consular services for West Berlin, extend international agreements to include the city, represent it in international conferences and organizations. These things had previously been done for West Berlin as of right; in future they would be done by virtue of the Soviet signature of the four-power agreement.

Immediate reactions to the agreement among the western Allies were mainly favourable, though in the United States doubts were raised by old hands in German affairs like General Lucius Clay and John McCloy, on the grounds that Brandt's new policies were going too far and too fast. Britain's foreign secretary, Sir Alec Douglas-Home, was delighted.[10] Forecasting the agreement, the *Guardian* predicted: 'Although the Russians can always tread on West Berlin, they are now even less likely to; they would have more to lose ... they would provoke a global crisis which is precisely what they want to avoid.'[11] The weekly *New Statesman* called the agreement 'a break in the clouds'; the permanent threat to West Berlin 'the awful vulnerability of its umbilical cord with the West', had been ended.[12] The paper believed that the DDR had needed to be put under severe Soviet pressure. Only a few weeks previously Ulbricht's successor, Erich Honecker, had declaimed against the 'imperialist' West German state, predicted increasing antagonism to it and indicated his dread of increased human or political contact between the two parts of Germany.[13] The British Foreign Office was pleased. It pointed out that there had been the fullest co-operation between Brandt's government and the western powers, the size of the Soviet consulate-general in West Berlin would be restricted and the apparent writing-off of four-power rights in East Berlin was a simple recognition of irreversible facts. It recognized that the other side could violate the spirit of the agreement, but scarcely a hard-and-fast written undertaking.

The western powers recognized, however, that East Berlin could – as a result of the agreement – gain in status. The British Foreign Office predicted that foreign embassies might move into East Berlin in 1973 – there was talk of a hundred United Nations member states doing this sooner or later. East Berlin could, in theory, become a magnet – while West Berlin withered. This danger cannot be immediately written off. In a simple but subtle way the *Sunday Telegraph* suggested that the Berlin agreement marked, not the end of the cold war but its transformation – 'Good may come of this, but it would be as well to realize that we shall never again, from an American President, hear John Kennedy's affirmation of faith: "Ich bin ein Berliner".'[14]

The mayor of West Berlin, Klaus Schütz, was utterly confident. Speaking in the City Parliament on 7 September he said that West Berlin now had 'the *status quo* plus' – the written agreement over communications was the first visible advantage for West Berlin in twenty-five years. The leader of the CDU opposition, Kiesinger, had admitted on 2 March 1969 that what mattered to the people of Berlin was concrete advantage; this had now happened. Schütz denied that East Berlin had been written off; four-power responsibility was not abrogated and the people of East Berlin still took no part in DDR elections. That West Berlin was not an integral part of the Federal Republic had been recognized in 1949. Finally, the fact that no more meetings would take place in Berlin of West German assemblies was not a reverse; their main point had been to stress links between West Berlin and West Germany and these links had now been materially strengthened by – at long last – a written agreement.[15] Twenty-five years of crisis were over – links with the West would be developed and strengthened and Berlin would stand on its own feet. In the course of a few weeks thirty different offices had opened in West Berlin to do business with Eastern Europe.[16] Schütz was well aware that Soviet pressure on the DDR would bring results. Thus Honecker had said on 19 October that the Berliners should expect no Christmas present.[17] But by 1 November, due to Brezhnev's visit to East Berlin, he was agreeing that transit problems should be satisfactorily solved without delay.[18] Schütz told the City Parliament that West Berlin's situation had been stabilized – 'We no longer need dream any dreams.'[19]

The opposite point of view needs consideration too; it was cogently stated by the one British newspaper that set its face, from the start, against Brandt's *Ostpolitik*, the *Daily Telegraph*. The paper's former correspondent in Germany, Reginald Steed, maintained that the principal aim of the Soviet Union was to undermine West Berlin's position.[20] The Russians had obtained a specific commitment about what the West Germans would not be allowed to do in West Berlin in the future. They would exploit their advantage in order to secure full recognition of the DDR and its acceptance into the United Nations and their next gambit would be to force the western powers out of Berlin. Steed foresaw diminishing confidence in West Berlin, with its falling population, its high percentage of pensioners and its perennial need of subsidies. He believed that the Russians and their East German minions could turn the screw again on West Berlin whenever they chose to do so; nothing would be easier than to rake up a specious excuse. Somewhat unfairly Brandt and his supporters were accused of employing a technique to push *Ostpolitik*, of asking: 'Are you in favour of the Berlin agreement and détente, or are you a Nazi?' In no single statement did Brandt argue in this back-handed manner.

Brandt's own summing-up of the four-power agreement on Berlin was balanced. He regarded a written undertaking by the Soviet Union on Berlin's communications as of cardinal importance. The city would continue to suffer from a sense of strain – its exposed geographical position ensured this. A heroic era had ended, but Berliners would soon realize that they faced a new challenge and would confront it with their usual aplomb. Their new mission was to be a meeting-place between East and West, a focus of cultural, economic, diplomatic and above all human interest. He believed that they would have the chance of working more successfully and living a little better.[21] There was no reason, he thought, why cultural contact with the East should not increase. Why not, for instance a Tchaikovsky 'week' with Herbert von Karajan conducting the concert's and three great Soviet soloists taking part? West German money would still be needed for investment, but it was the Berliners who should decide how to do more for themselves. It was necessary to 'live with the Wall', but possible to 'take away some of its stark brutality', for it to 'be made transparent'. The drain of young people away to the West was unfortunately continuing, but Berlin had always found new settlers in days gone by. Brandt made the interesting suggestion that foreign workers should have their own communal representation, a kind of 'communal nationality'. Everyone who came to Berlin should be fully at home there.[22]

The debate about the four-power Berlin agreement will go on, for success is a relative term in the context of a city with Berlin's strangely isolated position on the wrong side of the Iron Curtain. Axel Springer took the unusual step of seeking an audience in Britain, in the columns of the *Daily Telegraph*. He accused Brandt of flirting with the East and claimed that Soviet aims remained as before. They were: to separate West Berlin completely from the Federal Republic, turn it into a separate political entity and impose East German control of Berlin's access routes. He wrote: 'Once the new agreements on Berlin are concluded, the Soviets will allow a certain period for consolidation – probably even of co-operation. Then they will squeeze again, with the final goal of extinguishing Berlin as a symbol of hope and freedom.'[23] He foresaw a *pax sovietica* in Central Europe, which 'would mean a new Dark Age in our time'. The coming European security conference would be the next gambit, followed by Soviet pressure for an American withdrawal from Europe. Franz-Josef Strauss went further; earlier he had said: 'I am ashamed; the flag has been lowered.'[24]

But the balance of opinion was in favour of the Berlin agreement. As one writer saw it: four-power responsibility for Berlin and for questions affecting Germany as a whole had been confirmed, the DDR's legal claim to all Berlin had been dropped, West Berlin's transit traffic was safeguarded by a written agreement, West Berliners now had added chances of visiting East Berlin and there was no more talk of West Berlin becoming an independent political entity.[25] The DDR, admittedly, had hived off West Berlin from the Berlin question as a whole, had confirmed that it was not a part of the Federal Republic, had gained in negotiating status and would become an integral factor in any all-European security solution. But – it was West Berlin that had previously been in a position of weakness.

Brandt pointed out that the new agreement fulfilled the three essentials laid down by President Kennedy ten years earlier – the rights of the three powers confirmed, free access to Berlin ensured and the freedom and viability of West Berlin consolidated.[26] The close ties between Berlin and the Federal Republic would survive and he would visit the city whenever he wished. There was now 'a fair chance for a future without Berlin crises'. The Berliners, on the whole, accepted this. Out of every hundred letters from West Berliners to the city administration, sixty considered easier entry into East Berlin as the most important facet of the new agreement.[27] The safeguarding of the city's communications with the West ranked next. The outside world tended to forget that for twenty years West Berliners, with few exceptions, could not travel to the DDR and that for ten years, save under the 1963–6 pass agreements, they could not go into East Berlin. The desire for increased human contact was strong in West Berlin; a few telephone lines between East and West Berlin had been restored in March 1971, but since mid-December over 150 lines were functioning. West German youth supported *Ostpolitik*; at a youth congress in Stuttgart supporters numbered 139, opponents 23.

Western governments welcomed the Berlin agreement. In particular, Holland's foreign minister, Dr Luns, pointed out that another Rapallo treaty was not on the cards: 'There have been basic changes in the power-postures of Germany and the Soviet Union during the last thirty years. Russia has become so much more powerful than Germany, that only the presence of strong American forces in Europe allows Germany to have political freedom of action with regard to Russia. In other words, if Germany were to go too far, the United States can apply a very powerful brake.'[28] Of the two British statesmen in closest touch with Brandt, Lord George-Brown, former foreign secretary, found it 'sensible and absolutely right, with a considerable effect on Soviet thinking, and giving away nothing that is critical for us'. The big change was that in the past it had been impossible to get any sense whatever out of the Russians on the German question.[20] Harold Wilson approved completely of Brandt's *Ostpolitik*, which in his view owed much to the stamp of Brandt's own personality: 'Kosygin and Brezhnev believe in dealing with the Germany of today, but it has to be Brandt's Germany. Because of him and his policies there has, I believe, been a genuine change of Russian view about Germany.'[30] But as Wilson saw it, Brandt would have to move circumspectly, always attentive to Berlin's interests, never getting out of line with German public opinion. Another former British foreign secretary, Michael Stewart, felt that Britain must give Brandt's foreign policy every possible assistance: 'We must not discourage his *Ostpolitik*, but at the same time not urge him to go too fast, and we must not be so forthcoming to the Russians that the Germans forfeit bargaining-counters.'[31] *Ostpolitik* was realistic and recognized that present European frontiers had come to stay. So had the present political constellation: 'Only a process in the Soviet Union comparable to the Reformation can bring about a real change for the better in Central Europe.'

Here, indeed, was a note of pessimism that may be justified. One acute observer had seen Berlin, four years before the agreement, as 'a stranded ship'.[32] A year earlier another writer had felt that the city had 'lost its formerly all-pervading sense of purpose'.[33] The Wall had curtailed it mentally as well as physically, had deprived it of its glamour and cocky self-assurance, dowered it with 'an inarticulate malaise'. If the four-power agreement produced only a further degree of 'normalization', would the effect on the Berliners be a deadening one? One target of communist pressure in West Berlin would be its increasingly frustrated youth; baits for it were East German technological progress, welfarism extending to pegged food prices and rents, and East Germany's amazing strides in the field of sport – the 1972 Olympics were a tremendous triumph for the DDR. There was much to admire in the DDR, where a few years ago there had been nothing at all. Here was a reminder that Brandt's *Ostpolitik* would succeed only if pursued in a positive spirit, with the broad approval of the German people and the resolute backing of the Federal Republic's allies.

Brandt's first action after the signing of the Berlin agreement was to accept an invitation from Mr Brezhnev to meet at Oreanda, on the Crimea. The only feathers ruffled were those of the French – President Pompidou was expecting Brezhnev in Paris in October and Brandt's pre-emptive visit hinted at unwanted German self-awareness. The sixteen hours of talks were highly confidential and neither side had any interest in leaking details. For Brandt two key topics were implementation of the Berlin agreement – clearly the DDR would stage a go-slow – and diplomatic recognition of the DDR, which Brezhnev was bound to bring up and Brandt to reject. The meeting was cordial – journalists saw Brezhnev thumping Brandt on the back, the two men went swimming in the Black Sea and one conference session lasted up to 2.30 am. Brandt gave nothing away, at least, over recognition of the DDR. A note of comedy was supplied by the puritanical Soviet press – *Pravda* painted out a bottle of beer and a cigarette in Brezhnev's hand, from a photograph of him and Brandt chatting at a small table; *Izvestia* painted out the bottle but left the cigarette. An apt little essay in Soviet regard for the truth!

On his return Brandt was looking at work on the Olympic stadium in Munich on 24 September when he was assaulted by a young man of twenty-two, who clouted him in the face shouting, 'That's for betraying Germany to Moscow!' As policemen over-powered his assailant Brandt called out: 'Let him be – leave him!' The man was a political crank who had been deprived of office in the extremist National Democratic Party, because his views were too violent! In a speech to the Metalworkers' Union Brandt referred to 'desk-bound criminals' who were often responsible for such acts of futile violence.[34]

The principal purpose in meeting Brezhnev was to speed up negotiations with the DDR on implementation of the four-power Berlin agreement. On 6 September in West Berlin he appealed to the East Germans not to drag their feet. Only the day before the People's Police had with their usual brutal callousness opened fire on a would-be escaper from East Berlin, for the fourth time during the year. The East Germans continued to create obstacles to the agreement. Thus they set the strictest interpretation on possible misuse of the access routes to Berlin, even stipulating that there should be no stops at the side of the autobahn to satisfy the calls of nature. They wanted around 130,000 East Germans who had escaped from the DDR since the Berlin Wall was built to be denied right of transit through their territory. They even threatened that the sons of such Germans should be blacklisted along with their parents, and press-ganged for military service in

the DDR if such people were caught on roads and railways to
Berlin. In addition they stipulated that no visits to East Berlin,
save on compassionate grounds, would be allowed at Christmas
1971, because the four-power agreement came too late to enable
arrangements to be made in time.

A visit to East Berlin by Mr Brezhnev at the end of November
brought progress. By mid-December the East Germans had
agreed that unwanted persons should be sent home but not
arrested, that refugees from the DDR who had become West
German citizens should be allowed transit to and from Berlin and
that visas should be granted to West German applicants for entry
into the DDR. Communications between the Federal Republic
and Berlin would be substantially eased. There would be through
trains and motor coaches in which parties would be covered by a
single collective visa. Lorries would be sealed on West Berlin or
West German territory and not opened in transit. The private
motorist would not have to get out of his car at East German
checkpoints in order to go through a detailed and wearisome
process of filling in forms for a visa. Dues that he had paid in the
past for use of the autobahn would now be settled by the federal
government in a lump sum. There would be no further arbitrary
searching of vehicles and persons. On 11 December 1971 the
implementary agreements were initialled in East and West Berlin.
A week later bulk visa charges, now payable by the federal
government, were fixed at 240 million marks (£27 million) for
each of the years 1972–5. West Berliners should have thirty days
in the year for visiting East Berlin and the rest of the DDR. A
formula was found for 'misuse' of access routes – it would be
held to occur when 'travellers distribute materials (such as
leaflets), pick up passengers, leave the prescribed routes without
cause or permission, and commit other punishable offences'.[35]
Travellers and vehicles could be searched only where grounds
existed to suspect misuse. The East Germans agreed to further
negotiations on a comprehensive traffic agreement.

The effect on movement between Berlin and the West was
considerable. On the autobahns through the DDR the only
regulation left to worry about was the rigorous enforcement of
the 100 kilometres an hour (62 mph) speed limit. The 150-mile
road journey from Berlin to Hanover, in the heart of the Federal
Republic, could now be made in three hours; it had previously

taken roughly double that time. At Easter 1972 the first holiday period for visits of West Berliners to East Berlin, 449,597 West Berliners crossed the Wall, 184,638 of them for day-visits, the remainder for up to three days. Over 20,000 West Berlin cars crossed into East Berlin. Hundreds of thousands more West Berliners made the speeded-up journey to West Germany. Later Klaus Schütz said: 'We can breathe more freely', and pointed out that West Berlin had now been included in the new trade agreement between the Federal Republic and the Soviet Union – something that had not happened even after Dr Adenauer's visit to Moscow in 1955.

The more promising political atmosphere played its part in IBM's decision to build a new plant in Berlin. At the end of 1971 a consortium, 'Berlin Consults', was formed to make technical know-how available to countries on Berlin's doorstep and two contracts were later negotiated with Poland – for building a meat-canning factory in Lodz and a textile factory outside Warsaw. Berliners began talking, with real optimism, of extending marketing activities to communist-bloc countries, and of possible links between the EEC and its East European equivalent, Comecon. The sort of prospects envisaged were the creation of an East–West power-grid in Berlin, an exchange of electrical power for oil and natural gas from the Comecon pipelines, direct communications with Poland through East Berlin and the reconnecting of direct rail routes through Berlin – broken by the East Germans when they built their tortuous ring railway.[36] There were conferences in West Berlin of the Transport Workers' Union and of nearly twenty thousand doctors, both attended by East German delegations.

By the end of 1971 Brandt's *Ostpolitik* was paying sufficient dividends for the chancellor to be sure of a fair degree of support in the Federal Republic. It had not been an easy year in other fields; as we have seen, he had hoped that he would be able to devote increased attention to other problems during the scheduled second half of his term of office. The most pressing were the unity of his SPD, the state of the West German economy and the domestic reforms that he had promised when becoming chancellor.

Electorally the SPD had not had an easy time in the *Länder*.

In Hamburg and Bremen, traditional strongholds, the party polled 55 per cent of the votes and were well satisfied. The Bremen result, coming in October 1971 was especially gratifying, since the SPD vote rose by 9, the CDU vote by only 2 per cent. But Lower Saxony and Schleswig-Holstein provided sharp setbacks in June 1970 and May 1971. In Schleswig-Holstein and the Rhine-Palatinate the CDU achieved an absolute majority and increased their strength in North Rhine-Westphalia, Bavaria and the Saar. In April 1972 they sealed success in the *Länder* with a convincing win in Baden-Württemberg, increasing their vote by 9 per cent and securing here, too, an absolute majority. These successes gave the CDU control of the Bundesrat, the federal upper house.

These results were the more surprising in that the CDU seemed in a state of disarray and prophets of gloom were predicting the party's disintegration. Kiesinger was increasingly taking a back seat – he was nearly seventy and was already hinting at retirement in 1969. Erhard had slipped into the shadows and Gerhard Schroeder, an obvious choice as Kiesinger's successor was not in the best of health. The dynamic Strauss could not overcome the distrust of a large section of the electorate. On 4 October 1971 the CDU elected Kiesinger's successor, Dr Rainer Barzel, by 344 out of 520 votes. His opponent Dr Helmut Kohl, received 175 votes, but his candidature was a matter of form. The CDU did not wish to be seen to be suffering from too oppressive a lack of talent.

Barzel was forty-seven years old, a refugee from East Prussia and a Roman Catholic. He had served in the air arm of the German navy, studied law after the war, joined first the small Centre Party, then the CDU. Dr Adenauer noticed him, found him a seat in the Bundestag in 1957 and made him minister for all-German affairs in 1962. He resigned when Adenauer retired a year later and concentrated on a career in the Bundestag as a trenchant, sometimes aggressive speaker. His closest associate in the CDU leadership was Strauss, and the view was expressed that Strauss was using him as a kind of front runner. One commentator called him 'an image-maker's model of a modern politician – smooth, charming, articulate, self-controlled, ambitious, ruthless and unpredictable'.[37] Only the last adjective may be questioned: with his shrewd analytical mind Barzel was a careful planner and astute tactician. The tendency to underrate him prompted the dismissal of his election as merely giving 'the old doll a new head'.[38] His strength lay in party management and direction of policies from the floor of the Bundestag.

Brandt had to contend with dissatisfaction among his left-wingers, particularly in youth groups, and with the busy recruiting by the re-formed Communist Party. The *Jusos* were especially active in Hesse and West Berlin; so were left-wing trade unionists in the Ruhr, while a minor schism was taking place in the Bavarian branch of the SPD. The impression grew that Brandt was not firmly in charge of the party, partly because he had to concentrate on foreign affairs, partly because he accorded kid-glove treatment to argumentative ministers and let decisions ripen rather than hammering them out in endless debate. This was a change of style for the SPD, which had liked in the past to reassure itself by protracted internal discussions; it induced fretfulness among the rank and file. At the end of 1971 there were rumblings inside the cabinet, where the minister of economics, Karl Schiller, was becoming increasingly unpopular. There were worries about the government getting a bad press – the immensely powerful Springer group was consistently hostile. Perhaps the SPD's worst enemies were inertia in its own ranks and over-concern with the adverse trend in *Länder* elections.

To stop the party from 'fraying at the edges',[39] the SPD held an 'extraordinary party conference', from late November to mid-December. In his principal address Brandt ran through the, by now, familiar features of his foreign policy, offering one new thought – that co-existence demanded a conscious effort by the West Germans to develop their own political perspective. This was something that had been totally missing during the Adenauer era; the German political perspective was always assumed to be a corrollary to that of the western alliance. He noted that, in 1971, twenty-five thousand Germans would have been repatriated from Poland, against five thousand in 1970. For Brandt, believing in helping human beings, this meant much. He admitted that there were clouds on the economic horizon – prices and wage demands were rising, world monetary problems were irking even countries with stable currencies. But there was full employment, and jobs for more than two million foreign workers; the rise in real incomes between 1969 and 1971 had been the highest since the war; there had been legislation to increase pensions, speed up town planning, protect rent-payers. The conference took steps to prevent members in future supporting other political parties, particularly the Communist Party; this was the 'edge' of the SPD most subject to fray.

One of Brandt's advisers believes that he did not, in spite of his duties as Chancellor, neglect his party. On the contrary:

First and foremost he made people understand that a modern party was needed. In conferences he was the unifying factor. He had time for all shades of opinion and showed tolerance and understanding. He did not allow himself to be over-worried by the new left or younger members who wanted radical change – he regarded this as natural for young people, a phase of their lives which they would grow out of. The most important thing about his wise, middle-of-the-road philosophy was that it gave the SPD the chance to expand – the party came to terms with the churches and business circles. They stand a good chance now of getting a bigger share of the women's vote, which has been solidly conservative since the war.[40]

Brandt's own view was short and to the point: 'Our party has its differences, like any other, but I would call it child's play compared with what goes on in the Labour and Conservative parties in Britain. I am not worried about our youth; it would be more unhealthy if they had no ideas, rather than divergent ones. One can live with this situation.'[41]

The Brandt government were readier than any predecessor to help in the field of education. Their targets were three million places in kindergartens against an existing one million, regular schooling from the age of five by 1980, the doubling of the education budget from 3 to 6 per cent, the increase of university students by 100,000 between 1972 and 1975 to 650,000, an expansion of secondary education in line with the precept of 'equal opportunities for all'.[42] These targets were perhaps over-ambitious. It has been argued that more should have been done about half-day schooling, still the rule in backward areas, and less about increasing the number of university students. The universities concentrated too much on inflating their numbers, too little on looking after their students. An outstanding example of top-heaviness was Munich University, with over thirty thousand students. Most lacking in direction was the Free University of West Berlin, where domination of 'the professors' gave way to something approaching student anarchy. Universities were infected by Herbert Marcuse's destructive philosophy of rejection. Authority was senselessly flouted, student committees interfered in administration, wild demands were made for a blanket radicalization of university management and students set themselves apart from and often against the remainder of the community. But these were signs of the times. European youth was going through a period of frustration, due to a sense of insecurity that it would not admit. Undue influence was asserted by a small proportion of extremists. The cult of violence became interwoven with a vague spirit of revolt. All this did not help the 'silent majority' of hard-working but insecure students. A ferment of the soul may be fine in theory; an anarchy of the mind during its most formative period is mainly negative. That, too, the Brandt government had to live with.

Along with education reform, the SPD promised to overhaul the tax system. The FDP, with its mainly middle-class support, modified the reforms introduced in May 1971, which were castigated for 'milk and water orthodoxy, with a token 2 per cent on the very top people's income tax' and for ill-advised adjustments that actually led to skilled men with two children and a moderate income being taxed more than before.[43] The SPD promised to extend the operation of *Mitbestimmung* – workers' co-partnership rights – but met opposition from the FDP. The attractive but inchoate idea of a redistribution of wealth in the interest of the have-nots produced talk but little action, talk of electoral reform died away and SPD proposals for making abortion a less undignified and under-the-counter business were put on ice. Much domestic legislation went into the pipeline and stayed there.

In the economic field the SPD record was more satisfactory. The national income continued to grow by 6 per cent a year. The year 1970 was a good one, with full employment, wages rising faster than prices and the mark showing immense strength. In 1971 there was a slowing-down of growth and the government took some mildly reflationary measures; in addition the cost of living index rose by 4 per cent, double the average of the previous three years. German industry showed increasing nervousness, particularly when some leading firms cut their dividends. But the trade unions moderated their wage claims and the floating of the Mark in May 1971 halted the inflow of 'hot' money. At the end of 1971 the minister of economics, Karl Schiller, was forecasting a steady upswing during 1972, a healthy trade surplus, a greatly increased contribution to developing countries and more co-operation in the international monetary field. Schiller had taken over finance, in addition to economics, earlier in the year, when the minister of finance, Moeller, resigned. The German press called him the 'super-Minister'; there was speculation about his becoming Brandt's nominated 'crown prince' and successor.

Brandt was satisfied with progress in the domestic field early in 1972. As he put it: 'People abroad have been essentially interested in our foreign policy – that's why they suppose we have concentrated too much on it. A real crisis in domestic affairs would attract attention in the outside world; we avoided that. It's easier to set down aims in foreign policy in the right order – one, two, three. In domestic affairs, one has to look a long way ahead, and results take time. Maybe, our own publicity has not been as good as it should be, and we did not present our aims clearly enough.'[44] The same thought came from one of Brandt's advisers – SPD domestic policies were badly marketed.[45]

It was, however, his *Ostpolitik* and not domestic policies that produced a real crisis for the Brandt government in 1972. The new CDU leader, Barzel, was in Moscow just before Christmas 1971 and had long talks with Kosygin and Gromyko. He was quick to exploit them on his return to Bonn, explaining that the Soviet Union intended to use the treaty with the Federal Republic to her own advantage. There was nothing new in this thought: the Soviet Union's whole history has been one of the exploitation of agreements signed with her. Where the Federal Republic was concerned she had been more generous than usual, agreeing to a West German consulate in Leningrad and signing an air transport agreement that opened the Moscow route to German air traffic. Barzel, however, insisted that the Soviet Union must do three things before the Bundestag ratified the treaty: give official recognition to the expanding EEC, admit the

German right of self-determination and provide for greater freedom of movement and information throughout Germany. He was sharply critical of his own government for not doing more to get the Berlin Wall removed, or at least to secure an undertaking that East Germans would not be shot at when trying to cross it.

On 9 February 1972 the treaties were defeated in the Bundesrat by a single vote. This defeat meant that the government would have to obtain an absolute majority in the Bundestag for ratification – in fact, a minimum of 249 votes. On 28 February Dr Herbert Hupka, a refugee from Silesia, announced that he would leave the SPD. A few days later an FDP member, Baron Knut von Kuehlmann-Stumm, decided to abstain from voting for the treaties. This brought government support down to 249, the minimum figure. The Polish government was not helping either: it announced that there were only 10,000 Germans left in Poland to be repatriated, whereas the German Red Cross estimate was of at least 180,000 and up to 300,000.

Confusing reports were coming in about popular support for the government. On 10 February the Institute for Applied Social Science estimated that 56 per cent of West Germans supported *Ostpolitik*, against 62 per cent in March 1970. A snap poll by the Wickert Institute showed on 6 March that 50 per cent of the electorate would vote CDU in a federal election, only 44 per cent SPD and 3 per cent FDP. The danger of the FDP failing to clear the 5 per cent hurdle in the next election was obvious: if this happened the SPD, standing alone against the CDU, could hardly hope to win. Early in January the Wickert Institute placed the two main parties neck and neck with 45 per cent each, and the FDP with a relatively comfortable 6 per cent. On 13 March, however, the Allensbach Institute gave the SPD 50 per cent, the CDU 44 and the FDP 5 per cent. Allensbach had 53 per cent still supporting *Ostpolitik*. One comment was that political psychologists thought Brandt 'too earnest, too concerned with foreign affairs, and too distant. Perhaps he should start kissing a few babies.'[46]

For the SPD there were other ominous storm-signs. There were mutterings about the budget, which now envisaged a deficit up from £324 million to £880 million. According to one assessment inflation was now running at a rate of 5.8 per cent a year.[47] Then on 23 April came the CDU victory in the *Land* election in

Baden-Württemberg. The party was emboldened to make the decision, next day, to introduce a 'constructive motion of no-confidence' in the Bundestag with the deliberate intention of bringing down the government.

The phrase, and the parliamentary manoeuvre involved, require explanation. Under the federal constitution a government need not fall, indeed cannot resign, when losing a straight vote in the Bundestag. The framers of the 1949 constitution were determined that the history of the Weimar Republic should not recur; governments then had fallen and immediately been replaced by short-lived multi-party coalitions. There were only two ways for a post-1949 federal government to end its term of office prematurely. It could call for a vote of confidence, lose it and under Article 68 ask for a dissolution of the Bundestag and new elections. The federal president would, in this instance, be the court of appeal; he was committed to giving his assent within twenty-one days. It was also possible for the federal government to fall if the Opposition were able to bring its own vote of no confidence and install a chancellor with a majority in the Bundestag. This was what the CDU proposed to do on 24 April 1972.

The Bundestag debated on 26 April. On the previous day there had been a great wave of popular feeling in favour of Brandt. The trade unions threatened sympathy strikes in a dozen centres of industry. SPD left-wingers, so often a nuisance to the leadership, closed their ranks and marched with the party. A newspaper like the *Neue Ruhr Zeitung* of Essen was literally besieged with delegations and telephone calls. In Essen, a city of three quarters of a million inhabitants, the schools packed up for the day; workers collected, discussed and came to consult; municipal services ended.[48] 'At that moment,' the editor of the *Neue Ruhr Zeitung* said, 'I realized that Brandt meant more to the ordinary people of Germany than Adenauer ever had done.' The Bundestag debate produced a typical fighting speech by Brandt. *The Times* wrote: 'Herr Brandt is not the world's leading political orator, but he lived up to his reputation that he is at his best with his back to the wall by making a resounding defence of his *Ostpolitik* and his Government's economic and social record. It was a memorable performance by the Chancellor, who revealed not the slightest sign of anxiety over his political fate tomorrow.'[49]

When the Bundestag voted on the Opposition's motion of no

confidence on 27 April two Free Democrats joined the Opposition and there were three abstentions. The no-confidence motion was supported by 247 members, just two less than were needed to replace Brandt's government with one led by the CDU. Even though he came within an ace of success, Barzel was at once blamed. One supporter recalled that he was a big success with women at dinner-parties – 'They find him charming and capable of discussing all sorts of other things than politics. But how do we invite thirty million German women to dinner?'[50] A phrase bandied about was that while Adenauer never forgot the refugees, Barzel never forgot that the refugees had votes. Barzel himself refused to regard this as a personal defeat and was determined to try again.

Curiously, practically no one noted that even had Barzel secured the necessary 249 votes it would have been impossible for him to form a viable government. Brandt had been governing with a majority of six, which was whittled away by doubts over the eastern treaties. How could Barzel have governed with a majority of one, which depended on this same factor of doubt? Feeling in the country, moreover, remained predominantly in favour of the treaties. More than fifty thousand Berliners cheered Brandt on 29 April when he spoke outside the Schoeneberg Town Hall and eight thousand people marched in Bonn to demonstrate their support. A counter-demonstration by radical right-wingers was a flop. The *Daily Telegraph* castigated Brandt for 'the reckless haste and ill-conceived methods with which he and his advisers pushed through his *Ostpolitik* treaties',[51] but he had in fact taken two and a half years to negotiate them and reach the threshold of ratification. Barzel's claim that he could improve on them was denied by Radio Moscow; the Soviet government would not negotiate any change of the treaty with the Federal Republic.[52] Non-ratification of the treaties would not only have set relations with the Soviet Union and Poland at risk; it would have destroyed the four-power agreement on Berlin, the East–West German agreements on traffic and on passes for West Berliners and the Soviet–German treaty on trade.

On 30 April Brandt failed to secure a majority in the Bundestag on the budget – there was a 247–247 stalemate. He offered Barzel talks on a bipartisan approach to the eastern treaties and on 30 April Barzel told the West German news agency, DPA, that he was ready to work for an all-party declaration on foreign policy: 'If all concerned show goodwill, good nerves and composure, and if all take a little time, it should be possible to create this.' Talks began two days later, in an atmosphere that was, at least superficially, surprisingly friendly. The two men were photographed drinking a glass of beer together; a conscious effort was being made to show that party differences might be bridged over in the national interest. The talks, moreover, produced a codicil to the treaties, in the form of an all-party declaration, on 9 May. Its second clause pointed out that 'the treaties do not pre-empt a peace treaty for Germany and do not create a legal basis for the frontiers existing today'. This wording made clear that frontiers would have in any event to be confirmed in a final peace treaty and that current recognition of them was not in itself a new step. The all-party declaration also laid down that the treaties did not abolish the German people's fundamental right of self-determination. Brandt commented drily on the codicil that it was 'the work of lawyers, who are unique people in their way'.[53] The codicil was shown to the Soviet ambassador in Bonn, Valentin Falin, and its contents communicated by him to Moscow. The Soviet Union, evidently, would not object to it.

The all-party declaration was expressly designed to resolve the doubts of the Opposition about the treaties. In theory the CDU could now let the treaties be ratified – some party members strongly favoured this. But Barzel, more tactician than states-man, still hoped to bring the Brandt government down. This hope was stimulated by the news, on 8 May, that a right-wing SPD member of the Bundestag, Günther Müller, had quarrelled with his party – he left the SPD on 17 May. Müller's quarrel had nothing to do with the eastern treaties; he was incensed by socialist youth in his native Bavaria and accused the SPD of failure to enforce discipline. But his virtually certain defection meant that the Brandt government would no longer have a majority at all in the Bundestag.

The debate on ratification of the treaties was scheduled to take place in two parts, on 10 and 17 May. The temptation to back-track at the last moment was too strong for Barzel and on the morning of 10 May the CDU forced a procedural vote in the Bundestag, to change the agenda and defer ratification. The vote ended in a tie, and the CDU realized that they had committed an elementary blunder. A tie meant that the motion to change the agenda was lost and the ratification debate would go on. Had the CDU merely voted against the agenda, it would not have been carried and the ratification debate could have been postponed. The procedural motion defeated its own ends.

Brandt's speech on 10 May was impressive. He looked tired before he rose to speak but his fatigue fell away as he moved into top gear. He indulged in no histrionics, but it was a moving speech. Much in evidence was his gift of emphasis, modulating at exactly the right moment his strong voice with its grating undertones. He spoke for an hour and a half, finishing on a high key, with just the right admixture of emotion. In spite of his government's numerically shaky position he showed no sign of nerves or doubt. On a previous occasion in the Bundestag he had been accused of accepting, in his *Ostpolitik,* injustices committed twenty-five years earlier. He had countered with: 'At all events my government cannot, after twenty-five years, win the Second World War.'[54] On 10 May he strove to show that the treaties answered the bitter questions left unsettled by the war. On the ruins of a bloody past, mistrust, ignorance and fear had been created: 'Much time will be needed to dismantle this, but a beginning has to be made. This is not a peace treaty; West Germany cannot make one alone with East or West. But I believe that the peace achieved between peoples in the West can also be achieved in the East.' Where Poland was concerned mutual mistrust went much further back than 1939 – the partition of Poland in 1772 had marked the beginning of a policy, with German participation, that had put an independent Polish state in jeopardy. Berlin and its people were being helped by the treaties, no essential German interest was being sacrificed, a chance was being offered of the two German states being brought closer together and the federal government had the support of Nato and friendly western powers.

On 17 May the Bundestag voted on ratification of the treaties. Up to the last moment it was expected that Barzel would allow a free vote to his supporters, which would have ensured a convincing majority for the treaties.[55] But the Bavarian CSU wing of the party led by Strauss announced two hours before the debate that it would, in that event, vote solidly against the treaties. The CDU was seriously split – so much had Barzel achieved by his misplaced parliamentary tactics – and it was therefore decided to abstain. This, Barzel thought, was the only course on which the CDU as a whole could agree; party unity would be vindicated. In the event 248 voted for the treaty with the Soviet Union, with 10 against and 238 abstentions. The treaty with Poland was ratified by 248 with 17 against and 230 abstentions. The joint foreign-policy codicil – designed to make the treaties palatable – received 491 votes, with five abstentions. Because it had not obtained a clear majority of votes in the Bundestag, the government still required the assent of the federal upper house. This, as it happened, was forthcoming, as a result of CDU abstentions. The four-power agreement on Berlin was signed by the foreign ministers of the Soviet Union, France, Britain and the United States on 3 June. The traffic agreement between the two German states had been initialled three weeks earlier, and now entered into force.

So the eastern treaties were at last finally through and safe. Brandt had shown undeviating determination and his nerve never faltered. He believed that his policy was right and had a much wider measure of support in the country than in the Bundestag. The weekly paper *Der Spiegel* had already reported that readers' letters were overwhelmingly favourable – they included gibes at Barzel, often in the form of exceedingly poor doggerel verse.[56] During the ratification debates thousands of letters flooded into the SPD offices in Bonn and the Federal Chancellery. The vast majority of them were favourable to Brandt. The author of this book organized a small independent poll by appealing for views on *Ostpolitik* while broadcasting on the West German radio network. Of the forty letters that arrived thirty-two were friendly to Brandt's policies, four were against and four came from cranks who were not interested in *Ostpolitik* at all. Only one letter among those identifiably from the under twenty-five age group was unfavourable; among the friendliest were some from refugees from the lost eastern provinces, admitting that there was no hope of reversing history and asking for a fresh start in relations with Eastern Europe.

More significantly, perhaps, an estimated twenty thousand new members joined the SPD during the three-week period that ended with ratification of the treaties. One reason was the resignation from the all-party organization, Indivisible Germany, of its founder, Wilhelm Wolfgang Schütz. He believed that its aims were being traduced for party purposes by the CDU, which had ceased to be an integrated party with an honest programme and had degenerated into a collection of pressure groups and lobbies.[57]

Brandt could possibly have consulted the Opposition more fully at an earlier date. This view was expressed by CDU members of the Bundestag who were not unalterably opposed to the treaties.[58] Yet Barzel could have requested consultation at any time. Brandt's own answer was that the treaties were the logical outcome of a general policy of *rapprochement* begun by the previous CDU–SPD coalition government.[59] His concept of *Ostpolitik* had been under consideration for more than two and a half years; it should have been a matter for individual sense of responsibility, not a shuttlecock of party political manoeuvring.

The SPD–FDP coalition had lost its working majority in the Bundestag. Brandt could now count on only 248 votes out of 496 and there was no sign of this situation improving. Minority government is always possible, but new federal elections were not due until the autumn of 1973. Minority government for a period of nearly eighteen months would be frustrating, and not in the best interests of the country. It would mean the postponement of domestic reforms, over which the FDP had already acted as a brake – even proclaiming this as its natural duty when in alliance with the SPD. As early as 18 May the FDP chairman, Walter Scheel, indicated that there should be an early federal election.[60] He undertook to examine this question in talks with the CDU Opposition. The immediate CDU proposal was a pause of at least three weeks, while the current political situation was carefully considered. Brandt and the SPD would have expected an early election to be much in their favour. In May the Allensbach opinion poll showed that 50 per cent would vote for Brandt, only 32 for Barzel, as chancellor. Over 50 per cent approved of the eastern treaties, only 25 per cent definitely opposed them. Views about an early election were divided, partly due to eager expectation of the Olympic Games – Strauss said rightly that Germans did not want to be bothered with politics until the Games were over.

Six years earlier Brandt had told *Der Spiegel* that the federal constitution was not a Swiss cheese – presumably gruyère, with its myriad holes.[61] But he believed then that it should be possible to call new elections with the approval of a two thirds majority in the Bundestag. In 1972, however, this was not possible. To secure new elections the government had to lose a vote of no confidence, which it might have to bring against itself. The federal president, on application, could then order new elections, at an appropriate time. Brandt's dilemma was understandable: if he lost a vote of no confidence, the CDU might yet be in a position to bring a 'constructive' motion and form a new govern-ment. If he felt strong enough Barzel would not hesitate to do so. The Olympics apart, German public opinion would move steadily in favour of new elections, as opposed to governmental deadlock in Bonn. The weekly *New Statesman* gave a fitting if slightly comical example of this mood: 'In a small village in the hills, I found a priest blessing two tractors, four cars, 10 bicycles and a child's tricycle. "Even if the 'Sozis' [SPD] get in again, and my people would not want that, there should be an election", he told me. "Everyone who does honest work feels that what is being done at Bonn is morally questionable".' His words could have suggested to Brandt that early elections were not only desirable but vitally necessary. The eastern treaties were out of the way. The Olympics came next; then elections. This was the logical order in which things had to happen in 1972.

Interim Report

Brandt must have heaved a sigh of relief when the treaties with the Soviet Union and Poland were ratified and the way was cleared for talks between the two German states. In public he was at pains not to over-emphasize his satisfaction; privately, he admitted deep relief that he could turn his mind to other matters.[1] There were plenty; 1972 was to bring a series of problems, serious or merely irritating, but all looking like reverses for the government.

First, the SPD–FDP coalition had lost its majority in the Bundestag. There was a straight choice – to carry on minority government until the autumn of 1973, when elections were due, or to engineer earlier elections. Brandt and his advisers put a bold face on it; thus the view of Egon Bahr:

> We would love fresh elections – next week would do us best, but it will not be possible to get them before the autumn anyway. We can, on the other hand, perfectly well carry on as a minority government, for the Opposition won't find it easy to block legislation which the public wants – the raising of pensions, for instance, or budgetary allocations of any useful kind. If the CDU block legislation just to make life difficult for us, we shall make their responsibility clear and they will pay for it at the next elections. It's a struggle all right, but we'll get through one way or the other.[2]

Brave words, but without a parliamentary majority really effective government was not possible. There were additional risks – of ebbing public confidence in the government and further defections from the FDP. Elections were the only way of ending an uncomfortable stalemate – there was no 'crisis of democracy' and there had been no attempted CDU *coup d'état*.[3] Nor could one talk of sinister intrigue to unseat Brandt, or compare Barzel and Schroeder with men like Papen and Schleicher, who helped Hitler to power by undermining the Weimar Republic. It remained a nuisance for Brandt to organize a vote of no confidence in his own administration, something that could not be done until the parliamentary holidays were over and that actually happened on 22 September.

In the meantime Brandt had suffered a sharp setback, the British Labour Party's final decision to desert the European cause. The Labour Party had already voted against the European Communities Bill at Westminster, a vote against joining Europe. On 29 March the party's shadow cabinet decided to back a national referendum, as a last-ditch attempt to prevent Britain's entry into the Common Market. A referendum was out of keeping with British democratic practice and had been rejected by the Labour Party's national conference in the autumn of 1971. One leading British paper called Labour's reversal of its decision, for purely tactical reasons, a 'squalid little episode';[4] for Brandt it was a bitter disappointment and only small consolation to hear Roy Jenkins telling the BBC he 'would back Brandt very strongly in his *Westpolitik*, which involves the enlargement of the European Community'.[5] Brandt's failure to retain the support of British Labour was to bring undeserved criticism and gibes. A few months later he was to suffer a more personal pang of disappointment when, in September, the Norwegian people opted by a narrow majority to stay out of the Common Market. Speaking in Interlaken, Brandt called it a 'regrettable setback', although 'the decision of a free people must be accepted'.[6] He understood Norwegian hesitation: farmers and fishermen were worried by the Common Market's agricultural policies and by the fear of their coastal waters being fished-out. It would have been a matter of personal pleasure and pride to have welcomed the Norwegians into the Community. Brandt had once been asked if he was a sensitive person, and answered: 'It's hard to judge oneself; at all events I'm not a rhinoceros.'[7] As was his way, he masked his feeling over Norway's decision.

There were also troubles inside the SPD. Least worrying was the defection of Günther Müller, Bundestag member for Munich, who organized the breakaway 'Social Democrats 1972'. The municipal elections in June showed that Müller had little support. Of more importance was the growing unrest of SPD left-wingers, especially among young people. This unrest took unpleasant forms. Thus on 13 August West Berlin police had to use tear-gas and truncheons to disperse a 'new left' mob that attacked a conventional protest demonstration against the Berlin Wall. Admittedly there were right-wingers demonstrating but ceremonies of wreath-laying and speech-making at the wall had been taking place for a decade. More sinister was the growing anti-Semetic trend among the 'new left'; an example of it was the slogan '*Schlagt die Zionisten tot, macht den nahen Osten rot*' ('Beat the Zionists to death, make the Middle East red'). Leaflets with a similar message were handed out in Munich after the murder of the Israeli athletes in September.[8]

Mention has already been made of the universities, which – according to one authority – 'the Marxists view as a springboard for their campaign to effect radical changes in the present structure of society'.[9] At the Free University of West Berlin a militant minority of the 'new left' had secured a position of dominance. The worst consequence of this was that students were learning too little, or next to nothing.[10] An eminent outside observer put the trouble in Berlin down to 'an alliance between a mindless, pink administration which makes a virtue of appeasement, and a violent radical group of students which uses Nazi tactics'.[11] The troubles at the universities simmered on during 1972, the backcloth to left-wing violence of a more obviously anti-social kind. This centred on the so-called 'Baader-Meinhof gang', or 'Red Army Group'. These urban guerillas burgled banks, bombed police buildings and newspaper offices and assaulted American servicemen. Their least harmful activity was the distribution of revolutionary literature of a Maoist brand. By ill-fortune for Brandt, the Baader-Meinhof gang became active only after his government came into power and was at the same time manifestly an offshoot of the 'new left'. The SPD, somewhat unfairly, was blamed for a chapter of violent incidents, for police failure to track down the offenders and, latterly, for alleged police brutality. Police are under *Länder* authority, but the SPD still bore the brunt of the blame. The Springer newspapers were in the van, not without cause: bombs were planted in their Hamburg offices and there were bomb-scares in their Berlin headquarters. An accusing finger was pointed at the government for failure to carry out social reform and get at the root of social discontent. In a left-wing backlash the government was blamed for a manhunt in which 150,000 police took part, and even for the shooting, by mistake, of a British businessman in Stuttgart.[12]

Law and order was already an issue of national importance when the murder of the Israeli Olympic athletes took place on 6 September. Eleven athletes at the Games in Munich were gunned down by Palestinian Arab terrorists, nine of them after having been held prisoner, trussed up like chickens for the slaughter. The Olympic Games were to have been a special feather in the German cap; vast sums had been spent on staging them and the whole world's attention had been focused on German efficiency and sense of occasion. For Brandt this tragedy was particularly poignant, chiefly because it was Israelis who were murdered. He had always stood out for maximal restitution to the Jews who survived Hitler's holocaust and maximal efforts to effect a reconciliation between them and the German people. In 1960 he was in Israel and had expressed his sincere admiration for the state and its people, using the phrase 'They are in the same camp as we are'. He had knelt at the Warsaw ghetto in the sight of thousands of onlookers. He had defended the resumption of diplomatic relations in the face of Arab objections.[13] He had been invited to Israel in February 1972, finally went there in June 1973; and invited the Israeli prime minister, Mrs Golda Meir, to Bonn.

Brandt did what he could to avert the tragedy. He tried to enlist the help of Arab governments, including that of Egypt. He personally had a telephone call put through to Cairo, to ask President Sadat whether, in the event of the hostages being flown out at gun-point, Egypt would accept them. Sadat was not prepared to lift a finger to help. The West German government contacted the Israeli government in Jerusalem, learning that they would not give way to the kidnappers' demand for the release of two hundred terrorists imprisoned by the Israelis. The Israelis preferred active attempts to rescue the captured athletes in Munich rather than to allow them to be flown to a terrorist base, most probably in Libya. The German authorities offered the terrorists a plane to take them out of the country if they surrendered their nine captives. They offered money, although the $5 million paid by Lufthansa earlier in the year to Arab hijackers probably provided the finance for the Munich operation. They offered substitute hostages; both the former SPD mayor of Munich, Dr Jochen Vogel, and the federal minister of the interior, Hans-Dietrich Genscher, volunteered for this dangerous role.[14] In the end they tried to rescue the Israelis, but botched the attempt. For that they were roundly criticized in much of the outside world. Only the Israelis expressed approval for efforts first to secure the release, then the rescue of the captives, and refused to blame the Germans for their failure.

Brandt spoke on German and British television of his sadness and horror. For the chancellor, insult was added to injury when a leading Israeli citizen wrote asking how he, a Nobel Peace Prize winner, had failed to offer himself as a hostage to the terrorists.[15] Brandt's answer was that the terrorists had already refused to accept substitute hostages and that a head of government could not lightly make such a gesture. His son, Peter, did in fact tell his father that he was ready to be a hostage and thus represent him.[16]

In the *Frankfurter Allgemeine Zeitung* Brandt wrote that responsibility was shared by the federal and *Land* governments. Bavaria was responsible for security precautions in the Olympic village, and for the conduct of the attempted rescue. For intermediate efforts to secure their release by negotiation, federal and *Land* authorities shared responsibility. He called for joint security measures by all European governments and for the drafting of a United Nations convention against terrorism.[17]

Munich was a blow to Brandt's election chances, even though Bavaria was ruled by a Christian Democratic (CSU) *Land* government. A British newspaper quoted Hans-Dietrich Genscher as having coined the slogan 'Out of the stadium, and into the election campaign!', which would now boomerang.[18] Brandt paid tribute to countries that gave the Germans credit for doing the best that they could[19] and he told the BBC that his energies had been primarily directed towards averting bloodshed.[20] Did this betray defensive thinking? On 29 October Palestinian hijackers seized a Lufthansa plane and threatened to blow its passengers up unless the three Arabs captured after the Munich murders were released. At once they were flown out of Germany and on to Libya, to a hero's welcome by Colonel Gaddafi and his regime. Brandt told his cabinet on 31 October that he understood Israel's anger and frustration this time. But he had to give priority to the protection of human life; his government could not deliver passengers and crew of the Lufthansa plane to their deaths. He called again for international measures to combat terrorism. This time opinion in the outside world was divided; on the one hand the Germans were criticized for indecent haste in releasing the Arab murderers, on the other they were excused for taking no chances with desperate men. Two blots on German handling of the situation were failure to stop the passengers being flown to Libya and the fatuously silly statement of a government spokesman that Israel 'should not export her quarrels'. This was precisely what the Arabs, and not Israel, were doing. Once again the incident represented a reverse for the Brandt government.

Brandt had meanwhile to compete with trouble of a more predictable kind in his cabinet. Schiller, minister of economics and finance, was increasingly at odds with other members of the cabinet and was becoming increasingly disgruntled. On 2 July he offered his resignation, to become effective on 7 July. This was a heavy blow to Brandt, who had given him something approaching a 'super-ministry' by adding finance to economics, and to the SPD who regarded him as a trump card in the elections. Schiller still retained the reputation he had won as minister of economics in the 'big' coalition from 1966-9. He was shrewd and able; he was expected to combat inflation, clear bottlenecks and produce the goods as Erhard had done in a less complicated era. For he was operating at a time of world inflationary trends, with a world currency problem looming in the foreground. Even the best doctor cannot cure the ailments of those who are not his patients.

Like many able men, Schiller had his drawbacks. Didactic and professorially certain of the rightness of his own opinions, he did not make himself amenable to his cabinet colleagues. Towards the end of 1971 he had been at loggerheads with his state secretary, Philip Rosenthal, who resigned in protest against policies that he considered had no content of social reform. Early in 1972 Schiller had been criticized for his appointment of a Professor Eberhard Machens as head of the Federal Geological Institute in Hanover. The Professor was Schiller's brother-in-law and there was an accusation of nepotism. In May 1972 he had moved out of line with the rest of the cabinet by calling for cuts in public expenditure and increases in taxation. Apparently without consulting Brandt, he was proposing unpopular measures when federal elections were almost certain in the autumn. Commentators called him 'utterly tactless' and wrote of his 'bullying tactics'.[21]

By the end of June Schiller had been engaged in a still more crucial argument with the rest of the cabinet. The pound was floated, there was an alarming inflow of foreign exchange into Germany and on 26 June the president of the Federal Bank, Dr Karl Klasen, had advised Brandt to impose foreign exchange restrictions – which Schiller had discouraged. On 28 June Schiller had been confronted by Dr Klasen at a cabinet meeting, and on 29 June the cabinet had voted to introduce controls over the movement of foreign capital under the 1961 external trading law. Schiller was incensed, and was later to maintain that he had French backing for introducing a joint float of European currencies, without Germany having to impose foreign-exchange restrictions. This claim has been contested; it was held that France would co-operate in the joint float only if Germany tried out controls and they proved ineffective.[22] Schiller had taken offence with, it must be admitted, some reason; he believed that Brandt should have helped him to fight inflation by supporting budgetary cuts, should have defended him from the attacks of cabinet colleagues, and informed him of the Federal Bank's views. He fired in his resignation, in a letter of quite unprecedented length, running to around four thousand words. There was something Thermopylaean in the way he was ready to confront the serried ranks of his enemies, whom he accused of staging 'a demonstration against the minister of economics and finance' and 'a war of attrition, rich in personal defamations'. He had not a single supporter in the cabinet. The reason – infallible and oracular in his views, totally unbending, he deemed support to be superfluous. His resignation still brought criticism of Brandt. Had he, perhaps, been too hesitant about dispensing with Schiller's services? Did he simply let events take their course, instead of trying to steer them? If he appeared to handle the affair with a lack of decisiveness, the main reason was probably his ingrained aversion to getting rid of a subordinate; one recalls a phrase that he had used on a previous occasion – *'Ich kann ihn nicht einfach auf der Strasse setzen*' ('I can't just put him on the street').

Schiller's resignation came at an awkward time for Brandt, who was holidaying in Norway and busy planning his strategy for the unavoidable federal elections. He replaced him by taking Helmut Schmidt from the Ministry of Defence. This appointment had a deeper significance: he had refused to nominate Schiller as his 'crown prince' precisely because Schmidt would be the better choice. Experience in the economic field could help to groom Schmidt for future leadership. German newspapers predicted gloomily that the departure of Schiller meant that the SPD were jettisoning the free-market economy. Schiller sought to increase the unease by announcing on 17 August that he would not seek re-election for the Bundestag as an SPD candidate – a veiled hint there that he might just be prepared to do so in a different party. Brandt, perhaps nettled by accusations that he was indecisive in handling his cabinet, retorted by comparing Schiller to 'one of those very intelligent army recruits who insists it is everybody else who is marching out of step'.[23] A week later Schiller's post on the party praesidium was taken by Jachen Vogel of Munich, clearly marked out for stardom. The only other repercussion was an investigation into the magazine *Quick*, which had published the text of Schiller's letter of resignation, a confidential document. There were police raids on *Quick's* offices in Bonn, instituted by the public prosecutor's office and drawing the mildly disapproving comment from Brandt that he doubted whether the end justified the means.[24] Physical action against newspaper offices inevitably causes apprehension, but none of the heavy-handedness shown in the *Spiegel* case ten years earlier was apparent on this occasion. Comment died down quickly; the Schiller crisis turned out to be less damaging than expected.

It had one almost comical sequel. When the federal election campaign was fully under way the CDU first hinted, then positively stated that Schiller had come over to their side. Early in November he did indeed have private talks with Barzel, in a Hamburg hotel.[25] The country was at once flooded with CDU posters depicting Schiller and ex-Chancellor Erhard as twin champions of economic stability, while Barzel told the Sunday newspaper *Bild am Sonntag*[26] that Schiller would join in a campaign 'to restore stability and counter inflation'. On 13

November the CDU general secretary, Konrad Kraske, had to explain that Schiller had not yet accepted Barzel's offer; on the same day Schiller stated 'there was no discussion of concrete forms of co-operation or particular functions'.[27] More was to come. A leading member of the FDP, Karl Moersch, told journalists that Schiller had tried to join his party after resigning from the cabinet and had asked the party leader, Herr Scheel, for the post of minister of economics. In the meantime Schiller had put out feelers for a directorship of a tobacco firm. The CDU leadership were embarrassed. Franz-Josef Strauss, who had in the past referred to Schiller as 'minister of inflation',[28] was thoroughly unhappy about efforts to enlist such an awkward recruit. Schiller had worked with him in the coalition but Strauss 'described himself as the backroom-boy cook who concocted the magic potion, and Schiller, the waiter, who merely dished out but collected all the tips'.[29] Inappropriately, Strauss had been trying to lure the FDP into an alliance with the CDU after the elections, at the precise moment when Schiller appeared to be angling for a position of power within the FDP!

In the event Schiller became no more than an onlooker in the 1972 election campaign. This had started earlier. Possibly the first shot in it was a sudden attack in the West German press on Brandt for having his private swimming-pool rebuilt; the alleged cost was £7,000. Brandt's residence was an official one, the pool was in frequent use and the attack petered out; it was June, the weather was fine, the German public was just not interested. On 6 August Brandt forecast fresh elections before the end of the year. On the same day he suffered a minor setback when Finland announced it would seek diplomatic relations with the DDR before receiving a reply from Bonn to its letter of intent. On 20 August he made an important statement of policy in Bonn, on the twentieth anniversary of the death of Kurt Schumacher. SPD policy, he said, would never become 'something abstract'; its primary aim was a truly social and democratic community. Nor would the idea of German nationhood be given up for one moment, although there were two existing German states. Brandt urged his listeners to think beyond day-to-day issues, to think about human dignity and human values, the generation gap, the environment, the lot of the old people, the strains and stresses between industrialized and developing communities.

On 22 September he secured his 'simple' vote of no confidence in the Bundestag, enabling Federal President Heinemann to order federal elections for 19 November. *Der Spiegel* asked Brandt whether corruption was involved in the defections from the government coalition that had made new elections necessary. He answered: 'For me there can be no doubt about that.'[30] He was sharply criticized for this answer. What inspired it was almost certainly the endless leaks from the Federal Parliament designed to discredit his foreign policy. Well-informed journalists called these leaks a bad national joke, since they were always made to papers of the Springer group that were violently opposed to *Ostpolitik*.[31] Paul Frank, state secretary in the Foreign Ministry, said: 'For the first time we have managed to quote the Head of Government and the Foreign Minister of a super-power on the basis of stolen official documents. In all seriousness, we can't go on like this. . . .' Brandt's disgust and anger were understandable; only, it does not pay to have a thin skin in politics.

Brandt's principal electoral address came on 12 October at an extraordinary party conference of the SPD in Dortmund. Some time before it had been said that he would have to display the skill of a surf-rider to win the next election, after being brought to power in 1969 by the improbable combination of disappointed liberals, old-guard socialists and impatient youth.[32] In an election campaign finesse is generally of less use than straight, hard hitting. In Dortmund Brandt pulled no punches. He attacked the CDU for putting party before country, for subservience to its Bavarian branch, for seeking to make capital out of the Olympics tragedy, for intolerance towards youth and for not having the guts to sign the nuclear non-proliferation pact – when ninety-eight other states had already accepted it. He called the CDU a party in which Sancho Panzas predominated, but with a 'secret chancellor', Franz-Josef Strauss, the 'last Prussian from Bavaria'. There was a brief mention of Schiller; Brandt called his resignation 'a victory of vanity over sense'. He paid a handsome tribute to his FDP allies, calling Scheel 'a better foreign minister than Willy Brandt could ever be under Kiesinger'. Liberalism and social democracy had quite enough in common to produce effective government and to work together to create a new political centre. He promised good administration, tempered by imagination, compassion and a lasting desire for social progress.

Party tactics became clear during the campaign. The SPD set out to exploit Brandt's considerable personal popularity. Election posters showed him smiling or reflective, sun-tanned, healthy and handsome. 'If this were a presidential election,' one paper wrote, 'there is no doubt that Chancellor Brandt would win hands down. He has come to bestride Germany – East and West – like a colossus. He has completely taken over the mantle from Konrad Adenauer of statesman and father figure.'[33] Wherever he went he attracted huge crowds, with a big proportion of enthusiastic young people. The SPD's favourite slogans were 'Vote for Willy – who else is there?' and 'Willy must stay!' Brandt's own catchword was 'Germans, we can be proud of our country' – a subtle appeal to all those who believed that the new democratic Germany would expunge the memory of the old. The party made much of Brandt's *Ostpolitik*. The successful conclusion of the talks between the federal and DDR governments on 6 November helped. The DDR had already proclaimed an amnesty of political prisoners; seven thousand had been released and three hundred allowed to cross into the Federal Republic. Now the DDR permitted the first family reunions: twenty-four women rejoined husbands or fiancés who had previously escaped to West Germany. More political prisoners would be free to leave too, if they chose, by the end of 1972. The Soviet Union, for her part, undertook to grant 1,800 exit permits to Russians of German descent who wished to leave the country. On 5 November the first party of eight people, three of them children, passed through West Berlin. The talks between the two German states produced a draft treaty ready to be ratified by governments and parliaments. For the rest, the SPD insisted that its domestic record had been underrated, that the country was economically more prosperous than ever and the floating and revaluation of the mark had helped to raise the standard of living. Inflation in West Germany was at least modest compared with that in Britain and other industrialized countries.

The CDU presented themselves as a team, rather than relying on their leaders – an exact reversal of party roles in the past, when Adenauer dominated elections and the SPD took refuge in

the defensive image of a 'collective'. Barzel decided to make inflation, running at about 6 per cent, the main point of attack –
socialism was 'making us all poorer', prices were rising three
times as fast as under CDU governments, building costs had
bounded 40 per cent in three years. His summing up was; *'Dieses
Land ist nicht in Ordung'*, a dull equivalent for 'something is
rotten in the State of Denmark'.[34] He was unimpressive, in spite
of polish and a certain sleek persuasiveness. He limited himself to
two to three meetings a day, retired to bed regularly at 10 pm,
had little time for the press and left 'personality cult' tactics to
Strauss in Bavaria, land of the loud mouth and big fist pounding
the table.

The FDP were essentially concerned with survival. They
polled only 5.8 per cent of the votes in 1969; if they failed to
reach the 5 per cent mark they would cease to be in the Bundestag. For the first time they were campaigning on a federal level as
proclaimed junior partner of the SPD and had lost their right-
wing conservative supporters. As party leader Scheel depended
largely on middle-class voters with an equal antipathy to socialism
and the Catholic Church, and on the argument that a third force
in Parliament could act as a brake on either big party.

Compared with the election campaigns of 1965 and 1969, that
of 1972 was relatively sober, almost staid. Brandt would not
indulge in personal attacks; Barzel, after early polemical
fireworks, followed his example. Inevitably the campaigning had
some unpleasing features. The Young Socialists produced an
unofficial election poster showing Barzel and Stoltenberg, the
CDU prime minister of Schleswig-Holstein, perched on the back
of a huge poisonous insect wearing the mask of Strauss.[35] Young
Socialists were also responsible for a few physical assaults on
people sporting the CDU colours. CDU posters in Bavaria showed
Brandt with his head immersed in a beaker of brandy with the
caption: 'Do you want a man like this as chancellor?' – a
reminder of the old 'Willy *Weinbrand*' jest about Brandt being a
drunkard. CDU officials were found distributing a letter by a
former Gestapo agent accusing him of murder in the 1930s, and
the *Frankfurter Allgemeine Zeitung* carried an advertisement
linking him politically with Horst Mahler, a lawyer connected
with the Baader-Meinhof urban guerrillas.[36] In Bavaria Strauss
threatened to name him as a 'Norwegian partisan' and offered to

retire to Alaska to grow pineapples there if asked to become chancellor. One curious feature of the CDU campaign was the organization of bus-loads of young supporters, armed with carefully vetted 'heckling slogans', giving Barzel and his henchmen 'a chance to score with well-rehearsed quips'.[37]

The trade unions backed the SPD more openly than in the past, but industry contributed heavily to the CDU campaign; the SPD maintained that CDU election expenses were three times their own. On the day before the election the *Bild Zeitung* filled four of its twelve pages with advertisements demanding the government's overthrow. For the SPD there were private campaigns, mounted by intellectuals like Günther Grass and Heinrich Böll, costing perhaps £65,000 – a drop in the ocean compared with the massive sums given to the CDU by industrialists. The press was divided, but the Springer group waged a bitter campaign against Brandt, who spoke of the 'monstrous misuse' of the press on 17 November in Bonn.

There were no last-minute surprises. In Paderborn, an old Nazi stronghold, Brandt was heckled violently on 18 November. He countered by bringing on to the platform a young woman from the East German town of Erfurt, who had just arrived in West Germany. 'What matters to me,' Brandt told his stodgy audience, 'is to improve the fate of human beings in a divided Germany.'[38] Almost on the eve of the election he was able to announce that a 'hot line' would in future link his office in Bonn with that of the East German prime minister in East Berlin, but the possible effect of this was spoilt by the blowing-up of a would-be escaper on the East German frontier by an automatic booby-trap device. A small help for Brandt was the announcement, on 17 November, that talks between Nato and the Warsaw Pact would take place on 31 January 1973, on mutual balanced force reductions. This might help détente, but the subject was esoteric for the electorate.

The outcome of the 1972 elections was bound to be in doubt up to the last moment. Back in May Brandt had got a 52 per cent personal popularity vote in an Allensbach Institute poll, published in *Der Stern*.[39] Barzel was nowhere. But on 21 July a Wickert poll gave 51 per cent to the CDU and 35 per cent to the SPD in a federal election, supposedly due on 3 December.

Brandt was still ahead of Barzel, with 49 per cent against 28 per cent. Summer holidays intervened; in September Allensbach put the two main parties neck and neck, while the Emnid Institute in Bielefeld gave the two-party Brandt government a narrow lead. It was noted that both Barzel and Brandt 'look a little battle-weary before the battle'.[40] *The Times* stuck its neck out only two days before the elections and suggested a 50 to 50.5 per cent vote for the two government parties, 47 to 47.5 per cent for the CDU. It suggested, too, that Brandt's contribution would rest on the fact that 'many look on him as a sort of secular saviour, who has redeemed the German people and made their country respectable again'.[41]

A record poll was expected on 19 November, in spite of snow and sleet all over the country during the preceding two days. For the first time the two main parties were fighting on absolutely even terms – always before the CDU had been certain to emerge as much the stronger. Some observers believed that this was the coming-of-age election in the history of the Federal Republic. What had previously been routine was, this time, turned into a matter of much more personal choice. This time men and their ideas counted most.

The election had one novel feature: it was computerized, so producing an accurate picture within an hour and a half of polling ending at 6 pm. Half an hour later Barzel conceded victory in a short but dignified telegram – a famous victory too. For the first time in the history of the Federal Republic the SPD emerged as the strongest party, with 45.9 per cent of the vote and 230 seats in the Bundestag – a gain of over 3 per cent and 6 seats. The CDU vote dropped from 46.1 to 44.8 per cent and their seats from 242 to 224. That of the FDP rose sensationally, from 5.8 to 8.4 per cent, their seats from 30 to 42. The changes may look small, but they were decisive; the government majority, only 12 in 1969 and altogether ended in the intervening three years, rose to 48. This was a clear-cut working majority. Brandt was in for a second term but probably this time a full four-year term.

It was a tremendous personal triumph. There had been a record 91 per cent poll and this should have helped the CDU. But the German people chose Brandt, in spite of age-old prejudices against the *Sozis*, in spite of the prosperity that made small men potential capitalists, in spite of the great weight of money used by the other side. A survey carried out by *Der Spiegel* a week earlier had shown that voters gave Brandt 75 points for trustworthiness, against 50 for Barzel and 42 for Strauss.[42] But Strauss scored 76 points for aggressiveness and Barzel 49, Brandt only 13. One begins to understand why Brandt was given a clear vote of confidence: the man in the street saw mirrored in him the qualities that today count for more than all the gifts of Machiavelli's 'Prince', loyalty and modesty.

The FDP owed much to Scheel's stamina and optimism and to ineffective CDU leadership. For one cause of the latter party's lack of success was the disapproval of well-to-do middle-of-the-road voters over Barzel's shoddy tactics in trying to block the eastern treaties, and over his mistaken efforts to prove that they were being impoverished by SPD–FDP 'misrule'. Brandt had faith in his FDP allies; in mid-August he was forecasting a 'good seven per cent' for them.[43]

The elections hinged on the SPD's successful efforts to increase its all-round popularity marginally and on Brandt's personal appeal to youth. The young did not subscribe to the view that he was starry-eyed and obsessed with a sense of mission; they welcomed his reasoned idealism. There were more than four and a half million people with the right to vote for the first time, half of them in the eighteen to twenty-one bracket that had not voted at previous elections. The SPD gained ground among women, Catholic workers and farmers. The overall gain was 3 per cent – as in previous elections under Brandt's leadership. The computers, working overtime, produced an analysis that suggested a big switch of votes among the three parties that mattered. Their picture was of four million voters who changed sides. If true, this implies a greater readiness to exercise freedom of choice, much in the interest of West German democracy.

The reactions of the outside world were predictable. Brandt's victory was welcomed by every country outside Germany save China.[44] The Poles were delighted; Russians, Czechs and East Germans voiced pleasure in guarded terms. President Pompidou of France sent a telegram of 'very warm congratulations'. Every important newspaper in the western world, from the *New York Times*, through *The Times* to *Le Monde* and the responsible press of smaller countries, offered favourable editorial comment.

Here, then, is an appropriate moment to assess the man and what he has achieved. Brandt was sixty years old in December 1973; he is robust, durable, resilient. Adenauer, the only other statesman of real stature thrown up in Germany since the war, was after all seventy-three years old when he began to govern the Federal Republic. Brandt should have a major part to play in Germany and Europe for some time to come.

First, the man. His story speaks for itself: he set out in life with considerable ambitions but an invariably pragmatic approach to their achievement. He decided to learn at school, and go on learning afterwards. He did so. He decided to be a leader of men, and he was. How? The real answer is embedded in the mystery of human personality, but of one thing one can be sure – he realized that one must first convince those whom one may later lead. He mastered every subject before he expressed a view on it and he invariably spoke with authority. Human beings recognize a clear mind and a strong will; Brandt, learning to think for himself and fend for himself from childhood onwards, had both. And if his childhood left him with a certain loneliness, it bred sturdy independence, ability to think out ideas on his own, yet always sift the thoughts of others and learn from them. Journalism further developed his instinctive gift for analysis and selection and helped, too, to develop two outstanding characteristics – to 'get the job done, and to get it done right'.[45] Believing in decentralization, he was always ready to delegate tasks to others; he praised a little sparingly but refused to forgive mistakes only if the blunderer would not admit them. Nothing irritated him so much as clumsy efforts to cover up.

One adviser[46] was impressed most by the fact that he did not, as a person, change – his energy, enthusiasm and wholly remarkable industriousness stayed with him. So did his sense of personal loyalty to those whom he regarded as friends. Two stories are typical. To an old lady in West Berlin, a radical socialist in her youth, who took an encouraging interest in his political career, he sent each Christmas a gift of yellow roses.[47] And in 1971 when he learnt that an old friend of 'the emigration', whom he had not seen for years, was out of a job in London he found something to offer him in Germany.[48] Personal loyalty governed all his dealings – 'He stands four-square by every minister, by every underling; this is with him a solid and enduring principle, and he could never stab one of his ministers in the back, in the foolish way that Adenauer did with Erhard, during his speech at the Guerzenich Hall in Cologne.'[49] It could be argued that the breach with Schiller in 1972 was the exception to this rule of conduct, but it is an open question whether it was the minister and not the chancellor who first showed a lack of sense of solidarity. Schiller's fellow ministers would certainly give Brandt the benefit of the doubt!

A phrase of his offers a clue to his industriousness – 'The only thing that grows on its own is the jungle'.[50] An entirely self-made man, he has never ceased to value individual effort. To him laziness is unbearable, and intensely boring; exercising his brain is as necessary as exercising his body. One thinks of the catch-line in a René Clair film: *'Le travail c'est obligatoire, car le travail c'est la liberté.'* A piece of French persiflage, maybe; in Brandt's view the sober truth. Work was no obsession, but when he needed to work, everything and everybody else was put aside.

Interest in other people, and tolerance of them, these qualities too Brandt has in unusual measure. Other people's ideas, he has said, are a vital part of one's own experience.[51] And other people's well-being should be one's own essential interest – 'Politics only make sense to me if they serve people – and peace'.[52] Tolerance is something you do not preach, unless you are priest or prig; Brandt simply practises it. He is a man who instinctively respects the opinions of others.

The chronicle of his virtues – there are others not mentioned here – raises the inevitable question; is he perhaps a little bit too good to be true? Fifty years ago British schoolboys were regaled by two thoroughly 'healthy' journals, the *Boys' Own Paper* and *Chums*. In content and appearance they were as like as two peas. Stories always had a happy ending; heroes always made good. Brandt's story has a curious, even embarrassing similarity to those printed in these two papers. Perfection does not belong to politics, and Sir Lancelot surely has no place on the cabinet bench in the Bundestag. Even to be merely human, Brandt must necessarily have shortcomings.

His first marriage was a failure; even so, it seems to have left no scars and remains an isolated setback in personal relationships. He has stayed, since early youth, a little shy, a little wary. It would be wrong to talk of a barrier of reserve, for he can so often

be utterly at his ease with people. It is revealing that in several
hours of talks with the British prime minister in the summer of
1972 there was never a difficult moment, though Mr Heath is
proverbially subject to moods. The two men probably recognized
what they had in common, and the periodic instinct to be a
loner.

An occasional slowness to make up his mind, take decisions,
assert his authority – possibly, for instance, he should have got
rid of Schiller earlier – a tendency to succumb to delayed-action
effects of strain, these can hardly be regarded as serious personal
failings. But one which, his confidants agree, he does possess is an
inclination to think too well of people and trust some too far.
Those round him have noticed how often he has been let down,
how downcast he has been immediately afterwards, yet how
quickly he has been prepared to repose his trust in others once
more. Gullibility? Or calculated tolerance? One can take one's
choice, but it may be – as some advisers believe – that
unpleasantness is something that he thrusts away from himself.
The toughness of fibre shown in the political field is something
that he does not want to display in personal relationships. He
could pursue his *Ostpolitik* with relentless single-mindedness –
one friend even called it ruthlessness.[53]* But he could never
hunt an enemy down; he would only put him out of his mind.
Yet it actually makes him suffer that people can be ill-willed and
stupid.

Brandt the man necessarily remains a somewhat enigmatic
figure. This is a question of deliberate choice. Since he was a
small child he has carefully cultivated self-discipline and developed an instinct not to reveal himself. Men who have spent long

* It should not, however, be thought for one moment that Brandt does not have
fierce critics. An American journalist with two decades of experience told the
author that he believed that Brandt's image had been cunningly devised. It was a
mere façade and behind it the real Brandt was a strange amalgam of bad as well
as good qualities. He believed him to be sly and a single-minded careerist. A
liberal member of the nobility accused Brandt of having undermined the SPD;
he had turned it into 'something which is not any more the old SPD that I have
known and respected. Entirely different forces are taking it over, and let nobody
say that the *Führer* does not know about this; he knows very well what he is
doing.' Yet another accusation made against Brandt is that he is obsessed with
a sense of mission, which leads him periodically into a cloud-cuckoo land.

Accusations of this kind are likely to be made against any national figure.
The author found that these particular ones were not backed by any worthwhile
factual evidence.

hours, even days in his company agree that while he talks freely, gaily, openly, he virtually never speaks of himself. Yet this technique of self-concealment does not prevent him from appearing entirely at his ease.

His achievements as a statesman are plain enough. An assessment here is no more than an interim report and nothing like as detailed as a final balance-sheet. But he has already done much for Germany, in five main respects.

First, his contribution to Berlin. Up to 1955 he was no more than an active and determined younger Social Democrat. But as president of the City Parliament for two years, and as governing mayor for nine, he became the outstanding figure in Berlin's postwar political life. His devotion to duty, staunchness in the face of danger and ability to give of his best in a serious crisis will never be forgotten by the Berliners. He will always be 'our Willy' to them, and they will owe him a lasting debt of gratitude, too, for safeguarding their communications with the West and re-establishing the first tenuous links with the East through his *Ostpolitik*.

Secondly, he held the Social Democratic Party together when it was suffering from the cumulative effects of long years in the political wilderness. The revival in SPD fortunes in the 1960s is now regarded, retrospectively, as a matter of course. But the party's morale was very low when he became their candidate for the chancellorship in 1961; their leadership group consisted of ageing and discouraged men. Brandt gave his party courage and confidence, and maintained both in the face of disappointing election performances in 1961 and 1965.

In the third place, he played the major part in bringing the SPD to power. His work at the Bad Godesberg conference in 1959, in giving the party a new image and new programme, was invaluable. Until then the SPD were condemned to isolation and impotence by their refusal to accept the mixed economy guided by Erhard and by their failure to give wholehearted support to a full West German contribution to the western alliance. Brandt knew that the party had to broaden their appeal or they would never poll more than about a third of the popular vote. He realized, too, that they should make their peace with the churches, and take more trouble over the women's vote, traditionally conservative until 1972. There would never have been a 'natural' swing to the SPD without policies being realistically revised. Credit for revision belongs to Brandt and Wehner. Neither would have succeeded without the other, for the left wing of the party remained strong, stridently vocal and well armed with its slogans of 'true socialism' and 'radical reform'. Some admirers of Brandt claim that his work in helping to transform the SPD was the outcome of a mature political philosophy that he had fully worked out by the age of twenty-five, and that a 'red thread' ran through his thinking thereafter; one supposed proof of this was furnished in his book *In Exile*. This theory leaves out of account the fact that the book was a collection of extracts only, selected many years after it was written. The facts all point to Brandt being a pragmatist in his political thinking.

Fourthly, he produced, in his *Ostpolitik*, a rational coefficient to the *Westpolitik* instituted by Adenauer and accepted by all the main political parties. The issues involved in *Ostpolitik* have already been endlessly debated; the view of a British Sunday newspaper puts the matter in a nutshell:

> It can be argued that Herr Brandt has surrendered a principle and got little in return. The East Germans, and behind them the Russians, have made only a few slight concessions in the matter of human, administrative and trading contacts across the border. But they are real concessions, whereas the reunification of Germany, short of some new world cataclysm, has become an impossible dream. Post-war international relations are difficult enough, but it is better that they should be based on present realities than on a vanished past or an imaginary future.[54]

Brandt jettisoned dogmas that no longer had any practical application. His *Ostpolitik* is the first attempt to end diplomatic trench-warfare in Central Europe and to bring benefits to its peoples – rather than seek political advantage or victory. The road ahead for the protagonists of *Ostpolitik* will be difficult; for the progress that Brandt desires in East–West human relations will be regarded with hesitation and suspicion by the Soviet Union and her East German satellite. Paradoxically, too, Brandt cannot too openly express his suspicions of the other side. Were he to do so, factually and bluntly, he could prejudice the chances of successful détente. Periodically he must mask his feelings – something that does not come naturally to him. *Ostpolitik* will really succeed only if it is pursued with skill and finesse, and the full backing of the western alliance. The cold war is not yet finally over.

Brandt's fifth main achievement is less easily defined. It has been described, in vague terms, as the institution of a new era of German history, in which Nazism has at last become a thing of the past. The men who served Nazism, however half-heartedly, have gone and their places have been taken by men who fought against Nazism. Germans can consider their country's grim past with fewer inhibitions and her future with more confidence. More important may be the renaissance of liberalism, dormant and despised for a hundred years of German history. During most of that time the State, in German eyes, has been all-important; the individual has mattered little. Leading postwar German 'liberals' have blithely explained that 'liberalism' is moribund and unneeded.[55] But liberalism, in present-day terms, does not mean a party programme; instead it means belief in freedom and the individual, social and spiritual tolerance, the pursuit of the 'better life' in the fullest sense of the phrase. Brandt gave an idea of what he understood by this word in a speech in Cologne in March 1971.[56] In it, he listed his basic aims:

> More humanity in our society
> Equal opportunities for all
> Greater social justice
> More freedom for the individual
> More security, both at home and for our country
> Greater participation of the citizen in the life of the community.

Elsewhere he has said that 'the best citizen is the best patriot'.[57] The individual, as a rational being, is the fundamental element in the abstraction of the State. He is what counts. Obvious though this may sound, it is a truism that the Germans ignored for the best part of a hundred years. Brandt has put it into simple words: 'The State, that's the lot of us.'[58] It is this attitude that the writer Heinrich Böll was recalling when he wrote: 'Willy Brandt is the first German chancellor who has led us away from our tradition as a *Herrenvolk*, a master-race ... using the spur and the whip.'[59] The community comes before caste.

In a personal interview Brandt gave some idea of the way in which he would like to see the German community developing.[60] Materialism was, perhaps, its biggest enemy, although it may have passed its peak in the late 1960s. The Federal Republic was no longer 'just an economy, and not a political entity'. Interest in social and cultural life was growing; simple people were reading books and listening to music; simple people, again, were showing a greater sense of independence and civic responsibility. But materialism out of control meant the using up of resources, the debasing of human values, the pollution of the environment. The old Marxist notion of setting free the forces of production needed to be revised. Economic growth had limits and limitations, but human values were capable of almost infinite development. Social insecurity, he thought, was the second enemy of the community. Uncomfortable questions were being asked, and they did not come from 'bad people'. There was profiteering and corruption; a rat-race for promotion; an automatic, unconscious divorcing of ideals from daily existence. The younger generation, he believed, was sceptical because it did not accept conventional yardsticks of social values. The cult of violence was a third enemy of the community, sometimes in ambush. Its threat could be contained. But the threat was a real one – the anarchists of the Baader-Meinhof gang had been 'technically brilliant' – it was alarming how they managed to accumulate arms, know-how, a knowledge of objectives that struck at the roots of ordered society. Anarchy had to be countered – 'Society must make itself more effective, must always be prepared to act.' A modernized system of criminal control was being developed; it must be applied, in the interests of the community.

He did not see economic difficulties as comparable to the problems that upset the rhythm of organized and democratic existence. But it 'could well be necessary to find a new philosophy to counter inflation'. No policy of *laissez-faire* would do. The aim should be to guide the economy into a condition of price stability. Increased productivity could be used to reduce production costs. Competition, where it was genuinely free, should be encouraged. Technical progress must go on: 'To strike against a real improvement in the means of production is to retard the progress which we all want, and need.'

'Our nation,' Brandt said some years ago, 'needs fewer phrases and more veracity.'[61] Like Brandt himself, his compatriots and country have reached a stage where nothing more than an interim report is possible. What, then, of their progress and potential?

A striking assessment was that of Marion, Countess Dönhoff, in *Encounter* magazine in December 1971. The countess, an enlightened liberal, was at the time editor of the weekly *Die Zeit*. Her article 'Is Our Society Disintegrating?' began in a gloomy vein – 'Scarcely a week goes by in Germany without some occurrence which seems to be symptomatic of some sickness in our society.' She noted the increasing incidence of police round-ups and leaks of confidential information to the press, of refusals to carry out military service and of the vandalizing of buses, trains and other public property, above all of criticism of capitalist society – some of it callow and violent but some of it reasoned and necessary. She could have added to her list: there was the 'programmed suicide' of environmental pollution,[62] the social stresses caused by the 2.3 million foreign workers in the Federal Republic, the plummeting birthrate (down by 6 per cent in 1971) and what was called the 'civil war on the autobahn' – in 1972 one man shot a 'rival' driver dead; another leapt from his car and stabbed a pedestrian.[63] But Countess Dönhoff believed that such things were inevitable concomitants of 'the greatest bloodless revolution in the twentieth century'. Reforms went ahead in every field and greater demands than ever before were being made of society – for 'emancipation from the hypertrophy of narrow commercial interests, the priority of the general public interest, participation and co-determination, and the greatest possible measure of freedom and social justice'.

Political imperfections are easier to diagnose than social ones. While right-wing radicalism is less of a danger than ever before in the history of the Federal Republic – the neo-fascist NPD scored under 1 per cent in the 1972 elections – the far left has displayed disruptive and destructive symptoms. Its loud-mouthed exponents should study the stories of Brecht, dying disillusioned, or Solzhenitsyn, the personification of the persecuted but enduringly courageous intellectual. Rudi Dutschke and the anarchist activists, at least, have lost something of their appeal. But Brandt's *Ostpolitik* postulates the need to come to terms with the existence of two separate German states, and their differing natures. The reasoned support of the 'far left' is as necessary as that of the western alliance.

Political imperfections must necessarily include apathy and ignorance. Stupidity and disinterest can be laid, fairly and squarely, at the doors of the oligarchies that rule the 'democracies' of Western Europe. France's oligarchy has watched the Mediterranean slip out of Europe's orbit. Britain's has still barely noticed the fact that the Soviet Union has become, after the United States, the key naval power in the world. West German political ignorance may not be so crass, or so inexcusable. The reason is that the West Germans have, so far, been in the front line of the East–West confrontation. Yet the debates and man-oeuvrings in Bonn when Brandt presented his *Ostpolitik* in the form of draft treaties were conducted – at least by the CDU opposition – as a kind of mad charade of party politics. The outside observer was made painfully aware of an underlying sense of irresponsibility.

Ostpolitik reintroduces the subject of the inadequacy of Nato. Whatever political equalization can be achieved in Central Europe must depend on the strength of purpose, and strong right arm, of the western alliance. Nato countries spent $88 billion on defence in 1960, only $80 billion ten years later. Costs had risen by 25 per cent during the decade, so the relative decrease in Nato spending was 32 per cent. Yet Nato countries were getting richer all the time, at an average 4.5 per cent a year.[64] Throughout the decade about 60 per cent of Nato costs went on soldiers' pay, pensions and other non-military expenditure; the Warsaw Pact figure was 25 per cent. Dr Luns of the Netherlands, speaking in London, said that only a very 'precarious balance of force' still existed in Europe, and it was gradually shifting to the advantage of the Warsaw Pact – 'It reminds me of the 1930s.'[65] Nato experts admitted that the alliance suffered from too great a dependence on the United States, too much reliance on the nuclear deterrent, a lack of terrain and the partial non-participation of France. The manpower under Nato command was reduced by a quarter between 1966 and 1972 by the withdrawal of France from the integrated command, the halving of Canada's contribution and the reallocation of United States troops.

Behind the diminished reality of Nato, the fading image of the United States. The war in Vietnam has brought decreased confidence in the country, and in Americans themselves: Watergate, Black Power and the Che Guevara cult have contributed. Most Germans used to regard the United States as the undisputed moral as well as military leader of the western alliance. Few do so still with the old certainty of mind. The United States' own crisis of confidence has left Western Europe, in 1974, more leaderless than a decade earlier, and it has not become politically more united in the meantime. The 'sated' societies of West European countries demand more – whether in consumer goods, money or a share in government – while wishing to contribute less. Technological development alone has enabled their demands to be met, so far.

At least the 'new' Germany should play its full part in the solving of the awesome social, political and military problems that confront Western Europe. Inevitably those problems have reacted on the German government of the day – it is only human nature to blame one's own administration for monetary inflation, the rising prices of the necessities of life, and the now palpably apparent threat to living standards. Brandt was himself one of the first statesmen to admit the seriousness of the world energy shortage – he said that, 'although we shall not starve', all hope of economic growth must be jettisoned until the situation is stabilized. But for the longer-term future it is more significant that German militarism is dead; so is that old, wild Messianic belief in the superiority of all things German. Europeanism has superseded the idea of the omnipotent nation-state. And President Kennedy was right when he told a German audience: 'I would not diminish the miracle of West Germany's economic achievement. But the true German miracle has been your rejection of the past for the future.'[66] By 1973 Willy Brandt had worked for forty years to make a fairer future possible. He has proved himself to be the right man to lead his people into it.

Postscript

'Brandt shakes Europe' was the slogan carried by newspaper posters all over London on the morning of May 7, 1974. The chancellor's resignation had been announced shortly after midnight in Bonn. Nor was it a threat or a political tour de force; next morning the Federal President, Gustav Heinemann, accepted his resignation without demur. For one brief week, a caretaker administration carried on under Walter Scheel. On May 15 he was elected Federal President by a comfortable majority. On May 16 Helmut Schmidt, until then Federal Minister of Finance, was elected chancellor in the Bundestag. In a surgical sense, a quick, clean operation had been performed, and a protracted, nagging crisis avoided.

The proverbial straw which broke the camel's back was, in this instance, the revelation that Herr Günther Guillaume, an official in the Federal Chancellery who acted as link man with the SPD, had allegedly been spying for the East Germans and was a former officer of the East German army. Guillaume 'came west' from East Germany in 1956. After working as a photographic salesman, he joined the SPD in 1957 and progressed steadily as a party and then government official until securing his Chancellery post in 1970. Inevitably, Guillaume came into close contact with Brandt, owing to the chancellor's tenure of the chairmanship of the SPD. He handled confidential and secret documents and apparently enjoyed Brandt's full confidence. A jovial, earthy character, he seemed on the surface to have none of the characteristics of the spy of either fact or fiction.

Guillaume, according to the inadequate official accounts of his activities that were given during the next month, had been under close surveillance since the late summer of 1973. It was already known then that he had been an officer in the East German army and had failed to state this both when applying

309

for West German citizenship and when enrolling in West German government service. The political security office of the Bonn government, the Office for the Protection of the Constitution, queried his appointment to a Chancellery post, but was evidently overruled. Guillaume was arrested on April 24, on suspicion of passing secret information to the East Germans. Yet more than a month later, on May 26, semi-official reports were circulated that no incriminating evidence had come to light that he had spied successfully for the East Germans, or had even spied at all.

Brandt readily admitted responsibility for Guillaume's activities, as a member of his Chancellery staff, and indicated that 'classified' information had still been made available to him, after he had been placed under surveillance. There were two explanations of this apparent anomaly. The first was that Brandt had, in all good faith, cooperated with the West German counter-intelligence service, the Bundes-Nachrichtendienst (BND), in the hope that Guillaume would incriminate his East German masters. The second was more sinister; it was that the BND had used Brandt in the deliberate intention of provoking a political scandal. The BND was staffed largely by men originally chosen by ex-General Gehlen, who had worked for the Nazis and, as a fanatical anti-communist, opposed Brandt's *Ostpolitik*. There was talk of a systematic leakage of secret information to the press and of open disloyalty to Brandt among members of the government service and even officials of the Chancellery.

Where Guillaume was concerned, all was conjecture, and virtually all remained so for the time being. For Brandt, it seemed politically to be the end of the road. His friends and admirers wrote and spoke of a tragedy of Shakespearean dimensions, of a man beyond rescue who would be forced to leave party politics as well as the field of government affairs. In some quarters he was complimented on at least knowing when to leave high office, and his behaviour was widely contrasted with that of President Richard Nixon. There was a tendency to discover explanations which had allegedly been 'obvious' for a long time past—the chancellor had begun losing his grip six months earlier, he was *amtsmüde* (weary of the responsibilities of office), he was disappointed that his *Ostpolitik* had not brought more resounding results, disappointed too with his western allies and his own party, disappointed with himself. Only a little credence was given to stories that Guillaume, who once distributed photographs of slightly top-heavy females in the nude, had 'procured' women for Brandt on his official journeys abroad—including, absurdly, Swedish girls who smoked cigars. These stories led to claims that Brandt resigned because he was in process of being blackmailed—claims which Brandt denied at once and unequivocally.

Out of all this emerged a picture of a Brandt, deeply disillusioned, depressed and waiting for a chance to 'bow-out' and save himself further pain and embarrassment. This was the picture of a man who had readily committed political suicide—for a full 'come-back', on the West German political stage, looked out of the question. Was this picture a true one?

Certainly, there was cause for disillusionment. During the first four months of 1974, problems had multiplied for Brandt's Government. His *Ostpolitik* stagnated, for the East German regime was in no mood to make the slightest concession to the Federal Republic—one should perhaps note that the East Germans were at first embarrassed and silent over Brandt's resignation, but later offered the fatuous explanation that it was expressly designed to poison the atmosphere between the two German states! Brandt's *Ostpolitik*, in any event, depended on Soviet support. But the Soviet Union, engaged in the Middle East in building up Arab armed strength and in trying to sabotage Dr. Henry Kissinger's peace-making efforts, was not disposed to press its client in East Berlin. The Soviet Union's interpretation of détente, one should recall, was a severely circumscribed one, leaving the Soviet leaders free to press the western nations at every weak point continuously and relentlessly.

Brandt had so often insisted that a successful *Ostpolitik* depended on the strength and unity of the Western Alliance. Never had this strength and unity been less apparent than during the last quarter of 1973 and the first half of 1974. The western world had been rocked by the energy crisis which became apparent in October 1973, and by the blatant use of oil blackmail as a political weapon by the Arabs. The Middle East war of October 1973 created a rift between the United States and its NATO partners, for there was a total failure on the part of the latter to produce a credible back-up for the American effort to promote a fair and full Middle East peace settlement. America's European partners showed themselves primarily interested, where the Middle East was concerned, in the sale of their arms and the safeguarding of their individual oil supplies. One uses the word 'individual', since the rest of the Common Market Nine immediately deserted Holland, when the Arabs imposed an oil ban on that country for allegedly being too friendly to Israel.

Paradoxically, the Labour victory in the British elections of March 1974 had been a further source of worry to Brandt. For the Labour Party had committed itself to re-negotiating Britain's terms of entry into the Common Market—a devastatingly empty phrase—and to holding a national referendum which would probably result in an under-informed British electorate opting for a so-called economic independence which would amount to economic isolation. Brandt, as he made clear to me times over, set immense store on British involvement in Europe.

During the last quarter of 1973 and the first months of 1974, Brandt had faced growing domestic problems. As in the rest of western Europe, inflation was the main enemy. And, as in other European countries, there was no national unity in combating it. The students were increasingly restless, the unions were in militant mood. Certainly, West Germany was in better trim than her European partners. The scale of inflation was lower—a mere 7 to 8 percent a year against 15 to 20 percent elsewhere. The will to work remained much greater—from 1970 to the end of 1973 West Germany lost, proportionately, one-tenth as many working days as Britain from strike action, and one-eighth as many as the United States. In April, however, Brandt had to issue a ten-point appeal to the SPD to pull itself together. The party was losing ground in Land and municipal elections—thus on May 6 the CDU vote in the municipal elections in the Saar was up by 10 percent. There is nothing new about a swing against the government; what was new for the SPD was that the swing was coming when it had been in office for such a short time, and when—so recently—there had been predictions of SPD rule for a decade, or even longer.

Here, certainly, were reasons for Brandt to be disillusioned and depressed. But it may be that a purely personal factor played the biggest part of all in his resignation. All his life he had sought to trust people close to him, to believe the best of them

—in spite of the inner layer of reserve in his own character which would always be a built-in obstacle to truly intimate friendship and a total barrier to self-revelation. All his life Brandt wanted to believe in human decency, and—possibly a defect in a politician—to give the benefit of the doubt to people close to him who failed to match-up to his own expectations. All his life he had set standards of loyalty and team work.

Guillaume's treachery, in a personal sense, could have had a far-reaching psychological effect on Brandt. So could the ensuing prevarications and manoeuverings of his own followers. A self-imposed loneliness can make for extreme vulnerability under such bizarre circumstances. Brandt, certainly, was very vulnerable. All his life he had bottled up his feelings, doubts, emotions, above all his inmost thoughts whenever his own person and interest were concerned. It is understandable that a man who had, throughout life, to fight every inch of the way for what he wanted and what he believed in, would be bitterly and totally disappointed when forsaken, so brazenly and at so critical a moment. The view that he was only waiting for an excuse to quit is, on the whole, untenable. His personal crisis of confidence was forced upon him.

At this moment there is no 'last line' to be written about Willy Brandt. He helped to see a worthy successor, the tough and efficient Helmut Schmidt, into the office of chancellor. He himself retained, at least for the time being, the chairmanship of the SPD. He set an example in integrity which could be more important for Germany and Europe than an aptitude for discharging his duties as head of a government. Standards of conduct are slipping in the western world, and there is a valuable lesson to be learned from the manner in which the man who had fought so hard for success left the forefront of the political stage. There are other fields left for him to conquer, but this is not the time or place for their description.

Notes

Except when an English edition is cited, all translations are by the author.

CHAPTER 1

1 Willy Brandt, as told to Leo Lania, *My Road to Berlin* (London 1960), p. 19.
2 *Ibid.*
3 Personal friends of Brandt, in conversation with the author.
4 Personal friends of Brandt, in conversation with the author.
5 Brandt, in conversation with the author.
6 David Binder, 'Willy Brandt. A German Life', *New York Times* (November 1969).
7 Frau Paula Bartels-Heine, in letter to the author.
8 Frau Luise Flägel, a cousin of Brandt's mother, in letter to the author.
9 Brandt, in conversation with the author.
10 Bartels-Heine, in letter to the author.
11 Flägel, in letter to the author.
12 Brandt, as told to Lania, *op. cit.*, pp. 21–2.
13 Brandt, in conversation with the author.
14 Bartels-Heine, in letter to the author.
15 Flägel, in letter to the author.
16 Brandt, as told to Lania, *op. cit.*, p. 27.
17 *Ibid.*
18 *Ibid.*, p. 25.
19 Brandt, in conversation with the author.
20 Brandt, as told to Lania, *op. cit.*, p. 28.
21 *Ibid.*
22 Binder, *op. cit.*
23 Brandt, as told to Lania, *op. cit.*, p. 29.
24 Brandt, in conversation with the author.
25 *Ibid.*
26 Brandt, in BBC 'Late Night Line-Up' interview with Lord Chalfont (1 December 1970).
27 Manfred Beer, in *Die Welt* (31 October 1969).
28 Douglas A. Chalmers, *The Social Democratic Party of Germany* (New Haven 1964), p. 4.
29 David Childs, *From Schumacher to Brandt. The Story of German Socialism* (London 1966), p. 4.
30 *Ibid.*, p. 5.
31 *Ibid.*, p. 8.
32 Sir Stephen King-Hall, *German Parliaments* (London 1954), p. 18.
33 Alistair Horne, *The Price of Glory* (London 1962), pp. 10–12.
34 Brandt, in interview with Lord Chalfont.

35 Brandt, in conversation with the author.
36 Bruno Römer, Brandt's deputy in the SAJ, in letter to the author.
37 *Ibid.*
38 Hanno Drechsler, *Die Sozialistische Arbeiterpartei Deutschlands* (Meisenheim 1965), p. 66.
39 *Ibid.*, p. 160.
40 *Ibid.*, p. 174.
41 *Rote Fahne* (KPD newspaper) (13 April 1929).
42 Hanno Drechsler, *op. cit.*, p. 332.
43 Brandt, as told to Lania, *op. cit.*, p. 43.
44 Chalmers, *op. cit.*, p. 14.
45 Brandt, as told to Lania, *op. cit.*, p. 48.
46 *Ibid.*, p. 49.
47 Brandt, in BBC interview with Lord Chalfont.
48 Brandt, as told to Lania, *op. cit.*, p. 50.
49 Jan Peter Berkandt, *Willy Brandt* (Hanover 1961), p. 10.
50 Brandt, in interview with Lord Chalfont.
51 Berndt Brugge, in *Lübecker Nachrichten* (10 March 1972).
52 Brandt, in conversation with the author.
53 Brugge, *loc. cit.*
54 Brandt, *In Exile* (London 1971), p. 57.

CHAPTER 2

1   Berndt Brugge, in *Lübecker Nachrichten* (10 March 1972).
2   Brandt, *In Exile* (London 1971), p. 161.
3   *Ibid.*
4   *Ibid.*, p. 162.
5   Brandt, in BBC 'Late Night Line-Up' interview with Lord Chalfont (1 December 1970).
6   Fabian von Schlabrendorff, *The Secret War Against Hitler* (London 1966), p. 23.
7   Lewis J. Edinger, *German Exile Politics* (Berkeley 1956), pp. 8–10.
8   Brandt, *In Exile*, p. 163.
9   Johan Cappelen, in letter to the author.
10 Brandt, as told to Leo Lania, *My Road to Berlin* (London 1960), p. 59.
11 Terence Prittie, *Germans against Hitler* (Boston 1964), p. 132.
12 Brandt, press conference in Oslo (9 December 1971).
13 Edinger, *op. cit.*, p. 73.
14 *Ibid.*, p. 74.
15 Carola Stern, *Ulbricht* (London 1965), p. 69.
16 *Ibid.*, p. 73.
17 Edinger, *op. cit.*, pp. 42–3.
18 *Marxistische Tribüne*, 1:5 (1936).
19 Brandt, in letter to the author.
20 Gunter Markscheffel, 'First Meeting with Willy Brandt, and the Consequences', monograph sent to the author.
21 Herbert George, a friend of Brandt, in conversation with the author.
22 Brandt, *In Exile*, p. 60.
23 Hanno Drechsler, *Die Sozialistische Arbeiterpartei Deutschlands* (Meisenheim 1965), p. 332.
24 *Ibid.*
25 Brandt, *In Exile*, p. 60.
26 Brandt, in conversation with the author.

27 Otto Bauer, author of *Die illegale Partei* (Paris 1939), coined this phrase.
28 Joachim Unger, in conversation with the author.
29 Fritz Benke, in letter to the author.
30 Unger, in conversation with the author.
31 Brandt, in conversation with the author.
32 'Aus der Organisation', *Marxistische Tribüne* 2: 7 (1937).
33 Brandt report, dated 1937 (probably March), 'Einige Fragen unserer praktischen Arbeit draussen und drinnen'.
34 Hugh Thomas, *The Spanish Civil War* (London 1961), p. 73.
35 Luis Bolin, *Spain. The Vital Years* (London 1967), p. 162.
36 Thomas, *op. cit.*, p. 73.
37 *Ibid.*, p. 260.
38 Bolin, *op. cit.*, p. 210.
39 Brandt, *In Exile*, p. 141.
40 George Orwell, *Homage to Catalonia* (London 1966), p. 60.
41 *Ibid.*, pp. 61–2.
42 Brandt, *In Exile*, p. 141.
43 *Ibid.*, p. 142.
44 Thomas, *op. cit.*, p. 103.
45 Brandt, *In Exile*, p. 141.
46 Orwell, *op. cit.*, p. 75.
47 Brandt, *In Exile*, p. 149.
48 Bolin, *op. cit.*, p. 231.
49 Brandt, as told to Lania, *op. cit.*, p. 77.
50 *Ibid.*, pp. 78–9.
51 Brandt, as reported in *Marxistische Tribüne* (July 1937).
52 Walter Padley MP, in conversation with the author.

CHAPTER 3

1 Brandt, as told to Leo Lania, *My Road to Berlin* (London 1960), p. 26.
2 Herbert George, in conversation with the author.
3 Walter Padley MP, in conversation with the author.
4 Frau Irmgard Enderle, in letter to the author.
5 Brandt, in letter to the author.
6 Brandt, in conversation with the author.
7 Winston Churchill, in *House of Commons* (27 January 1942), vol. 377, cols 592–619.
8 Ernest Bevin, in *House of Commons* (29 July 1941), vol. 373, cols 1,357–71.
9 Letter in Willy Brandt Archives, Bonn.
10 Memorandum in Brandt Archives.
11 Letter of 13 July 1939, in Brandt Archives.
12 Report of FDJ meeting (24 July 1938), in Brandt Archives.
13 Carola Stern, *Ulbricht* (London 1965), p. 80ff.
14 Brandt, in *Det Zoda Arhundre* (December 1939).
15 *Ibid.* (January 1940).
16 Stern, *op. cit.*, p. 86.
17 Inge, editor of *Perspektiv*, in letter to the author.
18 Brandt, 'A Short Study of Latvia under Soviet Occupation', in Brandt Archives.
19 Brandt, 'Memorandum on Finland', in Brandt Archives.
20 Johannes Andenaes, *Norway and the Second World War* (Oslo 1966), p. 14.

21 Johan Cappelen, in letter to the author.
22 Scheflo, in letter to the author.
23 George, in conversation with the author.
24 Brandt, *Norwegens Freiheitskampf* (Hamburg 1948), p. 12.
25 Hermann Lehmkuhl, *Hitler Attacks Norway* (London 1943), p. 18.
26 Rolf Italiander, 'Die neuen Herren der alten Welt',
    in Akzente des Lebens (Bremen 1970), p. 412.
27 Brandt, as told to Lania, p. 104.
28 Italiander, *op. cit.*, p. 113.
29 Brandt, in conversation with the author.
30 *Ibid.*
31 *Ibid.*
32 *Ibid.*
33 Brandt, *Norwegens Freiheitskampf*, p. 48.
34 Roy Walker, *A People Who Loved Peace* (London 1946), p. 24.
35 *Ibid.*, p. 25.
36 Brandt, *Norwegens Freiheitskampf*, p. 64.
37 Brandt, memorandum in Brandt Archives.
38 Helmut Müssener, *Die Deutschsprachige Emigration in Schweden*
    (Stockholm 1971), p. 117.
39 Brandt, *Norwegens Freiheitskampf*, pp. 98–9.
40 Müssener, *op. cit.*, pp. 120–21.
41 *Ibid.*, pp. 135–6.
42 Johannes Andenaes, Olav Riste and Magne Skodvin (eds), *Norway and
    the Second World War* (Oslo 1966), p. 110.
43 Edinger, *op. cit.*, p. 247.
44 Brandt, memorandum of mid-1945, in Brandt Archives.
45 Müssener, *op. cit.*, p. 272.
46 *Ibid.*, pp. 355–8.
47 Yvonne Jerlin, 'Willy Brandt. Die Stockholmer Jahre', privately
    circulated thesis, p. 22.
48 Müssener, *op. cit.*, pp. 274–9.
49 Brandt, *Zur Nachkriegspolitik der Deutschen Sozialisten*
    (Stockholm 1944), p. 9.
50 *Ibid.*, p. 15.
51 Müssener, *op. cit.*, p. 276.
52 Brandt, *Nach dem Siege* (Stockholm 1944), p. 39.
53 *Ibid.*, p. 42.
54 *Ibid.*, p. 43.
55 *Ibid.*, p. 45.
56 *Ibid.*, p. 24.
57 *Ibid.*, p. 53.
58 *Ibid.*, p. 55.
59 *Ibid.*, p. 165.
60 *Ibid.*, p. 246.
61 *Ibid.*, p. 286.
62 *Ibid.*, p. 211.
63 Letter to George (30 June 1941).
64 Letter to George (5 October 1942).
65 Letter to George (30 June 1941).
66 Bruno Kreisky, in letter to the author.
67 Letter to George (14 August 1943).
68 Brandt, in BBC 'Late Night Line-Up' interview with Lord Chalfont
    (1 December 1970).

69 Enderle, in letter to the author.
70 Brandt, in conversation with the author.
71 Brandt, as told to Lania, *op. cit.*, p. 134.
72 *Ibid.*, p. 136.

CHAPTER 4

1   Yvonne Jerlin, 'Willy Brandt. Die Stockholmer Jahre' (Stockholm 1970), p. 38.
2   Brandt, in *Die Neue Gesellschaft*, 4 (1969).
3   Letter to 'Theo' (dated 22 June 1945); in the possession of Herbert George.
4   Letter to George, dated 'beginning of July 1945', with report enclosed.
5   Letter to Jacob Walcher (dated 14 August 1945).
6   Letter to George (dated 23 August 1945).
7   Brandt, *In Exile* (London 1971), p. 233.
8   Brandt, as told to Leo Lania, *My Road to Berlin* (London 1960), p. 146.
9   *Ibid.*, p. 149.
10 Sir Elwyn Jones, 'Judgement in Nuremberg', in *World Jewry*, 15: 1 (1972).
11 *Ibid.*
12 Dr Leo Kahn, 'Achievement and Failure at Nuremberg', in *Wiener Library Bulletin*, 24 (1972).
13 Brandt, in conversation with the author.
14 Brandt, *Verbrecher und Andere Deutsche* (Oslo 1946), p. 18.
15 *Ibid.*, p. 29.
16 *Ibid.*, p. 167.
17 *Ibid.*, p. 163.
18 *Ibid.*, p. 7.
19 *Ibid.*, p. 142.
20 *Ibid.*, p. 173.
21 *Ibid.*, p. 322.
22 David Childs, *From Schumacher to Brandt. The Story of German Socialism* (London 1966), p. 19.
23 Theo Pirker, *Die SPD nach Hitler* (Munich 1965), p. 37.
24 Letter to George (dated 14 April 1946).
25 Letter to Walcher (dated 30 April 1946).
26 Letter to George (dated 15 August 1946).
27 Letter to Walcher (dated 11 June 1946).
28 Brandt, *In Exile*, p. 239.
29 *Ibid.*, p. 235.
30 Letter to George (dated 12 November 1946), enclosing round robin of 1 November.
31 Brandt, in conversation with the author.
32 Brandt, in first brief meeting with the author.
33 Brandt, as told to Lania, *op. cit.*, p. 160.
34 *Ibid.*, p. 161.
35 *Ibid.*, p. 163.
36 Brandt, in conversation with the author.
37 Brandt, as told to Lania, *op. cit.*, p. 167.
38 Brandt, in letter to the author.
39 Brandt, reports in Willy Brandt Archives, Bonn.
40 Letter to George (dated 5 May 1947).
41 Inge Scheflo, in letter to the author.

42 George, in conversation with the author.
43 Bruno Kreisky, in letter to the author.
44 Frau Irmgard Enderle, in conversation with the author.
45 Brandt, *In Exile*, pp. 246–8.
46 Letter to George (dated 11 December 1947).
47 Brandt, in BBC 'Late Night Line-Up' interview with Lord Chalfont (1 December 1970).
48 Erich Brost, in conversation with the author.
49 Brandt, *In Exile*, pp. 248–51.
50 Prittie, *Konrad Adenauer. A Study in Fortitude* (London 1972), p. 128.
51 Lewis J. Edinger, *Kurt Schumacher* (Stanford 1965), pp. 135–6.
52 Dean Acheson, *Sketches from Life of Men I Have Known* (New York 1961), p. 172.
53 Lord Pakenham (later Earl of Longford), *Born to Believe* (London 1953), p. 182.
54 Prittie, *op. cit.*, p. 129.
55 Lance Pope, in conversation with the author.
56 Brandt, in conversation with the author.
57 Charles Thayer, *The Unquiet Germans* (London 1958), p. 145.
58 Brandt, in conversation with the author.
59 Otto Theuner, in conversation with the author.
60 *Ibid.*
61 Letter to George (dated 10 January 1948).
62 Brandt, in conversation with the author.
63 Brandt, as told to Lania, *op. cit.*, p. 164.
64 Richard Loewenthal and Brandt, *Ernst Reuter. Ein Leben fuer die Freiheit* (Munich 1957), pp. 370–80.
65 *Ibid.* p. 382.
66 Denis Healey, *The Curtain Falls* (London 1951), p. 11.
67 Brandt, as told to Lania, *op. cit.*, p. 174.
68 *Manchester Guardian* special correspondent (10 March 1948).
69 *Ibid.* (12 April 1948).
70 Brandt, in conversation with the author.
71 *Ibid.*
72 *Ibid.*
73 Pirker, *op. cit.*, p. 97.
74 *Ibid.*, p. 98.
75 Loewenthal, 'The Germans of the Cold War', in *This is Germany* ed. Arthur Settel (New York 1950), p. 53.
76 *Ibid.*, p. 52.
77 Brandt, in conversation with the author.
78 F. S. Northedge, *British Foreign Policy, 1945–61* (London 1962), p. 139.
79 Philip Windsor, *City on Leave* (London 1963), p. 129.
80 Brandt, as told to Lania, *op. cit.*, p. 203.
81 Theuner, in conversation with the author.

CHAPTER 5

1 Brandt, speech at SPD borough and local conference, Berlin (14 January 1949).
2 Ewan Butler, *City Divided* (London 1955), p. 75.
3 *Ibid.*, p. 81.
4 *Manchester Guardian* (22 June 1949).
5 Brandt, as told to Leo Lania, *My Road to Berlin* (London 1960), p. 265.

6 Konrad Adenauer, *Memoirs*, 1 (London 1966), p. 174.
7 Article 26 of the Electoral Law (15 June 1949).
8 Note of the Allied commandants to Ernst Reuter (30 June 1949), from Wolfgang Heidelmeyer and Günter Hindricks (eds), *Documents on Berlin 1943/63* (Munich 1963), p. 117.
9 Article 23 of the Basic Law of the Federal Constitution.
10 *Manchester Guardian* (22 October 1949).
11 Brandt, as told to Lania, *op. cit.*, p. 209.
12 *Ibid.*, pp. 210–12.
13 Shepard Stone, in conversation with the author.
14 David Childs, *From Schumacher to Brandt. The Story of German Socialism* (London 1966), p. 35.
15 *Ibid.*, p. 32.
16 Brandt, in conversation with the author.
17 Theo Pirker, *Die SPD nach Hitler* (Munich 1965), p. 129.
18 *Ibid.*, p. 128.
19 Brandt, in conversation with the author.
20 Sir Christopher Steel, General Robertson's adviser, in conversation with the author.
21 D. C. Watt, *Britain Looks to Germany* (London 1965), pp. 100–105.
22 William Henry Chamberlin, *The German Phoenix* (London 1964), p. 204.
23 *Berlin Stadtblatt* (18 July 1950).
24 *Ibid.* (15 February 1951).
25 *Ibid.* (10 April 1951).
26 *Ibid.* (20 October 1950).
27 *Ibid.* (20 August 1950).
28 *Ibid.* (28 November 1950).
29 *Ibid.* (26 November 1950).
30 *Ibid.* (14 January 1951).
31 *Ibid.* (15 March 1951).
32 Abraham Ashkenazi, *Reformpartei und Aussenpolitik* (Cologne 1968), p. 93.
33 Pirker, *op. cit.*, p. 130.
34 Prittie, *Konrad Adenauer A Study in Fortitude* (London 1972), p. 211.
35 *Manchester Guardian* (2 June 1952).
36 Helga Grebing, *The History of the German Labour Movement* (London 1969), p. 185.
37 Philip Windsor, *City on Leave* (London 1963), p. 152.
38 Brandt, in conversation with the author.
39 Brandt, as told to Lania, *op. cit.*, p. 236.
40 SPD pamphlet, *The Soviet Sea Around Us* (Bonn 1960).
41 *Manchester Guardian* (27 September 1952).
42 Hans Dollinger, *Willy! Willy!* (Munich 1970), p. 63.
43 Brian Connell, *Watcher on the Rhine* (London 1957), p. 245.
44 Prittie, *op. cit.*, p. 141.
45 Prittie, in *Manchester Guardian* (4 September 1953).
46 Richard Hiscocks, *Democracy in Western Germany* (London 1957), p. 92.
47 Brandt, as told to Lania, *op. cit.*, p. 236.
48 Brandt, in speech to Berlin SPD, Willy Brandt Archives, Bonn.
49 Pirker, *op. cit.*, pp. 200–201.
50 In *Vorwärts* (29 April 1955).
51 Brandt, speech to Hochschule für Politik in Berlin (21 January 1955).
52 Brandt, in radio interview for RIAS (Radio in the American Sector) (16 December 1956).
53 Brandt, speech in Stockholm (27 March 1956).

54 Brandt, speech in Berlin (30 October 1956).
55 Brandt, speech in Berlin (1 November 1956).
56 Heli Ihlefeld, *Willy Brandt. Anekdotisch*, revised edn (Munich 1971), p. 72.
57 Sir William Hayter, *The Diplomacy of the Great Powers* (London 1960), p. 48.
58 Prittie, *Germany Divided*, p. 129.
59 *Ibid.*, p. 151.
60 John Mander, *Berlin. Hostage for the West* (London 1962), p. 59.
61 Brandt, in conversation with the author.
62 Hayter, *op. cit.*, p. 20.
63 *Ibid.*, p. 28.
64 *Ibid.*, p. 30.
65 *Ibid.*, p. 32.
66 *Ibid.*, pp. 68–9.
67 Brandt, in *Neuer Vorwärts* (13 July 1956).
68 Rolf Schwedler, in conversation with the author.
69 Brandt, in conversation with the author.
70 Jan Peter Berkandt, *Willy Brandt* (Hanover 1961), p. 50.
71 Brandt, as told to Lania, *op. cit.*, p. 243.
72 *Ibid.*, p. 258.
73 *Der Spiegel* (9 October 1957).
74 Franz Neumann, in letter to the author (21 April 1972).
75 Jens Feddersen, editor of the *Neue Ruhr Zeitung*, in conversation with the author.

CHAPTER 6

1 Erich Brost, in conversation with the author.
2 Dietrich Spangenberg, in conversation with the author.
3 Shepard Stone, in conversation with the author.
4 Spangenberg, in conversation with the author.
5 Stone, in conversation with the author.
6 General Barksdale Hamlett, in letter to the author.
7 Senator Otto Theuner, in conversation with the author.
8 Senator Rolf Schwedler, in conversation with the author.
9 *Die Tat* (6 October 1957).
10 Brandt, in conversation with the author.
11 Heli Ihlefeld, *Willy Brandt. Anekdotisch* (Munich 1968), p. 62.
12 Brandt, in conversation with the author.
13 Walter Henkels, *Gar Nicht so Pingelig* (Düsseldorf 1965), p. 109.
14 *Manchester Guardian* (12 December 1958).
15 Brandt, in conversation with the author.
16 Abraham Ashkenazi, *Reformpartei und Aussenpolitik* (Cologne 1968), p. 116.
17 Hans Adolf Jacobsen and Hans Dollinger (eds), *Hundert Jahre Deutschland*, SPD pamphlet, pp. 115–17.
18 Konrad Adenauer, *Memoirs* 2 (Stuttgart 1966), p. 315.
19 *Manchester Guardian* (16 September 1957).
20 Adenauer, *op. cit.*, p. 319.
21 Brandt, as told to Leo Lania, *My Road to Berlin* (London 1960), p. 267.
22 Brandt, in conversation with the author.
23 Helga Grebing, *The History of the German Labour Movement* (London 1969), p. 164.

24 Theo Pirker, *Die SPD nach Hitler* (Munich 1965), pp. 273–4.
25 *Ibid.*, p. 276.
26 Brandt, speech at SPD *Land* Berlin conference (13 April 1958).
27 Ashkenazi, *op. cit.*, p. 176.
28 *Manchester Guardian* (13 November 1959).
29 Pirker, *op. cit.*, pp. 280–81.
30 Grebing, *op. cit.*, p. 166.
31 *International Affairs*, 34 (1958), p. 297.
32 *Ibid.*, p. 298.
33 *Ibid.*, p. 301.
34 *Ibid.*, p. 302.
35 *Ibid.*, p. 303.
36 Memorandum on London visit, Willy Brandt Archives, Bonn.
37 Ihlefeld, *op. cit.*, p. 73.
38 *Ibid.*, p. 74.
39 Central Office of Information, *Russia and the West 1945–63* (London 1963), p. 33.
40 Prittie, in *Manchester Guardian* (3 May 1958).
41 *The Soviet Sea Around Us*, SPD pamphlet (February 1960).
42 Ashkenazi, *op. cit.*, p. 129.
43 *Der Spiegel* (22 January 1958).
44 *Ibid.*
45 Ihlefeld, *op. cit.*, p. 63.
46 Prittie, in *Manchester Guardian* (5 July 1958).
47 Prittie, in *Manchester Guardian* (8 December 1958).
48 Brandt, in conversation with the author.
49 James Macgregor Burns, *JohnKennedy* (New York 1959), p. 90.
50 Brandt, in interview with the author (2 September 1960).
51 Brandt, as told to Lania, *op. cit.*, p. 254.
52 *Ibid.*, p. 272.
53 Hamlett, in letter to the author.
54 Grebing, *op. cit.*, p. 168.
55 Fritz Sänger, in letter to the author.
56 Ashkenazi *op. cit.*, p. 181.
57 *Manchester Guardian* (13 June 1960).
58 Pirker, *op. cit.*, p. 295.
59 Brandt, *Mit Herz und Hand* (Hanover 1962), pp. 11–18.
60 Pirker, *op. cit.*, p. 299.
61 Brandt, *Mit Herz und Hand*, pp. 25–6.
62 *Die Welt* (23 November 1960).
63 Brandt, in conversation with the author.
64 *Manchester Guardian* (5 September 1960).
65 *Der Spiegel* (8 February 1961).
66 Brandt, *Begegnungen mitKennedy* (Munich 1964), p. 41.
67 Burns, *op. cit.*, p. 197.
68 *United States Department of State Bulletins* (14 August 1961).
69 Philip Windsor, *City on Leave* (London 1963), p. 238.
70 *United States Department of State Bulletins* (14 August 1961).
71 Richard Hottelet, 'Berlin and Beyond', *Orbis*, v: 3 (1961).
72 Opinion Surveys of Federal Ministry for All-German Affairs (1957, 1959).
73 Prittie, 'Satellite Statehood', in *The New Republic* (15 August 1960).
74 *Ibid.*

CHAPTER 7

1   Richard Hottelet, 'Berlin and Beyond', in *Orbis*, v: 3 (1961).
2   Senator Otto Theuner, in conversation with the author.
3   Walter Ulbricht, East Berlin press conference (15 June 1961), reported in *Neues Deutschland* (16 June 1961).
4   Eleanor Lansing Dulles, *Berlin. The Wall is not Forever* (Chapel Hill 1967), p. 54.
5   James O'Donnell of *Saturday Evening Post*, in letter to the author.
6   Dulles, *op. cit.*, p. 49.
7   *Ibid.*, p. 55.
8   Prittie, in *Manchester Guardian* (13 July 1961).
9   *Ibid.*
10 Geoffrey McDermott, *Berlin. Success of a Mission?* (London 1963), p. 29.
11 Brandt, *Begegnungen mit Kennedy* (Munich 1964), p. 58.
12 *Ibid.*, p. 66.
13 Brandt, in conversation with the author.
14 Theo Pirker, *Die SPD nach Hitler* (Munich 1965), p. 308.
15 McDermott, *op. cit.*, p. 32.
16 Senator Rolf Schwedler, in conversation with the author.
17 Brandt, in conversation with the author.
18 *Ibid.*
19 McDermott, *op. cit.*, p. 31.
20 O'Donnell, in letter to the author.
21 Brandt, in conversation with the author.
22 O'Donnell, in letter to the author.
23 Ferdinand Friedensburg, in *Monitor* (6 September 1971).
24 Brandt, in conversation with the author.
25 Brandt, in *Stern* (11 August 1972).
26 David Binder, 'Willy Brandt. A German Life', *New York Times* Brochure, (November 1969).
27 Brandt, *Begegnungen mit Kennedy*, pp. 72–3.
28 Binder, *op. cit.*
29 O'Donnell, in letter to the author.
30 This information was given in confidence, so names must be withheld.
31 Brandt, *Begegnungen mit Kennedy*, p. 77.
32 *Ibid.*, p. 79.
33 Brandt, in conversation with the author.
34 McDermott, *op. cit.*, p. 73.
35 Brandt, in conversation with the author.
36 Philip Windsor, *City on Leave* (London 1963), p. 243.
37 Brandt, in conversation with the author.
38 General Lucius Clay, in letter to the author.
39 Brandt, *Begegnungen mit Kennedy*, p. 120.
40 Prittie, in *Manchester Guardian* (13 January 1962).
41 Otto Frei, 'The People of East Berlin', *Atlantic Monthly* (December 1963).
42 Otto Frei, in *World Today*, 17 (London 1961), p. 465.
43 Prittie, in *Manchester Guardian* (14 September 1961).
44 Willy Brandt Archives, Bonn.
45 *The Times* (15 March 1961).
46 Prittie, in *Manchester Guardian* (23 March 1961).
47 Prittie, in *Manchester Guardian* (26 July 1961).
48 *Der Spiegel* (8 March 1961).

49 Heli Ihlefeld, *Willy Brandt. Anekdotisch* (Munich 1968), p. 94.
50 Emlyn Williams, *Christian Science Monitor* (28 June 1961).
51 Prittie, 'The West German Elections', *Atlantic Monthly* (August 1961).
52 Fritz Sänger, in letter to the author.
53 Ihlefeld, op. cit., p. 94.
54 Prittie, in *Manchester Guardian* (23 September 1961).
55 Prittie, in *Manchester Guardian* (22 September 1961).
56 Dr Erich Mende, in conversation with the author.
57 Henry Wallich, 'Berlin's Economic Future', *Atlantic Monthly* (December 1963).
58 Karl Schiller, *Report on Berlin Economy 1961–2*, 1280 (13–14 April 1962).
59 Brandt, in conversation with the author.
60 William Henry Chamberlin, *The German Phoenix* (London 1964), p. 156.
61 Rainer Hildebrandt, *It Happened at the Wall*, pamphlet (Berlin 1967).
62 Hans Werner, Count Finck von Finkenstein, *Die Welt* (20 April 1967).
63 *Manchester Guardian* (30 December 1961).
64 *Jerusalem Post* (19 November 1960).
65 Ihlefeld, *op. cit.*, p. 79.
66 Chamberlin, *op. cit.*, p. 256.
67 Report on visit to United States, Willy Brandt Archives.
68 Brandt, *Begegnungen mit Kennedy*, p. 162.

CHAPTER 8

1 Frau Landerer (Brandt's secretary for many years), in conversation with the author.
2 His name, for reasons of confidence, cannot be given.
3 Landerer, in conversation with the author.
4 Shepard Stone, in conversation with the author.
5 Herbert George, in conversation with the author.
6 Landerer, in conversation with the author.
7 General Sir Rohan Delacombe, British commandant, in letter to the author.
8 General Sir David Peel-Yates, British commandant, in letter to the author.
9 George McGhee, in letter to the author.
10 The Rt Hon. Harold Wilson MP, in conversation with the author.
11 Brandt, in letter to the author.
12 Heli Ihlefeld, *Willy Brandt. Anekdotisch* (Munich 1968), p. 118.
13 Dr Günther Struwe, in conversation with the author.
14 Brandt, in letter to the author.
15 Ihlefeld, *op. cit.*, p. 125.
16 *Ibid.*, p. 130.
17 Dietrich Spangenberg, in conversation with the author.
18 Ihlefeld, *op. cit.*, p. 123.
19 *Ibid.*, pp. 130–31.
20 Brandt, in conversation with the author.
21 *Ibid.*
22 Peel-Yates, in conversation with the author.
23 Stone, in conversation with the author.
24 Brandt, in conversation with the author.
25 Prittie, in *Manchester Guardian* (2 April 1966).
26 Michael Hilton, in *Daily Telegraph* (8 October 1961).

27 Brandt, *Begegnungen mit Kennedy* (Munich 1964), p. 186.
28 *Ibid.*, pp. 212–15.
29 General Barksdale Hamlett, in letter to the author.
30 Hilton, in *Daily Telegraph* (28 August 1961).
31 Rüdiger Altmann, *Das Deutsche Risiko* (Stuttgart 1962), p. 48.
32 David Shears, *The Ugly Frontier* (London 1970), p. 14.
33 Gerhard Schroeder, at CDU congress in Dortmund (4 July 1962).
34 Schroeder, on North German Radio (8 October 1962).
35 E. H. Carr, *German–Soviet Relations between the Two World Wars* (Baltimore 1951), p. 65.
36 Abraham Ashkenazi, *Reformpartei und Aussenpolitik* (Cologne 1968), p. 195.
37 Erich Lüth, in letter to the author.
38 Brandt, *Koexistenz. Zwang zum Wagnis* (Stuttgart 1963), p. 113.
39 *Ibid.*, p. 115.
40 Brandt, speech in Tutzing (15 July 1963), Willy Brandt Archives, Bonn.
41 Ihlefeld, *op. cit.*, p. 19.
42 Fritz Sänger, in letter to the author.
43 Brandt, speech to Berlin City Parliament (9 January 1964), printed in *Brandt Reden 1961–5*, ed. Hermann Bortfeldt (Cologne 1965), p. 28.
44 Paul Henri Spaak, *Why NATO?* (London 1959), p. 13.
45 Hilton, in *Daily Telegraph* (13 December 1963).
46 Hilton, in *Daily Telegraph* (10 June 1966).
47 Prittie, 'NATO in the Doldrums', *Atlantic Monthly* (December 1964).
48 Brandt, in speech to Berlin City Parliament (17 September 1964).
49 Brandt, in speech to SPD delegates in Berlin (15 January 1965).
50 Eleanor Lansing Dulles, *Berlin. The Wall is not Forever* (Chapel Hill 1967), p. 209.
51 Jesse Lukomski, *Ludwig Erhard. Der Mensch und der Politiker* (Düsseldorf 1965), p. 297.
52 Brandt, in speech to SPD party conference (16 February 1964).
53 *The Times* (11 July 1965).
54 *New York Times* (21 August 1965).
55 Neal Ascherson, in *Observer* (5 September 1965).
56 Norman Crossland, in *Manchester Guardian* (11 September 1965).
57 *Le Monde* (14 September 1965).
58 *Sunday Times* (1 August 1965).
59 *The Times* (29 July 1965).
60 Prittie, 'The Atlantic Report, West Germany', *Atlantic Monthly* (August 1964).
61 Ascherson, in *Observer* (5 September 1965).
62 *The Times* (10 September 1965.)
63 *New York Times* (3 August 1965).
64 Crossland, in *Manchester Guardian* (3 September 1965).
65 Ihlefeld, *op. cit.*, p. 19.
66 *Ibid.*, p. 140.
67 *Ibid.*, p. 85.
68 *Der Spiegel* (29 September 1965).
69 Brandt, in conversation with the author.
70 David Childs, *The Story of German Socialism* (London 1966), p. 153.
71 Brandt, in conversation with the author.
72 Ashkenazi, *op. cit.*, p. 196.
73 Prittie, 'The Atlantic Report. Berlin', *Atlantic Monthly* (June 1966).
74 *Ibid.*

NOTES

75 Brandt, in conversation with the author.
76 *Ibid.*
77 *Ibid.*
78 Ivor Montagu, *Germany's New Nazis* (London 1967), p. 13.
79 Klaus Harpprecht, *Willy Brandt* (Munich 1970), p. 42.
80 *Ibid.*, p. 33.
81 Brandt, in conversation with the author.
82 *Ibid.*
83 Ihlefeld, *op. cit.*, p. 80.

CHAPTER 9

1 Brandt, in conversation with the author.
2 Fritz Lamm, *Die grosse Koalition und die nächsten Aufgaben der Linken* (Frankfurt 1967), p. 6.
3 *Ibid.*, p. 2.
4 Ralf Dahrendorf, *Für eine Erneuerung der Demokratie in der Bundesrepublik* (Munich 1968), p. 163.
5 *Ibid.*, p. 131.
6 Lamm. *op. cit.*, p. 16.
7 Helmut Schauer, in Lamm, *op. cit.*, p. 59.
8 Hermann Schreiber and Sven Simon, *Willy Brandt. Anatomie einer Veränderung* (Düsseldorf 1970), p. 116.
9 *Berliner Morgenpost* (12 October 1967).
10 *Nürnberger Nachrichten* (29 August 1969).
11 *Frankfurter Allgemeine* (15 July 1969).
12 Brandt, in conversation with the author.
13 Ivor Montagu, *Germany's New Nazis* (London 1967), p. 97.
14 Hans Dollinger, *Willy! Willy!* (Munich 1970), p. 92.
15 Dr G. F. Duckwitz, in conversation with the author.
16 Erich Lüth, in letter to the author.
17 Dr Günther Struwe, in conversation with the author.
18 *Ibid.*
19 Dietrich Spangenberg, in conversation with the author.
20 Frau Landerer, in conversation with the author.
21 Heli Ihlefeld, *Willy Brandt. Anekdotisch* (Munich 1968), p. 37.
22 David Binder, 'Willy Brandt. A German Life', *New York Times* brochure (November 1969).
23 Dr G. F. Duckwitz, in conversation with the author.
24 Brandt, speech in Bundestag (6 December 1966), in *Bonner Rundschau* (7 December 1966).
25 Brandt, *A Peace Policy for Europe* (London 1969), p. 105.
26 Brandt, at SPD conference in Bonn (25 February 1967).
27 Brandt, interview with *Mann in der Zeit* (24 April 1967).
28 Brandt, at press conference in Berlin (9 June 1967), in *Tagesspiegel* (9 June 1967).
29 Brandt, on Deutschlandfunk (2 July 1967).
30 Prittie, *Manchester Guardian* (19 August 1963).
31 *Die Welt* (14 October 1967).
32 *Bayern Kurier* (26 August 1967).
33 *Donau Kurier* (3 October 1967).
34 *Nürnberger Zeitung* (26 May 1967).
35 *Münchener Merkur* (14 October 1967).
36 Kurt-Georg Kiesinger, in *Rheinische Post* (27 July 1968).

37 Kiesinger, on Südwestfunk (25 August 1968).
38 *Der Spiegel* (19 December 1966).
39 Brandt, in *Aussenpolitik* (11 August 1967).
40 Brandt, speech at the Free University in Berlin (6 October 1967).
41 Brandt, *A Peace Policy for Europe*, p. 110.
42 Brandt, AP interview (6 February 1967).
43 Brandt, *A Peace Policy for Europe*, p. 37.
44 Michael Stewart, in conversation with the author.
45 George Brown, in conversation with the author.
46 *Ibid.*
47 Brown, *In My Way* (London 1971), p. 252.
48 Rt. Hon. Harold Wilson MP, in conversation with the author.
49 Ursula Schmieder, *Die grosse Koalition und die nächsten Aufgaben der Linken* (Frankfurt 1967), pp. 25–31.
50 Brandt, *A Peace Policy for Europe*, pp. 88–9.
51 *Ibid.*, pp. 90–92.
52 Nato *Report on the Future Tasks of the Alliance* (London 1967).
53 Alastair Buchan, in brochure *The Soviet Threat to Europe* (London 1969).
54 Adalbert Weinstein, *ibid.*
55 Erich Mende, *Was soll aus Deutschland werden?* (Munich 1968), p. 218.
56 M. Azaroff of the Soviet embassy, London, in conversation with the author.
57 Brandt, interview on German Zweites Programm (25 August 1968).
58 Brandt, interview with Frankfurt weekly paper *Publik* (6 December 1968).
59 *Die Welt* (12 February 1968).
60 Brandt, interview with *Die Welt* (3 September 1968).
61 Abraham Ashkenazi, *Reformpartei und Aussenpolitik* (Cologne 1968), p. 205.
62 Rt Hon. Harold Wilson, MP *The Labour Government 1964–70* (London 1971), p. 682.
63 *Ibid.*, p. 368.
64 Brandt, in conversation with the author.
65 *Ibid.*
66 Norman Crossland, of the *Guardian*, in letter to the author.
67 *Der Spiegel* (6 January 1969).
68 Ihlefeld, *op. cit.*, p. 20.
69 *Ibid.*, p. 107.
70 *Abendzeitung* (11 September 1969).
71 *Der Spiegel* (15 September 1969).
72 *Süddeutsche Zeitung* (27 September 1969).
73 Dollinger, *op. cit.*, p. 105.
74 *Der Spiegel* (27 October 1969).
75 Binder, *op. cit.*, p. 32.
76 Klaus Harpprecht, *Willy Brandt* (Munich 1970), p. 28.
77 *Bayern Kurier* (18 October 1969).
78 *Ibid.*
79 *Frankfurter Rundschau* (21 October 1969).
80 *Süddeutsche Zeitung* (21 October 1969).
81 Ihlefeld, *op. cit.*, p. 10.
82 Hans Adolf Jacobsen and Hans Dollinger, *Hundert Jahre Deutschland 1870–1970* (Berlin 1969), p. 408.
83 Brandt, in conversation with the author.
84 Ihlefeld, *op. cit.*, p. 10.

CHAPTER 10
1 Report from paper's 'own correspondent'. *Tagesspiegel* (22 October 1969).

2 Denis Foster, in *Financial Times* (11 October 1972).
3 *Ibid.*
4 Rt Hon. Harold Wilson MP, in conversation with the author.
5 *Süddeutsche Zeitung* (5 October 1969).
6 Hans Dollinger, *Willy! Willy!* (Munich 1970), p. 107.
7 Heli Ihlefeld, *Willy Brandt. Anekdotisch* (Munich 1971), p. 32.
8 *Ibid.*
9 *Die Zeit*, (23 October 1969).
10 Ihlefeld, *op. cit.*, p. 70.
11 *Ibid.*, p. 58.
12 Volker Kaiser, in letter to the author.
13 David Binder, 'Willy Brandt. A German Life', *New York Times* brochure (November 1969).
14 Karl Jaspers, *The Future of Germany* (Chicago 1967), p. 1.
15 Kurt Sontheimer, *The Government of West Germany* (London 1972), p. 69.
16 *Ibid.*, p. 131.
17 *Ibid.*, p. 61.
18 'Germany 1967', *Atlantic Monthly* special (November 1967).
19 Dollinger, *op. cit.*, p. 113.
20 *Süddeutsche Zeitung* (15 January 1970).
21 Frau Landerer, in conversation with the author.
22 Lord George-Brown, in conversation with the author.
23 Dr Joseph Luns, in letter to the author.
24 Wilson, in conversation with the author.
25 Dr G. F. Duckwitz, in conversation with the author.
26 Brandt, interview with French IV network, ORTF (29 January 1970).
27 Brandt, speech to Foreign Press Association in London (3 March 1970).
28 Brandt, speech at dinner in London (2 March 1970).
29 Federal Press Office publication, *Aufbruch in die 70er Jahre*, for all these figures.
30 Brandt, *The Policy of Détente* (London 1970), p. 115.
31 Brandt, speech to Overseas Club in Hamburg (7 May 1969).
32 Brandt, speech at Eleventh Congress Socialist International (16 June 1969).
33 Brandt, interview with *Der Stern* (2 November 1969).
34 Brandt, interview with *Stuttgarter Nachrichten* (3 December 1969).
35 Brandt, interview with *Westfälischer Rundschau* (9 January 1970).
36 *Der Spiegel* (16 February 1970).
37 Hans Ulrich Kempski, in the *Süddeutsche Zeitung* (20 March 1970).
38 *Der Stern* (15 March 1970).
39 Hermann Schreiber and Sven Simon, *Willy Brandt. Anatomie einer Veränderung* (Düsseldorf 1970), p. 122.
40 Claus Jacobi, in *Welt am Sonntag* (22 March 1970).
41 Brandt, in interview with second German Television network (4 December 1969).
42 *Der Spiegel* (16 February 1970).
43 Brandt, in BBC 'Late Night Line-Up' interview with Lord Chalfont (1 December 1970).
44 Hermann Poerzgen, *Frankfurter Allgemeine Zeitung* (11 August 1970).
45 Bernhard Leverenz, *Was soll aus Deutschland werden?* (Munich 1968), p. 188.
46 Georg Bruderer, 'Some Aspects of the Soviet Union's Ideological and Psychological Warfare', *The Soviet Threat to Europe*, pamphlet, (London 1969).

47 Lothar Reuel, *Die Welt* (15 August 1970).
48 Reginald Steed, *Daily Telegraph* (16 November 1970).
49 His name, for reasons of discretion, cannot be given.
50 His name, for reasons of discretion, cannot be given.
51 Brandt, speech at Mannesmann steel plant, Mülheim (30 April 1970).
52 Duckwitz, in conversation with the author.
53 *Ibid.*
54 *Ibid.*
55 Brandt, interview with Terry Coleman, in *Guardian* (5 May 1971).
56 Boris Kidel, 'Brandt and Auschwitz Survivor Clasp Hands', *Observer* (13 December 1970).
57 Axel Springer, 'Statt Versöhnung mit Polen eine Kluft in unserem Volk', *Die Welt* (8 December 1970).
58 Erich Mettler, *Neue Zürcher Zeitung* (11 August 1970).

CHAPTER 11

1   Norman Crossland, in *Guardian* (1 March 1972).
2   Associated Press report, *Die Welt* (20 October 1971).
3   *The Times* (21 October 1971).
4   *Daily Telegraph* (22 October 1971).
5   Jonathan Steele, in *Guardian* (21 October 1971).
6   Brandt, in conversation with the author.
7   *General Anzeiger* (14 April 1971).
8   Brandt, to Terry Coleman of the *Guardian* (5 May 1971).
9   *Jasmin* magazine (January 1972).
10 *Guardian* (4 September 1971).
11 Michael Lake, in *Guardian* (24 August 1971).
12 Sebastian Haffner, in *New Statesman* (3 September 1971).
13 Erich Honecker, at SED congress in Berlin (16 June 1971).
14 Douglas Brown, in *Sunday Telegraph* (29 August 1971).
15 Klaus Schütz, speech to West Berlin City Parliament (7 September 1971).
16 Schütz, speech in Brussels (25 October 1971).
17 Honecker, *Neues Deutschland* (19 October 1971).
18 Schütz, statement in West Berlin (2 November 1971).
19 Schütz, speech in West Berlin City Parliament (20 February 1972).
20 Reginald Steed, *Daily Telegraph* (8 September 1971).
21 Brandt, in conversation with the author.
22 Brandt, in conversation with the author.
23 Axel Springer, in *Daily Telegraph* (21 December 1971).
24 Franz-Josef Strauss, to the *Bild Zeitung* (22 August 1971).
25 William Born, 'Ideologische Auseinandersetzung geht weiter', in *Die Entkampfung Berlins*, ed. Rolf Heyen (Hamburg 1972), p. 32.
26 Brandt, *ibid.*, p. 63.
27 Günter Struwe, *ibid.*, p. 35.
28 Joseph Luns, in letter to the author.
29 Lord George-Brown, in conversation with the author.
30 Rt Hon. Harold Wilson MP, in conversation with the author.
31 Michael Stewart, in conversation with the author.
32 Amos Elon, *Journey through a Haunted Land* (London 1967), p. 88.
33 Fritz René Allemann, in *Survey* (Journal of Soviet Studies) (October 1966).
34 Crossland, in *Guardian* (9 October 1971).
35 *Financial Times* report, quoting text of agreement (23 December 1971).

36 Hanns-Peter Herz, Berlin senator, in conversation with the author.
37 Richard Davy, *The Times* (27 April 1972).
38 *Frankfurter Rundschau* (5 October 1971).
39 *Frankfurter Allgemeine Zeitung* (20 December 1971).
40 Dietrich Spangenberg, in conversation with the author.
41 Brandt, in conversation with the author.
42 SPD party report (*Bildungsbericht*), (end 1970).
43 *The Times* (30 June 1971).
44 Brandt, in conversation with the author.
45 Dr G. F. Duckwitz, in conversation with the author.
46 Colin Chapman, in *Guardian* (14 March 1972).
47 *The Economist* (22 April 1972).
48 Jens Feddersen, of the *Neue Ruhr Zeitung*, in conversation with the author.
49 *The Times* (26 April 1972).
50 *Guardian* (28 April 1972).
51 *Daily Telegraph* (1 May 1972).
52 Radio Moscow (29 April 1972).
53 Brandt, in conversation with the author.
54 Heli Ihlefeld, *Willy Brandt. Anekdotisch* (Munich 1971), p. 32.
55 *The Times* (18 May 1972).
56 *Der Spiegel* (8 May 1972).
57 W. W. Schütz, in conversation with the author.
58 Thus Dr Erich Mende, in conversation with the author.
59 Brandt, in conversation with the author.
60 *Guardian* (19 May 1972).
61 *Der Spiegel* (19 September 1966).

CHAPTER 12

1 Brandt, in conversation with the author.
2 Egon Bahr, in conversation with the author.
3 Heinz Möller, in *German International* (May 1972).
4 *The Economist* (8 April 1972).
5 *Listener* (8 June 1972).
6 Brandt, speech in Interlaken (29 September 1972).
7 Heli Ihlefeld, *Willy Brandt. Anekdotisch* (Munich 1971), p. 134.
8 *The Times* (8 September 1972); also *The Bulletin of the Association of Jewish Refugees in Great Britain* (November 1972).
9 *Washington Post* (2 April 1972).
10 Professor Helmut Jaesrich, in conversation with the author.
11 Professor Hugh Trevor-Roper, in letter to the author.
12 *New Statesman* (30 June 1972).
13 Brandt, interview with Cairo newspaper, *El Ahram* (12 December 1969).
14 The Federal Chancellery, letter to the author.
15 The name of the Israeli cannot, for reasons of discretion, be given.
16 The Federal Chancellery, letter to the author.
17 Brandt, *Frankfurter Allgemeine Zeitung* (11 September 1972).
18 Norman Crossland, in *Guardian* (8 September 1972).
19 Brandt, *Frankfurter Allgemeine Zeitung* (11 September 1972).
20 Brandt, on BBC 'Olympic Grandstand' television programme (5 September 1972).
21 Thus *The Times* (5 June 1972).
22 *The Economist* (22 July 1972).

23 *Financial Times* (18 August 1972).
24 *Sunday Telegraph* (13 August 1972).
25 *The Times* (14 November 1972).
26 *Bild am Sonntag* (12 November 1972).
27 *Daily Telegraph* (14 November 1972).
28 *The Economist* (18 November 1972).
29 Hella Pick, in *Guardian* (15 November 1972).
30 *The Times* (26 September 1972).
31 Thus Crossland, in *Guardian* (26 April 1972).
32 Roland Delcour, 'Schwarzbrot oder blonder Kolosz?', in *Blickpunkt Deutschland*, ed. Werner Höfer (Hanover 1970), p. 40.
33 Malcolm Rutherford, in *Financial Times* (17 November 1972).
34 *Financial Times* (9 October 1972).
35 *Süddeutsche Zeitung* (4 October 1972).
36 *New Statesman* (17 November 1972).
37 Anthony Terry, in *Sunday Times* (12 November 1972).
38 Boris Kidel, in *Observer* (19 November 1972).
39 *Der Stern* (25 May 1972).
40 *The Economist* (23 September 1972).
41 Lothat Reuel, in *The Times* (17 November 1972).
42 Quoted in the *Guardian* (15 November 1972).
43 Brandt, in conversation with the author.
44 Mark Arnold-Foster, in *Guardian* (21 November 1972).
45 Frau Landerer, in conversation with the author.
46 Dietrich Spangenberg, in conversation with the author.
47 James O'Donnell, in conversation with the author.
48 For reasons of discretion, no name can be given.
49 Spangenberg, in conversation with the author.
50 Ihlefeld, *op. cit.*, p. 46.
51 Brandt, in conversation with the author.
52 Ihlefeld, *op. cit.*, p. 20.
53 Jens Feddersen, in conversation with the author.
54 *Sunday Telegraph* (12 November 1972).
55 Dr Friedrich Middelhauve, in conversation with the author.
56 Brandt, speech at opening of Fellowship Week, Cologne (21 March 1971).
57 Ihlefeld, *op. cit.*, p. 20.
58 *Ibid.*, p. 20.
59 Heinrich Böll, in letter to the author.
60 Brandt, in conversation with the author.
61 Ihlefeld, *op. cit.*, p. 20.
62 Brandt, speech at Lindau (26 June 1972).
63 *Observer* (16 April 1972).
64 *The Economist* (25 March 1972).
65 As reported by David Fairhall, *Guardian* (28 March 1972).
66 President John Kennedy, speech in the Paulskirche, Frankfurt (25 June 1963).

Bibliography

ABSHAGEN, Karl-Heinz, *Schuld und Verhängnis*. Stuttgart, Union, 1968.

ADENAUER, Konrad, *Memoirs*. Vol. 1 London, Weidenfeld, 1966. Vols. 2–4 Stuttgart, Deutsche Verlagsanstalt 1966, 1967, 1968.

ALLEMANN, Fritz René, *Bonn ist nicht Weimar*. Köln, Kiepenhauer & Witsch, 1956.

ALTMANN, Rüdiger, *Das deutsche Risiko*. Stuttgart, Seewald, 1962.

ANDENAES, Johannes, *Norway and the Second World War*. Oslo, Tanum Forlag, 1966.

ASHKENAZI, Abraham, *Reformpartei und Aussenpolitik*. Cologne, Westdeutscher Verlag, 1968.

AUGSTEIN, Rudolf, *Konrad Adenauer*. London, Secker & Warburg, 1964.

BALFOUR, Michael & MAIR, John, *Four Power Control in Germany & Austria*. London, Oxford University Press, 1956.

BARING, Arnulf, *Aussenpolitik in Adenauers Kanzler-Demokratie*. Munchen, Oldenbourg, 1969.

BERKANDT, Jan Peter, *Willy Brandt*. Hanover, Verlag für Literatur, 1961.

BINDER, David, 'Willy Brandt. A German Life'. *New York Times* publication, 1969.

BOLESCH, Hermann Otto & LEICHT, Hans-Dieter, *Willy Brandt*. Tübingen, Horst Erdmann Verlag, 1971.

BOLIN, Luis. *Spain. The Vital Years*. London, Cassell, 1967.

BONHOEFFER, Dietrich, *Letters and Papers from Prison*. London, Fontana Books, 1959.

BRANDT, Willy, *Verbrecher und andere Deutschen*. Oslo, Aschehong, 1946.

Norwegens Freiheitskampf. Hamburg, Auerdruck, 1948.

My Road to Berlin. London, Peter Davies, 1960.

Germany, Israel & the Jews. Berlin, Press Office, 1961.

Plädoyer für die Zukunft. Frankfurt, Europäische Verlagsanstalt, 1961.

Mit Herz und Hand. Hanover, Verlag für Literatur, 1962.

The Ordeal of Coexistence. Cambridge (Mass), Harvard
University Press, 1963.
Begegnungen mit Kennedy. Munchen, Kindler Verlag, 1964.
Friedenssicherung in Europa. Berlin, Berlin Verlag, 1968.
Aussenpolitik, Deutschlandpolitik, Europapolitik. Berlin, Berlin
Verlag, 1968.
In Exile. London, Oswald Wolff, 1971.
BRANDT, Willy & LÖWENTHAL, Richard, *Ernst Reuter. Ein Leben
für die* Munchen, Kindler Verlag, 1957.
BRANT, Stefan, *The East German Rising.* London, Thames &
Hudson, 1955.
BRAUN, Otto, *Von Weimar zu Hitler.* New York, Europa Press, 1940.
BRENTANO, Heinrich von, *Germany and Europe.* London, André
Deutsch, 1964.
BROWN, George, *In My Way.* London, Gollancz, 1971.
BURKE, Arleigh, *Nato after Czechoslovakia.* Washington, Centre for
Strategic & International Studies, Georgetown, 1969.
BURNS, James MacGregor, *John Kennedy. A Political Profile.*
New York, Harcourt Brace, 1960.
BUTLER, Ewan, *City Divided.* London, Sidgwick & Jackson, 1955.
CARR, E. H., *German Soviet Relations between the Two World Wars.*
Baltimore, Johns Hopkins Press, 1951.
CHALMERS, Douglas A, *The Social Democratic Party of Germany.*
New Haven, Yale University Press, 1964.
CHAMBERLIN, William Henry, *The German Phoenix.* London,
Robert Hale, 1963.
CHILDS, David, *The Story of German Socialism.* London,
Pergamon, 1966.
CHRIST, George, *The Myth of Munich.* London, E. D. O'Brien
publication, 1969.
CLAY, General Lucius, *Decision in Germany.* New York, Doubleday,
1953.
CONNELL, Brian, *Watcher on the Rhine.* London, Weidenfeld &
Nicolson, 1959.
COOKRIDGE, E. H., *Gehlen. Spy of the Century.* London, Hodder &
Stoughton, 1971.
DAHRENDORF, Ralf, *Für ein Erneuerung der Demokratie.* Munchen,
Piper Verlag, 1968.
DAVIDSON, Basil, *Germany. What Now?* London, Frederick Muller,
1950.
DEUTSCHKRON, Inge, *Bonn and Jerusalem.* Philadelphia, Chilton, 1970.
DILL, Marshall, *Germany.* Ann Arbor, Univ. of Michigan Press, 1961.
DOLLINGER, Hans, *Willy! Willy!* Munchen, Wilhelm Heyne
Verlag, 1970.

DRECHSLER, Hanno, *Die Sozialistische Arbeiterpartei Deutschlands.* Meisenheim, Verlag Anton Hain, 1965.

DULLES, Eleanor Lansing, *Berlin. The Wall is not Forever.* Chapel Hill, Univ. of North Carolina Press, 1967.

EDINGER, Lewis, *German Exile Politics.* Berkeley, Univ. of California Press, 1956.

Kurt Schumacher. Stanford, Stanford Univ. Press, 1965.

ELON, Amos, *Journey Through a Haunted Land,* London, André Deutsch, 1967.

FEST, Joachim, *The Face of the Third Reich.* London, Weidenfeld & Nicolson, 1970.

FLACH, Karl Hermann, *Erhards schwerer Weg.* Stuttgart, Seewald Verlag, 1964.

GOYKE, Ernst, *Willy Brandt. Der Bundeskanzler,* Bonn, Ergo Verlag, 1971.

GRASS, Günther, *Speak Out!* New York, Harcourt Brace, 1969.

GREBING, Helga, *The History of the German Labour Movement.* London, Oswald Wolff, 1969.

GROSSER, Alfred, *Die Bundesrepublik Deutschland.* Tübingen, Rainer Wunderlich Verlag, 1967.

HARPPRECHT, Klaus, *Willy Brandt. Porträt und Selbstporträt.* Munchen, Kindler Verlag, 1970.

HAYTER, Sir William, *The Diplomacy of the Great Powers,* London, Hamish Hamilton, 1960.

HEIDENHEIMER, Arnold, *Adenauer and the CDU.* The Hague, Martinus Nijhoff, 1960.

HEIDENHEIMER, Arnold, *The Governments of Germany.* New York, Crowell, 1966.

HENKELS, Walter, *Gar nicht so Pingelig.* Düsseldorf, Econ. Verlag, 1965.

HILDEBRANDT, Rainer, *It Happened at the Wall.* Berlin, Grünewald, 1967.

HISCOCKS, Richard, *Democracy in Western Germany.* London, Oxford Univ. Press, 1957.

HOWARTH, David, *The Shetland Bus.* London, Nelson, 1951.

IHLEFELD, Heli, *Willy Brandt. Anekdotisch.* Munchen, Bechtle Verlag, 1968.

JOHN, Otto, *Twice Through the Lines.* London, Macmillan, 1972.

KAISER, Karl, *German Foreign Policy in Transition.* London, Oxford Univ. Press, 1968.

KEMP, Peter, *Mine Were of Trouble.* London, Cassell, 1957.

KENNAN, George, *Realities of American Foreign Policy.* London, Oxford Univ. Press, 1954.

KING-HALL, Sir Stephen & ULLMANN, Richard, *German Parliaments*. London, Hansard Society, 1954.

KIRKPATRICK, Sir Ivone, *The Inner Circle*. London, Macmillan, 1959.

KITZINGER, Uwe, *German Electoral Politics*. Oxford, Clarendon Press, 1960.

KNICKERBOCKER, H. R., *Germany. Fascist or Soviet*. London, Bodley Head, 1932.

KOHN, Hans, *German History. Some New German Views*. London, Allen & Unwin, 1954.

The Mind of Germany. London, Macmillan, 1961.

LEHMKUHL, Herman, *Hitler Attacks Norway*. London, Norwegian Press Office, 1943.

LEMMER, Ernst, *Manches war doch Anders*. Frankfurt, Verlag Heinrich Scheffler, 1968.

LEONHARDT, Wolfgang, *This Germany*. Greenwich (Conn.), New York Graphic Society, 1955.

LILJE, Herbert, *Deutschland von 1955 bis 1963*. Hanover, 1965.

LÖWENTHAL, Richard, *Hochschule für die Demokratie*. KOLM, Markusverlag, 1971.

LUKOMSKI, Jesse, *Ludwig Erhard. Der Mensch und Politiker*. Düsseldorf, Econ. Verlag, 1965.

MACMILLAN, Harold, *Tides of Fortune*. London, Macmillan, 1969.

MANDER, John, *Berlin. Hostage for the West*. London, Penguin, 1962.

MATTHEWS, Herbert L., *The Yoke and the Arrows*. New York, George Braziller, 1947.

MCDERMOTT, Geoffrey, *Berlin. Success of a Mission*. London, André Deutsch, 1963.

MOMMSEN, Wilhelm, *Deutsche Parteiprogramme*. Munchen, Isar Verlag, 1951.

MONTAGU, Ivor, *Germany's New Nazis*. London, Panther Books, 1970.

MÜSSENER, Helmut, *Von Bert Brecht bis Peter Weiss*. Göteborg, Hedberg, 1968.

Die Deutschsprachige Emigration in Schweden nach 1933. Stockholm, Tyska, 1971.

NELSON, Walter Henry, *Germany Rearmed*. New York, Simon & Schuster, 1971.

The Berliners. New York, David McKay, 1969.

NORTHEDGE, F. S., *British Foreign Policy*. London, Allen & Unwin, 1962.

OFFICIAL PUBLICATIONS:
Bulletin, Bonn, *Die Deutschlandpolitik der Bundesregierung*. 1968.
Bundespresseamt, Bonn, *Für Frieden und Entspannung*. 1968.
Erfurt. March 19 1970.
Kassel. May 21 1970.

336

Aufbruch in die 70er Jahre. 1971.

Central Office of Information, London, *Russia and the West.* 1963.

Deutsche Institut fur Zeitgeschichte, Berlin, *20 Jahre DDR.* 1969.

Ministry for All-German Affairs, Bonn, *Schaut auf diese Stadt.* 1965.

Presse & Informationsamt, Berlin, *Zur Passierscheinfrage.* 1964.

SPD, Bonn, *The Soviet Sea Around Us.* 1960.

United States, Department of State, *Berlin.* 1961.

ORWELL, George, *Homage to Catalonia.* London, Secker & Warburg, 1938.

PAKENHAM, Lord, *Born to Believe.* London, Jonathan Cape, 1953.

PAUL, Ernst, *Die Kleine Internationale in Stockholm.* Bielefeld, Verlag Neue Gesellschaft, 1968.

PAUL, Wolfgang, *Kampf um Berlin.* Munchen, 1962.

PERRIS, G. H., *Germany and the German Emperor.* London, Andrew Melrose, 1914.

PIRKER, Theo, *The SPD nach Hitler.* Munchen, Rütten Verlag, 1965.

PRITTIE, Terence, *Germany Divided.* Boston, Little Brown, 1960.
Germans against Hitler. London, Hutchinson, 1964.
Adenauer. A Study in Fortitude. London, Stacey, 1972.

REUTHER, Dr Helmut, *Menschen unserer Zeit.* Luzern, Publikations-buro, 1969.

ROWSE, A. L., *All Souls and Appeasement.* London, Macmillan, 1961.

RUGE, Friedrich, *Politik, Militär, Bündnis.* Stuttgart, Deutsche Verlagsanstalt, 1963.

SCHILLER, Karl, *Berliner Wirtschaft und Deutsche Politik.* Stuttgart, Seewald Verlag, 1964.

SCHLABRENDORFF, Fabian von, *The Secret War against Hitler.* London, Hodder & Stoughton, 1966.

SCHMIDT, Helmut, *The Balance of Power*, London. William Kimber, 1971.

SCHREIBER, Hermann & SIMON, Sven, *Willy Brandt. Anatomie einer Veränderung.* Düsseldorf, Econ. Verlag, 1970.

SCHRÖDER, Gerhard, *Decision for Europe.* London, Thames & Hudson, 1964.

SCHUTZ, Wilhelm Wolfgang, *Rethinking German Policy.* New York, Praeger, 1967.

SEARLE, Patrick & MCCONVILLE, Maureen, *French Revolution 1968.* London, Heinemann, 1968.

SEIFERT, Jurgen, *Die Spiegel Affäre.* Olten, Walter Verlag, 1966.

SHEARS, David, *The Ugly Frontier.* London, Chatto & Windus, 1970.

SHIRER, William L., *The Rise and Fall of the Third Reich.* New York,

Simon & Schuster, 1960.

SONTHEIMER, Kurt, *The Government and Politics of West Germany*. London, Hutchinson, 1972.

SPAAK, Paul Henri, *Why NATO?* London, Penguin, 1959.

SPRINGER, Axel, *Von Berlin aus gesehen*. Stuttgart, Seewald Verlag, 1971.

STERN, Carola, *Ulbricht*. London, Pall Mall Press, 1965.

STERN, Fritz, *The Failure of Illiberalism*. London, Allen & Unwin, 1972.

STRAUSS, Franz-Josef, *The Grand Design*. London, Weidenfeld & Nicolson, 1965.

THAYER, Charles, *The Unquiet Germans*. London, Michael Joseph, 1958.

THOMAS, Hugh, *The Spanish Civil War*. London, Eyre & Spottiswoode, 1961.

VOGEL, Rolf, *The German Path to Israel*. London, Oswald Wolff, 1969.

VOGELSANG, Thilo, *Das geteilte Deutschland*. Munchen, 1966.

WALKER, Roy, *A People Who Loved Peace*. London, Gollancz, 1946.

WATT, D. C., *Britain looks to Germany*. London, Oswald Wolff, 1965.

WEYMAR, Paul, *Konrad Adenauer*. London, André Deutsch, 1957.

WILSON, Rt Hon. Harold, *The Labour Government 1964–70*. London, Weidenfeld & Nicolson, 1971.

WHEELER-BENNETT, Sir John, *The Nemesis of Power*. London, Macmillan, 1953.

WINDSOR, Philip, *City on Leave*. London, Chatto & Windus, 1963. *Germany and the Management of Détente*. London, Chatto & Windus, 1971.

WISKEMANN, Elizabeth, *Germany's Eastern Neighbours*. London, Oxford Univ. Press, 1956.

Books by Various Authors, Collections of Essays etc:
This is Germany. New York, William Sloane, 1950.
The Curtain Falls. London, Praeger, 1951.
Documents on Berlin, 1943–65. Munich, Oldenbourg, 1963.
The Issues on the Berlin-German Crisis. New York, Oceana, 1963.
Die Zeit Wilhelm II und die Weimarer Republik. Tubingen, Verlag Hermann Leins, 1964.
Die Bundestagswahl 1965. Munchen, Olzog Verlag, 1965.
Adenauer und die Folgen. Munchen, Verlag Beck, 1965.
Brandt Reden 1961–5, Köln, Verlag Wissenschaft un Politik, 1965.
Die grosse Koalition und die nächsten Aufgaben der Linken. Frankfurt, Verlag Neue Kritik, 1967.
Was Soll aus Deutschland werden? Munchen, Wilhelm Goldmann Verlag, 1968.

Hundert Jahre Deutschland. Berlin, Deutsche Buch-Gemeinschaft, 1969.

Blickpunkt Deutschland. Hanover, Fackeltrager Verlag, 1970.

Germany Democracy and the Triumph of Hitler. London, Allen & Unwin, 1970.

Menschen und Ereignisse, Berlin, Axel Springer Verlag, 1970.

Solidarität. Bonn, Verlag Neue Gesells chaft, 1971.

Aussenpolitische Perspektiven des Westdeuschen Staates. Munchen, Oldenbourg, 1971.

Die Entkrampfung Berlins. Rowohlt, Hamburg, 1972.

Gedanken über einen Politiker. Munchen, Kindler, 1972.

Index

WILLY BRANDT

181–190, 195, 197, 198, 200, 207, 215, 218–230, 236–238, 252, 256, 259, 270–277, 279, 281–289, 291, 293–298, 301–303

SPD Party Congress, 1950 at Hamburg, 88; 1952 at Dortmund, 96, 115; 1956 at Munich, 194, 115; 1958 at Stuttgart, 114, 115; 1959 at Bad Godesberg, 115–118, 302; 1960 at Hanover, 130, 131; 1964 at Karlsruhe, 182, 184, 185; 1966 at Dortmund, 191; 1967 at Bad Godesberg, 218; 1970 at Saarbrucken, 244; 1972 at Dortmund, 293

SPD Party Executive, 79, 98, 104, 107, 113, 129, 196

Speer, Albert, Nazi war criminal, 62

Spiegel, der, German weekly paper, 184, 222, 239, 281, 282, 291, 293, 298

Springer, Axel, owner of a newspaper-chain, 254, 265, 272, 286, 293, 296

SS, Nazi black-shirt élite organization, 58, 69

Stadtbahn, metropolitan railway in Berlin, 124

Stadtblatt, W. Berlin newspaper, 90, 91

Stakhanovite, Soviet system of work-norms, 93

Stalin, Josef, Soviet leader, 21, 34, 41, 55, 64, 79, 94, 135, 226

Stalingrad, 52, 56, 134

Stampfer, Freidrich, SPD politician, 39

Stang, Dr Nicolas, Friis, Norwegian friend of Brandt, 47

Stang, Fr Ragna Friis, Norwegian friend of Brandt, 47

Stauffenberg, Claus Schenk Count von, opponent of Hitler, 11

Steed, Reginald, journalist, 264

Stein Platz, square in W. Berlin, 106

Steltzer, Theodor, conservative opponent of Hitler, 11, 57

Stern, German weekly paper, 207, 238, 240, 296

Stewart, Michael, British Labour politician, 181, 210, 212, 267

Stockholm, 27, 37, 48–50, 52, 53, 57, 58, 60, 62, 68, 73, 74, 99, 100, 119

Stotenberg, Gerhard, CDU politician, 295

Stoosz, Paul, Lübeck fisherman, 15

Stoph, Willi, Prime Minister of DDR, 192, 206, 238–241, 243–247 259, 260

Storting, Norwegian Parliament, 20, 45, 50

Strasbourg, 202

Strauss, Franz-Josef, CSU politician, 153, 154, 178, 184, 197, 223, 230, 244, 260, 265, 271, 280, 292, 293, 295, 298

Streicher, Julius, Nazi war criminal, 61

Stresemann, Gustav, German Chancellor, 201

Struwe, Günther, adviser of Brandt, 201

Stuckart, Wilhelm, Nazi official, 154

Stuttgart, 90, 114–116, 266, 287

Sudetenland, German-speaking part of Czechoslovakia, 22, 38

Südwestfunk, German radio network, 206

Suhr, Otto, mayor of W. Berlin, 73, 97, 100, 111, 118, 195

Sundalsdal, valley in Norway, 46

Sweden, 1, 28, 37, 45–52, 59, 88, 160, 188, 204, 235

Swedish Aid Programme for post-war Germany, 60

Swedish Labour Party, 49

Swedish-Norwegian Press Agency, founded by Brandt, 49

Swedish Trade Unions, 53

Switzerland, 235

Szende, Stefan, friend of Brandt, born Hungarian and now Swedish, 20

Tat, die, Swiss newspaper, 110

Technical University, W. Berlin, 173

Tegelerwald forest, Berlin, 29

Tel Aviv, 165

Telefunken electronics firm, W. Berlin, 183

Tempelhof airport, W. Berlin, 111, 146

Terboven, Josef, Nazi Commissar in Norway, 50, 58

Tericki, town on Soviet-Finnish border, 43

354